The Promise of Private Pensions

The Promise *of* Private Pensions

◆ ◆ ◆

The First Hundred Years

Steven A. Sass

Harvard University Press
Cambridge, Massachusetts
London, England
1997

Library of Congress Cataloging-in-Publication Data
Sass, Steven A., 1949–
The promise of private pensions : the first hundred years / Steven
A. Sass.
p.   cm.
"A Pension Research Council book"—P. ii.
Includes bibliographical references and index.
ISBN 0-674-94520-4 (alk. paper)
1. Pensions—United States—History.   2. Old age pensions—United
States—History.   3. Individual retirement accounts—United States—
History.   4. Retirement income—United States—History.   5. Social
security—United States—History.   I. Title.
HD7125.S27   1997
331.25′2′0973—dc21
96-37847

To Ellen
and our family

◆ ◆ ◆

Acknowledgments

◆ ◆ ◆

Every author incurs many debts. But I have a special obligation to Dan McGill, emeritus professor of insurance and risk management and former director of the Pension Research Council at the University of Pennsylvania's Wharton School. This book was Dan's idea; with the support of the Pension Research Council, he engaged me to write a history of the U.S. private pension institution. Dan opened every door at his disposal, and in the world of pensions these doors are many. Because of his introductions, the entire industry cooperated in producing this history. Dan also served as my intellectual mentor and guide. His lectures, writings, and discussions are the foundation of my understanding of private pensions. Without Dan's insights and assistance, I never could have found my way through this complex and subtle *objet d'économique*.

Other members of the Pension Research Council gave generously to this project. Olivia Mitchell, the current director, read the manuscript, provided valuable suggestions, and served as a sage advisor. Other PRC members who read and improved the manuscript include Howard Young, former special consultant to the president of the United Auto Workers, Michael Gordon, legislative aide to Senator Jacob Javits during the battle over ERISA; Robert J. Myers, former chief actuary of the Social Security Administration; and Judith Mazo of the Segal Company. I also wish to thank the Walter Reuther Foundation for its generous financial contribution to the Pension Research Council in support of the publication of this book.

At the Federal Reserve Bank of Boston, Alicia Munnell and Lynn Browne, directors of research, gave me the time to complete the final chapter, write the epilogue, and revise the manuscript for publication. I thank them for their constant support and encouragement. John Campbell, Jane Katz, and Susan Schacht, colleagues on the staff of the Bank's *Regional Review,* stimulated my thinking and patiently served as sounding boards for my incessant musings on the workings of the pension institution. Joan Poskanzer, editor of the Bank's *New England Economic Review,* gave the entire manuscript a thorough editorial tune-up.

My editors at Harvard University Press — Michael Aronson, Camille Smith, and the Press's two anonymous referees — provided excellent advice in book making. The extended epilogue is one result and the book, I believe, is much better for it. Michael and Camille were an author's dream. Their good humor and sound judgment kept the process upbeat and lively.

Finally, I thank my family. My wife, Ellen Golub, and my children, Fran, Alex, Yoni, and Zoë, for the most part tolerated the time and attention I gave to the project. They also offered insights into the intergenerational and household-economy relationships that underlie a good deal of this history of private pensions. Ellen tolerated the most. She also taught me the most about people, societies, writing, and myself. Ellen has supported me when I needed support, and pushed me when I needed pushing. She has been my companion throughout the endeavor.

Contents

◆ ◆ ◆

Introduction: Setting the Problem		*1*
1	Pensions and Capitalism	*4*
2	Business Finds an Interest	*18*
3	The Logic of Pension Expansion	*38*
4	The Hard Actuarial Realities	*56*
5	The Public Character of Private Pensions	*88*
6	A Tale of Two Classes	*113*
7	The Pension Industry Reorganizes	*145*
8	ERISA and the Reformation of Pensions	*179*
	Epilogue: Pensions and Post-Industrial Capitalism	*227*
	Notes	*255*
	Index	*322*

The Promise of Private Pensions

Introduction

◆ ◆ ◆

Setting the Problem

Pension: An allowance made to anyone without an equivalent. In England it is generally understood to mean pay given to a state hireling for treason to his country.

—Samuel Johnson's *Dictionary,* 1755

The private pension is one of the great curiosities of modern economic history. Why profit-seeking enterprises provide lifetime incomes to retired employees is murky at best. These initiatives in personnel management have, nonetheless, evolved into huge and complex claims on the financial side of the corporate house. Labor unions, the investment industry, and the national government have also staked out important claims on corporate retirement income programs. Private pensions, as a result, have become a composite institution, composed of managerial, business, actuarial, financial, legal, and political subsystems. Though pensions today touch a great many people and social organizations, only a handful of practitioners understand the rationales that drive the various subsystems, and how they interconnect. Most curious of all, the private pension institution has become the largest owner of corporate stock. What began as management's instrument in the market for labor has emerged, via the market for capital, as its nominal master.

The private pension institution is of recent vintage. Prior to 1900, today's vast and complex pensioning apparatus existed in embryo only, and the elderly derived their livelihood from much simpler sources. They worked, drew income from personal investments, relied on their children, and took charity if necessary. Such was the case in all traditional societies. But this pattern rested on a crumbling economic foundation, whose twin footings were handicraft production and the centrality of the family in economic life.

By the dawn of the twentieth century, America was busily erecting a new industrial economy, with bureaucratic and mechanical structures of great intricacy, scale, and organization. Labor and capital were flowing out of the family economy and into these large corporate establishments. Once there, and under the control of rational, systematic management, the household's factors of production became far more fluid, supple, and productive. But detached from the family and traditional skills, labor and capital suffered dangerous new vulnerabilities. The elderly, in particular, found themselves out of step with the new bureaucratic and mechanized regime. The private pension institution emerged as a way for the new corporate employers to address this deficit — and needs of their own — in a rational, systematic fashion.

The task turned out to be far larger and more resistant to system than the employers had imagined. They were forced to engage outside businesses and specialists to service their plans, including the largest insurance carriers and trust companies and the most sophisticated actuaries, lawyers, and investment managers. The government and the labor unions also demanded, and won, a powerful voice in these employer pension programs. So the institution became a Byzantine mosaic, the product of shifting corporate strategies, union campaigns, congressional mandates, judicial and administrative decisions, and the manipulations of actuarial, insurance, legal, and investment firms.

The institution is also an accretion. Pension plans are carefully counterbalanced sets of commitments, stretching far into the future, running between the employer, perhaps thousands of workers, their unions, the government, and outside investment vehicles. These complex arrangements are continually fought over and adjusted. But because of these carefully counterbalanced commitments, a plan of a particular vintage will persist for decades after the conditions that produced it no longer exist.

The pension institution is today a financial leviathan. A third of the private workforce participates in a private pension plan at any one time. Perhaps two-thirds will accrue a benefit over the course of their working careers. The institution is perhaps the largest beneficiary of federal tax incentives and absorbs more corporate revenue than any other employee "fringe" benefit, with the possible exception of health insurance. Private pension funds, as a result, in 1993 held about $1.5 trillion in assets. Pension liabilities — the present value of future benefit payments — are perhaps even greater.[1]

The institution reached its high-water mark with the passage of the Employee Retirement Income Security Act of 1974, the nation's most ambitious attempt to bring order to its private pension system. ERISA strengthened the institution's commitments and extended its reach. But soon after enactment the nation's larger economic system itself began shifting. The pension had been the creature of big business, big labor, and big government. In the years since 1974 the power of each has declined.

The nation's households still need a retirement income system. They still transfer their labor and capital to corporate engines of production, their members are retiring earlier, and they are living much longer. How profit-seeking enterprises respond to these changes, and to what degree their response is a pensioning system at all, is yet to be seen.

Chapter 1

◆ ◆ ◆

Pensions and Capitalism

Before Corporate Capitalism

The elderly, traditionally, derived most of their income from work. Earning power peaked at a much earlier stage in life — usually between the ages of 30 and 40. But before machines and bureaucracies took production out of human hands — so long as handicraft methods survived in industry, agriculture, and business administration — aged labor maintained its economic value. The tasks involved had been done for generations, and skills and experience, acquired in youth, served age as partial compensation for declining strength and stamina. Society therefore expected its old people to produce, and they did so for as long as they could. In colonial America, estates left by the elderly often held tools for skilled but not especially strenuous crafts, such as tailoring, shoemaking, and weaving. During the nineteenth century, roughly 75 percent of all males over 65 were working. Of those who did not, most probably were disabled.[1]

Because of the small scale of handicraft production, American shops, farms, and business firms were family affairs. Whole families formed the basic unit of employment, even in early factories, and as long as production remained under familial control, the nature and pace of work could readily adjust to the infirmities that arrived with age. Even as a man's hand inevitably slowed, his eye weakened, or his mind lost its acuity, he could continue to produce. And if some aged parent, aunt, or uncle could not help the family win an income in the marketplace, they could contribute to the internal household economy. Grandmothers, especially, but grandfathers as well, contributed by cleaning, cooking, raising children, and producing goods for family consumption. Unless such elderly relations were crippled by physical or mental disability, this labor would not abruptly lose its value and bring on "retirement" from the workforce. And given the quality of medicine in the nineteenth century, death often followed not long after the onset of disability, keeping retirements short.[2]

Investment in the family enterprise also served as a powerful vehicle for transferring income from one stage of life to another. According to the "life-cycle" model of savings and investment, young adults rationally put money aside to support themselves during their years of decline. Family investment decisions are clearly quite complicated; but nineteenth-century family enterprises behaved as if saving — for old age or perhaps for bequests — was an important consideration. In the process of settling the continent, American families built equity in millions of farms, urban lots, and small business enterprises. Agricultural improvements by family farms were the largest component in national capital formation in the first half of the century. These asset values rose with demographic and economic expansion — as the population quadrupled between 1840 and 1900 and product, per capita, tripled. Thus, the heads of family enterprises found themselves in possession of valuable economic properties.[3]

The family enterprise institution also vested the old with powerful property rights vis-à-vis their adult children. Elderly parents held first claim on the firm and its assets, while their offspring remained dependent for their incomes and inheritance. Custom did mandate bequests to children at various times, most notably at marriage. But parents retained ownership over the main body of family assets and chose when they would transfer farms and businesses to their children. Throughout the nineteenth century, parents also continued to give birth to new children through their mid-to-late-thirties. So they needed their property to support minor children to the end of their fifties — to the dawn of old age and the need for assets to support themselves — and through the nineteenth century, the over-65 age cohort controlled more wealth than any other group. They could even command an income after transferring title to their offspring; nineteenth-century documents record numerous cases of parents passing property to their children in return for guarantees of financial support.[4]

The family was a unit of consumption as well as production, and this also served the interests of the elderly. To the extent that a family accrued income, the needs of all generations would be addressed. If a family succeeded, everyone would eat; if it was poor, all felt the lack. The large number of children in nineteenth-century families could spread any burden that arose in caring for parents. A disproportionate share of the elderly also lived in the countryside where the necessities of life — food, fuel, clothing, and shelter — were especially inexpensive. For all these reasons, a large group of socially dependent old people failed to appear in traditional society.[5]

Traditional America did allow an occasional pension. But it understood the term as any periodic payment, with no special connection to superannuation. The British government of the colonial period pensioned its "hirelings," as noted in the quotation from Samuel Johnson used as an epigraph in the Introduction. Churches gave pensions to clerical widows and orphans, starting with the Presbyterians and Moravians in 1741 and 1742. After the Revolutionary War, the United States granted annuities to generals, war heroes, and those disabled in battle; nearly fifty years after the conflict, the federal government pensioned the remaining veterans with noncombat disabilities. Except for the venal pension of Johnson's definition, these payments were given as a symbol of gratitude in return for service to one's community. A soldier's pay clearly provided no compensation for heroics on the battlefield or for time taken away from personal affairs. A minister's income was not a wage but a "living," given by the community to support the selfless activity of the clergy, and it was deemed proper that dependent widows and orphans not be deprived of that "living" should the minister die.[6]

This military and church provision stands in sharp contrast to the lack of pensioning elsewhere in traditional America. Bound tightly to reward for communal service, pensions remained outside the private interest economy. As long as the great bulk of the population used handicraft methods and worked within a family enterprise, the pension would remain anomalous, without the possibility of emerging as a significant institution.

The Rationalized Economy: Factor Markets and Industrial Production

Handicraft, family enterprise, and economic security for the elderly did not vanish overnight. Industrialization and bureaucratization, which changed everything, advanced slowly over the course of the nineteenth century and were far from complete at its close. Nevertheless, the new economy clearly had come to control the nation's central productive apparatus by the year 1900. The material life of the United States had come to rely on instantaneous electronic communications and a railroad network that moved huge tonnages over enormous distances with speed and economy. By relaxing the frictions of time and space, these transportation and communications systems opened mass urban markets to mass production and mass distribution systems. The big business enterprise occupied the center of this rationalized sector, and by 1903, one hundred of these huge corporations controlled 40 percent of private nonfarm assets. Steam and electrically powered machinery now set the tempo in manufacturing, transportation, and mining, even in smaller firms. Wherever bureaucracy and machinery flourished, the scale of enterprise threatened to eclipse the labor and capital resources of any one family, as handicraft techniques and the individual scale in business were absorbed by an expanding productive apparatus.[7]

By the turn of the century, American households had come to depend on capital and labor markets for investment and employment opportunities. Rather than produce goods for sale, households exchanged their "factors of production," their labor and capital, for wages, interest, and dividends. Financial instruments, such as life insurance in force and bank deposits, grew four- to fivefold over the last two decades of the nineteenth century, while reproducible tangible assets expanded only two and one-half times. The manufacturing workforce quadrupled between 1870 and 1910 — from 3.5 to 14.2 million — while the population just doubled. The nation came away from the transaction with far more goods in its consumption basket. Wages in manufacturing were fully 80 percent higher than average farm incomes in 1910 and urban living offered more variety, stimulus, opportunity, and freedom than rural existence. There are no good figures for the return on investment in family businesses at the turn of the century. But the great expansion of the New York Stock Exchange, following the Depression of 1893–1896, indicates the growing appeal of such financial instruments for those who could also invest in some family enterprise.[8]

Along with the new benefits, industrialism brought new unpleasantries. Those in the population working for wages fell subject to an employer's authority and the regimentation of bureaucracy and power machinery. For people born free and raised on the farm, it proved a difficult transition. Worse was unemployment, a new phenomenon. Families knew nothing of layoffs and dismissals, for what could be gained by idling members of the household? But to the modern enterprise, wages represented an avoidable cost. Unlike a family, a firm could cut expenses by disgorging some labor. So when industry slid into depression, or a company lost a market, or an individual could no longer contribute sufficiently, workers lost their jobs. Unemployment loomed as a particular threat to the older employee. Accident and disease wore down the human body far more swiftly in industry and city than in handicraft shops, American small towns, or family farms. Steady industrial progress further corrupted many a worker's productive powers, relentlessly obsolescing his experience and training. Nor did business support anything approaching that diversity of domestic employments which had prolonged the usefulness of older hands in traditional settings. Even if labor retained its market value when 50 or 60 years of age, it would not when 70 or 80. As Robert Margo has shown, workers over 50 in 1900 were not especially disadvantaged in keeping a job; but they had a much tougher time finding a new position once unemployed. Joblessness tended to become permanent, a status that denied older proletarians normal access to the necessities of life.[9]

The basic logic of capitalism would have everyone make individual preparation for old age unemployment. Under the regime of handicraft production and family enterprise, people accumulate capital as part of the normal rhythm of economic life. They build equity in their place of work and own well-established farms and businesses by the time they reach old age. But in the factor-market economy, workers would have to consciously create an estate for their old age by investing part of their income in the capital market. Financial instruments could also protect them against the risk of outliving their resources. Insurance companies issued annuity contracts and could bear the risk of excess longevity by pooling individual mortality experience. So from a purely theoretical perspective, wage and salary workers were quite capable of preparing for their own old age.

Whatever the inherent potential, individual arrangements were not especially successful. Wages and salaries had grown dramatically in the last half of the nineteenth century, and with them the potential surplus available for saving. But expenses for "necessities" and "decencies" had advanced with uncannily parallel quickness. Few families earning less than $800 did much in the way of saving in the early twentieth century, and most wage workers earned less than $500 a year. In 1910 only 45 percent of the elderly in industrial Massachusetts drew *any* income from savings. Those better-paid proletarians who did hold financial assets had them earmarked for other purposes as well: the purchase of consumer durables, educating and equipping children, insuring against premature death, and providing a cushion for periods of illness or unemployment. American insurance companies actually attracted a pitifully small annuity business, and the bulk was drawn from Europe.[10]

Saving for old age is a complicated responsibility, and many factors could explain the limitations of individual thrift arrangements. Effective provision must begin years before; embarking on a savings program thus requires accurate vision, a reasonably high valuation of future experience, and a healthy aversion to risk. The problem of vision was especially acute. The very concept of "unemployment" — of which modern old age retirement is part — did not enter the popular consciousness before the mid-1890s. American men measure their personal prowess in economic terms, and repress the idea of inevitable decline and elimination from the workforce. Even with adequate foresight, wage and salary workers must set aside a substantial portion of their disposable income each year to extend their standard of living into old age. Such discipline had to be maintained in anticipation of an event that could very well never materialize: death in middle age was common, and retirement rare, in the nineteenth-century economy.[11]

This saving process was an extended intertemporal transfer that carried significant risks. Workers exchanged money for financial claims on banks, corporations, and insurance companies; they husbanded these investments from afar during their active years of labor; and lived off the money these paper assets then yielded when old — after the money was translated into consumables. Assets, moreover, could vanish overnight in swindles, bankruptcies, and financial panics. Over 1,000 banks failed during the difficult years between 1893 and 1897, and many dependent aged in the early twentieth century reported they had owned, but subsequently lost, a comfortable nest egg. The cash these assets threw off also fluctuated far more than a worker's wage; the yield on prime commercial paper, a relatively safe security, ranged between 4.7 and 7.6 percent between 1891 and 1898, with the average yearly fluctuation being 1.5 percent. The power of money over commodities also varied, providing elderly investors with unexpected gains and losses. Consumer prices fell 10 percent, then rose 25 percent, between 1893 and 1903, and they moved relatively independently of changes in interest rates.[12]

Given these new vulnerabilities, it comes as something of a surprise

that nineteenth-century reformers and labor leaders seemed blithely un-
concerned with the problem of old age incomes. This reflects, in part,
the weakness of early labor organizations; they focused by necessity on
wage rates and union recognition, the broadest and most immediate
goals of the working class. More important, however, was the fact that
a significant population of workers grown old in wage employment
took time to develop. The gradual unfolding of the modern economy,
a transformation spread out across a continent and a century, softened
the spread of superannuation.[13]

During the early years of U.S. factory production, children and young
men and women operated the machinery. Children entered mills to
supplement the family income while young adults hoped to acquire
capital for a dowry, a farm, or a small shop of their own. Most employees refused to accept their proletarian status as permanent, and few
stayed on beyond middle age. Labor organizations from the Jacksonian
Workingmen's Party to the National Labor Union and the Knights of
Labor at the end of the century actually campaigned for a liberation
from wages and a return to family enterprise, not accommodation to a
permanent employee status. Through the second half of the nineteenth
century and into the twentieth, a massive influx of immigrants satisfied
well over half of industry's exploding labor requirement. Like their native-born predecessors, immigrant workers were primarily young and
enthralled by the family enterprise ideal. Most hoped to save start-up
capital out of their wages and gave little thought to growing old in the
employ of another. From the perspective of business, immigrants bore
unemployment far better than natives. As foreigners they stood on the
periphery of society, trading their labor for cash on a strictly contractual
basis. Their status entailed no right to relief if deprived of work, and
with the onset of industrial crises or excess age, many simply emigrated
home with their savings. The great surge of immigrant labor also allowed native white wage workers to move into secure and well-paying
positions. So few Americans with full social citizenship faced a penu-
rious old age.[14]

Lifelong proletarian careers thus came slowly to America, and the
nation only gradually accumulated a superannuated population. In
1900 most men over 65 worked in handicraft industries — mainly in
agriculture — where they could avoid the uniform performance standards established by bureaucracy and power machinery. More than 60
percent still lived in rural areas where they could remain productive,

live off assets accumulated earlier in life, and retain good access to the basic economic necessities. So no significant group of reformers, before 1910, agitated for improvements in the condition of the elderly.[15]

Various indicators, however, clearly pointed to a rapidly expanding problem at the turn of the century. The labor force participation of older men had remained roughly constant throughout the nineteenth century. But between 1890 and 1900 the percentage of men 65 and over who were out of the labor force jumped from 26.8 to 31.3 percent. The increase, in part, was the residue of the sharp depression of 1893–1896, which permanently separated many older workers from their employers. But it also reflected the declining proportion of the elderly working in agriculture. And this continuing occupational shift, as Jon Moen has shown, led to a continuing sharp decline in labor force participation through the prosperous 1900s.[16]

For some older people, withdrawal from the labor force was a new form of consumption attributable to rising incomes and successful household saving and investment programs. For many if not most, however, it reflected the inability to find a job that paid enough to warrant the effort. A key indication of increasing stress was the sudden rise in shared living arrangements with adult children. Throughout American history, young adults formed separate households and raised their children apart from their parents and in-laws. But by 1900 more than 60 percent of the elderly lived with their adult offspring, an inferior choice, and relied on the earnings of their children to maintain adequate consumption levels. These economic demands at times interfered with their children's and grandchildren's educations, and with their opportunities to invest or take economic risks.[17]

Corroborating the impression of increasing distress was the rapidly growing number of elderly people relying on society for economic support. The local almshouses, modest institutions designed to care for a community's indigents, had become repositories for the aged. Fifty percent of almshouse residents in 1910 were over 60 years of age, a sharp increase from pre–Civil War levels. The elderly had also become an important object of private charity. Philanthropy erected over 800 old age homes, the most visible form of this benevolence, between 1875 and 1919. Combining the population in homes with that in almshouses, society at the turn of the century sheltered perhaps one out of fifty citizens over the age of 60. This proportion certainly ran much higher in urban areas.[18]

But the most dramatic indication of change was not the size of the institutionalized population. As Carole Haber and Brian Gratton have shown, the proportion of institutionalized elderly did *not* rise sharply in the late nineteenth century. What did change was the tremendous expansion of "outdoor" cash assistance via the transformation of the military pensions into a general program of old age relief. The Republicans made military pensions their political instrument in 1890, and steadily expanded eligibility from the sick and wounded to include all aged veterans of Mr. Lincoln's army. The policy helped win elections in Northern states and expended the embarrassing surpluses piled up by the Republican tariff. But the program was conspicuously huge and expensive. It provided benefits to one million Americans by 1900 — three-fourths of whom were elderly and the rest disabled. Of 3.1 million Americans over age 65, one in four got benefits. (Recipients were primarily Northern, white, and native born.) The scheme cost $142 million a year, or 1 percent of GDP, and consumed 25 percent of the federal budget. A program of such magnitude involved more than the obvious partisan side-payments or communal gratitude for battlefield heroics. Only some genuine need, in addition to routine political payoffs, could support this enormous financial transfer.[19]

The spread of industrialism was thus catching up with the aged. For the American household, industrialism meant the export of capital and labor to the new factor markets, there to fetch what they could. Youth and middle age enjoyed the high wages, but often saw little need or safe opportunity for saving and investment. America's transformation, however, was pushing the elderly toward difficult straits. The shrinking traditional sector no longer absorbed their labor. The factories and bureaucracies provided fewer places. Deprived of family enterprises as investment vehicles, fewer than half held any cash-producing assets. And those with assets were dependent on the market for food, clothing, and sometimes shelter, and thus were far less secure than those in traditional circumstances. As seen in the growing numbers relying on children, on traditional relief institutions, or on military pensions, a growing portion of the elderly was sliding toward dependence.

The future, moreover, looked bleak. The number of aged wage and salary workers increased daily, both absolutely and as a proportion of the population. But the number of federal pensioners would peak in 1902, as the stock of Civil War veterans began to die off. The almshouse was universally regarded as inappropriate and demeaning as a final rest-ing home, and local charities were ill-equipped to care for the rising tide of superannuated labor. Industrialism had "distended" the structure of American institutions, to use Robert Wiebe's fine phrase, and this signaled a major economic crisis for the elderly in the coming century.[20]

Pensions in the Age of Pure Capitalism

Nineteenth-century employers, as a rule, had not involved themselves in the problem of old age finance. The standard labor contract imposed no obligation on the firm other than cash payment at the time of labor service. Moreover, the tremendous mobility of nineteenth-century labor prevented the enterprise from becoming the national bedrock of old age income security. Workers jumped incessantly from one job to another as the market for labor continually opened new opportunities. The result, for the firm, was a confusing jumble of past, present, and prospective employees. Nevertheless, a handful of nineteenth-century businesses found reasons to pay out retirement allowances. These few firms experimented with several pensioning programs, and by 1900 had accumulated a measure of experience. These enterprises, a tiny minority, had begun to ameliorate old labor's disadvantaged state.

Family enterprise, the primary employer throughout the nineteenth century, almost never provided superannuation relief. Prosperous families, of course, had often developed bonds of affection toward their household or business servants, and would support these employees through their old age. The earliest company pensions no doubt grew out of such personal attachments spawned by years of faithful service. The cut of the market economy, however, kept such human stirrings in check. Continued success in business required colder calculations, for too large an entrepreneurial heart guaranteed only bankruptcy. More important, traditional family businesses rarely confronted the problem of superannuated long-service workers. Family farms typically hired outside hands only during harvest and planting seasons. Commercial and handicraft establishments had notoriously short lifespans. Nor did wage workers look to their employers for long-term economic security. They relied on their handicraft skills or hoped to establish a business of their own. Little distinguished labor from other marketed commodities, little but its capacity for mischief, and the simple exchange of cash for current labor services suited the interests and ambitions of both parties.

But economic rationalization was transforming employment relations in capitalist firms. The process of mechanization and bureaucratization drew labor and capital out of the household, into larger and more complex and durable enterprises. Such firms not only hired more workers but assigned them more responsibility and retained them for longer periods of time. Salaried managers actually directed many of the nation's largest enterprises by 1900, and in some organizations, such as the railroads, "employment in the service is generally understood to be permanent." While rationalization created stronger attachments between employer and employee, it also set limits on the duration of the relationship. By standardizing the pace of production and steadily obsolescing skill and experience, it hastened older workers to the superannuated state. Rationalization thus lured capital and labor to a liaison at once long-term and terminal.[21]

As capital and labor fell into this web of interdependence, both parties sought to shape a relationship to suit their interests. Workers wanted status, security, and justice as well as high wages. Business sought loyal and vigorous employees, and feared lest its best workers respond to the calls of unionism, alternate employment, or entrepreneurial ambition. In the past, standard cash-wage contracting had effectively equilibrated differences between employers and employees. But as rationalization entangled the market's invisible hand, relations veered erratically from labor monopoly, to capital monopsony, to the highly unstable bilateral monopoly. Relations between capital and labor grew powerfully conflicted; suspicion and defensiveness characterized labor-management interactions; and vicious strikes and counter-strikes periodically broke up the production process. So employers gradually turned to more innovative, long-term arrangements. The private pension institution emerged as a byproduct of these employer efforts to establish a more stable and efficient employment relationship with labor.[22]

Among the new strategies adopted by nineteenth-century employers, the most popular was welfare capitalism. Its rationale was, essentially, that systematic displays of diffuse and "gratuitous" benevolence would create a loyal, vigorous, and stable workforce. Examples ranged from subsidized housing and English-language classes to recreational facilities, insurance benefits, and profit-sharing. The programs were extensions of the kindliness wealthy businessmen had traditionally shown their household and business servants, and most welfare capitalists claimed altruistic motives. In some instances this must have been the case. But in the competitive environment of nineteenth-century America, welfare capitalism could flourish only if benevolent displays enhanced productive efficiency or served some other commercial purpose. Capitalists could look after labor's welfare if doing so attached workers' interests to those of the firm, suppressed their entrepreneurial ambitions, or led them to pass up offers from other employers or resist the appeals of union solidarity.[23]

The Midvale Steel Company provides a good illustration of welfare capitalism as applied to the older worker. In testimony before the U.S. Industrial Commission in 1900, Midvale's president, Charles J. Harrah, reported: "we give [the superannuated employee] a job tending a gate, and he thinks he is doing a day's work sitting by a stove and challenging everybody that wishes to come in . . . [if he becomes fully] incapacitated from age or from work or sickness the company pays him his wages. That continues for life. . . . That is one reason they do not care to leave our employ. They know they will be looked after."[24]

Rational policy, not personal sentiment, directed Midvale's behavior. Harrah showed more condescension than compassion for the man keeping his gate. He wanted to retain young active workers and, to that end, let them "know they will be looked after." This required Midvale to care for its superannuated men and even to develop a pension roll. But the firm did all it could to keep its old and faithful servants in harness. Management saw to it that "men do not like to go on the pension list. They look on it as a disgrace." Only when an employee suffered from "paresis or locomotor ataxia," posing a positive danger to plant and personnel, did the company allow or compel retirement. Midvale's benevolence, while clearly advantageous to its aged employees, had tightly circumscribed bounds.[25]

Midvale's brand of ad hoc welfare capitalism was probably among the more liberal methods for dealing with aged labor. Although it is impossible to characterize standard nineteenth-century practice, most employers probably ushered their older workers out with a few dollars, a handshake, and some kindly advice. An 1889 survey of railroads, firms offering noncash benefits far more than American business as a whole, found that 85 percent of the companies surveyed — mainly small, subsidiary lines — provided neither pensions nor employment to their superannuated workers. Many of the remaining 15 percent, like Midvale, relied primarily on light work assignments.

The number of firms that put their initiatives into written, quasi-contractual documents further shows the limited spread of pensioning. Companies formalized their personnel policies to enhance their visibility and reliability, and thereby their effectiveness at winning employee allegiance. But by 1900 only five industrializing family firms had put such formal pension plans in operation: Alfred Dolge, Sherwin-Williams, John Wanamaker, Solvay Process, and Procter & Gamble. This paltry figure could reflect the extent of employer benevolence, or perhaps the number of older long-service workers then engaged in American industry. But in either case, nineteenth-century business was little occupied with the problems of the older proletarian.[26]

While only a handful of family firms formalized a pension promise, old age income security, far more than other benevolences, required such a written declaration of intent. Receipt lay far in the future, and firms not making a formal pledge could arbitrarily reduce or even eliminate an old man's means of support. All formal pension plans contained exculpatory clauses that released sponsoring firms from legal liability. The rules governing the first plan adopted by an American manufacturing firm, the Dolge plan of 1882, stipulated this quite precisely:

> It is distinctly understood that all and every of the provisions of this [plan by-]law are voluntary on behalf of said house of Alfred Dolge, and that this law does not, nor does any of the provision herein contained, confer any legal right or create any legal right in favor of any employee of said house mentioned herein, or of any person or persons whomsoever, nor any legal liability on behalf of said house of Alfred Dolge, or of said Alfred Dolge, either in law or in equity.

Nevertheless, firms with written plans, such as Dolge, placed their good names squarely behind the pension promise. Although they occasionally exercised their privilege to modify pension benefits, they did so only under extreme circumstances.[27]

Given the seriousness of this long-run commitment, it is hardly surprising that the nineteenth-century family enterprise had little use for the pension. Firms interested in welfare capitalism gravitated instead toward a similar but ultimately quite different form of deferred compensation — profit-sharing. According to Stuart Brandes, historian of American welfare capitalism, profit-sharing became "the most popular of welfare activities." By conflating the rewards of labor and capital, profit-sharing seemed to tie the interests of workers, quite directly, to those of the company. Business could then bypass welfare capitalism's polite indirection—"I am concerned for you, so would you please be concerned for me." Profit-sharing, moreover, channeled benefits straight to the active workforce, while pensions gave cash to the superannuated and just distant promises to the young and energetic.[28]

The pension, put simply, traded in a time frame far too long for most nineteenth-century employers and employees. Among the family firms installing pension plans, at least two—Dolge and Procter & Gamble—offered the benefit only as an extension of a preexisting profit-sharing plan. As long as ad hoc gratuities satisfied the minimum demands of employer benevolence, and pension plans did little for the enterprise, welfare capitalism expended more rhetoric than resources on the superannuated worker.[29]

Chapter 2

♦ ♦ ♦

Business Finds an Interest

Railroading was the one business to develop a serious pension practice in the nineteenth century, and the early history of the institution is largely a history of railroad programs. The railroads were at the vanguard of economic mechanization and bureaucratization, and were the first corporations to develop modern employment practices. Efficient operation required a large permanent staff, with periodic replacement of superannuated workers. As the nation's first big businesses, the railroads also had the huge size and strategic economic position to overcome a basic barrier to the development of private pension programs: the ability to make believable promises of payments to be delivered decades in the future.

Three major firms, each pursuing a distinct managerial purpose, established benchmark plans in the final quarter of the nineteenth century. These enterprises laid out the primary rationales behind private pensioning and defined the basic options in U.S. plan design prior to 1920. Welfare capitalism was one such larger managerial purpose, as it was with the handful of nineteenth-century family firms that had offered their workers a pension. But vogues of welfare capitalism came and went, and management often embraced initiatives other than old age allowances as a way to make peace with its workers. Because the pension served several managerial functions, it actually would enjoy a far more durable career — on the railroads and in business generally — than the strategy of corporate benevolence.

To "Permanently Attach . . . Better Men"

The modern pension institution first appeared in North America in 1874, with the installation of the Grand Trunk Railway of Canada Superannuation and Provident Association. This organization had nothing to do with welfare capitalism, for it explicitly excluded the proletariat, the target of all welfare-capitalist efforts, and restricted participation to "salaried officers, clerks, passenger and freight agents, telegraph operators, road masters, inspectors in any department and foremen in the mechanical department." Not that the Grand Trunk had no interest in the welfare of its manual labor force. One year earlier it had organized a trainmen's accident insurance program, the first in North America. That this insurance package omitted old age income protection, and that its 1874 pension scheme specifically excluded manual workers, clearly indicate that the Grand Trunk Superannuation Association operated outside the framework of classic welfare capitalism.[1]

To understand the Grand Trunk's purpose, one must examine British pension practices. The Grand Trunk directors resided in London, and the scheme they installed was standard on English railroads. The plan was compulsory for all employees who entered the service before the age of 37, and required a contribution of 2.5 percent of salary to a pension fund. Beginning at age 55 these workers could voluntarily retire on pension and receive, for each year of plan membership, one-sixtieth of final salary to a maximum of two-thirds of salary. The company matched worker contributions and met any plan deficit, up to 50 percent of total employee payments. In addition to its main purpose of assuring old age income, the scheme contained elements of a savings program. Should participants not remain in service until retirement — should they quit, be honorably discharged, become disabled, or die — the plan returned some or all of their contributions. Only workers dismissed for cause lost everything. Only those retiring on pension, however, benefited from the company payments and the interest on their own contributions.[2]

This strange and convoluted English design, first seen on the London and North Western Railway in 1853, was itself an imitation of Britain's recently established pension arrangements for civil servants. The government's Superannuation Act of 1834 satisfied an urgent bureaucratic need, and similar programs would soon give service to English, Canadian, and American organizations.

The government, by necessity, operated a widely dispersed organization that delegated power and responsibility to a large class of officials. Developing and controlling such agents had been a difficult task, and the promise of an old age pension emerged, in the early nineteenth century, as an important instrument to induce competent and faithful service. This somewhat resembled the rationale behind welfare capitalism; the essential difference was class. The civil service pension was directed at a highly differentiated complex of salaried officials, not the homogeneous proletariat. It rewarded investments in organization-specific skills and personal relationships, and the dutiful execution of official responsibilities over an extended length of time. The plans applied to both clerks and senior officials, and tracked individual careers from entry to exit. By necessity, the schemes paid great attention to employee equities — crediting individual account balances and specifying withdrawal rights. Benefits assumed the form of individual contractual rights and carried an official guarantee of payment.[3]

The civil service and its pension plan had a history quite distinct from that of welfare capitalism. It addressed a managerial problem — the effective operation of an extended administrative apparatus — that antedated industrialism and indeed existed in the earliest empires of ancient civilization, and would continue to bedevil enterprises that employed few if any manual workers. Prior to civil service, positions in government had been largely hereditary or dependent on political favor. The state had felt no obligation to support its superannuated servants. Gratitude, indeed, typically flowed the opposite way. Government office had been a prize piece of property, a royal gift passing through a network of personal allegiances to the king's ultimate delegate, and those in office fully expected to profit from their official positions. Twelfth-century vassals thus had exploited the king's serfs and eighteenth-century placemen had helped themselves to his taxes. Had such means of enrichment been denied, most "officials" would have turned to other pursuits, or other kings.[4]

Modern administrative reformers systematically strove to expropriate such property rights and place the duties of office above the interests of its holder. They would proletarianize the governing class and make administration a job. In the process they fashioned a new form of employment: the bureaucratic career. The term "career" derived from the

French word for "race course" and assumed its modern meaning early in the nineteenth century; the *Oxford English Dictionary* dates "diplomatic career" to 1803 and "public career" to 1815. The notion involved a lifelong professional or organizational pursuit that offered opportunities for personal advancement. Civil service reformers recognized the value of a loyal, vigorous, and experienced staff, and hoped to hold and promote men in diplomatic or public careers until they could work no longer. As the security and opportunity of government employment grew apparent, young men, especially those more able than well-connected, eagerly offered their services to the state. The pension emerged early on in the development of this bargain; it surfaced as the price to be paid in exchange for an administrative career.[5]

The cost of an official's pension was not met only by the state. Before the establishment of the modern civil service, certain British administrators had retired on pensions provided not by a grateful government but by their successors. As the government bureaucracy had solidified in the eighteenth century, incumbent officials took hold of their offices as pseudo–personal property, and held them out as pseudo–objects of commerce. When close to retirement, these placemen would trade their positions to ambitious young men in exchange for half their official salary. With the Superannuation Act of 1834, the government interposed itself between the two parties. It commuted the official's "property" interest into a pension claim against the Treasury and required all active employees to contribute a portion of their salaries to support the new program. Despite this dramatic redistribution of rights and payments, no player in the triangle suffered. Retiring allowances increased to two-thirds of final salary at age 65, with forty-five years of service, and the payments became far more secure. (In 1859 the scheme was liberalized to one-sixtieth of salary per year, for up to forty years of service, with retirement as early as age 60.) Young men still contributed to their predecessors' retirement income, but the price fell sharply and the cost was spread across their working careers. The state assumed new managerial and financial liabilities, but gained the greatest prize of all. By inducing officials to remain in service and capturing their desire for personal wealth, the pension was instrumental in creating a dedicated, career civil service.[6]

Railroads were the first modern enterprises to require large bureaucratic organizations, and they likewise adopted the pension to develop a loyal, experienced, and permanent administrative staff. The Grand

Trunk pension association, according to general manager L. J. Seargeant, aimed at securing "permanence of service, and the relief of the
individual from anxieties attendant upon the contemplation of the period of inability to provide for himself and his family — in fact it has
been thought that superannuation associations would permanently attach to the service better men and secure from them the better performance of their duties." Such associations encouraged longevity and loyal
service by basing rights on years of service and the circumstances of
separation. As officials aged and grew in experience and responsibility,
the plan held out the pension as an ever more graspable reward for
dutiful service.[7]

The Grand Trunk pension scheme also gave temporal shape to a railroad career, a critical contribution. It specified 55 as the minimum age
for voluntary retirement, marking the earliest permissible terminus to
the employment relationship. It also established age 37 as a fundamental turning point. Everyone younger was required to join and no one
older could enter the program; while the younger men scrambled for
a place in the collective enterprise, those off the corporate payroll at age
37 were permanently cut adrift. The plan then managed the triangular
trade in corporate careers across the employee's workspan. It taxed the
young in exchange for their career opportunity and it rewarded the old
for a career of reasonably selfless service. As employees typically valued
retirement benefits only after age 37, and as railroad promotions typically grew scarce at that age, the pension became a critical tool for
retaining valued middle-aged staff.[8]

Although the Grand Trunk scheme clearly served rational corporate
interests, Seargeant was not above cloaking the pension in the garb of
welfare capitalism. He claimed that "when an employe becomes, as it
were, part of the service, when performance of duty results in habits
which lead him to neglect [personal] opportunities, when sympathies
create an *esprit de corps,* and when the whole of those cooperating causes
lead to a lifelong work in the interests of one company, there seems to
be a moral claim upon the benevolence of employers who have benefited by faithful, if not brilliant services." The plan, of course, offered
no such benevolence to equally permanent, selfless, and even more
needy blue-collar workers. Only the officer class, the career employees
of the railroad, "earned" a Grand Trunk pension. The company thus
recognized this corps of loyal, responsible, and experienced executives

as a significant resource, a stock of human capital that had to be built and maintained systematically. The pension did just that.[9]

"Indemnity against Sickness"

In the United States, as opposed to Canada, the first railroad pension plans grew out of the welfare-capitalist tradition. The American Express Company, a railroad freight forwarder, set up the nation's first formal scheme in 1875 within this context of corporate benevolence. As explained in the minutes of the company's executive committee:

> Cases [are] constantly arising of application for assistance by employees of the Company, injured or worn out in the service. It [is] therefore Resolved:
> that all payments on account of the above named applications be charged to a separate account to be known as the Pension account, and not charged as heretofore to current expenses.
> Resolved:
> that the Genl Supt. is hereby directed to report to the Executive Committee names of such employees of the Co. as are now deserving of and entitled to such assistance and heretofore from time to time report such additional cases as may arise.
> Adopted.

American Express thus formalized an existing ad hoc welfare-capitalist program as a bureaucratic and bookkeeping convenience. The company extended old age "assistance" to anyone in the firm "injured or worn out in the service" and set allowances at half salary up to a maximum of $500. The Grand Trunk, by contrast, limited pensions to company officials, had no incapacity requirement, and allowed pensions up to a far more generous maximum of two-thirds of average pay. Through 1892 American Express spent nearly twice as much on pensions as the Grand Trunk Railway. But because its benefits were substantially lower and beneficiaries required proof of incapacity, its cost per participant was perhaps one-sixth of the Grand Trunk's expenditure.[10]

When the Baltimore & Ohio Railroad installed the second U.S. private pension plan, in 1880, it also did so as a manifestation of corporate benevolence. The B&O, in fact, provided old age income protection as part of the first formal and comprehensive employee benefit package in the railroad industry. Unlike American Express, the company carefully specified plan details, explicitly tied pension benefits to its wider welfare initiative, and actively publicized the program. The B&O, as a result, became the model for railroad welfare-capitalist practice, and other companies, over the remaining years of the century, would use its plan as their major point of departure when they reviewed their relations with labor.[11]

Prior to 1880 U.S. railroad executives displayed little interest in their blue-collar workers and allowed their conditions of employment to evolve ad hoc. As detailed by Walter Licht, "local officials handled recruitment, discipline, job assignments, compensation, promotions, and informal injury and death benefit awards, as well as other aspects of the work, in arbitrary and discretionary ways." The skilled — the engineers, firemen, and conductors — responded by organizing independent craft unions to protect themselves from the capricious decisions of local officials, and to win greater control over the terms of their employment. The less skilled experimented with even more aggressive forms of collective representation. The result was turbulence, indiscipline, and turnover so pervasive, writes Licht, that "the real question of labor supply was not whether an adequately large and competent pool of workers existed to staff the industry, but whether railway labor once mobilized could be retained." This era of corporate inattention came to a sudden end in 1877, in the midst of the 1873–1879 depression. Responding to an industry-wide pay cut, railroad workers as a class set out on a frighteningly violent nationwide riot, and were met by a similarly vicious response by management. Strikers and militiamen fought pitched battles and railyards burned to the ground; casualties numbered in the hundreds and property damage ran to the tens of millions. The event shocked the nation and forced management to recast its labor policies.[12]

It was to reestablish peace that the B&O turned to welfare capitalism. The railroads were already pursuing an "efficiency wage" compensation strategy — paying their workmen a premium wage. They did so not just to attract better workers but as a token of corporate benevolence, as part of what George Akerlof calls a "gift exchange" with labor. Already offering premium pay for premium service, the company could hardly expect to improve its relations with labor by raising wages further. After inquiries identified a pervasive insecurity as the workmen's primary complaint, management responded by stabilizing and rationalizing the lives of its employees. It removed much of the foremen's rough and arbitrary authority and began to routinize hiring, firing, and discipline. It was in this spirit of rationalizing benevolence that the B&O, in 1880, established an "Employe's Relief Association" to provide insurance protection, especially against accidents. The program functioned as a token of corporate benevolence, and the workmen, for their part, sorely needed the coverage. One in 120 American trainmen lost their lives each year and another one in twelve suffered injury. Railroad employment was so hazardous that life insurance companies typically refused to write policies on trainmen and several states actually forbade such coverage.[13]

After accidents, railroadmen would typically pass the hat among themselves. The amounts raised this way had never been sufficient, and the collections imposed an unpredictable strain on employees' finances. The workmen and their unions often formalized this process by organizing workmen's insurance societies; but these initiatives had not been very successful. "In a comparatively small portion of our country," reported R. F. Smith of the Pennsylvania Railroad, "more than four hundred of these and kindred associations failed and were wound up within the short period of eight years [1886–1893]." The companies themselves had thitherto been largely successful in avoiding legal liability for workplace injuries and deaths. But as explained by Dr. W. T. Barnard, the man who designed the B&O program, "one result of the indifference of railway management towards their subordinates has been to array against them agencies most potent in fermenting discontent — secret societies, brotherhoods and similar organizations; for it is a notorious fact that they owe their success mainly to the assistance and relief they hold out to their members and their families in case of sickness, disablement and death." Prior to 1880 various railroads had operated an informal "system of gratuities" for accident victims, with local officials distributing this corporate charity. But this, too, proved unsatisfactory. According to Smith, managers found the practice "essentially vicious, both in principle and results; as toward the employing company, inequitable and more and more impossible of proper and discriminating administration; as toward the employes demoralizing and necessarily inadequate."[14]

The workmen's insurance program installed by the B&O in 1880 was a major step forward. Barnard had carefully examined the Canadian plan, as well as others in England and Europe, and his design owed much to their influence. His B&O relief association thus insured workers against sickness and injuries incurred off the job, protection offered in some of these employer programs but otherwise unavailable. "Where men are employed in large numbers, and under thorough organization and discipline," wrote R. F. Smith, "it is feasible or safe to undertake indemnity against sickness." Observers on both sides of the Atlantic were also coming to the opinion that blue-collar railroad workers needed and could be provided with pensions. In 1880 the English Great Western Railway set up such a program and the Massachusetts Railroad Commissioners reported that "most railroad men agree that it is desirable to have some method by which employes of large railroad corporations can be insured in case of accident and death and have pensions when disabled or superannuated." So Barnard, an official in the vanguard of industry opinion, included a "pension feature" in his relief association.[15]

Barnard at first designed a curious pension arrangement. His plan allowed relief association members to deposit funds with the company on a regular basis and, upon retirement, receive a pension of ten cents for each dollar contributed, plus an additional half-cent per dollar for each year of membership in the relief association. The B&O in effect offered its employees an opportunity to purchase annuities. But despite what may have been the best intentions of the B&O, the offer was hardly a benevolent vehicle for universal old age income security. Should a worker enter the company's service at age 20 and contribute each year 5 percent of his income, he would receive as a pension less than 30 percent of his salary. Investing this sum at going rates of interest would generate an income stream 25 percent greater than the B&O pension. So workers surviving to retirement could enjoy higher old age incomes and leave the underlying asset to their widows and children. Should they not survive, their heirs would have their accumulated savings, as opposed to nothing in the B&O plan. Barnard's scheme made sense only for those who were close to retirement, had financial assets to purchase a B&O annuity, and expected to live in retirement for more than a decade. Thus it is hardly surprising that only one employee signed up, and the company discontinued the "benefit" in 1889.[16]

The pension was not the only feature of the B&O relief program to run into trouble. Far more controversial was Barnard's decision, following standard English and Canadian practice, to mandate association membership. Employees opposed this requirement, wanting to maintain their freedom. Union men also feared the competition for worker loyalty and encroachment on their fragile relief organizations. This opposition thus perturbed the goodwill the program was designed to create, and management, in the prosperous 1880s, usually sought consensus with workers and their representatives. The B&O ultimately decided to keep its insurance program compulsory, but it added new benefits to sweeten the package. The pension reappeared as one of these sweeteners, in 1884.[17]

The revised B&O welfare scheme offered free pensions to all members of the relief association. The plan allowed employees with ten or more years of service to retire voluntarily, at age 65, or if disabled at age 60. Allowances were one-half the employee's sickness benefit, with a modest 5 percent increase for each five years of association membership in excess of ten. The resulting pensions were low. Workers earning between $420 and $600 a year got fifty cents a day, not including Sundays and legal holidays; each quinquennium of association membership beyond the first two brought another two and one-half cents a day. After thirty years of service (and mandatory association membership), pensions approximated one-third of such a worker's wage. Replacement ratios were lower in other income classes, however, and workers earning less than $420 annually got but $90 a year, barely one-fifth of their former livelihood.[18]

The B&O plan of 1884 stood as welfare capitalism's high-water mark in railroad pension planning. Barnard tied his allowance tightly to his relief association and its larger purpose of pacifying blue-collar labor. Pensions accrued only to members of the relief association, which included only manual workers, and payments were a function of the employee's standard insurance benefit. As indicated by the meager allowances and limited increment gained from long service, the plan targeted the subsistence minimum, just enough to keep body and soul together. The B&O insurance plan viewed old age as an enfeebling illness, in conformity with the prevalent view at the time, and gave pensioners the same allowance it provided to the long-term disabled. Barnard's entire welfare initiative gave workers a protective safety net against the hazards of proletarian life. Should they die or become disabled — whether from accident, illness, or age — the B&O relief association would keep his family from destitution. The pension was a token of corporate benevolence, part of a larger gift of security, for which the company expected, in return, loyal and diligent service.

"The Utilitarian Side of the Sociological Problem"

The third and final pension rationale appeared in its fully articulated form in the Pennsylvania Railroad plan of January 1, 1900. Whereas the Grand Trunk pension had emerged in response to an ancient administrative problem, and the B&O had addressed a current social crisis, the scheme developed by the Pennsylvania was clearly forward looking. It addressed a concern specific to the large and highly organized big business enterprises that would dominate economic life in the twentieth century.

The Pennsylvania had perhaps the most advanced business organization in the world in 1900. It employed more workers than any other firm and boasted perhaps the finest staff of professional managers. The company encountered all the difficulties inherent in the new employment relationships and had the capacity to devise a modern and effective response. Its managers studied the personnel practices of the English railroads and the B&O, and adopted policies that developed executives and pacified proletarians. But the company's plan of 1900 gave the pension a new rationale in the American context. In addition to defining relationships with bureaucrats and brakemen, the benefit helped the enterprise maintain the efficiency of its highly tuned productive process.[19]

The work of the modern organized enterprise involves an extensive division of labor controlled by a central authority. Adam Smith's classic description of a pin factory crisply illustrates the gist of the matter: ten specialists, working in a carefully planned array, producing pins with remarkable efficiency. Smith saw the pin factory as a minor example of divided labor and held up the market, not the firm, as the master coordinator of economic specialization. It was industrialization, which brought a tremendous leap in the scale and speed of production and distribution, that shifted the balance toward managerial control. As Alfred Chandler argues, the organized enterprise handled the massive new volumes and breakneck velocities far better than Smith's invisible hand. Railroads were the first business organizations to manage such speeding economic systems, and the first to employ a highly divided and organized workforce. And the Pennsylvania Railroad, with "the most completely organized departments of any civil corporation in the country," was the first to appreciate the uses of the pension for maintaining organizational efficiency.[20]

Complex enterprises such as railroads divided labor two ways—horizontally by technical function and vertically by bureaucratic authority. The railroads became so tightly organized, even in the nineteenth century, that the smallest units of production required close coordination among various occupational specialists, and close supervision by several layers and divisions of management. The services provided by all these employees were essentially complementary, with the output of any one worker tied closely to the output of co-workers, and with limited ability to substitute the labor of one for another. One inefficient man thus degraded an entire group's performance. Massive train wrecks periodically illustrated the implications of an engineer's failing eyesight or a brakeman's weakened arms. Although less graphic in their effects on the organization, enfeebled managers steadily lost the respect of subordinates and cost the firm unnecessary expense and missed opportunities. It was therefore essential to remove older workers unable to perform their duties.[21]

This sharply defined, finely divided, and highly structured work apparatus crystallized first in U.S. railroads. And "the large enterprises that were to operate the American railroad network throughout the twentieth century," writes Chandler, "took their modern form in the 1880s." During that decade, management standardized the work day and established the essential medium of labor coordination—official railroad time. Unions likewise became significant players, doubling in number and for the first time commanding sizable membership lists. Written, collectively bargained contracts now commonly defined railroad wage rates and working conditions. As bureaucracy and the railroad brotherhoods exercised their influence, they sharpened the divisions of labor and strengthened the sway of seniority in personnel decisions. All collective bargaining agreements rewarded longevity; and corporate officials developed their own informal seniority system. Management generally supported these developments, as productivity typically increased with experience and the company hoped to restrict the discretionary authority of foremen and local officials. But as railroad labor practices grew more precise and rigid, and the numbers of older employees expanded, it became critical to eliminate the superannuated worker.[22]

As large, government-regulated corporations, railroads were sensitive to employee and public opinion. So they avoided summary dismissals. Residential homes were expensive, unpopular, and thus not an attractive option, and easing the load on older workers fell out of step with the tightening railroad work process in the 1880s. It became socially, psychologically, and administratively difficult, and undermined the new organizing norm of seniority, to assign employees who had risen through the ranks light work duty carrying lower pay and prestige. The major alternative to retirement on pension thus lost its appeal at precisely the time, and for precisely the reason, that a policy of eliminating the elderly became increasingly necessary. The downward inflexibility of wages, which came with the crystallization of corporate career employment relations, meant a mere decline in productivity could become an ongoing drain, as Edward Lazear argues in his brilliant article "Why Is There Mandatory Retirement?" Retirements also produced a chain of promotions in the generally static railroad organization. This gave heart to ambitious young workers and supplied managers with a fresh stock of rewards. Especially toward the top of the organization, where seniority had less sway and the distribution of work was less predefined, retirements gave managers valuable opportunities to restaff and reshape the organization. The pension also helped them promote younger men and pass over the old, for it provided an independent reward for long and faithful service.

Originally, pensions appeared on the Pennsylvania not as a means of retiring the elderly but as part of a welfare-capitalist initiative. John A. Anderson, the man who designed the company program, had been grouped with the B&O's W. T. Barnard, the other pioneer of railroad welfare planning, as a reformer "of broad humanitarian and christian views." His 1886 package of benefits for blue-collar workers was also quite similar to Barnard's on the B&O. But perhaps owing to the difficulties Barnard experienced, Anderson kept his insurance program voluntary. And because pensions were expensive, he included no formal old age income option. Nevertheless, the Pennsylvania informally assisted the superannuated in a manner quite similar to the B&O. Older workers unable to perform their duties could claim a benefit under the company's sickness insurance program, and after this coverage expired, after fifty-two weeks, the company continued payments using corporate funds. These allowances, a contemporary observed, were "tantamount to pensions paid out by the company." And Anderson was building up a pension endowment from all surpluses generated by the insurance program; upon accumulating a sum he considered sufficient, probably enough to pay benefits out of interest income, he hoped to make pensions a formal feature of his welfare program.[23]

The key innovation in the Pennsylvania's 1886 welfare scheme was not in benefit design but in corporate organization and control. During the earlier, somnambulant era of railroad labor-management relations, personnel policy toward blue-collar workers had fallen by default to foremen, unions, independent employee benefit societies, and evangelical organizations such as the YMCA. The B&O and Grand Trunk/ English railroads had then developed positive policies toward labor, but had pursued their initiatives at arm's length, through quasi-independent employee relief associations. Parliament had chartered the British and Canadian relief organizations as distinct legal entities; the Maryland legislature had done the same for the B&O. Because these relief associations had been modeled after and competed with existing labor organizations, elected employee representatives had exercised a critical influence. The Pennsylvania, however, diverged from this setup and decided to administer its welfare activities within the firm, through an internal "Voluntary Relief *Department.*" It allowed employee representation on the department's board of overseers. But it retained control and kept policy, administration, and financial decisions firmly in management's hands.[24]

The creation of the Pennsylvania Railroad relief department stood at the beginning of modern corporate personnel administration, an event of the greatest significance for the future of pension planning. Employee welfare management became an integral function of the firm and the distribution of benefits inevitably grew sensitive to the needs of the employer. General corporate managers readily proposed shifts in plan design that would condition labor to better serve their ends. Max Riebenack, the man responsible for the 1900 revision of the Pennsylvania pension plan, defined the impulse behind this corporate "welfare" policy as

> the desire of industrial concerns requiring for their adequate operation large forces of employees, with differing lines of employment, to subserve, maintain and develop corporate entity throughout its varied ramifications. The railways . . . were among the first . . . to perceive and act upon the question of concentrating the [welfare] interests of their employees within the purview and jurisdiction of corporate oversight and control, by affording, largely through their own revenues, avenues leading to the establishment of a standard of individual efficiency. In short, they have grasped the utilitarian side of the sociological problem.

The Pennsylvania's informal 1886 pension program thus based a worker's superannuation allowance on "the length of his faithful service with the company," not years of participation in a quasi-independent relief association. Bypassing the indirections of the benevolent association, the company could reward a corporate objective distinct from mere employee goodwill and stability. American personnel management, after originating in welfare capitalism, now attempted to affect more directly the utilization of labor in corporate settings. And the pension, more than any other welfare-capitalist instrument, served this new agenda.[25]

The transformation of the pension at the Pennsylvania began in 1889, with the organization of a committee to formalize the company plan. The first indication that the committee would entertain issues beyond the pale of welfare capitalism was the choice of Riebenack as chairman. As assistant comptroller of the railroad, Riebenack was a far more prominent and powerful figure in the Pennsylvania hierarchy than the superintendent of the relief department; the comptroller's office had contact with all parts of the enterprise, exercised general oversight of executive recruitment and promotions, and handled the company's circulation of funds. Riebenack also launched an extensive international study of "railway provident institutions" in the mid-1890s, the results of which were published by the International Railway Congress in 1905. This effort brought the assistant comptroller, an official typically focused on internal corporate matters, into contact with pension experts on both sides of the Atlantic.

The problem of the superannuated worker and the usefulness of pensions in shedding aging employees were steadily gaining attention in the 1890s. An early public reference appeared in 1893, when Samuel Barr, superintendent of the B&O relief department, quoted the arguments of "the celebrated Dr. Farr of England" for offering "superannuation" benefits. The contribution to organizational as opposed to individual efficiency is reason number four:

> In the first place, superannuation is a guarantee of fidelity; in the second place it encourages efficient officers; in the third place it retains good men in service; in the fourth place it induces men to retire when they become old or inefficient from any cause; and in the fifth place it prevents old employes from falling into disgraceful dependence or distressing destitution, which would be a public scandal and deter desirable persons from entering the service.[26]

The call for retirements became more pressing toward the end of the decade. Railroads and their insurance companies were blaming an upsurge in accidents on union seniority rules and the superannuated train-men thereby kept in service. As railroads became larger, faster, more complicated and finely tuned, and dependent on what Riebenack called the "standard of individual efficiency," their labor force was rapidly ag-ing. Fewer than 3 percent of Philadelphia's railroad workers were over 55 in 1880; twenty years later, about 1 percent of Pennsylvania Railroad workers were over 70. At precisely the wrong time, the railroads were becoming, in the words of the historian William Graebner, "holding institutions" for the aged.[27]

Severing employment relationships was the chief objective of Rie-benack's new pension program. English railroads were then forcing many older workers into retirement on pension, and the Pennsylvania Railroad's principal transportation officers said Riebenack's pension plan "would improve the service and is preeminently a necessity, on account of the position in which the Company is placed by having such a large number of employes of advanced years, who are physically in-capacitated from performing efficient service, besides tending to im-prove the esprit de corps of the service."[28]

For a benefit designed to raise employee esprit, in the traditional welfare-capitalist sense, Riebenack's pension requirements were unusu-ally stiff and the allowances low. A worker had to be 70 years of age with thirty years of service to get 1 percent of final ten-year average salary for each year of service; an American Express official termed the benefit "barely sufficient for board and washing." While benefit was similar to the B&O's welfare-based stipend, the Pennsylvania required its employees to retire and accept the allowance. The only provision for voluntary retirement was in the event of disability — hardly a voluntary circumstance. Such limitations on freedom had never earned employee goodwill, and Riebenack had not designed his plan with this purpose in mind. Riebenack still viewed the pension as an employee "benefit" to attach and motivate workers, and he included it as a matter of course in his survey of "railway provident institutions." But the plan broke dramatically from welfare-capitalist tradition and the company, as if to acknowledge this fact, housed the program in a department of its own, separate from the relief administration. Mandatory retirement was not really the striking feature of the Pennsylvania's new pension program; pensions were an essential feature in its new retirement program.[29]

As a concern for organizational efficiency pushed the Pennsylvania to a program of compulsory retirements, bureaucratic convenience in-sisted upon one fixed age of severance. The company pension plan allowed exceptions — earlier retirement in the event of disability. But the general thrust of corporate life was to routinize, and thereby rationalize, the conditions of employment and remove discretion from the hands of an employee's supervisor. This specification of a compulsory termination of the employment relationship led to a parallel restriction at the beginning. To assure a sufficient length of service to justify a pension — thirty years on the Pennsylvania — the company established a hiring limit at age 35. All employees then would be eligible for an incapacity pension at age 65.[30]

The salience of efficiency also led to a new view of pension finance. The Pennsylvania, in 1886, had figured pensions as a costly benefit and had begun to accumulate an endowment to relieve current operations from much of the burden. Prospects for a well-funded system vanished with the rapid increase in the number of older workers. But this same demographic shift, plus faster and heavier trains and tightening seniority practices, generated the urgent demand to eliminate superannuated workers. Because the railroad believed pensions helped accomplish this task, providing an economic benefit to the firm, old age allowances had a self-financing character. Whether or not the company gained financially depended on whether or not the pension was larger than the worker's excess compensation, the difference between his pay and his contribution to the firm. The Pennsylvania thus justified the cost of its pension plan on the basis of this organizational "demand," just as it felt increasingly unable to "supply" old age allowances as a welfare-capitalist benefit.

Because forced retirement was the new object of pension policy, Riebenack further insisted that "the pension allowance is purely an optional railway disbursement from railway revenues exclusively, the employe making no contribution whatever." Only in this way could retirements remain "absolutely subject to company direction and control" and responsive to the demands of corporate efficiency. Riebenack and his committee

> considered carefully contributory systems and rejected that idea because it meant participation by employees in management of the scheme which though useful in accident and sickness cases would not help in pensions. We also felt that it was worth what it would cost to have the whole plan entirely in the hands of the management to alter or modify as might seem best. About half our pensioners are retired

for disability [at either their or the company's instigation, but always with the company's approval] between 65 and 70 . . . We feel sure that the pension system tends to keep our best men.

Contributory systems, moreover, could not easily address the corporation's immediate need: retiring the current cohort of older workers. These men had no time to accumulate contribution credits and could be retired on a reasonable pension only through some awkward plan provision. So in exchange for a free hand in its retirement policies, the Pennsylvania assumed all liabilities and paid all allowances out of its operating budget; its plan would be noncontributory and "pay-as-you-go." England's foremost pension actuary, H. W. Manley, recommended just this policy and for precisely these reasons.[31]

The drive for organizational efficiency led the Pennsylvania Railroad to one final feature — the extension of its pension plan to all employees. This decision to retire all employees "whether members of the Relief Association or not" came rather late, in the 1898 revision of the projected plan. Riebenack may have made the change because British practice was moving in this direction or because operating officials within the firm had argued for such an extension. The performance of white-collar workers also declined with age. And as seniority and experience had pushed them up the company's supervisory hierarchies, their wages were as likely as those of blue-collar workers to exceed the value of their productive contributions. A younger replacement, moreover, would cost much less. And the retirement of a supervisory employee would trigger a beneficial chain of promotions and job eliminations below.[32]

The Pennsylvania plan of 1900 thus brought the entire corporate workforce under the pension program. All employees were compelled to retire at age 70. All received a pension equal to 1 percent of final ten-year average salary for each year of service, paid by the company. After working on the railroad for thirty-plus years, in specialized production and hierarchic roles, the employees of the Pennsylvania Railroad went into old age through a common administrative process.[33]

The dawn of the new century thus saw three different railroad pension designs, each serving a distinct business purpose (see Table 2.1). The Grand Trunk pension program helped define corporate career relationships, and included only salaried personnel. The scheme managed a complex transfer of human capital assets among the company and the

Table 2.1.   Salient characteristics of railroad pension plans

Characteristics	Company		
	Grand Trunk	B&O	Pennsylvania
Rationale	*Career*	*Welfare*	*Efficiency*
Funding	contributory	—	noncontributory
Benefits	high	low	—
Retirement decision	voluntary	voluntary	compulsory
Withdrawal rights	yes	no	no
Explicit minimums[a]	no	yes	yes
Restrictive maximums[b]	yes	yes	no

a. Minimum pensions arose where benefit formulas produced unreasonably small allowances. The Grand Trunk had little need for such a provision because its pensions were high and usually exceeded any reasonable floor. Minimum benefits, moreover, facilitated separations, while the Grand Trunk's primary interest was in lengthening service.

b. The B&O, in keeping with its limited purpose of providing insurance against destitution, placed a dollar cap on individual allowances. The Pennsylvania, pursuing a policy of retirement, sought to keep allowances in some relation to active income. It thus kept the door open for high money benefits. Despite the Grand Trunk's two-thirds maximum pension, its scheme allowed much higher benefits than the open-ended Pennsylvania arrangement. It would take sixty-seven years of service on the Pennsylvania to reach the Grand Trunk ceiling. The Grand Trunk included this feature in its plan to keep the relationship between active and retired income consistent with its purpose of extending corporate careers.

different employee generations. The young paid in; the company paid out; and anytime after age 55, these administrative workers could claim a generous pension reward. The B&O used the pension to smooth relations between the firm and the class of manual laborers. It appeared as part of a comprehensive insurance package that provided workers with a financial safety net against the hazards of railroad employment. Consistent with this purpose, employees disabled by age could retire, at age 65, on a rather meager allowance. The Pennsylvania, alone among the three, included all employees in its plan and made retirement the object of its program. It aimed to enhance organizational efficiency by severing, not strengthening, the employment relationship. Noncontributory funding was therefore essential, and, as employee attitudes played a secondary role in achieving the intended purpose of the plan, the benefits paid out were small.

The English program had focused on the corporate official and helped define a longitudinal career that fit an individual's cycle of vitality. The B&O had offered pensions to win the cooperation of labor as a class and assure the smooth and continuous operation of the enterprise. With the Pennsylvania, the interaction between organic personal and continuous industrial time became critical. The enterprise advanced with a coordination so swift and precise that it could tolerate no individual failure to keep pace. So management had to fit the human cycle to the corporate clock. And because this need existed throughout the organization, the efficiency impulse exerted a powerful leveling influence in pension design. Officers and laborers alike were brought into the scheme, and severed on a uniform schedule.

Chapter 3

◆ ◆ ◆

The Logic of Pension Expansion

Publicity generated by the Pennsylvania announcement ignited a vigorous pension movement which spanned the first two decades of the twentieth century. Many organizations apparently had been considering the pension idea, and decided to proceed upon learning of the Pennsylvania program. Other railroads dominated this early expansion, establishing one-fourth of all new plans through 1910. Thereafter the pension spread across the economy, and railroads accounted for less than 10 percent of plans established in the subsequent decade. This expansion, however, was far more quantitative than qualitative: through 1920, the design of the emergent American pension institution remained largely within the parameters established by the three nineteenth-century railroad pioneers.[1]

Follow the Leader

Within four years of the Pennsylvania announcement, eleven other railroads had rushed to install formal schemes of their own. The number grew to thirty-eight by 1919, and these schemes covered 75 percent of the railroad workforce. No other industry came close to this level of participation, and the 1.5 million workers in these plans formed the bulk of employees in America's private pension institution. Both quantitatively and qualitatively, the history of the pension thus remained a history of railroad plans through the early decades of the twentieth century.[2]

The railroads could choose from three distinct pension designs, and

Max Riebenack's 1905 survey, *Railway Provident Institutions in English-Speaking Countries,* provided ample documentation on each. Nearly all railroads, however, followed the Pennsylvania program. The industry standard became compulsory retirement at age 70 (or in some cases retirement at management's discretion); participation by all grades of employees; gratuitous, noncontributory funding; a benefit of 1 percent of final ten-year average salary for each year of service; and a hiring limit assuring that all employees qualify for an early retirement disability pension at age 65. The industry adopted the Pennsylvania design en masse because the firms all operated complex and accident-sensitive organizations, had been in business long enough to accumulate significant populations of older employees, and had institutionalized employment systems that gave these workers protections against summary dismissal. This constellation of factors led directly to the principle of compulsory retirement on pension.[3]

The other nineteenth-century pioneers in the railroad industry revised their plans along the lines of the Pennsylvania design. The B&O, by 1903, had extended coverage to all employees and, according to one report, had made retirement mandatory; in 1926 it adopted the Pennsylvania benefit formula — 1 percent of final ten-year average salary times years of service. The Grand Trunk introduced a Pennsylvania-type scheme — compulsory retirement and universal participation, noncontributory funding, and the Pennsylvania benefit formula — in 1908. In the mid-1890s American Express had been searching for ways to discourage retirements and reduce its pension expense. But after studying the Pennsylvania plan, the company reversed its focus and began to search out new additions to the pension roll. A memorandum from the company president, dated December 31, 1901, declared:

> [During] these days of strong competition from every quarter it is absolutely necessary that the *working organization of the company should be kept up to the highest standards* — We desire, therefore, that as soon after the first of January coming, as possible, you will take up the entire pay roll of your Department, go carefully over it, and finding on it a man or men of age or condition, mental, physical or otherwise unfitting him for the service called for by the position he occupies and if he is entitled to pension, see that he is reported to Executive Committee for same — or if not entitled to pension, that he is dropped from the service . . . the Company cannot afford, as pointed out to

you by our enclosure of January 27th 1897, to carry on its regular pay rolls at full salary month after month, and year after year, men who are blocking the way to the advancement of younger men entitled to the position and pay.[4]

The Pennsylvania plan did not altogether ignore other pensioning interests. It insured proletarians against the disabilities of age. It just assumed, as a matter of bureaucratic convenience, that disability commenced at age 70. While its benefits were low, at least one contemporary thought it induced white-collar workers to pursue corporate careers:

> A young man entering [the Pennsylvania's] service knows that the path is open for him to the head of any department that his abilities qualify him to fill, for he sees the offices, from the president on down, filled by men who have won their way from the ranks by their own efforts. To this outlook is now added another feature, "an anchor to windward." Of all that run, only a few can win the greater prizes, but to the others who have given the best years of their life and have served well in the positions that they have been called upon to fill, there is the consolation, that in their old age they will not be left penniless objects of charity.

And the pension plan brought an efficient end to the relationship between worker and firm. C. G. DuBois, a Western Electric official who surveyed current practice in 1905, found railroad managers exuding satisfaction with their multipurpose tool: "Interviews with the officials of important railways having pension systems showed an absolute unanimity among them on the subject to the effect that the pension system pays, that it ought to be supported entirely by the company and that its expense is not burdensome."[5]

Pensions as a Token of Benevolence

Most plans established in the first two decades of the century followed Riebenack by covering all workers and financing the plan with corporate funds alone. But corporate America paused before creating a stampede for the Pennsylvania design and key deviations signaled differing personnel management needs. Banks, insurance companies, and public utilities, which were far more dependent than the railroads on a career white-collar workforce, promised pensions at least half again greater, for a given final salary, than those the Pennsylvania provided. In the first decade of the century, when low-benefit formulas predominated, nearly half the non-railroad plans pursued the original B&O program of voluntary retirement with meager allowances. These sponsors were dependent on a blue-collar workforce, and the design of their plans suggests classic welfare-capitalist motives. Compulsory retirement, the hallmark of Riebenack's design, appeared in only one of four non-railroad plans established in the first decade of the century. This changed after 1910, however, indicating increased pensioning for organizational efficiency purposes. Forty-five percent of new installations, in both blue- and white-collar plans, then mandated a fixed retirement age.[6]

In the historical literature, the pension has appeared most often as part of the welfare-capitalist movement. Stuart Brandes's survey of corporate benevolence devoted a chapter to pension provision, and business histories generally interpret the program as an effort to build proletarian goodwill. But as the foregoing discussion suggests, the pension movement and the welfare movement were closely intertwined only in the century's first decade.[7]

As is always the case with welfare-capitalist programs, the motivation behind such pension plans ranged from sincere humanitarianism to the simple desire for labor control. The rise of large-scale enterprise had created tremendous personal fortunes and thus unprecedented opportunity for true philanthropy. The phenomenon also revolutionized the labor market, and pensions had a decidedly practical value in calming relations with workers. Identifying the basic impulse behind a particular plan is thus no easy task. Nevertheless, benevolence was perhaps never displayed more clearly than in 1901, in Andrew Carnegie's steelworkers' insurance program. Carnegie had just sold his company to J. P. Morgan's U.S. Steel combine, and thereupon retired from business. In the best of welfare-capitalist traditions, the steelmaster felt that "his former employees in Carnegie Steel . . . had some claim out of past association upon his pocketbook." His pockets bulging, Carnegie now bequeathed an economic security system quite similar to the old B&O program. His scheme provided insurance against disability due to accident, illness, or age, with $4 million earmarked for the pension program. To incapacitated workers over 60 with fifteen years of service, Carnegie promised a subsistence stipend of 1 percent of aggregate pay for each year of service. And in the best welfare-capitalist tradition of the nineteenth century, the scheme operated as a semi-independent company relief fund.[8]

Rarely were welfare-capitalist pension plans, especially those of a durable nature, products of such charitable endowments. In the large-scale enterprise — the locus of formal pension planning — altruism typically had little scope for action. In corporate environs, welfare policy slipped quietly to men that Robert Ozanne called "timekeepers," a transition paralleling the shift on the railroads from W. T. Barnard, an official full of nineteenth-century do-good, to Max Riebenack, the prototypical modern executive. Timekeepers, like Riebenack, often came from the financial side of the house and viewed benefit programs from a utilitarian perspective. Only if a welfare initiative yielded a clear advantage in the purchase or utilization of labor would they give their approval.[9]

In the first decade of the century, the primary focus of these executives was nevertheless welfare-capitalistic. The rise of large-scale enterprise had disrupted old arrangements and had created an urgent need to reorder relations with workers as a class. Giant enterprises enjoyed monopsonist power in many key labor markets, with great discretion over wages and working conditions. But large capitalizations and tightly coordinated production methods had created an ironic dependence on what Homer Hagedorn termed "an effective, contentedly immobile labor force." The cash-for-current-service labor contract, no matter how high the wage, could not deliver this stability and dependability. In industry as in railroading, grumblings, quits, strikes, and squabbles with minor officials held profit as a constant hostage. Like railroaders of the 1880s, industrial executives in the 1900s were determined to gain the control of the workplace with welfare-capitalist initiatives. The railroads had already established a modus vivendi with labor by the turn of the century and could proceed, with Riebenack, to the business of efficiency. Industry first had to attend to a more primitive need: the construction of institutions to convert "a body of disparate and perhaps grudging individuals," as John Pencavel has put it, "into an integrated and productive labor force."[10]

The municipal street railways, which installed more pension plans in the 1900s than any single non-railroad industry, provide an example. Their schemes were thought to follow the Pennsylvania design as they were noncontributory, specified 70 as the normal retirement age, and paid 1 percent of final average salary times years of service. But four of seven firms restricted participation to the low-paid staff, and all parted company with the Pennsylvania in the crucial area of compulsory retirement. Welfare-capitalist considerations, in other words, led to pensions in this industry. And what led to the new initiative was the recent electrification of municipal transportation systems, a transformation that greatly increased fixed expenses compared to the horse-drawn-trolley regime. Management had a greater need to retain seasoned workers and prevent disputes from disrupting service. But with no regulatory instruments other than the cash-wage contract, the urban rails became frequent scenes of violent flare-ups. Philip Taft wrote:

> Strikes of streetcar men were attended by street fighting and use of firearms in San Francisco in 1907; Cleveland in 1908; Philadelphia in 1910; and Buffalo, New York in 1913. In San Francisco, according to *The Outlook,* strikebreakers opened fire on pickets and "some twenty men were wounded, five it was said mortally." The professional who was recruited by private detective agencies in municipal transportation strikes was a tough breed who was ready to face danger, and not averse to creating trouble.

Street railway managers, in the 1900s, thus needed welfare capitalism far more than their counterparts in the railroads. Adding welfare carrots to the detective stick, they adopted programs that offered pensions as a token of fair and equitable treatment.[11]

The pillars of the welfare-capitalist upsurge of the 1900s, however, were the great national monopolies organized by J. P. Morgan — firms such as U.S. Steel, International Harvester, and American Telephone and Telegraph. George W. Perkins, Morgan partner and Harvester executive, made it clear that welfare capitalism was a "purely business question. Profit sharing, pensions, and the like, from a pecuniary standpoint, are a profitable thing." Perkins expected welfare programs to cut down on strikes and keep unions out of company plants. Corporate benevolence, he believed, would differentiate "good trusts" from "bad trusts" and calm public outrage over Morgan's monopolization program.

> If, as many of us have come to believe, co-operation in business is taking and should take the place of ruthless competition, — if this new order of things is better for capital and better for the consumer, then in order to succeed permanently it must demonstrate that it is better for the laborer; and if profit sharing, pensions, insurance, and the like

mean anything, they must mean co-operation between capital and labor,— co-operation in the broadest, most helpful and enduring form.[12]

The American Telephone and Telegraph Company provides an especially well-thought-out example of corporatist pension planning. In the nineteenth century the company had supported superannuated employees informally, on an "Awaiting Orders Payroll." But as the firm became a vast operating enterprise and as its workforce aged, this policy of casual relief fell victim to discrimination and abuse. Rapid growth, mergers, and intense competitive struggles meanwhile brought AT&T, like many of the nation's nouveau big businesses, to a state of corporate neurasthenia. As John Brooks reported:

> Poor service and heavy-handed competitive tactics had resulted in a terrible public image. Internal struggles for power had left its management largely devoid of aggressive and creative leadership. A concomitant of this lack was a demoralized employee force . . . plant work in the Bell System was notoriously dangerous . . . and jobs as operators were shunned by many respectable women because of the company's not wholly undeserved reputation for laxity in controlling the conduct of its male office employees.

The new management of the firm, installed by J. P. Morgan, ordered in response a stiff tonic of corporate welfare capitalism.[13]

AT&T's manufacturing arm, Western Electric, established the firm's first formal pension program in 1906. Company executives had carefully investigated current practice, examining the Pennsylvania's arrangement and the British National Telephone Company's contributory scheme for salaried officials. But Western Electric, like most contemporary manufacturers, avoided both compulsory retirement and employee contributions in favor voluntary retirement, low benefits, and company funding — the standard welfare-capitalist design. The AT&T pension was workman's insurance, not an instrument of organizational revitalization nor a cultivator of human capital. When pensioning spread to the entire AT&T system in 1913, the company still aimed its benefit program at wage workers. Walter S. Allen, the plan's chief designer, identified the telephone operators as "the class whose active interest and cooperation is most desired." These employees made up half the company's workforce and their "enthusiasm and interest . . . [was] most vital to the question of service." Allen understood that a pension plan could hardly draw operators into careers with the corporation, for they typically remained with AT&T for only three years. Nor did the company display much interest in pensions as a means of retiring the inefficient. The "object of a pension," according to Allen, was "to secure the fullest co-operation of the employes and to convince them that the company appreciates their services . . . Nothing could be done at so little expense to secure the feeling of the solidarity of the system as the adoption of this plan."[14]

AT&T, like many corporations of the period, was quite interested in lengthening employee tenures. Allen stated flatly that "the greatest problem which the telephone industry has to face is the short service life of the operators and the consequent difficulty in maintaining a satisfactory standard of service." The instrument he chose to lengthen service, however, was not the pension but a thrift plan with phased-in company contributions. The program was voluntary, contributory, and offered employees tangible returns within a relatively short period. Similar schemes sprang up at the time which shared these characteristics, including stock purchase at U.S. Steel and profit-sharing at International Harvester. Industry offered pensions to influence worker sentiment, but then turned to schemes with more immediate payouts to lengthen employee tenures.[15]

The American welfare-capitalist movement culminated not in a deferred compensation scheme but in the employee representation plan — the company union. Violent clashes, such as the 1914 Ludlow Massacre and the great steel strike of 1919, had demonstrated the persistence of industrial conflict even among America's foremost practitioners of corporate benevolence. John D. Rockefeller Jr. was among those most visibly shaken by the bloodshed. Colorado Fuel and Iron, scene of the Ludlow tragedy, was under his financial control. Although thitherto he had not taken an active role in corporate management, Rockefeller resolved to put CF&I's labor relations on a more cooperative plane. He retained as advisor William Lyon Mackenzie King, former Canadian minister of labor and future Canadian prime minister, and King developed the employee representation scheme. Once converted to the new program, Rockefeller forced his various interests, including CF&I and the Standard Oil companies, to add employee representation to their welfare activities.[16]

By reasserting family influence in the giant corporation, Rockefeller had reversed the flow of business history. His selection of a YMCA official to direct Standard Oil's new employee benefit program likewise smacked of an earlier era. But in one critical respect the Rockefeller-King initiative represented a clear advance. It recognized that the relationship between capital and labor was a political issue that required a political solution other than noblesse oblige. The company union, of course, was a solution more congenial to employers than to employees. Nevertheless it addressed the core of industrial relations where the assorted bundles of benefits and incentives had not. Rockefeller then spread his new gospel with publicity campaigns and through the "Special Conference Committee," a semi-secret group of ten giant corporations organized by Standard Oil. These efforts, and a need to improve labor-management relations induced by World War I, led American business to adopt the program rapidly, and by 1920 employee representation had emerged as the centerpiece of advanced industrial policy.[17]

Welfare capitalism had thus become a rich complex of initiatives, with employee representation, deferred compensation, insurance, and social uplift all flourishing under this one ideological umbrella. From the standpoint of business, welfare capitalism seemed reasonably successful. Most firms adopting the strategy were able to keep unions out of the workplace, although labor, according to Brandes, showed no real increase in loyalty or contentedness. But as welfare capitalism reached its historic crescendo in the 1910s and early 1920s, the pension became a secondary element in a much more ambitious program. Even among manufacturers and other large employers of manual labor, an increased use of compulsory retirement and the willingness, by some, to pay generous allowances signaled the rise of alternate concerns. As in the railroads, business encountered the pension as an aspect of corporate benevolence. But an interest in efficiency and in career development, in time, came to drive its interest in the instrument.[18]

Pensions in Rationalizing Industries

Few firms set up pension plans to develop career employment patterns in the first decade of the century. But installations with this end in mind, by universities, utilities, banks, and insurance companies, picked up steam in the 1910s. These were rationalizing enterprises; they processed information, not materials, and made decisions, not hard goods or commodity services. The firms in the rationalizing sector hired large numbers of professionals, clerks, and managers, members of the "new" middle class, to whom they delegated discretion and authority. The Grand Trunk Railway had restricted participation in its Superannuation Association to precisely such workers, and its high-benefit pensions helped define and reinforce career employment tracks. The scheme allowed the salaried staff to fulfill a key middle-class expectation — that a life of honest labor would yield a comfortable and secure old age — without deflecting their attention from the business of the firm.

An experienced white-collar staff was the core asset of rationalizing organizations such as universities, utilities, banks, and insurance companies. This corps of career employees had discretion and organization-specific "human capital," and could be replaced only with difficulty and expense. The pension paid for services of these human capital assets upon final receipt of their value by the firm. Allowances had to be high to be visible and influence individual career choices, to induce workers to cast their lot with the firm, learn its methods, and remain diligent and loyal. The resulting attraction of a comfortable retirement could be quite powerful. When the Carnegie Foundation for the Advancement of Teaching offered free pensions to professors at universities without secular affiliations and that adopted Carnegie's standardized admissions requirements, professors at nonqualifying institutions threatened everything from lawsuits to mass resignations until their schools complied. So powerful was the pressure that the Carnegie pension offer, leading to standardized college admissions requirements, has been called the most effective instrument of educational reform in the twentieth century, establishing a uniform national educational ladder from kindergarten to college.[19]

The appeal of high-benefit plans induced diligent and loyal service where salaried officials exercised broad discretion over corporate property and employers could not closely monitor performance. Leslie Hannah discovered that various English banks set up pension plans as replacements for fidelity bond arrangements that were common for employees handling cash. In contrast to fidelity bonds, workers absconding with funds would forfeit a pension whose value increased with income and age, and in line with their embezzlement opportunities. And the pension required no up-front employee investment. This expanded the firm's pool of labor substantially, to include the growing number of literate and numerate public school graduates who lacked the capital to put up as a fidelity bond. While American pensions do not seem to have grown out of fidelity bond arrangements, security concerns clearly had an influence among financial firms. Frank Vander-lip, vice president of New York's National City Bank and a leading figure in the American pension movement, explained: "if men are removed from anxiety for the future, they are much more apt to devote their best efforts exclusively to their careers, and to be in less danger of diverting their energies into side channels of money-making — which may easily lead them on to dangerous ground."[20]

The Grand Trunk plan for white-collar workers was distinguished not only by high benefits and restricted eligibility but by employee contributions, withdrawal rights, and voluntary retirement. This design in its entirety proved quite popular in Canada. But nearly 90 percent of American plans, with 98 percent of covered employees, were noncontributory in 1920. The banking industry accounted for most of the contributory schemes in the United States, and Latimer traced this to the influence of a few Canadian executives in U.S. banks. While contributory plans almost always involved withdrawal rights, they did not necessarily shift costs to the employee. A $1,000 salary with a compulsory 2.5 percent pension contribution was otherwise equivalent to a $975 salary and noncontributory funding. Banks, insurance companies, utilities, and universities were notoriously low-paying organizations that substituted status, security, career opportunities, and increasingly a pension, in place of cash income. Whether or not employees contributed to the pension program, they exchanged current income for future benefits. And this pattern grew out of employment relationships in rationalizing industries.[21]

The high pension/low cash salary combination in these white-collar industries contrasted sharply with the low pension/high wage profile found in the blue-collar group. Rationalizing enterprises relied heavily on career employees, and their pension plans managed the buildup of human capital assets. The schemes systematically deferred income payments to the completion of a career — a distinctly back-loaded compensation pattern. Low-benefit plans, by contrast, arose where large-scale plant and equipment formed the key assets of the enterprise. Firms had to assure continuous operation and paid high wages to keep workers on the job and out of the labor market. Management added pensions, along with other forms of insurance, because it believed security bought more employment stability than a fatter pay envelope.

As only contributory plans included withdrawal rights, the general adoption of the noncontributory format did limit the American pension institution's role as a savings vehicle. The Grand Trunk's contributory plan had returned employee contributions in case of death or separation prior to retirement, giving participants an investment interest in the pension fund. But American plans were essentially insurance instruments. Many U.S. firms with noncontributory schemes also sponsored employee thrift plans. In effect, they unbundled the employer and employee halves of the contributory program. This pattern altered the characteristics of employee savings arrangements and passed the issue beyond the scope of pension planning. But because of the availability of parallel thrift plans, the noncontributory format did not seriously impair the central purpose of high-benefit pension programs — drawing salaried officials into organizational careers.[22]

Thus the pension institution benefited from efforts to build a new corporate class, just as the impetus drawn from welfare-capitalist initiatives declined. Only one of four plans established in the 1910s functioned merely as disability insurance — providing a minimal old age income to employees no longer able to work. Nearly twice as many plans were driven by the need to attract white-collar workers and to reinforce organizational careers.[23]

Reconciling the Corporate Clock

The third rationale, facilitating compulsory retirement, spread beyond the railroads in the 1910s to become a driving force in the pension movement: about half of all plans established in the decade specified a mandatory date of retirement, and they included both white- and blue-collar plans. The inclusion of compulsory retirement varied, somewhat, from industry to industry. Of groups in the 1910s with seven or more plan profiles, the majority of schemes in insurance, petroleum, railroads, street railways, and utilities specified a mandatory date of retirement; those in metals and machinery were divided nearly equally between compulsory and voluntary retirement; most banks, food processors, and companies in the miscellaneous categories let employees determine their own date of separation. In most industries, however, the pension had become closely associated with mandatory retirement. This was the case both in the nation's manufacturing industries, where the instrument had originally appeared in the welfare-capitalist context, and among utilities and insurers, where the pension helped establish career employment relationships.

Several industrial categories — miscellaneous, food, and banking — were relatively immune to this rush to retire. The miscellaneous group included industries with few cases of company pensioning, and such novelty suggests entrepreneurial idiosyncrasy rather than business rationality. Their plans thus should probably be interpreted as the random noise surrounding all economic movements. Pension planning in the food industry, as we shall see in the next chapter, also did not always meet contemporary standards of rationality. So little about the underlying rationale can be learned from the shape of its plans. In the banking industry, however, neither qualification applies. Banks established more pension plans than any other industry by 1920, and their experience was generally satisfactory. These firms, presumably, chose voluntary retirement because it fulfilled a commercial interest.

Bank pension plans probably took their shape from the great discretion over cash and credit that banks *by necessity* delegated to their staffs. Because of this delegation, bank employees primarily needed honesty, judgment, and the confidence of management — qualities that tended to grow rather than decline with age. Nor were these attributes amenable to bureaucratization, the enemy of the elderly. The nation's great investment banks, nearly alone among those at the economic pinnacle, had remained partnerships for precisely this reason. A bank's vulnerability to embezzlement also suggests an unusual interest in security. Such considerations had exerted a powerful influence on England's high benefit/voluntary retirement design, and they had been voiced in America quite early by bank officer Frank Vanderlip. The pension's value in managing the firm's assets — both human and financial — thus provided sufficient reason for bankers to join the pension movement. Compulsory retirement, in contrast, appears not to have offered significant improvements in efficiency.[24]

The general adoption of compulsory retirement, however, reflected a broad-based demand to eliminate elderly workers. As William Graebner has outlined, the decade of the 1910s marked a watershed in the history of retirement policy. This in part was due to the gradually aging workforce in America's large mechanized and bureaucratized firms: the supply of light-duty jobs could not keep pace and the elderly refused to retire voluntarily. But the impulse to require retirement also arose from a sudden preoccupation with operational efficiency. Frederick Taylor's *Principles of Scientific Management,* published in 1911, announced the formal debut of the efficiency movement in manual employment.

The Taft administration's vigorous pursuit of administrative reform stimulated a similar concern in business bureaucracies.[25]

The association of compulsory retirement plans with industries most amenable to the efficiency movement suggests that a shift in business operations and culture, as well as demographic pressure, brought on the flood of retirement pensioning. Among the low-benefit, blue-collar plans, superannuation presented the greatest operational problems to railroad and mining concerns. Older workers in these two industries threatened safety as well as productivity, and they adopted compulsion with the greatest frequency. Likewise manufacturing firms with tightly coordinated operations — the metal and machinery makers — had far less tolerance for the elderly than the miscellaneous group that divided labor less finely and paced production with less precision. Among high-benefit plans, utilities and insurance companies showed a greater tendency toward bureaucratization than banks and merchandisers, and they were the ones to adopt compulsory retirement.[26]

The spread of scientific management spelled engineering control of the labor process, and this especially threatened the livelihood of the elderly. Older workers brought experience and a wide range of skills to the shop floor. Scientific management transferred control of the workplace to educated engineers, the enemies of shop-floor handicraft skill and traditions. Engineers championed instead a rationalized approach to the work process, with standardized, narrowly defined, and precisely interconnected work routines. They continually redefined shop-floor tasks and asked little from labor but a speedy adaptation to the new regime. There was serious concern that men over 45 were not up to the task, that they could not respond effectively to management directives. Some scientific managers in larger establishments hoped to redefine the production process and reemploy labor "superannuated" at age 45 in an expanded number of light-work assignments. Older machinists who lost their jobs, however, had an increasingly difficult time finding positions in the modern shops of the 1920s and 1930s. And those who kept their jobs looked forward to continued employment as second-class help.[27]

This early efficiency movement, in both factory and bureaucracy, held an overwhelmingly static vision of the economically rational world. It argued and searched for the "one best way" to shovel coal or coordinate a shipping department. Rationalization, however, was a dynamic enterprise. One way to shovel coal would always give way to another. And although old labor suffered much from the gospel of precision and static standards, it would suffer even more in an economy that changed technologies, policies, and efficiency norms on a continuous basis. In 1920 the threat had surfaced only in scattered areas.[28]

Academe most clearly illustrated the challenge posed by dynamic rationalization. The universities had been among the earliest participants in the pension movement, with Columbia, Harvard, and Yale all establishing plans for their professors in the 1890s. No industry, including the railroads, had installed more formal schemes in the nineteenth century. University plans had all followed the high benefit/voluntary retirement formula, a design meant to attract and retain personnel. But by 1905, the year Andrew Carnegie and his Foundation for the Advancement of Teaching announced their free pension program, facilitating retirement had become a second rationale in academic pensioning. At least three other universities had installed plans before the Carnegie program took over the field, and two included compulsory retirement provisions. Carnegie established his program to relieve suffering, to draw "able men" to the classroom, and also to facilitate the retirement "of many older professors whose places should be occupied by younger men." The Carnegie Foundation's new director, Henry C. Pritchett, was "less concerned with the pension as a retirement than as a recruitment device," writes Graebner; he believed scholars would follow the esoteric paths of scientific investigation only when their livelihoods *throughout* their lives were assured. Pritchett, nevertheless, also appreciated the pension's ability "to eliminate the inefficient."[29]

It was the dynamic nature of academic understanding — the product of the newly constructed research establishment that Pritchett hoped to advance — that caused obsolescence to lap at the heels of older academics. "An ideology of personal growth and professional progress," to use Graebner's characterization, created a constant flux in ideas. Graebner discovered that older elementary and secondary school teachers "were not disliked so much for their senility as for their backwardness, for the fact that they were trained in the old ways of the nineteenth century." Progress had stranded otherwise competent personnel as esoteric masters of obsolete technologies. And in higher education, especially, the leap to the twentieth century meant a career in a never-ending intellectual marathon.[30]

The shift in pensioning rationales, from improving relations with labor in the 1900s to improving efficiency in the 1910s, fits a larger course of American business history identified by Louis Galambos. Studying innovation in the early years of the century, Galambos found that the recently organized big businesses were too preoccupied with "boundary" problems to concern themselves with improving internal operations. These firms first had to define and legitimize relationships with customers, competitors, and the public at large. As with other boundary concerns, big business wanted direct access to the open labor market and the loyalty of workers it hired. It struggled against intervening labor monopolists — unions, ducal foremen, and inside labor contractors — and against allegiances to formerly independent operating companies. Only as corporate managers gained control over these boundary issues could they attend to the issue of efficiency — to getting more for less.[31]

The Galambos transition is strikingly demonstrated by the history of the pension at Standard Oil. In 1903, long before John D. Rockefeller Jr.'s crusade for the higher welfare capitalism, the firm had installed a semiformal pension plan of classic welfare-capitalist design. It allowed superannuated workers to retire voluntarily on a minimal allowance of 25 percent of final salary. Standard replaced this arrangement in 1918 with a plan featuring high benefits and compulsory retirement. The increase in pension allowances was clearly consistent with the younger Rockefeller's interest in strengthening the "gift exchange" between capital and labor. But nothing in this warm-hearted program suggested mandatory retirement. Both features, however, did suit the managerial program of Walter Teagle, who had just arrived as president of the company in 1917. Teagle had immediately instituted a vigorous campaign of corporate centralization and vertical integration, and he brought Rockefeller's new personnel office under his personal control. Teagle increased the responsibilities of corporate executives and at the same time demanded tighter coordination among the firm's various production units. The 1918 pension plan, with high benefits and compulsory retirement, assisted both initiatives.[32]

Other important plans initially installed under the auspices of welfare capitalism likewise came to mandate retirement at a specified age, usually 65. AT&T, for example, had originally specified only voluntary retirement or separation at the discretion of management. But the executive committee, using the latter authority, issued an order forcing retirement on all employees over 70, except top management. When U.S. Steel replaced the Carnegie program with a plan for the entire firm, in 1911, it required all employees to take the "benefit" at age 60. International Harvester, the agricultural machinery giant and acknowledged leader in the welfare-capitalist movement, heralded things to come when it included compulsory retirement in its comprehensive 1908 benefit program.[33]

Thus by 1919 the pension had been variously insinuated into the American business system. Begun as an instrument of boundary regulation, it matured into a basic element in the corporate employment relationship. By 1920 astute business people knew that pensions reduced neither strikes nor turnover. But the instrument helped structure the flow of human resources through the corporation, from recruitment through retirement. A fully articulated plan defined the oldest age of entry into an employment relationship and the manner of final termination. The pension created a pattern of expectations, strengthening the social contract between employees and employer. The promise of an assured lifetime income was balanced by the expectation that employees devote themselves permanently and exclusively to the sponsor's interest. In the words of Reinhard Hohaus, one of America's pioneer pension actuaries, a plan created an "atmosphere of permanence and stability on which wage-earners of the higher type set great store."[34]

The pension institution also did quite well in quantitative terms. Over three hundred plans, covering 15 percent of the nation's wage and salary workforce, had been established by 1919. This was up from thirteen plans in 1899. Ninety thousand retirees drew $55 million in pension payments in 1927 — equal to 3 percent of the covered workforce and 1 percent of covered payroll. The institution was also housed in the largest and most secure organizations in America. Eighty-seven of the two hundred largest corporations had pension programs, nine of the top ten. As the workforce of younger big businesses matured, they too would add plans. Thus in just one generation, the pension instrument had been established in American economic society.[35]

As a general solution to the mounting problem of old-age poverty, however, the private pension system of 1920 was clearly inadequate. Small and medium-sized business had not participated in the movement. They could bear neither the costs nor the risks. They had few older workers, and little need for career employees, rigid performance standards, or good public relations. In fact just four firms in 1924 — the Pennsylvania and New York Central Railroads, AT&T, and U.S. Steel — employed one-third of all pension plan participants. Only a small subset of all covered workers, moreover, would remain with their employer to retirement. For those who did and claimed a pension, only a handful had a company guarantee that benefits would never be reduced or eliminated. And no one had protection against inflation once retired.[36]

A private pension institution had arrived in the United States because it served the interests of the new giant enterprises that organized the economic landscape. It would require more history, however, before the pension would better serve the needs of others.

Chapter 4

◆ ◆ ◆

The Hard Actuarial Realities

The private pension institution emerged as a tool of organizational integration, helping managers accommodate labor to the nation's huge, complex, and ambitious new enterprises. This provision of old age pensions was itself an example of the aggressive integrationist impulse of these giant corporations. The sponsoring employers were absorbing responsibilities thitherto performed primarily by households and, to a minor degree, by financial intermediaries. But unlike the expansion of the firm into new areas of production and distribution, management took on these obligations with no close examination of future costs. It simply concluded that the benefits of a plan would comfortably outweigh its nebulous expense.

The 1920s, however, would reveal a financial calculus far tighter than anyone initially imagined. Costs rose steadily. If a sponsor's finances soured, its pension program became a burdensome, indeed treacherous commitment. Such difficulties in time forced corporate sponsors to look outside their organizations for help in designing, analyzing, and financing their plans. Historians generally view the 1920s as a period of increasing corporate integration. But in pension provision — an important contributor to this gathering economic cohesion — vertical "disintegration" and the emergence of new market relations became suddenly more common.

The Piper Calls

The sensational failure of the Morris Packing Company plan, in 1923, exposed the weakness of the U.S. private pension system and burst its growing social acceptance. After years of financial difficulty in the meat packing business, Morris ceased operations, sold its assets, distributed the proceeds to its shareholders, and stopped further payments to its pension program, a contributory plan with 3,500 participants and 400 retirees drawing benefits. The pension fund had taken 3 percent of employee earnings and $25,000 a year from the company since 1909. But the assets accumulated by 1923 were totally inadequate to pay the accumulated benefit promises. While the fund held $1.5 million, a sum four times larger was considered insufficient. Young workers, who had no hope of ever collecting a pension, then depleted the fund by exercising their right to withdraw from the program and receive a return of their contributions. The remaining participants, distraught over the loss of their livelihood and the rude termination of their pension plan, and now aggrieved by this hemorrhage of assets, finally sued. But by then all that remained were the company's oldest and most faithful servants, and just enough funds for fourteen months of benefit payments.[1]

Morris employees had dutifully paid in their contributions and had been led to believe that an obligation accrued upon their employer to make good their promised pensions. There was no disputing the facts. Corporate officers had often used pension promises to keep workers in harness during the company's long and difficult history. Management even had offered assurances that the "Morris millions" stood behind the annuity program. Employees, in response, had given labor and money that now could never be retrieved. But the court ruled that the participants had a claim only against the plan and not against its sponsor. It held Morris responsible only for its "official" pronouncements — in particular its formal pension plan document — not statements of its officers. As the document specifically limited the company's liability to the annual $25,000 contribution, the court denied all further participant claims. For the pension institution as a whole, the implications of the Morris decision were clear. The great majority of plan documents in 1923 likewise strictly limited corporate pension liabilities. So labor's sense of a pension claim against the employer, accrued over its years of service to the firm, had no legal foundation.[2]

Morris had designed perhaps the nation's most generous pension program, a fact that seriously compromised its finances. Allowances were set at 2 percent of final ten-year average pay for each year of service; retirement was allowed at age 55; and widows and surviving children of all employees, both retired and active, got half-pay pensions.

While no other plan had assumed such liabilities, most saw steadily rising pension charges. Each year more employees retired, usually with longer service and higher incomes, and relatively few on pension died off. U.S. Steel in 1915, after operating its new plan for but four years, raised its retirement age from 60 to 65 and demanded twenty-five rather than twenty years of service. Carnegie's scheme for university professors faced stringencies so great that it totally reorganized its program in 1918. In the early 1920s rumors of pension troubles at "several large corporations" floated through the business community, and after the Morris fiasco, with the stress on corporate finances intensifying, an air of anxiety spread among those responsible for managing corporate pension systems. Suddenly the pension appeared as an ever-expanding vortex of expense, each year sweeping away greater sums and absorbing a larger portion of total labor cost.[3]

Few companies in the 1920s felt the relentless upward pressure more than the Pennsylvania Railroad. The firm had explicitly launched its formal program in 1900 without accumulating a pension fund. The company figured its increased operational efficiency, the result of retirements, justified charging outlays as a current expense. And the cost, for twenty years, had been quite bearable. Payments totaled a mere 0.5 percent of payroll in the first two years of operation and stood at only 0.6 percent in 1917–1921. But then burdens climbed dramatically and, at the end of the 1920s, the company paid its 9,563 pensioners nearly 2 percent of payroll. When top management pressed pension superintendent E. B. Hunt on the future cost of the program, in 1927, he could only reply that "payments increase at an unknown rate for indefinite periods."[4]

Max Riebenack, designer of the Pennsylvania pension plan, had realized that pension payments would rise. Because of the thirty-year service requirement, the original cohort of retirees in 1900 had all been hired prior to 1870, and railroad employment had risen swiftly over the subsequent thirty years. Riebenack counted over three thousand additional employees who could be eligible for a pension within the plan's first decade. Although death would claim its share of both retirees and those active workers over 60, Riebenack had expected the pension roll to swell, on net. But the aging of the company's workforce plus declining mortality and turnover rates meant the proportion of workers who survived and retired on pension kept rising well beyond Riebenack's ten-year horizon.[5]

The Pennsylvania in fact faced generations of rising pensioner populations even if mortality and turnover rates stopped falling. Assuming that the firm's hiring rate had also stabilized in 1900 — that Pennsylvania recruited each year a constant number of entry-level workers who remained with the firm and died at constant rates — then the number of *new* retirees would increase each year for the next fifty years; it would rise until the entire active workforce had been hired under this new regime of stasis. The number of *pensioners,* however, would continue to rise; the burden on the plan would grow until all retirees had been hired in this steady-state regime. Only then would the plan be what the actuaries call "mature." Had Riebenack been aware of these dynamics, he could have anticipated an increasing pension burden lasting well into the latter half of the twentieth century.

The rise in the Pennsylvania's pension bill was actually delayed for twenty years. While the number of pensioners rose steadily, mergers and internal expansion added large numbers of fresh young workers to the payroll base. The growth of the pension-payroll ratio quickened after 1910, but the outbreak of World War I provided a final reprieve. The peak wartime demand for labor kept workers employed and off the pension roll. Even more significant was the wartime inflation. Allowances, once granted, held constant. So when the price level doubled during the conflict, inflation halved the real cost of pensions outstanding. New awards, of course, reflected the higher wartime and postwar wage rates. But because benefits were based on earnings over a ten-year period, it would take an entire decade to complete the adjustment.[6]

Pension payments, as a percentage of payroll, began climbing rapidly immediately after the Armistice. The key factor was not just the return to the inevitable maturation of the company plan and more normal macroeconomic conditions. What pressed the Pennsylvania Railroad in the 1920s was the sudden eruption of competition from trucks, buses, and automobiles. Corporate earnings declined, cash grew scarce, and, as hiring declined, the plan began to slide dangerously toward an "overmature" demographic profile. At the dawn of the interwar era, expanding cohorts of retirees, with rising benefit levels, had become an increasingly burdensome obligation on the company's income statement.[7]

By 1925 the Board of Officers of the Pennsylvania's Pension Department recognized "the grave necessity of having to make a reduction in our pension payments." Expenditures had jumped 13.5 percent in that year alone and pension superintendent Hunt feared a quadrupling over the next twenty years. Company officials responded with various proposals to stem the outflow—eliminating compulsory retirement, restricting incapacity pensions, calculating allowances over a longer salary base, and reducing the benefit factor from 1 percent to 0.9 percent. Opposition from within the firm, however, checked all efforts to cut expenses. Eliminating compulsory retirement, objected vice president A. J. County, "would disrupt the whole principle on which the pension plan has been adopted. I do not think it would appeal to very many people to keep men over seventy years of age operating trains or working in shops." The company's lawyers also decided that "changes in the regulations cannot be made to adversely affect those on our pension rolls, but can only apply to those added after a given date." Others pointed out that neither a fifteen-year salary base nor stricter regulation of early retirement would significantly reduce expenditures. Meeting the stiffest resistance was the proposal to cut the highly visible benefit percentage. Relations with labor were then quite testy, for management had just crushed the shopmen's brotherhoods, substituting company unions. The Pennsylvania's president, W. W. Atterbury, was aggressively promoting such unions as a means of achieving industrial cooperation and was presenting himself to the public as "an avowed exponent of [labor's] rights, privileges, and welfare." Unilateral reductions in pension benefits thus jeopardized Atterbury's image and the firm's larger labor strategy. So the board of directors, after reviewing its various options in 1927, decided to leave everything as it was.[8]

The Pennsylvania Railroad represented the general experience far better than Morris Packing. For most pensioning organizations, the first two decades of the twentieth century were robust years of expansion. These firms saw inflation and the demand for labor boom during the war and subside thereafter. And while most industries did better than the railroads in the 1920s, nearly all sponsors faced increasing outlays for pensions. The railroad's difficulties, though more severe than the norm, demonstrated that the Morris experience could not be viewed as an isolated irrelevancy. Periods of stasis or decline, inevitable in the lifespans of firms, sharply aggravated the burdens of pensioning. This was so because slack demand cut earnings precisely when operating managers, trying to lighten their payrolls and staffing levels, were trying to accelerate the flow of labor into retirement. Thus did management discover a crucial fact. The pension had emerged as a labor program and its cost was generally gauged against total payroll expense. But payments did not behave as a variable labor cost, fluctuating nicely up and down with the level of output and employment. Demography, the macroeconomy, and especially the competitive health of the firm were the determining factors. Outlays rose inexorably in the 1920s, for railroads especially, as additional pensioners and low rates of inflation created ever more costly obligations. And when pension expenditures did fluctuate with the output of a firm they did so perversely: pension outlays spiked when corporate revenues slid.

Not surprisingly, labor and its representatives also developed serious misgivings about company programs. Corporate plans in the mid-1920s covered about 15 percent of the nation's active workforce, but only a small number would ever enjoy a benefit. The typical participant had "no more than one chance in two of living to the usual age of superannuation retirement when his pension will be due," wrote Murray Latimer, the leading student of corporate pensions in the interwar era, "and the chance of surviving in the employment of a single company is much smaller still." As illustrated by the Morris case, the receipt of benefits also relied on the employer's continued solvency and its decision to neither reduce nor terminate allowances. The company nevertheless demanded a sacrifice of liberty and mobility, what the critic Louis Brandeis called the "new peonage," in exchange for this shadowy benefit. A labor consensus thus took shape in the decade that only a compulsory government pension program, similar to those in Europe, could protect aged workers and preserve democratic liberties.[9]

For both management and labor, the two principal parties to the pension institution, the newly recognized uncertainty and intractability caused much anxiety. Workers could hardly depend for their old age income on so poorly secured a promise that was contingent on employment with a single firm, with sufficient years of service, up to the date of retirement. Nor could management abide an expense with such an unknown and destabilizing potential for growth. Neither party, however, was quick to develop solutions to its problems. Labor had little influence, as the courts held pensions to be free-will corporate gratuities, beyond the legal grasp of active employees. Other than rail workers, few were represented by strong independent unions. Management's control was also more apparent than real. As seen at the Pennsylvania, past custom and competing policy initiatives thwarted efforts to cut costs even at highly stressed sponsors.

The Science of Reform

Despite this immobility the 1920s became a decade of pension reform. The agents of change came from outside the institution — from government, consultants, philanthropic foundations, and life insurance companies. These parties had imported advanced British pension techniques during the previous decade, and had formed themselves into a "disinterested" community of "scientific" pension experts. They had established their own criteria for evaluating pension plans and had developed innovative instruments to implement their ideas. Successful first in redesigning public-sector and academic plans, they then carried their programs to the corporate sector. The reformers made little progress at first. But they established a dialogue with corporate executives and, over time, succeeded in redirecting the institution's development.

These reformers established the critical notion of pension "soundness"— the elimination of risk and uncertainty for *both* employer and employee. They agreed that "soundness" could be achieved only if three key conditions were met. Most important, the pension expense could not be conceived as the cash paid out to retirees. As in other cases of long-term costing, the expense had to be matched, in time, with the firm's receipt of value. If a company produced woolens for thirty years, closed its plant, and purchased a button shop, one reformer asked rhetorically, could proper accounting charge a woolen worker's pension against the new button operation? Pension costs, all reformers agreed, had to be accrued — they had to be charged in conjunction with the employer's receipt of productive labor services. Expensing schedules could vary, as in the case of depreciating the cost of a machine. But the value of the future annuity had to be amortized, under the direction of a competent actuary, over the years of active work. As their second condition of soundness, the reformers insisted that the accrued expense be met by monies transferred to a secure and independent fiduciary. Finally, the reformers held that participants had to be vested with legal rights to their pensions, or to a cash withdrawal, after some reasonable period of service. These three conditions of soundness could be summarized as the actuarial, funding, and vesting criteria.[10]

In the 1910s the government sector provided the most vigorous arena of pension reform. State and local government had the nation's longest experience with employee pension plans, and agitation for a federal employee retirement system persisted throughout the decade.

An air of pessimism, however, engulfed many existing programs. New York City, for example, had exacted a percentage of employee salaries for a scheme that promised, like the Morris plan, excessively generous benefits. Its pension roll began expanding faster than its payroll, and by 1910 outlays exceeded intake. As the meager asset accumulations evaporated, the employees and the city's operating budget faced increased demands to pay the bill. The sordid and self-seeking squabbles that followed recalled the scandalous debates over the Civil War military pension scheme. So just as the Civil War veterans and the memory of their alliance with the Republicans were fading away, the association of "government" and "pension" again assumed a bad odor.[11]

The key figure to emerge out of this flurry of government work, especially from the perspective of the private sector, was George B. Buck. Employed at age 20 by the federal Efficiency Commission, Buck was assigned responsibility for designing the proposed civil service pension program. He quickly educated himself with British materials, the best available, and was influenced especially by the writings of British actuaries H. W. Manley and George King. Manley elucidated the theory of pension costing while King provided a method of extracting from personnel records the figures needed for the actuarial computations. Herbert D. Brown, Buck's colleague at the Efficiency Commission, also provided in-depth surveys of civil service retirement systems in Great Britain, New Zealand, and New South Wales. Congress in the end rejected Buck's design, but his work in Washington established his reputation. He proceeded to New York City, where he reconstructed the municipality's pension system and set up the nation's first consulting firm "specializing in the establishment and valuation of employee benefit funds." By the end of the 1920s Buck was offering actuarial advice to a wide range of public and private clients.[12]

The government plans that Buck designed paid scrupulous attention to the equities of each individual participant. "Mr. Buck has strong convictions," wrote his long-time assistant, Margaret Burt: "He believed firmly in individual thrift . . . He believed in individual life insurance but not in group insurance or the other fringe benefits so popular at present [1976] . . . He agreed with his old friend, Mr. Rahde, that employees should be paid their full salary and 'buy their own geraniums.'" So employees in his plans had their own accounts, built up preferably through their own contributions or by employer payments on their behalf. This concern for individual equities led Buck to reject the British practice of taking a uniform percentage of salary from all employees. Those entering his plans at age 20 paid less than those who entered at 40, for they had more years to contribute and accumulate interest. His design for the federal government called for contributions up to 8 percent of salary, with government paying only amounts greater than this cutoff. Tradition resulted in a more typical joint contributory format for New York City. The municipality also picked up the entire "past service" expense — the cost of pension credits already awarded for service prior to the installation of the new pension scheme. (Aside from this nigh inevitable assumption of preexisting obligations, Buck countenanced no intergenerational transfers.) All contributions were deposited in individual accounts, and to further safeguard the assets Buck insisted on the most secure investments: only those permitted the regulated insurance companies.[13]

Buck based pension allowances on final salary and designed contribution schedules so that the accounts contained, at retirement, the actuarial present value of this future stream of pension payments. In the parlance of insurance, Buck's program resembled a collection of individual "level-premium deferred-annuity" (LPDA) contracts: the commencement of *annuity* payments was *deferred* to the future — the date of retirement — and the contract was financed by a stream of *level payments* that continued until that date.

While Buck and others were putting government plans on a sounder footing, reform also went forward in academe. The Carnegie free pension system, a simple gratuity from the great man of steel, had dominated university pensioning since its organization in 1905. The program provided needed benefits and gave its director, Henry C. Pritchett, powerful leverage over American higher education. But the burdens of pension philanthropy soon overwhelmed Carnegie's bequest, initially $10 million, then raised to $15 million. A larger-than-expected number of professors, with higher-than-expected salaries and longevity, joined the roll each year, and ever more universities clamored for admission. These demands pushed Pritchett, a man initially absorbed in academic reform, to become a leading student of pensions. His annual reports provided acute discussions of the world's best practice, and criticism of industry's thoroughly unsound, nonactuarial, discretionary pay-as-you-go ("paygo") schemes. Pritchett soon became convinced, wrote Rainard B. Robbins, his long-time associate and a noted pension actuary, "that whatever the Carnegie Foundation could do to promote sound pension *systems* in colleges would be a far more valuable service than using its income to support liberal free pensions at a very limited group of colleges." After a dozen years of study, including close examination of the British Federated Universities Superannuation Scheme, Pritchett finally drew the Carnegie Foundation for the Advancement of Teaching out of the practice of philanthropy and into a more businesslike arrangement.[14]

The Carnegie Foundation opened a new chapter in American pension history in 1918. It then incorporated the Teachers Insurance and Annuity Association, a legal-reserve life insurance company regulated by the state of New York, for the express purpose of operating the nation's first "insured" pension arrangement. The new scheme rested on a unique and highly modified deferred annuity contract. Pritchett would have member institutions determine contribution levels and retirement dates, so TIAA allowed for flexible premiums and flexible commencement dates of the payment stream. The participant's ultimate benefit, determined at retirement, would be the actuarial equivalent of the funds in his or her account. Basing benefits on an account balance, as opposed to final salary, such plans became known as "money purchase" plans and appeared to participants more as a savings scheme than as an annuity arrangement. TIAA professors, however, could not cash out. The only cash "withdrawal right" came as a death benefit in the event of death prior to retirement. Nor could universities alter or influence the annuity once funds were in the hands of TIAA. Because Pritchett and Carnegie wanted to tie academics to the profession, not to any one institution, the annuity contract was a nonforfeitable arrangement between the professor and TIAA alone.[15]

In academe, as in government, a strict regard for individual equities in a secure, savings-type program thus emerged as the high road of reform. Carnegie's insurance company and Buck's New York City program both satisfied the basic requirements of pension soundness. They operated under actuarial control, gave participants explicit rights to cash or a pension, and were funded through segregated investments of the highest safety.

TIAA, however, could boast a greater degree of pension security. The trustees in Buck's scheme were the same government officials who employed the plan's participants. Should conflicts arise over administrative or financial decisions, workers stood at a disadvantage. While New York required employees to retire to capture the city's contributions, TIAA immediately vested its professors with rights to their employers' money. But the feature of Buck's program that most upset Pritchett and other reformers, and one that his New York program shared with industrial schemes, was its use of final salary as a benefit base. In Pritchett's system, the universities transferred their entire pension obligation to TIAA; TIAA then assumed responsibility for prudently investing contributions received and translating the sum accumulated, at retirement, into a lifetime annuity — standard life insurance exercises. New York City and its pension trustees had to set up funding programs designed to hit an unknowable target — the participant's final salary. Buck countered, with some justification, that pensions should bear a close relation to final pay. He also argued that periodic actuarial valuations and funding modifications could accommodate unexpected changes in salary, though the adjustments became costly as one got close to retirement. But his arguments were not accepted. In the new community of pension experts, whose primary object was to reduce uncertainty, final average formulas quickly fell out of favor.[16]

The reformers, of course, would all have been ecstatic had the Pennsylvania Railroad adopted Buck's program. Had the firm expensed and funded its accruing obligations, albeit on a final-salary basis, and had the company vested its employees with claims to these accumulations, it would have established a laudatory standard of "soundness" for corporate pension programs. It would have required a shift in focus: from pensions as the *price* of retirements paid by an enterprise capturing an offsetting gain, to pensions as the *cost* of retirement, met during the years of productive labor. The firm would need to recognize the obligations accruing to workers employed, and the railroad's initial cash expense would have been many times the sum paid out in 1900. Its expenditure for a sound pension program would be even greater, as it would have to fund this expense and also amortize, over time, the obligation the plan had created based on work contributed in the past.

Neither the Pennsylvania nor the corporate community, of course, had taken this path. So the Pennsylvania's pension expenditures and recognized obligations were small at first, and then began their precipitous rise. Payments to retirees went from $235,000 in 1900, to $960,000 in 1911, to $2.9 million in 1921, to $7.9 million by 1931. By the time an actuary arrived to evaluate the plan — as of year-end 1931 — the firm's accrued liability stood at $231 million, one-third of its "capital stock." Amortizing this mountainous commitment, while funding the firm's yearly accruing obligation, would absorb an estimated 7.9 percent of payroll.[17]

It clearly would be far more difficult to redeem the corporate pension institution in 1930 than in 1900. But only after three decades of experience did the magnitude of pension expense become clear. And only in the 1920s did the two basic forms of external assistance appear in America: the consulting pension actuary, such as George Buck, and the pension insurance company, such as Pritchett's TIAA. Both stood ready to rationalize the esoteric problems of pension provision, and employers availed themselves of these services in the 1920s. When they did, they radically reformed the conversion of work into old age income.

The Business of Reform

The movement for pension soundness hardly touched corporate America prior to 1920. Business was preoccupied with labor management issues, such as eligibility, retirement conditions, and benefit levels, and nearly all firms handled their programs as internally managed paygo affairs. The Standard Oil plan of 1918, which addressed the full range of pensioning purposes, had become the business community's model. It promised high benefits, assuaging manual labor and attracting career employees; and mandated retirement, which promoted organizational vitality. Pritchett nevertheless accused Standard of making all the mistakes "that have been pointed out by recent students of social insurance and pension principles." The plan was discretionary, paygo, and totally devoid of actuarial control. This pension arrangement, Pritchett prophesied, entailed hidden "financial liabilities that may seriously embarrass even the Standard Oil Company." But in 1918 Henry Pritchett, George Buck, and the other reformers exercised little influence beyond the public and nonprofit sectors.[18]

Stimulated by the Morris fiasco of 1923 and the steady increase in pension expense, corporate managers would address the problem of pension finance in the 1920s. But they would move cautiously. Pensions were an aspect of labor relations, a sensitive area. Even after sponsors recognized the need for assistance, they preferred to find counsel within the corporate sector and resisted advice from the new community of experts at capitalism's periphery. They sought help from the nation's giant life insurance companies, organizations specializing in handling life-contingent finance and carrying impeccable conservative credentials.

The insurers responded energetically, developing comprehensive solutions and becoming the decade's primary agent of corporate pension reform. Management nevertheless kept even the carriers at arm's length. The insurers at times seemed too intent on expanding their business, at others more concerned with equity for participants than the needs of their corporate clients. Management would thus be slow to entrust even the insurance companies with their employee pension programs.

The Metropolitan was the first life insurance company to enter the pension business, and it remained the leading pension insurer throughout the interwar period. Ingalls Kimball, director of the Metropolitan's Pension Division, traced his company's initial involvement with pensions to the tremendous growth of its group life insurance business between 1910 and 1919. Group life insurance, "under which all employees of a single employer may be protected through the issuance of one contract, had brought about an increasingly intimate contact between business men and the officers of life insurance companies. It was therefore natural that the advice of the life insurance companies should be asked with relation to the probable future cost of pensions under the plans that were then in operation." At the end of the 1910s, as a service to its group insurance clients, the Metropolitan began working up estimates of future pension expenditures.[19]

Upon surveying the corporate pension scene, insurance company officials recognized the merits of the reforms advocated by Pritchett, Buck, and their colleagues. They quickly became acquainted with these reformers; Metropolitan and Equitable executives indeed advised Pritchett on the design of the TIAA program. And they studied the ground-breaking British pension literature. Insurance industry officials agreed completely with the basic reform idea, that pension costs ought to be accrued: they should be recognized and met during the worker's productive years, not expensed as the allowances were paid out in retirement. "The actuarial concept," explained Metropolitan actuary J. D. Craig, "is that each generation shall earn and pay for its own pensions" over its "forty-five years of active labor." The Metropolitan also agreed that sound arrangements were contractual, contributory, and fully funded. Employees could be secure, argued the insurer, only if they held their accruing benefits by legal right. Sponsors had improved their relations with labor by eliminating arbitrary managerial practices and formalizing their original pension promise. They should extend this successful policy by granting labor full rights to the benefits earned. The

Metropolitan also urged employers to accept employee contributions to raise benefit levels, spread risk, and heighten awareness of the program. The final item on the reformers' agenda, the need for full funding, followed directly from the recognition of an accruing contractual liability.[20]

While analyzing corporate plans, the Metropolitan soon recognized a significant business opportunity. Sponsors clearly lacked the skills and facilities needed to maintain sound pension programs. But the Metropolitan had professional actuaries on staff to calculate the accruing cost; it was experienced in collecting and investing funds; and it could contractually relieve sponsors of their pension liabilities and guarantee employees their retirement income. So rare and delicate was this combination of functions that the government allowed only insurance companies to sell annuity contracts. The New York State Insurance Department, effectively the national regulator of the industry, further protected policyholders from excessive ignorance, ambition, or expediency on the part of the carriers. New York specified the key actuarial assumptions, set funding standards, and permitted only the most staid and sober of investments. Buck had restricted New York City pension investments to the Department's approved list of securities while Pritchett actually organized TIAA as a fully regulated insurance company. The insurance vehicle thus appealed to reformers as an attractive solution to the problem of pension risk and uncertainty, and the Metropolitan would have this perception spread to the industrial sector.[21]

The Metropolitan formally entered the pension business in 1920. It offered to sell, on a group insurance basis, noncashable, nonforfeitable single-premium deferred annuity (SPDA) contracts called "pension bonds" that paid ten dollars a year for life, beginning at age 65. (An SPDA contract converts a *single payment* into an *annuity* that commences in the *future*.) Participants held these securities, as they did TIAA certificates, as a "personal and permanent possession." An adequate old age allowance required the accumulation of pension bonds over many years, and high-paid workers needed several units each year to provide an income in retirement comparable to that in activity. The cost of pension bonds also rose as participants aged, for there was less time for interest to compound and the employee was more likely to survive to retirement. The pension bond scheme would not yield an allowance pegged to an employee's earnings at the end of his or her career. Instead, a steady accumulation of pension bonds — at a rate of say one per each $1,000 of income — would produce a pension benefit proportional to the employees' average salary over their period of plan participation. (If employers wished to credit service prior to the establishment of a plan, the insurer suggested they purchase the appropriate number of pension bonds over a period of years.)[22]

The Metropolitan claimed its bond scheme was the soundest available. Unlike Buck's and Pritchett's designs, pension bonds precisely defined both employee benefits and employer liabilities. Because Buck had based allowances on final salary, he could only estimate the accruing employee benefit and employer expense. The TIAA program had defined the annual pension expense, but could only estimate the allowance this money would eventually buy. But pension bonds allowed sponsors to transfer to the insurance company all further liability, including the risk of adverse mortality and investment experience, while employees knew the precise size of their future benefits and were assured of full funding. The Metropolitan also argued that the provision of pension bonds on a jointly contributory basis would resuscitate the "gift exchange" aspect of pension provision: it would "awaken a new type of loyalty, and give a disciplinary hold on employees based on genuine appreciation of the motives which actuate the employer in installing the Old Age Pension Plan. The old type of 'loyalty' based on the fear of losing Pension rights is eliminated."[23]

Although the Metropolitan was eager to restructure and assume management of corporate plans, it saw in pensions a much larger commercial opportunity. Poverty among the elderly was surfacing as an issue of major public concern and, as the representatives of labor took pains to point out, existing private pension arrangements were totally inadequate in addressing this new social problem. In other new areas of industrial risk, such as unemployment and workplace injuries, many states now required employers to provide workman's insurance. The extension of this "social insurance" framework to old age income maintenance seemed inevitable to the Metropolitan. The company, of course, did not want government to operate a public pension program. Instead it wanted government to make it an "obligation of the employer to care for the working people, and then leave it to him to work out the means of giving that type of insurance. In other words, whether that be done co-operatively or not. When I speak of co-operatively I mean through some type of insurance undertaking." Cooperation and preemption of government were hallmarks of corporate thinking in the

1920s, so the Met had a reasonable chance of winning business support for such a government pension mandate. And if Congress complied, several percent of national income would, for the foreseeable future, flow to the nation's insurance industry. The Met had designed its corporate pension scheme to suit such a mandatory system, so it could expect to capture a significant portion of this revenue.[24]

Success in selling complex pension contracts, let alone the notion of a government-mandated pension obligation, involved tremendous skill and persuasiveness. The Met therefore assigned some of its most sophisticated executives to the business and launched a vigorous marketing campaign directed at the nation's largest firms. If pensions were to be discussed by organizations such as the National Civic Federation, the National Industrial Conference Board, or even the Associated Industries of Massachusetts, the company sent speakers or provided meeting space. In 1923 Kimball organized and hosted a critical and well-attended pension conference for big-business executives. There Met officials hammered away at the idea of the accruing pension expense, showing with logic and anecdote why funds for retirement had to be gathered during the active years of work. Kimball presented charts, reproduced from Luther Conant's recent *Analysis of Industrial Pension Systems,* showing paygo payments in a simulated plan rising for fifty years. He pointed to mature English schemes where allowances amounted to 10 and occasionally 20 or even 30 percent of payroll. Kimball then proceeded to the virtues of advanced funding and insurance company administration. Finally, he campaigned for a state-imposed pension obligation to head off a publicly run program. Without modesty or shame, he campaigned for the Met's compulsory pension bond system, which he dubbed the "American Pension Plan."[25]

Throughout the 1923 conference, Kimball pushed his prestigious audience to endorse the Metropolitan's political program. The sanction of such an assembly, in the political climate of the day, would have gone a long way toward enacting the proposal. The corporate community was aware of the burgeoning movement for social insurance and applauded the insurer's effort to keep pension affairs in business hands. It positively refused, however, to sanction the Met's universal pension bond scheme. A. G. Mills, of Otis Elevator, told the insurers that "the industries in this country are varied and the employees varied, so widely that to have a uniform system, I think, is impracticable; but to say as a general principle that there should be a pension system applicable to employees of industrial organizations, I would say that there should. But I would not care to go into details of this plan or any other." Kimball nevertheless pressed for a consensus, for the shape of such a "pension system applicable to employees of all industrial organizations." But Standard Oil's Clarence Hicks then bluntly reiterated: "it is impossible and impracticable [to set up a general American Pension Plan]. For twenty years the [Standard Oil] company has been experimenting on plans. I do not know why it becomes suitable at this time to stop experimenting. If we had done this a week ago, we would not have had the benefit of what we did today." With that the meeting, and with it the insurer's campaign for a government-mandated private pension system, abruptly came to an end. Mills arose and presented a motion extending "hearty thanks" to the Metropolitan and asked "as many as favor that motion will please rise."[26]

Compounding this political failure, the insurer also had been unable to sell its individual corporate pension programs. After four years of trying, 1920 to 1923, the Met had "reinsured," or assumed the risk, of just one plan. That contract, moreover, made no use of pension bonds but merely reinsured a preexisting noncontributory scheme. The performance, reported the Metropolitan actuary Reinhard Hohaus, "by no means constituted a satisfactory showing in view of the effort that was made."[27]

But the Metropolitan was a resourceful enterprise, and after such a thorough rejection it adjusted its product to suit the market. Kimball and his associates had learned over the years that turnover in industry ran from 100 to 250 percent annually, and that corporations balked at providing pension bonds for transient employees. These generally young and inexperienced workers, moreover, had little interest in securing income for their old age. So the insurer's new designs gave sponsors more control over the program and provided few if any benefits to withdrawing employees. The Met also allowed voluntary employee participation. This spared employers the damage that a compulsory program, requiring employee contributions, could cause to the firm's relations with labor. A voluntary program, however, involved a significant increase in the insurer's marketing costs and meant that its pension plans would have to satisfy employee as well as employer demands.[28]

At the very 1923 meeting that laid the universal pension obligation to rest, Kimball wheeled out a modified pension bond scheme for the commercial marketplace. The variation had employees pay the full cost of a pension bond in their first year of plan participation. They continued this fixed contribution level until they withdrew or retired, the employer making up the balance as the premium rose with age. Although sponsors still provided for departing employees, they now made no contributions for those with less than two full years of plan participation. In an example developed by the Metropolitan staff, total contributions to the plan would approximate 5 percent of payroll, with the employer paying 2 percent and the employees 3. The bulk of the employer's 2 percent, however, went for long-service workers. For those who ultimately retired, the employer indeed contributed the bulk of the funding.[29]

The Metropolitan finally installed its first contributory plan in 1924, at the Western Clock Company of La Salle, Illinois. Other than TIAA, this was the first insured, contributory plan in the United States. This Western Clock contract, and those to follow, involved even more adjustments to the market than the Met's 1923 design. The two contribution streams of the 1923 program were essentially translated into separate employer and employee contracts. Employees again contributed the same amount each year of plan participation, but the payments were now made toward a separate "level-premium deferred annuity" contract (LPDA). This piece of the pension scheme paid participants at retirement an actuarially calculated "Income." For retirees, and *only* for retirees, Western Clock would add a company "Pension." The firm funded this benefit each year as accrued, buying single-premium deferred annuities and cashing in policies for withdrawing employees. With this contract the Met finally developed a "sound" pension program that spared employers any expense for leavers' pensions.[30]

Workers at Western Clock and elsewhere found such employer-subsidized retiring allowances attractive. They knew, however, that they were far more likely to separate from their employer, whether from death, disability, quits, or layoffs, than to survive to retirement. Like management, they therefore focused on their withdrawal rights. Employees also wanted access to their money should they face an emergency or simply discover that the plan no longer suited their needs. Since participation in the Western Clock plan was voluntary, as were most programs later managed by the insurance companies, the carrier had to respond to these demands.

At Western Clock and in most subsequent insured plans, an employee had three withdrawal options upon leaving the employer. He could choose to continue his contributions under a separate level-premium deferred annuity contract with the carrier. He could stop further payments and, in effect, commute his account balance into a paid-up single-premium deferred annuity contract (SPDA). Or the withdrawing worker could convert his position to cash. Pension reformers of the day excluded cash surrender options from their plan designs. This avoided adverse selection — as when an employee cashes out when diagnosed with cancer — thus allowing higher pensions to those who survived. A prohibition on cashouts would also prevent participants from squandering their accumulations and living out their days as dependents on society, or on their former employer. The Met's original pension bond scheme, designed in the spirit of reform, was purely an instrument of old age income insurance and had no cash withdrawal right. But bowing to pressure from employees, who could not be sold on the intangible value of old age income protection, the insured schemes of the mid-1920s allowed cash surrenders. The contract still favored annuities. Employees choosing either the LPDA or SPDA option got credit for company contributions, their own past payments, and interest on both; employees taking cash typically got only their own contributions. But as reformers feared, cash became the overwhelming disposition of employee withdrawal rights.[31]

The Met was able to enroll 80 percent of Western Clock's workforce by 1924, thanks in part to the cash withdrawal feature. The carrier had expended considerable sums in marketing, however, and had expected higher participation. One explanation given for the lukewarm response was the lack of interest credits on cash withdrawals. The Met parried this criticism by informing employees that retirement income was the object of the program, and that its policy lowered the premium needed to buy a given old age income. The Metropolitan initially thought this lower rate, once explained, would expand the demand for its product. But employees generally remained obdurate, and the insurer paid interest in an increasing number of plans it developed over the decade.[32]

The final stage in the Met's evolution came in precisely this area of marketing plans to labor. The insurer began by simplifying the "employee interface" of its contracts. The original contribution and benefit schedules had a confusing but actuarially fair specification based on age, sex, and salary relationships. In 1924, the Met defined a schedule based on income alone, as given in Table 4.1. The Metropolitan also dropped the term "group pensions" in favor of "group annuities," wrote Hohaus,

Table 4.1. Employee contributions and benefits, typical insured plan, late 1920s

Salary	Monthly contribution	Monthly benefit
Under $1,500	$3.00	$18.00
$1,500–2,099	4.50	27.00
2,100–2,699	6.00	36.00
2,700 and up	7.50	45.00

Source: Reinhard Hohaus, "Group Annuities," *Record of the American Institute of Actuaries* 18 (1929).

"to lend to insured retirement plans the atmosphere of financial soundness with which annuities are surrounded. The word 'pensions' has a wide range of meaning, and several unfortunate incidents in the operation of pension schemes about that time did not increase its prestige."[33]

In 1927 the Met finally found the key to success in marketing group annuities. The company discovered that bundling pensions with group life, health, or disability insurance enhanced the attractiveness of each individual program. The annuity–life insurance bundle had a low cost relative to separate insurance contracts purchased on a nongroup basis, and employees recognized this fact. The bundle also returned 75 percent of an employee's cumulative contributions in the event of withdrawal. Nonpension forms of group insurance were written on a term basis, and employees had objected to the lack of surrender values. The existence of a cash return thus overcame a major complaint against the insurer's existing products. Employees, of course, had no knowledge of the sums going to the various coverages. Pensions in fact accounted for 75 percent of the typical annuity–life insurance premium, and the package gave withdrawing participants a refund of these contributions, without interest. But as workers lacked this information, they were in no position to balk.[34]

Marketing annuities as part of a group insurance package finally opened the pension business to the Metropolitan. Contracts in force went from three in 1924 to eighteen by 1926 to forty-six by the end of 1927; premiums received rose from $240,000 to $930,000 to $2,350,000. By the end of 1927 the Met was managing more plans than all insurers in the world combined, and its group annuity contract served as the industry model. Insurers were also capturing an increasing percentage of new installations. They were convincing progressive businessmen to take an actuarial perspective and view pensions as an accruing expense. Independent experts, such as Murray Latimer, avidly recommended the industry's products to all current and potential sponsors. The insurers also extended the reach of the U.S. private pension institution beyond its original habitat — the large corporation.[35]

Group pension contracts, according to Hohaus, were "one of the most complicated branches of life insurance with little tradition or precedent either to assist or to handicap those experimenting in that field." But by the end of the 1920s the actuary was cautiously optimistic about the business. "Group Annuities will become a very important part of group insurance," he wrote, and "the actuary of an adventurous turn of mind will find much opportunity in Group Annuities to explore uncharted waters, and he may be assured that there are sufficient rocks and shoals, with an occasional glimpse of the gulf stream, for even the most adventurous."[36]

Settling Accounts

The insurance firms had entered the pension business claiming they could provide the nation's soundest retirement programs. Some employers may have been primarily interested in soundness. Certainly no sponsor wanted to repeat the Morris experience. But the slice of American business most attracted to insurance, the middling-sized enterprise, contracted out primarily because doing so was the least expensive, if not the only feasible way, to provide formal pension benefits. Many of these firms had supported superannuated employees on an ad hoc basis, but were too small and financially vulnerable to promise active workers a distant pension. To derive full value from a pension scheme, especially to induce loyalty and career commitments, the benefit had to be provided by a solid, permanent institution. As important were the insurer's cost advantages arising from economies of scale in plan design, management, and risk-bearing. The carriers could supply, off the shelf, expert actuarial, legal, financial, marketing, and administrative expertise. Their clients typically had none of these skills in-house. And because insurers pooled the experience of many plans, they could easily afford the risk that one or two investments would tank, or that an employee would live forty years on pension.[37]

The industry's success among middling-sized firms contrasted sharply with its performance with the Metropolitan's original target — big business. Insurance executives had clearly become recognized pension authorities and had convinced the large sponsors, as well as the small, to view pensions as an accruing expense. But of the twenty-two companies attending the 1923 conference, not one had insured its plan by the end of the decade. Insurers captured 32 percent of all installations in the last half of the 1920s, but these were the smaller plans, with only 13 percent of the new participants. The frustrated carriers even tried using government to force the pension institution out of the employers' hands. They appealed to the New York State Superintendent of Insurance, claiming that sponsors were illegally trading in life-contingent finance. But the superintendent demurred and merely offered to supervise plans, like TIAA, that chose to organize themselves as insurance companies. Free to manage their own programs, the largest sponsors avoided the insurance vehicle.[38]

The big companies resisted insurance company salesmen for two basic reasons. Unlike the smaller sponsors, insurance company management offered little in the way of cost saving. Second, and a position they shared with most of the smaller firms that insured their plans, they saw the carrier's insistence on soundness more as a burden than a benefit. Although insurers had significantly modified their contracts from their original strict standard, sponsors still found much objectionable.

The larger sponsors, though mere initiates in the mysteries of pensions, remained confident of their ability to manage their plans as efficiently as any insurer. They saw little need for third-party pension guarantees, and a few, like AT&T, considered their financial strength "as certain as the solvency of any life insurance company." American big business was also of sufficient size to capture most economies of scale in the pension business. Its personnel and comptroller departments were already handling most of the necessary administrative details; company treasurers could put pension funds to work within the firm, setting up "balance sheet reserves" to acknowledge the obligation; should sponsors choose to invest outside the firm, there was no shortage of securities or fiduciaries. Mortality among tens of thousands of employees was predictable within a narrow range, so the risk of adverse experience was small. While only AT&T seems to have employed a company actuary, consultants such as George Buck were available in the marketplace. Thus cost considerations, independent of an interest in soundness, would not bring big sponsors rushing to the Metropolitan's door. As explained by one big firm that did insure its plan, "the element of certainty was the prime factor — certainty of pensions being paid and certainty of maximum cost. Economy was a secondary, but important consideration." Until more sponsors chose or were forced to choose soundness, insurance companies would cater primarily to small and middle-sized firms.[39]

But the principles of actuarial soundness, as understood in the 1920s, conflicted with managerial interests in critical areas. First, the reformers' insistence on contractual plans ran smack against the fundamental business principle of avoiding fixed obligations. Management especially shunned commitments that were costly or poorly understood, or that threatened its authority. Contractual pension benefits were serious and open-ended financial claims that could lead to worker involvement in pension administration and retirement decisions. The Pennsylvania Railroad of 1900 had forsaken employee contributions precisely to avoid entanglements and to keep pension and personnel decisions in managerial hands. American business had followed the Pennsylvania and saw little reason to alter its course.

Sponsors also resisted the notion that they ought to send assets out of the enterprise to improve the security of their employee pension plans. According to U.S. Rubber's C. S. Ching, management was "not disposed to pay over money of the Company and the employees, year by year, in an amount determined by the Life Insurance Company [or an independent actuary] under a method which we could not understand." Although external investment did safeguard employee pensions in the event of sponsor bankruptcy, the alienated funds disappeared as a source of corporate investment, liquidity, or credit. The return on external investments, whether from insurance companies or the securities markets, also seemed low. Ching asked whether it was proper to invest at an "absolutely safe 3, 4, 5, or whatever percent, when you have a good solvent company that may be able to make more with the money? In other words, are you justified in taking the stockholders' money out of the business?"[40]

The new strict standards of soundness also demanded a conservative financial approach to future withdrawals. Insurance contracts were able to eliminate employer *payments* to terminating employees. But they required sponsors to pay premiums up front for all active workers and provided refunds for leavers only when they withdrew. A strict regard for soundness would require a similar procedure for uninsured schemes. But sponsors had their actuaries estimate a "withdrawal decrement" to adjust their contributions in advance. According to Latimer, this could reduce contributions in start-up plans by a third.[41]

The most serious conflict between the principles of actuarial soundness and management policy focused on the practice of basing benefits on unknowable final salaries. No expense and funding schedule could precisely meet such an open-ended obligation. Latimer spoke for most reformers when he declared: "final salary base ought never to be used, and that the majority of industrial pension plans now do so is a most ominous sign for their future stability." But only allowances based on preretirement earnings achieved management's basic objectives: providing aging blue-collar workers with basic economic security, motivating middle-aged white-collar workers, and retiring the superannuated. Benefits pegged to salary levels over an entire working career, although amenable to advance costing and funding, would be insufficient in times of inflation and excessive during deflations. Final-salary formulas, as compared to the actuarially sounder average-salary schemes, also skewed benefits to senior high-paid employees whose income and service to the firm continued to expand over time. Senior management, which benefited most from this arrangement, also controlled the basic decisions about plan design. They would not be quick to abandon a single, apparently "democratic" benefit formula that supplied basic allowance to long-service workers, induced career commitments, facilitated retirements, and gave unusually handsome allowances to themselves.[42]

On the most basic level, reformers differed from sponsors in their fundamental concept of the pension. For reformers, pensions were simply deferred wages. This concept grew in part from the actuarial models that equated future benefits with current contributions. Reformers also saw pensions as deferred wages because they took a social perspective and saw a universal need to spread income from the years of activity to those of retirement. Thus the reformers' earliest and truest expressions, such as TIAA and the Met's pension bond, required total deferment. Pension accruals were not only funded, contractual, and nonforfeitable, they were also noncashable. Management, in contrast, viewed pensions as an instrument to further its purposes in the labor market. To guard against other interpretations, it wrote exculpatory clauses into plan documents, shunned employee contributions, and even prevented the buildup of pension funds that could be seen as employee assets. The sums in question, according to C. S. Ching, were clearly the "stock-holders' money" to be used for the stockholders' purposes.[43]

Management had nevertheless come to embrace a portion of the re-formers' program by the end of the 1920s. It did so, however, for reasons more pragmatic than principled. What brought sponsors to reform was the need to understand, routinize, and control pension costs. To define the extent of their liabilities, many placed their programs under some form of actuarial supervision. Upon discovering the size of their commitments, many began funding programs to routinize pension expensing and to stave off unmanageable explosions of claims in the future.

The use of actuaries thus became common. By 1929 Latimer found that 163 U.S. and Canadian plans out of 297 reporting, or 55 percent, had been valued by an actuary. This represented a substantial increase over the 36 plans reviewed by an actuary in 1925, 17 percent of the total. One such actuary, Stanley P. Farwell of the Business Research Corporation, described his procedure upon arriving at a plan sponsor:

> Our first step is to calculate the accrued liabilities which usually are unknown. The result is often a very large sum . . . the next step is to see what can be done . . . to bring pension liabilities and required payments within amounts which the company in question can stand. Naturally one of the first things is to examine the pension plan. In some we commonly find provisions that will build up liabilities unduly without sufficient reason. Such provisions are retirement at the age of 50, or retirement with a service record of 15 years, or provisions for taking care of widows and orphans. The latter is a particularly expensive provision.[44]

This growing awareness of large and expanding pension liabilities pushed many corporate sponsors toward the second controversial issue of soundness, the decision to fund. The Pennsylvania Railroad, the pioneer of the modern American pension system, illustrates the process.

The 1926 directors' committee that had recognized the seriousness of the company's pension problem, and had rejected the idea of cutting benefits, also had recommended funding. The directors, however, had taken their definition of the company's liabilities from their lawyers, and came away with a distinctly nonactuarial understanding of the problem. After scrutinizing the plan document's exculpatory clause and carefully analyzing the slim record of pension case law, the firm's legal department concluded that the company might not have the authority to suspend pensions once granted. It therefore advised management to view all allowances in pay status as contractual obligations. So the directors' committee proposed that upon each retirement the company set aside funds sufficient to provide the entire annuity. The firm's "expense" would thus take the form of a single-premium *immediate* annuity (SPIA) for all future retirees, expensed as they retired. The Pennsylvania then joined with other railroads interested in funding on an SPIA basis, through the Railway Accounting Officers Association, to petition the Interstate Commerce Commission for permission to include, among their legitimate, recoverable expenses, "premiums paid to insurance companies for annuity policies or amounts credited to reserves or turned over to trustees to represent the carrier's provision for pensions to employees currently retired." The negotiations bogged down, however, as the ICC began inquiries among all railroads regarding an industry-wide pension system.[45]

An SPIA program — funding pensions as awarded — would have added stability to railroad finances and strengthened the company retirement system. Murray Latimer's examples of pension funding methods, given in Figure 4.1, are based on rather arbitrary assumptions. But they nevertheless show the basic relationships between expensing policies. Had the Pennsylvania funded according to an SPIA schedule in 1900, by 1926 its cash outlays would have been about 25 percent below paygo. But starting an SPIA program in 1926 would be a tremendous burden, as the firm would have to fund its existing retirees as well as all new pensioners upon retirement.

When compared to a strict actuarial expensing schedule — accruing (and funding) pension costs during the years of employee activity — the railroads' proposal was lukewarm reform at best. Latimer offered examples of the two most common *accrual* methods — single- and level-premium *deferred* annuity expensing (SPDA and LPDA). The methods are akin, respectively, to term and whole life insurance. The single-premium deferred annuity approach expenses the present value of the projected pension benefit earned in the current year; the level premium method, like whole life insurance, collects and invests funds in advance in order to keep premiums level over the course of the contribution period. Both recognize a pension expense for a given employee forty years earlier than either paygo or SPIA. And in both, the sponsor's total pension expense will equilibrate much earlier, and at a far lower level.

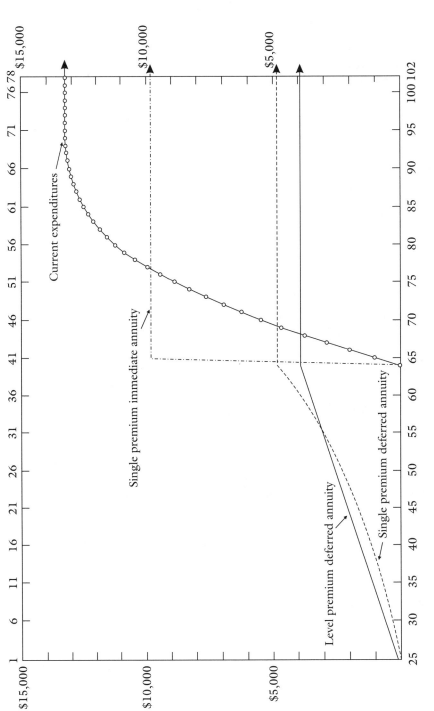

Figure 4.1. Annual charges into operating expenses each year for 40 years, under four methods of cost accounting, for an annual pension of $1 to each of a group of 1,000 entering employment at age 25 and surviving to age 65 (combined annuity mortality, 4 percent interest). *Source:* Murray Latimer, *Industrial Pension Systems in the United States and Canada* (New York: Industrial Relations

Latimer's SPDA model stabilized at 37 percent of paygo and his LPDA at 30 percent.

By the latter part of the 1920s, corporate officials in charge of pension operations had come to accept such actuarial expensing schedules as both proper and prudent. In 1928, the Pennsylvania's Hunt wrote: "the ideal system would recognize that each employe is a potential pensioner, and the Company would reserve such sums in relation to its current payroll as would provide funds for the payment of pensions . . . This, of course, would not be practicable for the reason that railroads generally are not prepared to take up the burdens which this ideal system would impose." T. O. Edwards, general auditor of the Southern Pacific Railroad and chair of the Railway Accounting Officers Association's subcommittee on pension accounting, stated flatly, in 1929, that "the only sound basis for financing a pension plan is on a full reserve."[46]

AT&T, which may have been the only noncontributory, uninsured sponsor to employ its own actuary, was also among the first to decide to fund pension benefits during an employee's active years of work. The firm applied to its regulator, also the Interstate Commerce Commission, to begin such an accrual program in 1927. The commission did not need to settle on a single treatment suited to many different firms, as it did in the railroad industry. But it was wary, as this additional "cost" would justify (currently) higher phone rates. The ICC finally approved AT&T's petition, but only after the company agreed to make pensions a contractual obligation and to fund the benefit externally, through transfers to a fiduciary. The regulator did not want to give the phone company the right to raise tariffs in exchange for an accounting entry. And to avoid further inflation of the rate base, the commission required AT&T to pay all pensions currently in "pay status" (the pensions of existing retirees) out of profits or from existing employee benefit funds. The company complied in full. Employees were given legal rights to their pensions upon meeting eligibility requirements; the company funded currently accruing pension expenses through transfers to its fiduciary, Bankers Trust; and pensioners on the rolls in 1927 were paid out of existing employee benefit funds.[47]

In November 1928 the ICC offered the railroads the same terms it had extended to AT&T. The railroads, however, found the conditions unacceptable. As the oldest pension sponsor, the industry had a far higher proportion of dependent workers on its rolls than the younger telephone company. It also had no surplus cash in its employee benefit funds with which to pay current allowances; the commission proposal thus meant a direct reduction in the industry's hard-pressed profits. And with their financials so poor, the companies were loath to give labor contractual pension rights. Both the railroads and the pension community criticized the decision. T. O. Edwards characterized the ruling as "manifestly unjust" as the ICC had in the past prevented the roads from accumulating funds in such an employee benefit pension fund. Latimer castigated the ICC for having "hindered rather than helped the development of American railroad pension systems." Not one railroad accepted the ICC conditions, and the 1.5 million railroad workers, nearly half of all pension plan participants, were thus denied the protection of sounder programs.[48]

In the private pension institution overall, sponsors only rarely awarded contractual pension rights. But the impulse to fund, as seen at AT&T and the railroads, flourished in the flush conclusion of the 1920s. The impulse found its fullest expression among the most prosperous sponsors. A few utilities and large manufacturers, enjoying especially good years and with few costly capital projects under way, began pouring funds into their pension plans. Seven such companies, with 500,000 employees, had accumulated $150 million by 1929; of this sum, two-thirds had been squirreled away since January 1, 1925. As shown in Table 4.2, over half the total of all U.S. and Canadian plans, 194 out of 352, had begun some funding program by 1929. Excluding the American railroad plans, nearly two-thirds of all schemes, with 70 percent of all participating employees, were funding. Had U.S. railroads been allowed to fund, up to 85 percent of participants might have had

Table 4.2. Pension funding ca. 1929, United States and Canada

Funding status	Number of plans	% of all plans	% of all except railroads
Funded:	194	55	63
Uninsured			
Noncontributory	104	30	34
Contributory	44	13	14
Insured	46	13	15
Unfunded	158	45	37
Total, all plans[a]	352	100	100

a. There were 307 plans outside the railroad industry: 194 funded and 113 unfunded.
Source: Murray Latimer, *Industrial Pension Systems,* tables 72, IV, and 75.

their benefits protected by some advance-funded pension accumulation as the Roaring Twenties came to an end.[49]

Business thus had responded to its new awareness of pension expense with a shift toward soundness. Between 1925 and 1929 the percentage of plans receiving actuarial advice rose smartly from 17 to 55 percent, funding grew from 39 to 55 percent, and some companies solidified participants' rights as their pension assets grew. A few guaranteed allowances once granted or to employees who satisfied the requirements for voluntary retirement. Eastman Kodak, in a bold stroke, vested workers with twenty years of service with rights to a pension. The company found the feature relatively cheap, popular, and also convenient, as it facilitated the elimination of unwanted workers.[50]

Despite such progress, the initial problems were such that it would take business decades, with reform at this pace, to put its pension house in order. The great majority of active employees, no matter how long their service, had no pension claim unless they survived in service to retirement. Nearly all plan documents still carried exculpatory clauses. Of the eighty-eight noncontributory sponsors using actuaries, only nine had acquired the habit of a periodic valuation. The rest had received but one actuarial review.[51]

Funding was also more apparent than real. Of the respondents to Latimer's survey, sixty-three firms with "funding" programs, employing about 500,000 workers, used balance sheet reserves to fund their pension plans. Such internal corporate accounts, of course, offered participants no more security than straight paygo arrangements should their employer run into financial difficulty. Forty-two firms, with 900,000 employees, had segregated trust funds. But many if not most of these trusts were revocable, meaning the sponsor could recapture the assets at will; and many if not most of the firms with segregated trusts, including AT&T and Standard Oil, "invested" their pension fund assets entirely in sponsor securities. Revocable pension trusts, holding nothing but sponsor securities, differed from balance-sheet reserving in form much more than in substance. Too many sponsors, with too many participants, meanwhile remained in straight paygo basis. Excluding the railroads, these firms were also the smallest uninsured sponsors. Including the railroads, they were the least stable financially and the most in need of reform. Murray Latimer estimated the unfunded liability of the entire corporate sector, as of 1932, at $2 billion, roughly 2 percent of U.S. Gross National Product and 1 percent of the value of all corporate stocks and bonds outstanding in 1929. He estimated the value of all pension assets, including balance sheet reserves and sponsor securities in pension trusts, at no more than 15 percent of the gross liability. Assets were now rising at about the same pace as liabilities. But domesticating the pension remained a serious challenge.[52]

From an historical perspective, structural changes in the pension institution were more significant than the uneven increase in soundness. The pension thitherto had been closely associated with the centralization of American economic life, with the integration of various business functions into large organizations. One of the great innovations of the Pennsylvania Railroad had been the internalization of human resource management, including the absorption of insurance functions from households, commercial carriers, employee and joint employer-employee associations. The Pennsylvania had seen the pension not only as an instrument of corporate organization but as a program to be managed exclusively by the firm. After 1920 this ambition fell away. The pension remained an important element in corporate labor policy, but the institution added new actors, interests, and control structures. It began a process of vertical disintegration that would stimulate, and complicate, the future growth of soundness.

The pension turned out to be far more complex than originally thought. The efficient management of a pension program demanded skills in actuarial analysis, plan design, marketing, and investment that far exceeded the standard capacity of even giant business enterprises. Only the major insurance companies had such resources in-house, and even they took several years to develop a solution both comprehensive and commercial. The Met's group annuity plan, bundled in a general group insurance package, was a significant business achievement. In a striking reversal, even the British would import this U.S. insurance innovation. The insurance carriers, because of such energy, their creativity, and the comprehensiveness of their programs, emerged as the decade's leading champions of external pension management.[53]

The insurance firms made many adjustments in their original programs to suit plan sponsors. Their efforts, of course, had not been sufficient to satisfy most corporate employers. The largest sponsors usually chose to control their programs themselves and to contract for specialized services only. Such employers would typically hire actuaries to evaluate their pension commitments; if pressured by government or employee sentiment, they would engage fiduciaries to manage their assets.

When possible, they avoided employee contributions and the attendant marketing, administrative, and legal complications. But whereas corporations circa 1920 had discussed pensions almost exclusively among themselves, and almost entirely as an adjunct to labor policy, a decade later they viewed the pension as a financial instrument and sought advice and services from actuaries and insurers.

The movement toward soundness gave firms other than the sponsors a place in the U.S. pension institution. It enfranchised participants, the retirees in particular. The state also came to play a significant role through its regulation of railroads and utilities and supervision of insurance companies. The pension had thus become far more complex than an internal administrative instrument. The 1920s saw the first transformation of the pension, in hindsight inevitable, from a management program to a complex social institution.

Chapter 5

◆ ◆ ◆

The Public Character
of Private Pensions

The Great Depression of the 1930s sent a massive shock wave through the nation's fragile private pension system. It cracked the corporate financial structure and shook the social, economic, and political foundations of the U.S. business system. Earlier jeremiads — such as Henry Pritchett's 1918 prophesy that unsound pensioning would embarrass even the great Standard Oil Corporation — proved prophetic. The Depression also brought Franklin D. Roosevelt and his "New Deal" to power. Roosevelt and his administration were consistently willing to reconstruct social institutions and redistribute basic social claims over the objections of the corporate community. They were especially eager to enhance the position of labor, and nowhere in economic society did the New Deal have a greater impact than in old age pensions. The Roosevelt administration laid a new institutional foundation for public and private pensioning that left an imprint far deeper than the Depression itself. This restructuring ushered in what Robert Paul, of the Martin Segal Company, has called the nation's second private pension institution.

The Socialization of Economic Security

The New Deal created an entirely new context for private pension planning. In the decade following Roosevelt's 1933 inauguration, the government launched a huge state-run social insurance scheme radical in both scope and principles. This program salvaged the battered private pension institution, but it did so on terms requiring substantial governmental participation in old age income provision. The administration then used the tax code to establish pension rights thitherto denied either in employer-written pension documents or in common law adjudication. The New Deal would give statutory status to labor unions, and this would assure workmen a voice in pension decisions. Acting primarily in the interest of labor, government thus reconstructed and became an ongoing player in the U.S. private pension institution.

In four short years, 1929 to 1933, corporate America's decade-long prosperity flipped upside down. Earnings of $10 billion turned to losses of $2 billion, unemployment moved from 3 to 25 percent of the workforce, and the corporate pension institution came under enormous stress. The number of pensioners doubled from 1927 to 1932, as retirement became a mechanism of wholesale "payroll saving." The comparatively high allowances drawn by these new retirees, the result of higher pay in the 1920s, further strained the institution. So did the greater life expectancy of these younger pensioners. As interest rates fell from 4 to 3 percent, the cost of deferred annuities (or of properly costed pension credits in uninsured plans) also jumped dramatically. The collapse of corporate profitability presented an especially grave threat to plans funded on a paygo, balance sheet reserve, or company-securities basis — plans dependent on the strength of the sponsor alone. In the Depression the institution thus saw its resources melt away as the demands upon it intensified.[1]

For the short term, the institution remained solvent. Pension contributions between 1927 and 1932 were twice the amount of allowances paid out, and assets rose by $135 million. The dominant position of the Metropolitan in the pension insurance business, and the strength of the industry's new group insurance cartel, the "Group Association" sponsored by FDR's National Industrial Recovery Act, assured the maintenance of "sound" group annuity rates and underwriting standards. But it was becoming increasingly difficult to remain optimistic. Many in the business community feared that the Depression was permanent, that capitalism had reached its final, stagnant end. In this scenario, continued unemployment would further bloat the pension rolls; and the collapse of profit and interest would frustrate attempts to lower costs by funding benefits in advance. More pressing than these anxieties about the future was the fact that many key sponsors in 1933 were already in serious trouble.[2]

As could have been expected, sponsors responded to the Depression by lowering their pension ambitions. Nearly 10 percent either discontinued or suspended part of their plans. The partial suspensions included halting new grants, eliminating further benefit accruals, and closing out new participants. A few of these hard-pressed firms even revoked pension trusts and recaptured the assets for general corporate purposes. Another 10 percent continued their programs, but reduced benefits. Still others, especially the petroleum giants, adopted a contributory format requiring employees to share in the costs and risks. Their new programs often took the form of "money purchase" schemes, which fixed employer and employee contributions and yielded whatever pension benefits the resulting sums could purchase from an insurance company. This arrangement further limited the risk borne by the pension sponsor, as it reduced its exposure to the fluctuating cost of deferred annuities.[3]

Amid all this retrenchment, a surprising irony of pension history was the vigorous growth of new plans as the Depression intensified. Despite the terminations, the number of plans actually grew between 1927 and 1932 at a rate exceeded only during the years of World War I. The new plans were typically installed by small companies that somehow dodged the full blast of depression, so coverage did not expand over this five-year period. Explaining this simultaneous contraction and expansion was sponsor conservatism. Existing sponsors retreated from pension commitments as a way to safeguard their beleaguered enterprises. Employers setting up new plans sought to secure old age incomes with funds not needed for investment in the midst of the Great Depression. The plans installed in the period were uniformly sound, with insurance companies managing all but one. The overwhelming majority were contributory and contractual, specified tight maximum allowances, and awarded benefits on the basis of the employee's current income, not the unknown final salary. Vesting employees with rights to their pension benefits after a given period of employment, a practice all but unknown in 1929 but essential in providing participant security, appeared in half of the new arrangements. In a parallel adjustment, an unusual number of sponsors reserved the discretionary right to retire any employee at will.[4]

While conservatism characterized the sponsors' response to the Depression, the need for old age income protection had never been more urgent. The percentage of the population over age 65 was rising faster than ever before, and a much larger proportion of these people were lifelong wage and salary workers. Depression unemployment struck these older employees particularly hard, and those holding onto their jobs felt pressure to retire from younger colleagues both laid off and stymied in low-level positions. The private pension institution in the best of times had been totally inadequate to meet society's old age income requirement. As the incidence of destitution among the elderly rose dramatically, the corporate instrument became even more peripheral to the national need.[5]

Prior to the Depression, labor had had neither enthusiasm for nor influence in pension matters. Few blue-collar workers had expected to live to old age, so except for the elderly, few had attended to old age income programs. Nor had the working class, in large measure foreign born or the offspring of immigrants, been in a position to influence political, legal, or corporate pensioning decisions. Nevertheless, various social reformers and union leaders had defended worker rights in corporate plans. The movement toward "sounder" programs in the 1920s had reflected their influence. Labor reformers also had been among the leading advocates of government pensions, and by 1930 they had helped establish old age pension programs in ten states. These victories, however, had been more symbolic than real. Sound corporate programs, as we have seen, were still the great exception at the end of the 1920s. And as for state pension schemes, income tests, meager allowances, and strict residency requirements severely limited their impact.[6]

The Depression, however, swelled the constituency of reform and swept into office a sympathetic administration and Congress. For millions of elderly Americans, general unemployment, the collapse of investment values, and the inability of their children to assist them had left the state as their sole source of hope. From 1930 to the end of 1934 another nineteen states established old age pension programs. These schemes, however, were of the restricted and highly limited character of earlier state programs. The national government, alone, had the necessary strength to provide a significant relief program. So labor turned to Washington for help.

Labor's new national political influence surfaced first and most directly in connection with the railroad pension system. The railroads had been the first industry to adopt pensioning en masse and had remained the institution's largest sector. But now the railroad plans were the weakest as well. They had had the misfortune to discover the accruing and accelerating character of pension expense from their own experience. As the 1920s had been financially difficult, the railroads had not been in a position to respond. The industry's seniority system, moreover, had translated any success in economizing on labor requirements into an increasingly old (and from a pension perspective, more expensive) workforce. The average age of railroad employees had jumped from 32 in 1920 to 42 in 1930. Then the Depression dealt the industry and its pension system a crushing blow. While railroad revenues had been flat at $5.7 billion per year between 1920 and 1929, they fell by half, to $2.85 billion, by 1933. Gigantic losses inevitably followed, as did "payroll saving" retirements. The number of railroad pensioners jumped 65 percent, from 34,000 to 56,000. After the layoff of 700,000 employees, 40 percent of the industry workforce, the average railroad employee in 1935 would be 46 years old. What is amazing, in the face of this pressure, is the small number of railroads that terminated or suspended their programs. The industry's pension system, however, stood at the brink of failure.[7]

The railroads attempted to address their pension problem at the end of 1931, when the major carriers and brotherhoods met to collectively bargain a response to the Depression. The parties agreed to a 10 percent wage reduction; but on pensions they could agree only on discussing the subject in future. The companies wanted cuts while the unions pushed for sounder programs. Most roads nevertheless matched the agreed-upon wage reduction with a 10 percent cut in pensions. This corporate-union maneuvering over pensions, however, proceeded no further: the rank and file suddenly preempted the collective bargaining process. Worker organizations sprang up around the country and formed themselves into the vibrant Railroad Employees' National Pension Association. RENPA immediately took the issue to the public arena, where railroad workers had enjoyed a long history of political success. Largely white and native-born citizens, unlike the semi-servile immigrants in manufacturing, they had for decades drawn Congress into the regulation of their affairs. They now turned to government to protect their pensions regardless of company policy or solvency.[8]

RENPA's proposal to Congress aimed primarily at expanding employment opportunities via a program of retirement. To facilitate the recall, retention, and promotion of younger workers, RENPA urged a reduction of the retirement age from 70 to 60. And to sweeten the process and broaden support across the rank and file, RENPA proposed an increase in pension allowances. The railroad seniority system had vested older workers with property rights to their jobs, much as officials in Britain's venal eighteenth-century bureaucracy had held claims on their positions. Jobs, of course, were the one commodity in critically short supply during the Depression. As young tax collectors in imperial Britain had pensioned off the incumbent officials, low-seniority railroad workers were only too happy to pay pensions to open opportunities for themselves. And they were more than eager to sweeten the pot. RENPA was so intent on retirements that it campaigned for paygo funding against the brotherhoods, who argued for soundness and a pension fund. RENPA contended that paygo allowed much higher immediate benefits at a given contribution rate, and it needed these benefits to facilitate retirements. In the Depression, this argument went far.[9]

What was truly radical in the RENPA proposal, however, was its call for government assumption of the railroad pension system. The organization argued that only the government, not the once-great railroad corporations, could operate their pension institution. RENPA viewed the railroads as a permanent economic fixture and their revenues as a solid foundation for a pension program. Individual companies might come and go, but the industry would stay. If a government mechanism was there to tax it, the railroads could finance these socialized insurance benefits.[10]

The carriers resisted RENPA's program, first in Congress and then in the courts. They objected to the increase in their pension costs, their inability to control administrative decisions, and the end of the loyalty a pension engendered and the fear created by the threat of its loss. The carriers failed in Congress; they lost the Senate by a vote of sixty-six to zero. But they won in the courts. In 1935 a conservative Supreme Court overturned legislation as fast as the New Deal could create it. And the Court ruled that the federal government had no constitutional authority to operate an industrial pension system or to promote railroad employment. But Roosevelt's landslide reelection in 1936, and his threat to pack the Supreme Court with justices sympathetic to his programs, convinced the carriers to reach an agreement with labor. After adjustments from both sides, Congress passed new railroad retirement legislation in 1937. A government program would henceforth provide pensions along the basic lines designed by RENPA. As the scheme focused benefits on the rank and file, most companies also established supplemental plans for their salaried staff.[11]

Thus did corporate America's first encounter with private pensions come to an end. Quite clearly, the railroads had not properly calculated their commitments before embarking on their pioneering adventure. Despite exculpatory clauses in their plan documents, they had not been able to extricate themselves from the widening vortex of pension liabilities. And after the Depression set in, they had been unable to prevent the socialization of their programs. Those sponsors which had followed the railroads typically employed workforces that were far younger and less competent politically. These firms thus had amassed far lighter pension liabilities, had been able to limit and fund their obligations prior to 1929, and faced no direct governmental challenge. They would keep control of their pension systems through the Depression. All corporate arrangements, however, would be profoundly affected by the New Deal's two major political achievements: the Wagner Act, which enfranchised the labor union, and the creation of a national Social Security system. The effects of the Wagner Act would take time to materialize; but the socialization of old age income provision would have a significant impact by the end of the decade.

The railroad workers, when agitating for pension legislation, had been primarily concerned with their own problems. In Washington, however, nearly everyone viewed the progress of their bill as a harbinger of a universal social insurance program. The nation as a whole, it seemed, suddenly became intent on government pensioning. A mass movement for old age pensions indeed crystallized in 1934 around Francis Townsend, a thitherto out-of-luck California physician. Townsend had advanced a simple, albeit impractical, pension panacea: a scheme of lavish government pensions to end both the Depression and poverty in old age. His $200 monthly benefit was so generous that corporate pensions, for all but the highest paid, look puny by comparison. After just one year of organizing, Townsend claimed 1,200 clubs, 25 million supporters, and 95 clerks to handle the mail. The phenomenon, like the spontaneous eruption of the railroad workers' pension campaign, demonstrated in clear political language the plight and politicization of older America.[12]

Nearly everyone in Washington, even the Republicans, was prepared to enact social insurance legislation by the summer of 1934. The nation agreed, for the moment, at least, that modern industrial societies all needed a universal, mandatory, state-administered security program. Although opinions varied as to the breadth of protection and the mechanisms to be used, socially insured retirement benefits were on every agenda. Using an *insurance* device implied a direct relationship between an individual's contributions and his or her benefits. The notion of *social* insurance made the program compulsory and skewed payouts to the lower-paid, assuring some minimum income for all.

Roosevelt himself took the initiative in social insurance. In 1934 he created a cabinet-level Committee on Economic Security and staffed it with disciples of Louis D. Brandeis and John R. Commons. Directed by Wisconsin's Edwin Witte and including Wisconsin's Arthur J. Altmeyer, the chief executive of the Social Security Administration from 1937 to 1953, this group designed a social insurance program that intruded as little as possible into the nation's individualistic economic ethos. "Only in a very minor degree," Witte insisted, "did [Social Security] modify the distribution of wealth and it does not alter at all the fundamentals of our capitalistic and individualistic economy." The design in many ways resembled that of the soundest private plans. It was compulsory and contributory; it accumulated a substantial pension fund to help secure future payments; it guaranteed a return of employee contributions in the event of death (either before or after retirement). Benefit values, moreover, were at least as large as cumulative employee contributions, plus interest; and over a broad range of incomes there was an "equitable" or close correspondence between contributions and benefits. Social Security did make a special accommodation for low-income participants and paid no pensions (and assessed no contributions) above a stipulated sum. But so did many corporate schemes. So close was the CES program to the best private designs that Social Security could conceivably eclipse, someday, the private pension institution.[13]

The community of pension sponsors resisted the CES design, fearing critical damage to their own programs. During the congressional debates they rallied around an amendment, proposed by Senator Bennett ("Champ") Clark, that would allow corporations with plans in no way less advantageous to their employees to opt out of the federal program. The Senate passed the Clark Amendment by a thumping fifty-one to thirty-five, but the House backed the administration and adamantly refused to allow such "contracting out." The Clark Amendment turned out to be the last and thorniest issue resolved by the congressional conference committee. Social Security finally cleared the Congress only after the President agreed to hearings on the Clark Amendment in the next session of Congress and, some say, to the amendment's actual passage.[14]

But prospects for the Clark Amendment were not promising. In the subcommittee set up to explore the issue, its supporters first were forced to agree that only private arrangements managed by insurance companies were as advantageous as the public program. For a time, the Met's 1923 "American Pension Plan" had life. But soon tortuous complications arose over measuring, pricing, and safeguarding pension credits. Nor could Clark's party assuage fears of adverse selection — that the private plans would carry the cheaper, younger lives and turn over to the government the substantially more expensive older workers. The New Deal majority, however, was primarily concerned with the social and political implications of contracting out. The constitutionality of the Social Security Act rested on the power of Congress to tax, and this seemed to require a universal levy. Social Security supporters, moreover, thought that any identification of the program with a poorer stratum of society would undermine its long-term public appeal.

While the arguments were still unfolding, support for the Clark Amendment evaporated suddenly. It was as though corporate America one day woke up and recognized both the reality and advantage of the liberal worldview. As one perceptive commentator observed, "I doubt if any campaign for a major amendment to law ever collapsed as swiftly as that for the Clark Amendment. With a great sigh of relief business admitted government to one more function it had proved it could not carry out itself, turning over to government hundreds of millions of liabilities incurred in good faith, but liabilities for which private resources are simply not adequate."[15]

The contracting-out campaign at an end, the community of pension sponsors turned their attention to the design of the new government program, generally seeking to restrict its economic significance. The more Social Security resembled a straight means-tested welfare system, providing just the minimum "adequate" benefit, the more they liked it. To keep expenditures down, business wanted flattish, subsistence-type benefits geared to need rather than past contributions. Should the return of prosperity alleviate the elderly's plight, such a welfare-oriented program could be cut back readily. The administration, however, was convinced that poverty was the final reward for most Americans, then and in the future. New Dealers viewed Social Security as a new institutional fact of American life and were concerned primarily with maintaining the dignity of the elderly recipients. A universal and "equitable," or contribution-based, social insurance mechanism provided such non-stigmatized participation. Agreeing that an insurance format enhanced the legitimacy of the old age income program, the administration hoped to maximize, and business hoped to minimize, Social Security's insurance component.

Business generally supported paygo financing, despite its apparent fiscal unsoundness. The administration wanted to fund Social Security through the purchase of government securities, building up a "pension fund" and backing the program with the full credit of the United States. The huge scale of the enterprise, however, meant that funding would provide the Treasury with a tremendous flow of revenue without the need to (explicitly) tax or borrow. It in effect gave the government a license to spend without the check of direct congressional taxation and, as put by an insurance company president, M. Albert Linton, "irrespective of market conditions" and without "the appraisal of the financial community." Business also pointed out that government bonds in Social Security vaults ultimately did little to improve program security. Future benefits would in any case be backed by a promise of government taxation. Bonds offered explicit recognition of the pension liability and access to all government revenues while the paygo plan was secured by an implicit intergenerational compact and the narrower payroll tax. These advantages, business argued, hardly justified funding's increased burden of current taxation and the fiscal freedom it gave the administration.[16]

On the two points at issue, adequacy versus equity and paygo versus funding, business soon found a slew of unusual allies. A social service bloc, led by Abraham Epstein and Isaac Rubinow, was primarily concerned with the "adequacy" of benefits in satisfying human requirements. Believing that those most in need of social insurance were also those least able to afford it, they wanted Social Security to redistribute income "inequitably." This party wanted contributions to flow to the needy today, not to a fund for future benefit payments. Also influential was the small but growing community of Keynesian economists, who emphasized Social Security's impact on aggregate economic demand. The Keynesians campaigned for high benefits to pump purchasing power into the economy. Believing lower-income people had a greater propensity to spend benefits on current consumption, they favored "adequacy" because it redistributed income in the macroeconomically proper direction. The Keynesians likewise abhorred the idea of funding, as it would merely augment the Depression's mound of stagnant savings. As reflected in the history of the Railroad Retirement Act, rank-and-file workers likewise favored paygo programs that boosted employment, conserved current wages, and skewed benefits to the lowest-paid. Finally, the still powerful Townsendite movement pressed for higher payments, and by the late 1930s many Congressional Republicans had adopted the Townsendite program.[17]

Together, these constituencies pushed through the important 1939 amendments to the Social Security Act. This legislation decisively shifted the program emphasis from equity toward adequacy. Benefit schedules were flattened, which skewed benefit/contribution ratios in favor of the lower income classes. Survivor benefits, which enhanced the "adequacy" of the program in serving human needs, replaced the original "equitable" lump-sum death benefit based on past contributions. The amendments also abandoned earlier funding ambitions and pushed Social Security much closer to paygo. The resulting program, around which a national consensus soon solidified, provided far more space for private pensions than had the original 1935 Act. By focusing its benefits at the bottom of the income scale, the government avoided direct competition with the career-inducing schemes. Benefits at the middle and bottom of the scale were not so high that firms pursuing an efficiency wage strategy for blue-collar workers — offering premium compensation in exchange for premium loyal and steady service — could not offer supplementary pensions as a token of corporate goodwill. The paygo decision also gave private plans more room in the financial markets; had funding continued, Social Security might well have driven up the national savings rate, reduced the return on investment, and rendered private pensions far more expensive. As a result of these benefit and funding decisions, the fortunes of higher-paid corporate personnel, in particular, were handed back to the private institution.[18]

Until the emergence of the 1939 consensus, the uncertainty surrounding Social Security had disrupted orderly pension planning. Contracting out had remained a possibility into 1936. Anxiety that an expanded Social Security program would eclipse the corporate schemes — a threat present in the original 1935 design — persisted until the passage of the 1939 amendments. Only at the end of the decade did the shape of Social Security, and conversely the scope of private programs, grow clear. When the dust settled, the government had taken over two functions thitherto performed by corporate plans. No longer would workers face destitution when superannuated, and thus stand in need of capitalist welfare. Nor did the lack of suitable old age pensions, at least for rank-and-file workers, impede a systematic corporate retirement policy. Indeed, the public program all but institutionalized 65 as the universal age of retirement. Of the three initial pensioning purposes, the only one undiminished by the arrival of Social Security was the desire to induce career employment.[19]

Government's preemption of old age pension provision was thus dramatic, and most contemporaries predicted dampened corporate enthusiasm for private plans. It is therefore quite surprising to find the private institution continuing its vigorous growth. New installations had proceeded rapidly through the economic collapse of 1929–1932, but they expanded at their fastest rate thus far between May 1932 and the end of 1938. Nearly three hundred employers started pension programs in this period, a figure nearly matching the total number of plans in 1929. These schemes also continued the pattern begun in the 1920s; they were typically reinsured and sponsored by smaller employers. The total number of participants thus edged up in the 1930s, and the institution accelerated its spread into the mainstream of American business life.[20]

The gradual spread of pension concepts and experience — movement down a pension learning curve — certainly explains some of this acceleration in institutional development. However, new practical considerations also stimulated this growth. While Social Security partly preempted two original uses of corporate pensions, the program ironically made the instrument far more effective in the third — drawing personnel into career employment relationships. Private plans had traditionally discriminated in favor of key corporate personnel by basing benefits on final salaries and by awarding pensions only to those surviving in the firm to retirement. Those promoted up the organization tended to stay to retirement and see their final incomes rise far above those of their subordinates; those grubbing about the bottom tended to move on or be dismissed. The recent interest in pension soundness and the dominance of insurance had deflected the institution from this purpose by eliminating final salary formulas and by returning to separating employees at least their own contributions. But with the rank and file now largely taken care of by Social Security, the bulk of private funds could focus more directly on career employees. The government program indeed had raised public consciousness of the problem of old age income while failing to satisfy the needs of middle- and upper-income groups. Pension sponsors could now meet this demand and do so using far fewer dollars. Benefit levels of programs established in the late 1930s were half as large as those in the plans of 1929; but combined with Social Security, they afforded a significantly higher retirement income.[21]

While Social Security helped the private pension function as a career-inducing instrument, it also complicated plan administration. To efficiently skew company funds to the career employees, corporate benefits had to be "integrated," or calculated in conjunction with the government allowance. Because Social Security payments flowed disproportionately to lower-income workers, benefits from integrated plans, conversely, would service the higher-paid. Already in 1938, before the 1939 amendments would skew Social Security benefits even more sharply toward lower-paid employees, a significant portion of all sponsors had integrated their plans. Integration, however, was a tricky business. As Social Security benefits were determined by a quirky method, the integrated private pensions could rarely be expressed as a simple formula. Moreover, observers confidently predicted further Social Security benefit increases and design changes that any integrated plan would need to accommodate. These complications made it even more difficult for sponsors to manage their plans and encouraged the use of external expertise. The arrival of Social Security thus further stimulated the growth of the pension industry.[22]

Considering the size and implications of Social Security, the political response of the community of pension sponsors, aside from the Clark Amendment imbroglio, was notable for its moderation. Acceptance of the New Deal initiative involved a thoroughgoing reconceptualization of private efforts at old age income assurance. It demanded recognition that government's role in the provision of security was permanent and legitimate, not a passing response to the Depression. Acceptance meant acknowledging that individuals and corporations were unwilling or unable to satisfy the new need for retirement income; that the nation, using democratic government, had established an intergenerational social contract to solve what private initiative had not. The most clear-sighted business people also understood that a significant private institution remained possible only with the socialization of basic old age pension benefits. Government would handle pension functions separable from the firm — retiring aged labor from the workforce and assuring these people a basic standard of living. Remaining to the sponsors was the pension function that they themselves most valued — attaching workers to organizational careers and then releasing these higher-paid personnel in an orderly fashion.

With the arrival of Social Security, the cash income of the elderly would come increasingly from three financial sources — government pensions, employer pensions, and individual savings. And cash was essential, for the only necessity that most elderly households now produced for themselves was shelter; they owned their homes, but purchased food, clothing, and medical services. Income from employment fell steadily, and the image of the pensioner sitting on a "three-legged stool" became an industry cliche. In the years following the passage of Social Security, each leg of this stool, for most elderly Americans, would grow in inverse relation to its age. Individual savings, the ancient support of the elderly, would supply an ever smaller portion of the pensioner's purchasing power. Social Security, the most recent leg, would become the financial foundation of old age. Occupational pensions would stand in between. And at the end of the 1930s, the private institution enjoyed significant room for future expansion.

Taxes and Consequences

The purposeful entry of government into the provision of old age pensions pushed the older corporate programs upward in the firm. Private pensions would henceforth be tied tightly to the need to reward key employees, and plan benefits would flow more swiftly to the higher-compensated personnel. A second New Deal initiative, a "soak the rich" tax program that the administration presented to Congress a few days after its Social Security bill, inadvertently reinforced this effect. As part of the ongoing battle between New Deal reformers and the business community, the Democrats passed a revenue act greatly raising taxes on high-income earners: the Treasury now wanted 70 percent of taxable income over $100,000. Suddenly, this upward jolt of taxation made pension plans attractive as shelters for high personal incomes. The instrument thus found a new purpose — the avoidance of tax. The schemes that sprang up quickly in the late 1930s functioned not just to attach key employees to the firm; they also served to reduce tax levies on owners and top corporate executives.[23]

Pension plans had enjoyed tax relief since the origin of the federal income tax in 1913, with the bulk of the benefits going to the sponsors. Corporations had always been allowed to deduct pension payments and deferred annuity premiums as ordinary and necessary business expenses. (This was true even though pensions were quite *un*ordinary and therefore perhaps *un*necessary.) Contributions to pension funds organized separately from the corporation had been made deductible in 1918. Three years later, Congress had exempted from taxation profit-sharing and stock bonus trusts established for the exclusive benefit of "some or all employees," and the Internal Revenue Service had extended this exemption to pension funds. Since 1921, employers therefore deducted their current year's pension contributions, pension trusts paid no tax on their investment income, and employees were taxed only upon the actual receipt of pension payments. Responding to the increased interest in soundness at the end of the 1920s, the 1928 Revenue Act granted tax relief to sponsors shifting balance sheet reserves to a trust or insurance company. Even though these assets funded liabilities accrued in previous years, Congress allowed sponsors to deduct the sums transferred. But to limit the use of this provision as a tax avoidance stratagem, the deduction had to be spread over a ten-year period.[24]

While sponsors had dutifully taken their legitimate tax reliefs, tax avoidance had not been a significant purpose behind pension planning. With Roosevelt's dramatic tax increase, however, avoiding taxes levied on plan *participants* became a major reason to set up a pension scheme. The tax-saving potential especially appealed to proprietors of small, closely held firms. These businessmen not only had high incomes to protect but held the necessary corporate control to install the appropriate plan. Such firms were the traditional customers of insured pension plans, and quick-witted insurance agents soon began promoting their wares as tax-saving instruments. One New York Chartered Life Underwriters luncheon seminar on the tax advantages of pension plans demonstrated this new interest: it drew a crowd of two hundred, the organization's largest attendance for such a meeting. The Internal Revenue Service was soon flooded with pension trust inquiries — the second New York division alone received one thousand requests in 1937. Although it is impossible to know the extent to which private pensions had simply become tax-dodging instruments, both the interest and the potential clearly were present.[25]

No treasury easily accepts the avoidance of taxes. The New Deal especially resented losing revenues from high-income employers — its primary political opponent — through sharp readings of the tax code. The

Internal Revenue Service therefore developed, and the tax courts upheld, various regulations restricting the use of the pension tax reliefs. The tax preferences had been granted to plans benefiting employees, not owners, so the IRS ruled that "devices of whatsoever nature for withdrawing profits or paying salaries to officers are not pension trusts within the meaning of the act." The Service also limited pension allowances, and thereby deductible contributions, to some measure of reasonableness. But the control of tax abuse by regulation quickly grew unwieldy. The procedure took too much time and the courts could always overrule IRS regulations or their specific applications. As tax-avoiding pension schemes multiplied in the late 1930s, so did the task of maintaining a regulatory system.[26]

When tax receipts for the year 1936 fell far below expectations, the administration asked for a congressional investigation of the various new schemes of tax evasion and avoidance. President Roosevelt wrote Congress on June 1, 1937, claiming "that there is a well defined purpose and practice on the part of some taxpayers to defeat the intent of Congress to tax incomes in accordance with the ability to pay through a legal though highly immoral avoidance of the intent of the law." Included in Roosevelt's list of particulars was abuse of pension reliefs. "The revenue acts," he wrote,

> have sought to encourage pension trusts for aged employees by providing corporations with a special deduction on account of contributions thereto, and exempting the trust itself from tax. Recently this exemption had been twisted into a means of tax avoidance by the creation of pension trusts which include as beneficiaries only small groups of officers and directors who are in the high income brackets. In this fashion high-salaried officers seek to provide themselves with generous retiring allowances, while at the same time the corporation claims a deduction therefor, in the hope that the fund may accumulate income free from tax.
>
> Thus in one case $43,000 is annually appropriated by the corporation to a pension trust for the benefit of its two chief owners. One of the co-owners will retire at the age of 65 with a monthly pension of $1,725, and the other will retire at 60 with a monthly pension of $1,425.[27]

In the resulting hearings, held by an ad hoc Joint Committee on Tax Evasion and Avoidance, Treasury officials presented their case. Undersecretary of the Treasury Roswell Magill entered into the record a written brief, prepared by Deputy Revenue Commissioner Charles T. Russell, and then discussed the pension problem with the committee. The administration officials reiterated the argument presented in the President's letter — that pension tax reliefs were not necessarily advancing the purpose Congress intended, and that the use of pensions to shelter corporate officials from tax served no social goal. The Treasury also urged that tax relief be restricted to irrevocable pension trusts. Current law allowed all tax benefits — the deduction of contributions and the exemption of trust income from tax — even if the plan document allowed the sponsor to recapture the plan's assets. Revocable personal trusts received markedly different treatment (the grantor paid tax on trust income), and current law all but invited corporations to use pension funds to juggle income between tax years. The Treasury thus proposed three statutory requirements for all tax-favored pension plans: the irrevocability of pension trusts; limits on allowances granted; and a requirement that plans include employees generally and not be restricted to owners and managers.[28]

Congress did not act on the administration's proposals in 1937. Although the Treasury had identified a burgeoning interest in pensions as a tax-avoidance mechanism, it had admitted that abuse had not become a serious problem. Its proposals were anticipatory reforms. A more important reason for inactivity was that Congress and the administration, pursuing political as well as fiscal agendas, focused on more sensational forms of abuse and evasion. Treasury witnesses and their congressional interrogators spent far more time discussing the incorporation of yachts, which had allowed various well-known businessmen to deduct the acquisition and operating costs of their pleasure craft. The administration's serious discussion of pension problems, Russell's written report, was merely entered into the record. Undersecretary Magill, who testified before the committee, had no great command of the subject, and his limited testimony centered on the revocability of tax-exempt pension trusts. And while revocability focused on reliefs provided to corporate sponsors, the committee was investigating the avoidance of personal income taxes. Lacking urgency, spice, or a clear connection to the committee's central concerns, pensions went straight to the congressional back burner. Congress did return to the issue in 1938, but then it merely required irrevocable trusts and the submission of various documents to qualify a plan for tax relief.[29]

As the 1938 amendment in no way restricted pensions as mechanisms for avoiding personal income taxes, the revenue hemorrhage expanded. The Treasury still believed Congress had intended to protect only bona fide employee trusts, so it responded with a new and tougher set of regulations. Section 165 of the revenue code required tax-exempt employee benefit trusts to be for the "exclusive benefit of *some or all* employees." To prevent arrangements serving just the top executive group, the IRS demanded the participation of "all or a large percentage of the total number of the employer's clerks or workmen (as distinguished from persons in positions of authority)." If the plan was not all-inclusive, the government wanted to know who was left out and why. Such efforts, however, met stiff resistance. Pension consultants and insurance agents claimed that Congress specifically had included "some or all" to sanction top-tier plans. So they continued constructing schemes that blatantly discriminated in favor of high-paid officials. They also integrated private and public benefits, awarded credits for past service, and included a host of similar allowable features that skewed benefits up the corporate ladder and challenged the administration's revenue agents. The industry won a great victory in 1939, when the Board of Tax Appeals approved the Albert W. Harris plan that limited participation to company officers.[30]

As Treasury officials became enmeshed in pension regulation, they were drawn to two additional issues. The first involved the enormous potential for tax avoidance created by the general lack of vesting of active workers with legal rights to their pension benefits. Making pension awards contingent upon actual retirement, the IRS came to understand, all but guaranteed that top-tier personnel received an inordinate proportion of pension plan benefits. High-level officers were far more likely to stay to the end of their careers and retire on pension; lower-level employees typically left much earlier and, without vesting, simply forfeited their claims. The lack of vesting also created problems in tax theory. It was generally believed that pension expenses were deductible because pensions were a form of compensation. Compensation, however, was normally the property of the employee. Treasury officials thus became struck with the "incongruity of nonvested compensation" and its implications for tax policy. For these practical and conceptual reasons, the administration added vesting to its pension reform agenda.[31]

Treasury officials also grew concerned with the funding of tax-favored plans. To protect the fisc from tax avoidance, existing statutes restricted the amounts that sponsors could contribute to their pension funds. But the law demanded no minimum funding level. Government had no assurance, in effect, that the tax-favored plan would ever pay the young rank and file their promised pensions. The issue, once again, was whether or not a particular scheme was a bona fide *employee* benefit plan. To provide such assurance, the Treasury had to protect itself against insufficient as well as excess funding. But what was the appropriate level of contributions? On matters like this, current law required only the slightest pretense of actuarial precision. It allowed deductions for contributions covering "the pension liability accruing during the year" and for a portion of contributions accrued in the past. But the statutes established no standards for measuring these liabilities. The IRS, Treasury argued, now had to supervise pension costing techniques. The administration's final objective was thus to place costing and funding regulations on a proper actuarial footing.[32]

It was not until 1942 that Roosevelt's Treasury again approached Congress about pension taxation. Motivated by a sudden rash of suspicious inquiries about setting up small-company plans, the administration returned to the Congress for statutory restrictions. This time Treasury officials offered Congress a far more detailed analysis of pension policy than they had five years earlier. A revived U.S. economy, stimulated by the outbreak of war in Europe in 1939, had led many proprietors to shelter their incomes in discriminatory pension plans. With America itself now in the war, the IRS feared an avalanche of tax-avoiding schemes. Randolph Paul, Undersecretary of the Treasury, thus began the campaign by reiterating the administration's basic premise. Pension plans enjoyed tax preferences only because they advanced a social purpose—the provision of benefits to rank-and-file employees. But many of the newer plans, he continued, were mere tax avoidance schemes for high-paid executives. To shift the instrument back to its original purpose, Paul suggested four new requirements to qualify for tax relief. Favored plans, he proposed, would feature full and immediate vesting, general employee participation (that is, no discrimination against the rank and file), a $7,500 cap on yearly allowances, and minimum funding requirements.[33]

Although the administration laid a stronger case before Congress in 1942 than it had in 1937, it also met far stiffer resistance. Conservative legislators, including Senator Robert Taft, complained that the administration was inappropriately using the tax code to advance its social program. Practicing pension professionals, who understood pension mechanics in great detail, traveled to Washington to point out difficulties in the Treasury proposals. Especially influential were consultants H. Walter Forster and Arthur S. Hansen. In addition to these politicians and technical experts, plan sponsors lobbied vigorously against the Treasury proposals. Because of their large numbers of employees and shareholders, these firms carried significant political weight. AT&T, the nation's largest private employer and pension sponsor, indeed led the campaign against the Treasury proposals. The telephone company considered its plan a bona fide employee benefit program, not a frivolous tax avoidance scheme, but it threatened to terminate should Congress enact the new proposals. Taking this threat at face value, AT&T's employees and their union officials wrote letters and traveled to Washington to testify in favor of the status quo.[34]

Of the reforms proposed by the administration, the participation requirements drew the least criticism. Both Forster and Hansen pointed out difficulties in defining the relevant employee group, of which some minimum percentage or representative cross-section would have to participate. But Congress *did* expect to get a social return for its tax favors. Most Congressmen expected pension plans to benefit those who most needed help, the middle- and lower-income employees, and many expressed contempt at employers who excluded the rank and file. The large corporate sponsors such as AT&T, moreover, included substantially all employees in their schemes and could readily satisfy the proposed participation tests. Congress thus stipulated that plans receiving tax relief establish trusts complying with a revised section 165 of the revenue code. Section 165 trusts now were for "the exclusive benefit of employees or their beneficiaries," language specifically omitting the phrase "some or all." Participation had to be either (1) 70 percent of all full-time employees; (2) 80 percent of employees in voluntary plans, with at least 70 percent of full-time employees eligible to participate; or (3) such that the IRS determined was a bona fide employee group. The statute also insisted that plan benefits not discriminate in favor of officers or highly compensated employees.[35]

The pension community fought the Treasury's proposed $7,500 allowance cap with more determination. AT&T's plan, and those of many other big businesses with well-paid executives, clearly fell afoul of the proposed limitation. AT&T currently had retirees drawing more than $7,500 a year, and many in the firm's management looked forward to pensions substantially in excess of this figure. The company argued that such high pensions were needed for the critical and delicate task of retiring top executives — a legitimate corporate function and not part of a tax-avoidance scheme. Pension consultants further pointed out that existing antidiscrimination provisions gave the IRS sufficient power to control tax evasion. The Service, they claimed, did not need this arbitrary limit on allowances. These arguments swayed Congress, and the 1942 Revenue Act included no cap on pensions paid by tax-exempt trusts.[36]

It was the administration's mandatory vesting proposal that met the most intense hostility. Most plans had no vesting and the Treasury recommendation could bring tremendous change to these programs. Some recently established plans did vest employer-financed benefits, but only for employees above a certain age or after some lengthy period of service or plan participation. Opposition to the Treasury proposal became so fervent that Paul abandoned the idea of full and immediate vesting and instead recommended mandatory vesting for employees over 40 with fifteen years of service. The sponsors, nevertheless, still complained bitterly. As the Metropolitan Life Insurance Company had discovered in 1923 when it had unveiled its pension bond scheme with full and immediate vesting, sponsors vehemently resisted paying anything to separating employees. Vesting not only increased pension costs by some unknown amount, but by facilitating quits it frustrated a purpose behind many corporate plans. Congress listened to these arguments and introduced no vesting requirement in the 1942 Act.[37]

While efforts to control discrimination brought the Roosevelt administration and the business community into conflict, placing pension costing and funding on an actuarial basis brought the two parties together. Treasury officials consulted freely with leading pension professionals when drafting the funding regulations — section 23(p) of the revenue code. The collaboration was quite successful, and the significance of the 1942 Revenue Act owed much to this cooperative effort. The statute and the companion Bulletin issued by the government resulted in the codification of best professional practice and, based thereon, the arrival of modern regulation of pension costing and funding.[38]

Section 23(p) of the 1942 Revenue Act imposed the first funding obligations on tax-favored plans. The cost of benefits accrued in the *current year* — what the actuaries called the "normal cost" — now had to be funded in the current year; pay-as-you-go and terminal funding thus were excluded from the community of tax-favored plans. The actuarial profession recognized various costing methods, each yielding a different normal cost pattern (and therefore differing measures of the accumulated past service liability). All commonly recognized methods were sanctioned by the statute. The act allowed the standard accrued plan benefit method, akin to the insurers' single-premium deferred annuity, which figured annual (or normal) cost as the actuarially discounted value of benefits credited each year. Congress also permitted costing techniques that smoothed pension costs over time — the level premium deferred annuity method found in many insurance company contracts and the level percentage of payroll method. These smoothing techniques could generate more tax relief than the standard APBM: sponsors could claim deductions at a faster rate and have more trust income accumulating free of tax. But because these methods were "sounder" than the basic APBM program and were currently in use, Congress allowed them to continue.[39]

The new section 23(p) also revised the tax treatment of contributions funding credits for past service. Previous law had exercised little control over these huge liabilities. Deductions for past-service contributions just had to be spread evenly over a ten-year period, a jerry-rigged procedure accommodating the transfer of balance-sheet reserves to a trust or insurance company. Nothing, however, limited the percentage that could be funded and invested tax-free in any one year. The new law required precise actuarial estimates of the unfunded "past service or other supplementary pension or annuity credits." It then limited both contributions and deductions to 10 percent of the total amount. Nothing required sponsors to amortize this initial plan cost (or the cost of a revision). But if the sponsors chose to extinguish their past-service liabilities, they had to follow an actuarial accounting and amortization schedule. Premiums paid to insurance companies likewise came under this actuarial scrutiny, causing insurance to lose one of its competitive advantages over trusteed programs. Whereas the entire premium had been deductible in the nonactuarial regime, payments in excess of the permitted amount — normal cost plus 10 percent of the unfunded past-service liability — could no longer be deducted in any one year.[40]

As important as statutory requirements was what the IRS was able to do with them. Despite the apparent precision of the 1942 Revenue Act, the legislation required IRS regulations, and therefore a measure of IRS control, over various aspects of pension plan management. The Service, for example, declared that interest on the unfunded past-service liability had to be included in the calculation of the annual normal cost; and it specified what forms of property, other than cash, were acceptable as contributions to qualified plans. The new nondiscrimination mandate, and the elimination of the "some or all" appellation from the permitted employee beneficiary class, also demanded administrative interpretation. Among the features that had to pass muster were methods of integration with Social Security and the award of credit for past service. To prevent officers from funding their own pensions and then terminating the scheme or allowing it to die, the Service issued a series of regulations that required qualified plans be more permanent undertakings.[41]

The new complexity of pension regulation tremendously expanded the authority of the IRS pension chief. Isadore Goodman, who held this position from 1957 to 1977 and before that served as technical advisor to the previous chief, was responsible for volumes of regulations, rulings, and opinions testing whether a plan indeed was a bona fide scheme benefiting employees in general. The practice of prudent sponsors and pension advisors in seeking IRS approval *before* installing or modifying a plan only augmented his influence. Gossip and speculation spawned an industrial folklore over what Goodman demanded in a plan for prior approval. And among Goodman's supposed extra-statutory tests was vesting after twenty years of service, a requirement that the Treasury had not been able to enact in 1942. Although Goodman's benchmark still left significant room for discrimination, it nonetheless pressed a measure of vesting on the private pension institution.[42]

The Revenue Act of 1942 brought to an end this burst of legislative reform. The Treasury's two recommendations for tax-preference qualification bypassed by Congress — mandatory vesting and pension maximums — would not be enacted for another thirty years. What Congress had done in 1942 nevertheless marked a watershed in the history of private pensions. The essential new requirement for plan qualification — broad employee participation — became the pillar in the government's campaign against discrimination and tax avoidance. Business executives could no longer dream of installing a plan for just themselves. Placing all tax-favored plans on an actuarial basis established a minimum standard of soundness throughout the entire institution. From that time forward, at least "normal" pension costs would be recognized and funded.

The Public Character of Private Pensions

The consistent purpose of pension tax regulation, like the administration's initiative in Social Security, was to benefit rank-and-file labor. Viewed from the perspective of the private pension institution, however, the two government programs had antithetical effects. The government's own pension program pushed the private institution up the corporate hierarchy; the Revenue Act of 1942 pulled it back down into the ranks. Social Security preempted the need for benevolent employers to provide blue-collar workers with basic old age support; but the IRS prevented corporate plans from becoming just tax-favored savings vehicles for wealthier individuals. Approaching private pensions from two different directions, government policy in the 1930s thus defined an intermediate *public* role for employer-sponsored plans: they would provide *socially* needed supplementary retirement income to an upper-middling segment of the population. Social Security would provide the basic leg of the elderly's new three-legged stool; the combination of tax benefits, IRS regulations, and employer interests would maintain private pensions as the intermediate support for middle-class Americans. Even should tax avoidance be a sponsor's primary aim, tax regulations would force the plan to serve the public purpose as well.

Government thus became a critical new player in private pensions. In most ways the institution benefited. The enactment of Social Security removed enormous liabilities from the institution's balance sheet. Because corporate decisionmakers now received a disproportionate share of the private benefits, they developed a greater personal stake in the institution. The tax regulations also imposed a salutary measure of actuarial and financial discipline upon the plan sponsors. The arrival of government, however, brought significant administrative overhead costs. Integrating a plan with Social Security and satisfying IRS qualification and funding requirements were complicated tasks involving expensive expertise. As IRS regulations changed periodically, the need for such expertise was continually refreshed. The active presence of government thus stimulated the expansion of the pension-servicing industry. In both the traditional area of plan design and the new necessity of regulatory compliance, sponsors had to rely more than ever on external professional advisors.

The entry of government furthered the institution's ongoing disintegration. Responsibilities to provide income for the elderly had shifted out of the household economy, first to employers and then to insurers, and now to government as well. Social Security could have reintegrated the social portion of this activity. It could have effectively become the nation's centralized pension agency, all but eliminating the *private* pension structure. But it did not. The Social Security Administration became merely another organization, albeit one of gargantuan proportion, in a larger public/private institution. The granting of systematic tax favors brought government into the nation's pension system from another direction, with the Treasury now serving the private institution as regulator, as well as financier.

So the private pension institution did not merely survive the Great Depression of the 1930s. It was thoroughly reorganized by New Deal reforms. The pension emerged in 1942 as a far more complex piece of property, serving a clear public purpose, as well as employer and employee interests. Decisions involved not only employers but the government and the increasingly sophisticated pension-provision industry. And the labor unions legitimated by New Deal legislation would soon take a seat at the table. The nation's second private pension institution was thus a complex collaboration that in time would prove much sturdier than the first.

Chapter 6

♦ ♦ ♦

A Tale of Two Classes

The maturation of a vigorous American state, first in the New Deal and then in World War II, had the unintended effect of returning issues of class to the center of the pension institution. The earliest pension plans had been designed for either blue-collar or managerial personnel. But employers steadily had submerged this class differentiation beneath an overriding concern for organizational efficiency and benefit security. By the late 1920s, most firms subjected all employees to the same corporate clock. Nearly all new installations and major plan revisions based benefits on relatively nondiscriminatory career-earnings formulas and provided rank-and-file laborers with withdrawal rights and contractual guarantees from third-party insurance companies. Disrupting this harmonizing trend were dramatic New Deal initiatives.

By assuring basic retirement incomes, Social Security usurped the labor-focused "welfare" function from corporate pension programs. By establishing collective bargaining as the basis of U.S. labor relations, the Wagner Act derailed management initiatives, including the pension, designed to incorporate wage workers into a company-wide personnel system. Meanwhile, the New Deal's aggressively progressive tax policy made the pension shelter far more valuable to owners and managers, who paid income tax, than to workers, who typically did not. The sharp run-up in government levies, first for relief and public works, then for military expenditures, intensified this upper-class tax-planning interest. As private pensions became especially attractive to owners and managers, the institution quickly learned to serve this clientele. The more successful elements of the working class, those organizing unions under the Wagner Act, also used their new bargaining strength to assert their own claims to private pensions. Naturally, labor and management pulled the second, post–New Deal pension system in different directions. But rather than overtax the institution, these class forces, for a time, added strength and variety.

Top-Tier Pensions

For plans in existence prior to 1935, Social Security was the immediate stimulus for a sharp redirection of the benefits flowing from corporate plans toward management personnel. The government program promised rank-and-file workers roughly 30 percent of their career-average pay, but replaced far less income for managers earning more than the $3,000 taxable "wage base." After the 1939 and then the 1950 amendments, Social Security allowances also replaced significantly less income of those at the top of the wage base. As corporate pensions originally had paid between 30 and 60 percent of salary, failure to integrate the plan with Social Security would create unnecessarily high allowances for rank-and-file employees and dramatic contrasts in replacement rates.[1]

The Wagner Act, and the subsequent organization of American labor, likewise deflected corporate plans toward managerial personnel. Unionization made compensation and working conditions areas of overt labor-management conflict and subject to collective bargaining. Firms now had little incentive, and perhaps not the legal right, to unilaterally extend pension benefits to unionized or unionizing blue-collar workers. The fierce conflict with labor also heightened the need to secure the loyalty of the white-collar staff.

Whereas pension institutions had formerly taken decades to change, corporate executives responded to the new situation with lightning speed. Of the 515 functioning plans identified by Murray Latimer in 1938, 70 percent had been newly installed or had been changed significantly since the election of Franklin Roosevelt in 1932. Of these 350 sponsors, not all had been brought under Social Security; the government had not finalized the system's design and, prior to 1940, had not paid a benefit. But half of Latimer's 350 sponsors, 35 percent of the private pension universe, had already integrated their schemes and refocused their resources toward the higher income earners. Because of Social Security and the Wagner Act, most major corporations organizing plans in the late 1930s and early 1940s — primarily firms in young industries such as autos, rubber, aluminum, and glass — actually excluded wage workers altogether. Coverage rates thus dropped by nearly half, from 78 percent of a sponsor's workforce before 1930 to 41 percent in plans established in the 1930s.[2]

The salaried-only plans established by large corporations in the late 1930s were typically "excess" group annuity arrangements organized and operated by a major life insurance company. Pension amounts were based on career-average earnings and typically replaced a comfortable 40 to 50 percent of this sum. Social Security dramatically lowered the cost of providing this old age income benefit, as is clearly reflected in the benefit formula: for earnings within the Social Security wage base the plans replaced income at one rate (often 1 percent per year of service), and for earnings that exceeded the Social Security wage base, they replaced at a higher rate (often 2 percent per year of service). The nation's large insurance companies had an off-the-shelf product — the group annuity — that delivered such a pension allowance. Their contracts also allocated benefits to employees individually and specified detailed withdrawal rights, for sums contributed by the employee, that especially appealed to career white-collar workers. The group annuity contract also included financial inducements to stay with the firm — the portion of the benefit paid by the corporate employer.[3]

The sharply rising tax rates on high personal and business income in the late 1930s made pension plans suddenly quite attractive as tax shelters. Corporate executives and their salaried staff came to appreciate this aspect of their plans. But for the future of the institution, these tax advantages were far more important to owners and managers of small and mid-sized businesses. A large number of plans set up in the late 1930s and early 1940s were clearly tax planning devices that integrated their benefits, excluded the rank and file, and shifted control of the assets, via insurance company arrangements, from the firm to the individual plan participants. Schemes set up for just a few executives or a small number of managers were often too small to satisfy an insurance company's group underwriting requirement. So a common alternative was to fund such plans with a standard insurance company product for individuals — individual level-premium annuities. The firm paid for such policies directly, without first passing taxable income to the participant, by sending the funds to a plan trustee who bought and held the contracts. These programs became known as individual trust plans, and Walter Couper and Roger Vaughn, in 1954, wrote that "it does not do very much violence to the facts to say that pension plans based on individual plans were developed as programs designed chiefly to benefit senior executives and that they sometimes involved elements of tax avoidance of the kind that played an important role in stimulating the restrictions imposed by the Internal Revenue Act of 1942 and subsequent Treasury regulations."[4]

Individual annuities were significantly more expensive than group contracts. Sales commissions typically ran to 25 percent of the first year's premium and 5 percent of the second year's. Group annuity commissions varied with the size of the plan, but even on the smallest and most expensive contracts commissions came to less than one-third of these amounts. Individual trust plans also bore gross administrative expenses in excess of 15 percent, as opposed to 2 to 5 percent on group annuity contracts. Policy cash values thus began at low levels and built up only slowly. The insurers also assumed adverse selection, as purchasers of individual annuities typically lived unusually long lives, so the carriers demanded higher premiums for a given annuity amount. For all these reasons, individual policies were a costly way to purchase retirement income.[5]

For top-tier plans, individual annuities nevertheless had certain advantages. Individual annuities generated more tax benefits, a significant consideration: their level-premium format pulled tax deductions forward in time and socked more funds into tax-sheltered investments. Unlike group annuities, individual trust plans let firms base benefits on final average salary. Individual annuities were sold in discrete units of monthly retirement income, typically in ten-dollar amounts, and the plan would take out additional contracts as a participant's salary rose. Because of the shorter amortization period and the greater likelihood of survival to retirement, these additional annuity contracts taken out later in life became rather expensive. But management-centered plans appreciated this feature, as it skewed payments to top officials whose incomes rose sharply throughout their careers.[6]

Well-paid executives paid far more attention to accumulating assets than blue-collar workers living paycheck-to-paycheck, and individual annuity contracts offered liberal settlement options that enhanced their value as investment vehicles. Upon retirement, the participant could choose either a straight life annuity; an annuity reduced in amount but with a guaranteed number of payments; or a joint and survivor annuity, again reduced in amount, covering the lives of the participant and his or her spouse. These settlement options attenuated the influence of the participant's own mortality and gave greater assurance of an ultimate payout. By allowing a choice of annuity options, carriers faced increased adverse selection — participants in bad health would select joint and survivor or guaranteed-payout annuities — and this raised the cost of retirement income. Liberal settlement options thus exchanged pension value for asset protection; they traded old age income insurance for investment security. As upper-income earners were more concerned with preserving than outliving their wealth, individual annuities served nicely.[7]

Because of their significance as investments, individual trusts, like the Grand Trunk Railway plan of 1874, paid scrupulous attention to participant equities. They therefore allowed leavers to continue the policy on their own. Cashing out, however, presented problems. During the early years of an individual annuity contract, commissions and loadings depressed cash values far below the premiums paid. Transient employees rarely emerged from such plans in a happy frame of mind. Industry opinion indeed viewed individual trusts as unsuitable for production workers because of their notoriously high turnover. Managers did not suffer so much from this problem, as they typically had longer tenures with a firm. But should they die prematurely, they would leave a disappointing death benefit. Individual trusts thus typically included life insurance, using a combined annuity–life insurance contract known as a retirement income policy. These contracts typically carried a minimum $1,000 death benefit for each $10 unit of monthly retirement income, paying beneficiaries the greater of the policy cash value or this $1,000.[8]

The shift in the pension institution toward top-tier arrangements began in the late 1930s. But the coming of World War II catalyzed the process and rushed into being this managerial portion of the second U.S. pension institution. The Treasury, as we have seen, had grown suspicious of the sudden interest in management-oriented plans and had pushed its 1942 restrictions through Congress to forestall a massive wave of tax avoidance. As government officials had expected, U.S. incomes, profits, and taxes all surged as Europe and then America mobilized for war. Many businessmen suddenly earned far more than they could reasonably spend, but were seeing much of their new abundance carted away in wartime taxes. With the dramatic increase in the corporate excess profits tax in 1942, subject firms paid a confiscatory 90 percent of their marginal income.[9]

The nation's prosperous folk were also those with the greatest ability to buy tax-saving advice. The nation's insurance agents, who had learned their lessons well in the late 1930s, were only too eager to guide such clients into pension tax shelters. During normal times, the 1942 reforms in pension tax law might have discouraged these businessmen from setting up corporate plans. But the government now financed up to 90 percent of the pretax cost, so many launched programs that included a significant portion of their workforces. The law leveraged as well as thwarted discriminatory intentions; corporate control groups could get their pensions, and improved labor relations, at ten cents on the dollar.

The government provided two further wartime stimulants to the private pension institution. To finance the conflict, Congress not only drove the top corporate and individual tax rates skyward but spread the burden across the population. Whereas 6 percent of the nation had paid tax in 1939, nearly 75 percent did by 1945. The tax relief offered by a pension plan thus became valuable to the workforce in general. The government's wage-stabilization program also furthered the pension's new appeal. To limit inflation, the War Labor Board systematically fought employers attempting to lure or keep labor by raising cash wages. But the WLB allowed, indeed encouraged, the use of noninflationary compensation such as pension benefits. Employers soon discovered that pensions were especially useful in retaining personnel. This effect seemed strongest in the managerial ranks, where key staff could not easily be replaced. These employees were also those suddenly faced with a significant income tax liability.[10]

The war economy thus provided managerial and tax-sheltering plans with an ideal environment. The institution would cover 6.5 million employees in 1945, triple the 2 million of 1938. The number of plans grew much faster, as the pension spread to smaller firms. In the 27 months between September 1942 and December 1944, the IRS approved over 4,000 new plans, or eight times the 515 programs in place in 1938. Between 1940 and 1945 the number of insured plans more than quadrupled, to 6,700 from 1,530. Individual trust plans were the most vigorous in this sector, rising tenfold from 440 with 15,000 participants to 4,550 with 180,000; by 1945 such plans were three times as numerous as traditional group annuities. Individual trust plans typically benefited a small group of key employees and covered, on average, just forty lives. Group annuities, on the other hand, averaged over 700 participants and covered six times as many lives as individual trusts.[11]

The incidence of integration increased sharply over the course of the war. According to Conference Board surveys of larger sponsors, 80 percent had integrated their plans by the end of 1943, up from 65 percent in 1939. Plans established in the early part of 1944 tilted even more toward management, with 90 percent integrated and/or limiting participation to salaried employees. Less than a quarter of all employees participated in the plans established from 1940 through 1946, and one could expect the sharpest top-tier slant among small and closely held corporations.[12]

Although wartime conditions soon came to an end, the experience demonstrated the usefulness of the pension as an instrument of compensation. Tax rates came down after 1945, reducing the value of pension tax shelters and the de facto level of government pension funding. But the nation soon drifted into the Cold War and the hot Korean conflict, so taxes stayed high and broadly based. Wage flexibility returned after 1945, albeit gradually, and the benefit's grip on compensation design subsided. But executives now understood firsthand the value of the pension in retaining key personnel. Few sponsors eliminated their programs, and the number of plans and total coverage remained stable after the end of the war. The private pension, which in the 1930s seemed threatened with elimination, socialization, or serious curtailment, emerged in the postwar era as a widely recognized management tool.[13]

Labor Plans

Labor had great political success in the 1930s, winning the right to organize and a Social Security system that provided a basic old age income. In the 1940s, however, labor's political standing and its status in the new public-private pension system came into question. Large corporations were integrating the rank and file out of much of their preexisting claims in private pension programs. Enterprises establishing new plans often excluded them outright. As pension schemes became tax-planning devices, government tax treatments designed to benefit the rank and file were increasingly usurped by business owners and managers. The Revenue Act of 1942 would counteract some of this sharp shift away from labor, although it would let employers exclude wage workers, as a class, from qualified plans. The sharpest blow to labor, however, was the declining real value of its Social Security benefits. And as this one great legacy from the New Deal weakened in the 1940s, workers increasingly turned to the second, the union movement, to reassert their pension claims.

What undercut Social Security in the 1940s was a vicious inflationary spiral set off by the wartime economy. Consumer prices in 1948 were two-thirds higher than they had been in 1941, and worker compensation had nearly doubled. As Social Security defined its tax base and benefit schedules in a 1930s framework, the inflation quickly eroded the value of its revenues and allowances. The average Social Security benefit replaced 30 percent of the average wage in 1940; but that figure fell to 22 percent in 1945, and to 19 percent by 1950. The original 30 percent had hardly maintained retirees in comfort. Indeed 50 percent replacement was often cited as the minimum acceptable retirement income. But within one decade of the great national compromise of 1939, the low level of Social Security benefits had gutted the purpose of the government program.[14]

The contraction of Social Security replacement rates now threatened to return the American elderly to poverty and social dependence. The tremendous demand for labor during the war had kept large numbers of older people employed. But the need for labor slackened with the return of peace. The paychecks stopped coming and the need for retirement income emerged anew. The Depression had decimated personal savings while the immature corporate pension systems still supported relatively few retirees. With Social Security payments so low, the elderly fell back on a federal, means-tested old age welfare program that had been established alongside the Social Security insurance scheme in 1935. This Old Age Assistance program had been set up primarily for those unable to gain coverage under Social Security's insurance scheme — those already old and poor, or those working in jobs not included in the program. As these populations shrank, Social Security was expected to dominate the public provision of old age income. But because of the wartime and postwar inflation, Old Age Assistance was growing rapidly as a welfare supplement for those without adequate retirement incomes, and was actually distributing larger sums than the Social Security insurance program.[15]

The foundation of the second U.S. pension system — the notion that private pensions served as Social Security supplements — thus came into question with the rapid decline in Social Security benefits. While employers were busily constructing their supplementary plans, largely benefiting managerial employees, the government fell down in its responsibility to provide a basic allowance for all. As the federal presence receded, the American union movement, revitalized by New Deal reforms, emerged as the primary champion of labor's pension interests. There was little prospect of restoring Social Security replacement rates in the conservative climate of the immediate postwar years. So while the unions remained a key defender of the national social insurance program, they soon developed a strategy that involved active participation in the private as well as the public pension arenas. They would fashion their own pension programs over the course of the 1940s and 1950s and, as they did, they would complete the design of the second U.S. pension institution.

Prior to 1945 unions had little to do with corporate pension arrangements. Labor leaders generally had opposed company plans, recognizing that employers use pensions to discipline workers and wean them from unions. The International Association of Machinists, in a judgment typical of the time, said in 1928 that "our bitter experience of the past causes us to look upon all pension plans by private corporations as being prompted by sinister motives." Unionists had much preferred individual self-reliance or a national social insurance program. As the economy had slipped into depression, labor had become increasingly involved in efforts to enact and liberalize Social Security. As for corporate plans, union leaders had attempted to remove their insecurity and coercive potential. They thus had urged strict contractual and contributory arrangements and third-party, insurance company management. The strong trend toward insurance and group annuities, which sponsors had been adopting for reasons of their own, had thus won labor's grudging acceptance.[16]

Quite apart from the evolving corporate pension movement, several of the nation's largest and most successful unions had established plans of their own by the 1920s. Most of these sponsors had been traditional craft organizations — brotherhoods of the skilled and largely native-born Americans who worked for a great many small firms over the course of a lifetime. Their employers had had neither the resources nor the long-term employment relationships that would lead them to set up ongoing pension and welfare programs. Since the middle of the nineteenth century, the stronger brotherhoods thus had taken the responsibility of insuring themselves. Their schemes typically had provided death and disability benefits first. But as more union members had grown too old to work, pressure had developed to provide some form of assistance — an old age home, a lump sum grant, or a life annuity. Many of the superannuated had been founding fathers of the organization, if not the actual fathers of younger members. This had intensified the pressure for a program. In terms of the various rationales identified for early corporate sponsors, these union plans had been essentially of the "welfare" variety: they had aimed at keeping those disabled by age from destitution.[17]

True to their origin in welfare policy, most union programs had paid very modest benefits and required applicants to demonstrate both poverty and the inability to work. In the 1920s those who met all requirements would be awarded allowances in the order of $30 per month. Like the original B&O Railroad plan, which also had grown out of welfare considerations, union pension benefits had been relatively flat, or invariant with regard to income or service. These welfare plans had set their allowances according to minimum standards of adequacy — the amount necessary to keep pensioners out of poverty. The union schemes had specified a minimum period of membership to qualify for a pension (often fifteen years) and a longer period to gain the entire benefit (often twenty-five years).[18]

Earlier commentators, including Murray Latimer and Charles Dearing, have argued that these early programs had given the unions "extensive experience" with pension operations. These writers based their assertions on the fact that 40 percent of all union members in 1928 had been covered under some form of old age maintenance program. Their larger claim, however, cannot be sustained. Fully half of this coverage had only allowed members to retire to some distant old age home or on the meager cash value of some other forms of insurance. Although annuities had been the fastest-growing form of union old age assistance through the 1920s, only 20 percent of the movement's membership had participated in a bona fide union pension plan. The great bulk of this participation had been concentrated in just ten international organizations. Railroad Brotherhoods, with a goodly portion of this "covered population," had merely offered voluntary individual annuities as supplements to corporate programs. The remaining coverage had centered in just three areas: the carpenters and joiners, the electrical workers, and the typographers and pressmen. The labor movement, moreover, had been in decline. From a high point of 5 million members in 1920, a vigorous employer offensive had brought union membership down to 3.5 million by 1924 and had kept it at that level through the remainder of the decade. When viewed from this perspective, prospects had been bleak for the union pension movement.[19]

Labor's actual pension experience had also been highly irregular. In terms of benefit design, most plans had barely emerged out of the primitive phase of old age homes and commutations of life insurance policies. The union sponsors had also lacked the necessary central organization to administer their programs properly. While the use of flat benefits had reduced the need for reliable bookkeeping, testing poverty, disability, and union loyalty demanded far more bureaucratic efficiency than union offices had been able to muster. Administration of the certification process thus had devolved into the hands of local union officials, opening the gates for widespread corruption. These officials had gained tremendous power over older members through their ability to grant or withhold a union pension. Decentralization also had bloated claims against the plan, as these local leaders had much to gain and little to lose through liberal interpretations of plan requirements.[20]

While union pension liabilities had grown all too quickly, plan assets had never been adequate. These schemes had not developed on an actuarial basis, but had proceeded in a quasi-paygo fashion. At their annual conventions, the organization membership had set contribution levels with an eye on current benefit disbursements. At the end of the 1920s the typical union plan thus had just two to three years' benefits put away. Nor were the assets secure. These plans explicitly allowed the union to dip into the pension fund when faced with some "emergency," and labor leaders quite regularly took advantage of this opportunity. In 1928, 40 percent of the pressmen's pension fund thus had been transferred to the union treasury for general union purposes. Union officials also used their influence to borrow pension money for their personal business ventures. Another 20 percent of the pressmen's pension fund thus had been invested in the president's playing card company.[21]

The best that could be said for these early union plans was that they were immature. As in the case of contemporary railroad plans, the Depression then had cut short any opportunity for further development. Benefit applications had multiplied rapidly in the 1930s, absorbing the available resources. The unions had responded by tightening eligibility requirements, raising contributions, cutting benefits, and then terminating allowances altogether. Of the thirteen international unions sponsoring plans in 1929, just four paid benefits in 1949. The Depression thus had destroyed the initial union pension program. In the postwar period labor would build a second pension system. But it would do so as part of the employer institution.[22]

While the Depression had destroyed the old union pension structure, it had brought compensation from the public sector. Social Security addressed essentially the same pension burden as had the union systems. The legislation had limited public responsibility to *employee* pensions, restricting participation to wage and salary workers and excluding the self-employed. Funding also had been based on the employment relationship — the government had divided the cost evenly between the employer and the employee. The government program, especially after 1939, had emphasized the adequacy of benefits and therefore had indirectly given pension credit for past years of service so that those already old could retire on a decent allowance. Because Social Security addressed labor's essential pensioning interest, and because of the global nature of its scope and resources, American workmen thenceforth would look to government, not their unions, as the primary source of old age income.

A resurgent union movement, also spawned in the Depression, nevertheless would take a critical position in the second U.S. pension system. The Wagner Act of 1935 had given workmen the right to form unions and bargain collectively, changing the basic framework of labor relations. A revitalized labor leadership had taken the Wagner Act, and the new and militant working class consciousness abroad in the nation, and had launched the most sustained and long-lasting organizing drive in American history. Union membership, which had fallen to a nadir of 3 million in 1933 (11.3 percent of employees in nonagricultural establishments), had reached 10.5 million in 1941 (28.8 percent), and 13.5 million by 1944 (36.6 percent). The transition to collective bargaining, however, had been far from smooth. Management had bitterly resisted the great union upsurge. In labor's camp a militant Congress of Industrial Organizations (CIO) had broken away from the old American Federation of Labor (AFL); the AFL, sticking by its traditional program, had preferred organizing workers on the basis of skill; the CIO, more conscious of class than craft, would unionize all workers in an industry whether skilled or not. Further complicating the scene had been fierce intra-union battles — especially within the CIO — between Communist and non-Communist factions. Labor relations in the 1930s thus had been marked by intense and often violent struggles over the nature and jurisdiction of the new labor organizations. And as long as such fundamental boundary issues remained open, nothing so mundane as supplemental pensions would receive much attention.[23]

Before the institutionalization of collective bargaining could advance very far, America had entered World War II. To stabilize the economy, the government had imposed a thoroughgoing system of wage and price controls that had brought the key collective bargaining issues under federal jurisdiction. This bargaining hiatus, and management-labor cooperation in the war, cooled passions all around. Labor relations in the postwar period thus were far less bloody than they had been in the 1930s. It was then that labor and management resolved their basic boundary issues and defined a stable collective bargaining regime. The process of resolving these issues and defining the new relationship was naturally quite rough. As described contemporaneously by Benjamin Selekman,

> the union aggressively presses to extend its scope of action; and management strives with equal determination to contain it within bounds. The modes of joint dealing generally reflect the responses of leaders on both sides to the sheer newness of the relations into which they suddenly have found themselves plunged by legal compulsions and organized force. These developments have been marked particularly in the large-scale plants of basic industry, long strongholds against the entry of unionism.[24]

The CIO, which organized those "large-scale plants of basic industry, long strongholds against the entry of unionism," would be the key organization in establishing labor's post–New Deal pension program. It played this role because of the three main labor movements it was the most sensitive to the new possibilities in collectively bargained employment relationships. In terms of basic strategy, the AFL relied on a monopoly of craft skill; the Communists looked to class consciousness and a future revolution; only the CIO made do with worker solidarity and the Wagner Act. Labor's new collective bargaining rights, however, provided a firm platform from which to assert pension claims. Bargained plans, moreover, were far sturdier than the old stand-alone union programs. Like Social Security, they involved employer participation. Collective bargaining also framed a continuing employment relationship, both a prerequisite and a stimulus for employer-based programs. The CIO early on recognized the promise of bargained plans. And as inflation eroded the real value of Social Security benefits during and after World War II, pension and welfare benefits became key items on its bargaining agenda.[25]

The two parties were hardly prepared to agree on pensions or other innovative labor arrangements immediately following the war. In addition to the tensions over collective bargaining and the rifts within labor's camp, a more basic anxiety gripped workers and managers alike: both expected a quick return to depression. Intent on keeping their firms lean and flexible, management were determined to hold down labor costs and maintain their "right to manage" the productive process. Labor leaders likewise feared depression. But they used the new Keynesian economics to justify policies exactly opposite to those developed by business. Higher wages and expanded union job control, they argued, would maintain aggregate demand and fend off the downturn. Workers, who "had become both restive under wartime wage controls and fearful of the impact of reconversion on take-home pay," eagerly supported the union leadership. Thus, while business desperately tried to hold the line, labor aggressively pressed for more security and higher cash compensation. The return of peacetime bargaining thus resulted in the disastrous strike wave of 1945–46. Work stoppages in 1946 alone absorbed over 100 million manhours, triple the amount in any previous year, and one-year contracts remained the rule until the end of the decade.[26]

Franklin Roosevelt's successor, Harry S Truman, saw little choice but to intervene. The Wagner Act had organized the nation's key labor markets as bilateral monopolies; as such, no automatic market mechanism, based on rational calculation and marginal adjustment, led to stable wages and employment levels. The economy needed some form of external intervention to secure production continuity and appropriate pricing, and Truman did what he could to supply this outside guidance. He seized or threatened to seize whole industries. He encouraged activism in his key labor agencies, from the National Labor Relations Board to the Federal Conciliation Service. In a half-dozen major disputes, he established ad hoc fact-finding boards to investigate and recommend terms of settlement. An increasingly conservative nation meanwhile returned a Republican Congress in the 1946 elections. The new body lost little time enacting the Taft-Hartley Act of 1947, an extensive pro-management revision of the Wagner Act. While this political jockeying affected the bargaining strength of the bilateral monopolists, the two parties were groping toward an accommodation. The pension emerged in this process, as it had on the B&O Railroad, as a token of fair dealing and mutual endeavor. But it did so, in the context of the New Deal's labor system, in a collective bargaining framework.[27]

Critical to the emergence of the negotiated pension program were two fortuitous circumstances present during the jelling of postwar labor-management relations. The first was the spiral of rising prices that had gutted the real value of Social Security and corporate pension programs. The new federal labor laws restricted management's ability, and incentive, to provide production workers with adequate corporate benefits. Blue-collar employees now required special treatment, and it was unclear whether management could unilaterally install or reform a plan for their organized or organizing workers. Unions, which now stood between a company and its labor force, also would gain much of the credit should a firm establish or liberalize an existing corporate plan. So pensions almost inevitably became an issue to be dealt with and settled at the bargaining table.

The second fortuitous circumstance was the unparalleled strength of the United Mine Workers, a union with a particular interest in pensions. Led by the charismatic John L. Lewis and enrolling 80 percent of the nation's miners, the UMW dominated its industry as did few other labor organizations. So strong and secure was the union, it had provided funds and leadership to the fledgling CIO. Lewis had served as the federation's first president; his lieutenant, Philip Murray, had headed its steelworkers' organization and, in 1940, had succeeded Lewis as president of the CIO. The mine workers had been brazen enough to challenge the U.S. government during World War II and in the immediate postwar period, and only the government could seriously challenge its power. Lewis's miners meanwhile needed pensions more than most other workers. While their union wages were quite sufficient in cash-poor Appalachia, mining was a hazardous occupation full of injury, morbidity, disability, and death. After a lifetime of exposure, one could hardly expect aged miners to work in the pits. Coal mining, moreover, was a declining industry with dramatically rising labor productivity. Employment in the bituminous fields thus had dropped precipitously from a high of 700,000 in 1923 to 416,000 in the late 1940s; it would fall to 250,000 by 1955. As there were few employment alternatives in the coal fields, the supply of labor would have to go down so that the labor market would clear at UMW wage levels. The union, in other words, needed pensions to retire older workers.[28]

With both the means and the incentive to act, the UMW demanded an employer-financed welfare and pension fund in 1945. The owners refused, and the union backed down. Lewis made the welfare fund the union's top negotiating priority in 1946, but the operators rejected all union demands. So the UMW called a strike on April 1, effectively halting U.S. coal mining. On May 22, as the strike began to choke industrial production, President Truman invoked the War Labor Disputes Act and seized the nation's coal mines. One week later, on May 29, Secretary of the Interior J. A. Krug signed a contract with the UMW providing a $.05 per ton royalty for the United Mineworkers Welfare and Retirement Fund. The actual benefits and plan's financial policy were left up to the three trustees — the chairman from the UMW (Lewis himself), one from the government (from the private owners after the War Labor Disputes Act expired on June 31, 1948), and a neutral trustee selected by the other two. The parties immediately ran into trouble in selecting the third trustee, in setting the retirement age and pension benefit, and in deciding whether to fund the plan or to pay as they went. Lewis called two strikes protesting the delays — one against the government and the second against the reinstated owners. Each operator won injunctions directing the men back to work, and each saw Lewis and the union fined for ignoring these orders. The union ultimately won its sympathetic third trustee, favorable benefits and retirement conditions, and paygo financing. But because of the turmoil, the first pension check was not mailed until September 1948. Payments were subsequently suspended in September 1949 and only restored for good in July 1950.[29]

In many ways, Lewis had established a classic union pension plan. The scheme formed part of a general welfare program that also included disaster, medical, death, disability, and survivor annuity insurance. The fund also gave generous credit for past service and paid a flat $100 per month. When added to a $50 Social Security benefit, this represented a very ample retiring allowance. Although the employers had argued for funding — and therefore less generous current benefits — the UMW insisted on a paygo policy. The UMW program, like those of earlier unions, would thus bear a chronic "past service" liability. In 1955 Lewis himself estimated the deficit for current retirees alone at $1.25 billion, eight years' contributions to the fund. But he insisted it would be "a crime of the highest order" to deprive those now alive and in need merely to "sequester and secrete these great sums of money" in a pension fund. Lewis justified a paygo policy on the stability of the industry and the UMW's position within it: "It is not necessary to build up an enormous reserve to safeguard the payment of a pension for the life expectancy of an individual, when the fund is a going concern and has an annual revenue, and when any protection to that fund through experience can be brought about gradually with the distribution of the load over succeeding generations of men in the industry."[30]

Like the early union (and corporate) paygo plans, pension costs rose steadily and strongly, and they pushed the program off balance. As listed in Table 6.1, pension payments rose by 90 percent, from $42 to $70 million, in the five years 1951–1955. As a result, the union negotiated an increase in the royalty per ton to $.20 in 1948, $.30 in 1950, and $.40 in 1952. The plan trustees tightened eligibility requirements in 1953 and discontinued disability and survivor annuities in 1954. Even expenditures on the medical program, a great source of pride for the union, declined in 1954 and 1955 as pensions came to absorb nearly 60 percent of all spending. As pensioners were given free medical benefits and were high users of such services, retirees absorbed an even larger portion of the UMW program.

Despite the political and financial stress surrounding the UMW program, Lewis's scheme had enormous effect. "Psychologically," wrote a perceptive union official, "it is likely that the miners' welfare fund was the single most influential force in the negotiated pension movement." No other national union so dominated its industry or won pensions immediately following the war. Not until the end of the 1940s would the economy stabilize and relations ripen between the big CIO unions and their employers. Only then did these unions win pensions. Because of the turmoil in the coal fields, this timing difference was not so favorable to the miners as would seem at first glance. UMW retirees began receiving a steady stream of pension checks only in 1950. The later CIO plans would kick in then as well. But their designs, with three more years' gestation, would benefit from the delay.[31]

The typical CIO experience is most clearly illustrated by the United

Table 6.1. United Mine Workers' welfare and retirement fund activity,
1946–1955

Year ending	Total receipts	Total expenditures	Pension payments	Hospital & medical	Balance in fund
5/29/46–6/30/50	$230	$179	$43 (24%)	$20 (11%)	$ 51
6/30/51	130	82	42 (51%)	25 (30%)	99
6/30/52	126	126	51 (40%)	50 (40%)	100
6/30/53	131	139	59 (42%)	56 (40%)	92
6/30/54	135	133	64 (48%)	52 (39%)	94
6/30/55	129	119	70 (59%)	43 (33%)	103

Note: Dollar amounts in millions; percentages of expenditures in parentheses.
Source: Louis S. Reed, *Welfare and Pension Plans Investigation Hearings before a Subcommittee of the Committee on Labor and Public Welfare,* 84th Cong., 1st Sess. (1955), p. 1032.

Auto Workers. Along with John L. Lewis, the UAW's Walter Reuther was labor's primary champion of pension benefits. Reuther, however, faced stiffer opposition. The UAW bargained with employers larger and stronger than the coal mine operators. Firms like General Motors, Ford, and Chrysler bargained separately with the UAW and each exercised much greater control over its labor situation. The development of pensioning in the auto industry thus required significant accommodation to corporate requirements. A UMW-style plan — a multiemployer paygo program with a union-dominated pension fund — was not a reasonable expectation. In autos, as in other big-business industries, blue-collar pensioning would develop on a company-by-company basis.[32]

Reuther and his welfare initiatives were also opposed from within the union. The UAW's strong left-wing faction viewed collective bargaining — and negotiated employee benefits — as passing historical phenomena. These militants had achieved many of the union's most dramatic successes, often while ignoring central UAW directives and violating collectively bargained contracts. In the process, they had developed a significant following among the rank and file. The union's left wing presented a key barrier to the process of "normalizing" relations with management. The companies indeed refused to develop more complex arrangements with the UAW until the union disciplined these wildcat strikers and contract violators, providing what management called "company security," and led workers into a more cooperative relationship with the firm. Thus Ford wrote to the UAW, before we could entertain any thought of an Employee Retirement Plan we had to answer two basic questions. The first was the question of company security. If the company's ability to go on as a profitable progressive institution would be threatened, it was obvious that such a program could not be considered.

On the other hand, if our employees were not encouraged to their best efforts and top efficiency by fair treatment, good working conditions, good wages, and a reasonable sense of security in their jobs, the ability of the company to succeed in competitive enterprises would be also placed in danger.[33]

Despite the difficulties, Reuther began the process of establishing "long-term relationships of 'normal' collective bargaining" immediately after World War II. According to Benjamin Selekman, the 1946 agreements he negotiated in the first year of his UAW presidency "marked the transition to permanent continuing joint relationships, and spelled out mutual rights and obligations with explicit particularity." In return for a 15 percent wage increase from Ford, for example, the UAW recognized "that the primary objective of the Company in entering into this Agreement is the promotion of orderly and peaceful relations with its employees and the attaining of efficient and uninterrupted operations in its plants." Wildcat strikes at U.S. Ford plants fell to 27 in 1946, from an annual average of 203 since 1943.[34]

In the next contract negotiations, in 1947, Ford and the UAW actually announced tentative agreement on the first pension plan for U.S. auto workers. Although the UMW success clearly had stimulated the union leadership to demand a plan, the Ford-UAW design was in the traditional corporate mold. The agreement called for modest earnings-related pensions — 1 percent of final earnings times years of service, offset by Social Security. The plan was voluntary and contributory, with employees paying 2.5 percent of their first $3,000 of income (through the Social Security wage base) and 5 percent of any above; Ford put in 5 percent of payroll plus additional past-service contributions. As was common in such designs, employees received a full return of their contributions, plus interest, in the event of death or withdrawal. While the miners had forced employers to finance a traditional union program, the auto workers had negotiated just a traditional corporate plan.[35]

External events, however, unraveled the 1947 Ford-UAW agreement. Congress passed the National Labor Relations (Taft-Hartley) Act during the contract negotiations, over President Truman's veto. The new statute gave employers stiff "company security" provisions, including the right to sue unions and their officers for contract violations. Ford thus got more from Congress than it had from the UAW, and it gave nothing in return. The bargaining back in Detroit thus began to drift, and after another two months of negotiations, the parties announced a surprising settlement. They had agreed to two contracts — one with pensions and a modest raise, the other without pensions but a larger wage increase — and put the final choice to the rank and file. The union leadership campaigned vigorously for the pension plan, but was opposed by the union's left-wing faction. The election embarrassed Reuther, as the membership voted for cash by a three-to-one margin.[36]

When Ford and UAW negotiators returned to the bargaining table in 1948, they were further apart on pensions than ever before. The chastened union leadership now insisted on a UMW-style program. They demanded a noncontributory plan (funded by royalties on production) with the resulting assets managed by a joint labor-management board. The company, absorbed in corporate America's growing assertion of its prerogatives, now resisted bargaining over pensions at all. Management claimed that retirement programs were discretionary instruments, included in bargaining only if the firm so chose. Inasmuch as Ford commented on the union's proposals, it rejected them out of hand. Management insisted that production workers contribute to any future plan and that the company manage the pension assets. There was little common ground between the two positions, and little developed during the negotiations. Although the UAW kept its plan on the table right up to the signing of the contract, it settled for increased wages and insurance, but no pension benefits.[37]

While the two parties hardened their positions, forces external to the bargaining process were becoming quite conducive to the establishment of labor pension programs. The government set the stage in 1948, when the National Labor Relations Board's Inland Steel decision declared pensions to "lie within the statutory scope of collective bargaining." After the Supreme Court upheld this position in 1949, management had to bargain in good faith and could no longer treat pensions as discretionary gratuities. Meanwhile inflation abruptly came to a halt in 1949. This eased workers' demands for higher cash wages and increased their receptivity to pensioning. The public, which blamed unions for the rising cost of living, would not tolerate another round of wage increases: the costs of a pension program, however, went largely unnoticed. In union politics, CIO moderates were meanwhile gaining the upper hand over their left-wing rivals. Reuther established his clear leadership in the UAW only at the 1949 national convention. By year end, he and like-minded CIO officials began purging their federation of Communist influence. With mainstream unionism in the ascendancy, the prospects for increased cash wages now distant, and the NLRB Inland Steel decision in place, pensions became the CIO's primary bargaining issue in the 1949 contract negotiations.[38]

But pensions remained thorny, complex, and expensive. Rather than digest the benefit as inevitable in the evolution of bargained employment relations, the industrial system nearly choked on the issue. At least one astute observer, Clark Kerr, thought pensions simply too esoteric for the rough-and-tumble of labor bargaining. U.S. Steel meanwhile estimated that the proposed United Steelworkers' plan, in addition to the heavy current "normal cost" charges, involved an immediate $1 billion liability for past-service accruals. Disputes over who should fund and who should invest pension assets also raised fundamental economic and political differences. So negotiations during the summer of 1949 in autos, steel, coal, and other basic industries began to freeze up over pensions. The Federal Mediation and Conciliation Service failed to find a basis of compromise, prospects for continued economic stability grew dim, and three days before the strike deadline in steel, on July 12, President Truman intervened. He established a special Steel Industry Board to conduct an investigation and recommend settlement terms and won a contract extension to give his board time to do its work.[39]

The Steel Board report, issued on September 10, was the defining document in the history of collectively bargained pension plans. Although put together in haste, and showing signs of it, the report commanded widespread support. U.S. industrial relations were quickly coming apart over the pension issue, with the coal miners about to strike to preserve their program and the UAW and other unions threatening walkouts to win plans of their own. The Board recommendations seemed to be the country's only avenue of escape from another cycle of unrest and inflation.[40]

The Steel Board proposals not only tried to draw a compromise between management and labor, but did so in a fashion that served the public interest. The Board thus opposed union demands for inflationary wage increases. But it recommended new pension and welfare benefits that it valued, respectively, at $.06 and $.04 per hour. The Steel Board was in part fighting wage inflation with noncash compensation, repeating the strategy that government had found so successful in World War II. But more important, the Board sanctioned pension and welfare benefits because it saw them as essential employer obligations. Providing adequate social insurance had become a recognized social responsibility with the enactment of Social Security. Employers, who provided livelihoods to a majority of Americans and thus were basic social institutions, shared in this obligation; Congress had recognized this by requiring them to pay half of the taxes supporting Social Security. The Steel Board would now draw them further into the nation's social protection network, finding that "a social obligation . . . rests upon industry to provide insurance against the economic hazards of modern industrial life, including retirement allowances, in adequate amount as supplementary to the amount of the security furnished by Government." The Board then took the common definition of an adequate pension — $100 per month — and recommended that the steel companies make up the difference between this figure and a worker's Social Security allowance. As Social Security benefits had remained at their deflated, Depression-era levels, half the burden of providing an "adequate" pension would lie in the private sector.[41]

The Steel Board justified this extension of employers' responsibility for social protection with the flawed and fiercely contested "human depreciation" theory of pensions. It reasoned that "human machines, like the inanimate machines, have a definite rate of depreciation." The Board blamed industrial work for this gradual loss in human earning power and, as compensation, demanded pensions from the enterprise benefiting from that labor. This use of accounting concepts was far from precise, and it generated more heat than light. But the theory allowed the Steel Board to argue that "insurance and pensions should be considered part of normal business costs." Like a depreciation charge, it continued, "this obligation should be among the first charges on revenues." The Board here advanced a position differing significantly from the typical views of management and labor. The collective bargaining parties normally viewed pensions as a fringe benefit offered only by the most profitable firms. But the Steel Board insisted that pensions were a basic labor cost, that a portion of employee compensation *ought* to be old age income insurance. In the board's conception, employers had an obligation to pay, and workers had a right to receive their benefit.[42]

The United Steelworkers accepted the entire SIB package. The union gave up not only its wage demands, which were little more than bargaining chips, but also a long-held position on integrating employer pensions with Social Security. Labor leaders had bitterly opposed firms that reduced company pensions by the retiree's entire Social Security benefit. Employers contribute just half of Social Security's revenues. So employers could claim credit and reduce company pensions, they argued, by only half of the government allowance. But the unions accepted the Steel Board formulation to win a program that paid adequate pensions. This integration formula also aided the unions in their campaign, as leaders of the American working class, to raise Social Security benefits. As big business would now directly benefit from such an increase, corporate influence would swing behind the liberalization movement.[43]

U.S. Steel accepted the Steel Industry Board proposal, including its $.10 per hour cost, but insisted on one key change. It demanded that the pension and welfare plans be voluntary and contributory. U.S. Steel clearly wanted to avoid, or share, the $1 billion past-service liability and the future costs and risks of a pension plan. The company argued that the plan should preserve "an individual's right to spend or save as he sees fit." It also insisted that "no one unwilling to contribute towards his own old age requirement has the moral right to demand that others make that provision for him." U.S. Steel, in other words, flatly rejected the social responsibility assigned to it by both the Steel Board and the union. And here the bargaining process came to a halt. Unable to reach a settlement by the September 30 contract deadline, 500,000 steelworkers then went on strike to win pension benefits.[44]

The breakthrough came not in steel, a mature industry with a large overhang of older workers, but in the much younger and more vigorously growing auto industry. When the Steel Board issued its report, on September 10, the Ford-UAW talks had been deadlocked for some time over pensions. Two days before the deadline in steel, on September 29, Ford and the UAW signed a Memorandum of Agreement on Retirement and Health and Security Programs based on the Steel Board package. Ford agreed to pay pensions, for the duration of the contract, of $100 per month, reduced by Social Security benefits, to all eligible UAW retirees. The program was noncontributory, granted full pension credit for past service, and would cost the company $.0875 per hour. This settlement naturally put great pressure on the steel industry, and on November 31, Bethlehem Steel finally signed an agreement that included a similar plan. The rest of the steel firms soon came to terms, establishing a pattern for other CIO industries. So by 1952, after the completion of the so-called fourth round of postwar labor negotiations, pensions had become a fixture in CIO labor contracts.[45]

As pension planning spread through the CIO industries, company and union negotiators refined the design of the bargained single-employer program. It soon became clear that CIO plans would be funded. Chrysler demanded a paygo program in its 1950 negotiations with the UAW; John L. Lewis and his mine workers had actually opted for such a system, over employer objections. But Reuther and the UAW insisted on what was called full funding — payment of the accruing normal costs plus the amortization of past-service liabilities. The policy secured the program and reassured young workers that there would be pensions for them. Chrysler and the UAW failed to reach a compromise, and this dispute precipitated a strike. The UAW won the battle, and funded pensions became a CIO shibboleth.[46]

A second issue settled was whether CIO plans would be defined-benefit or defined-contribution programs. The Ford-UAW negotiators had overdefined their scheme, specifying both a benefit ($100 monthly, less Social Security), and a contribution ($.0875 per hour). But after Congress raised Social Security benefits in 1950, it became clear that one of these conditions had to be relaxed. The firm saw that far smaller contributions were needed to support the new benefit level; the union, conversely, saw that the contractual contributions could support far larger pensions. Such confusion in fact would result whenever experience deviated sharply from the original actuarial projections. In the large, single-employer plans being negotiated in the early 1950s, the issue was soon resolved in favor of fixing benefits and allowing contributions to fluctuate. The unions were essentially interested in assuring adequate benefits and were not eager to bear investment risks and responsibilities. The CIO unions retired from pension finance in exchange for negotiated benefit levels. A few contracts, such as the General Motors–UAW pact of 1950, specified the speed at which the past-service overhang had to be amortized. But most agreements merely set a contractual benefit level and allowed the employer — and the IRS — to regulate funding.[47]

The 1950 increase in Social Security benefits also brought a third major adjustment in CIO pension design — the relaxation of full integration. The maximum government pension actually rose quite dramatically — from $46 in 1949 to $80 in 1950, $85 in 1952, and $108.50 in 1954. As a result, retirees without sufficient service to earn a pension in excess of the higher Social Security amounts were often "integrated out" of a company allowance. Many of those who continued to receive the initial integrated $100 monthly benefit simply refused to understand why a rise in Social Security caused their corporate pensions to decline, and then vanish, by 1954. Workers viewed the two allowances as independent, largely because of the contractual and equity elements consciously built into both the labor contract and the federal social "insurance" program. Subsequent refinements in the plan design, again led by the 1950 GM-UAW plan, thus dropped the full reduction for Social Security. Some plans called for 50 percent integration — reducing corporate benefits by 50 percent of the government amount. But most followed the GM program, simply fixing the benefit over the course of the contract, implicitly taking Social Security into account.[48]

By the end of the fourth round of postwar labor negotiations, CIO single-employer plans had become standardized affairs. They were funded, noncontributory defined-benefit plans, paying modest benefits and granting full credit for past service. They made retirement from blue-collar employment a relatively smooth transition and a reasonably comfortable prospect. In the larger context, these fourth-round contracts signaled a broader stability in U.S. labor relations. Confidence in the economy and the recession of labor radicalism had created a general climate of mutual accommodation, with management and labor finally viewing their relationship as workable. Fourth-round contracts thus were multiyear pacts, breaking the previous pattern of annual renegotiation. The UAW agreements extended for a full five years. The rise of bargained pension plans clearly benefited from this growing moderation. Pensions likewise supported the new stability. But if the CIO unions had not won these programs in 1949, labor would not have gained the benefit as quickly in the slower-paced milieu that followed. Just as society's door slid shut on rapid structural change, bargained pensions slipped nimbly into the new arrangements.[49]

Although change would come more slowly in the 1950s, the CIO's great success in pensions pushed the AFL to organize plans. These craft unions also had members who faced old age with neither work nor adequate savings. While the enactment of Social Security and the restoration of benefit levels in 1950 had assuaged the problem's urgency, government allowances were hardly an adequate replacement for a good union wage. Older AFL members needed supplementary allowances as much as their CIO brethren. Younger AFL workers also needed pensions to facilitate retirements and reduce the competition for work. Such accumulations of needy elderly workers, and pressure for retirements from the younger members, had been the traditional stimulus of union pension interest. So with the CIO example before them, AFL unions proceeded to establish pension programs.[50]

Since AFL unions had not stressed pension development in the years during and immediately after World War II, their pension planning was largely based on CIO initiatives. Most critical was the decision to establish plans within the collective bargaining framework. Unlike the old stand-alone union schemes, employer support became a critical and contractual ingredient in labor's new programs. Because AFL craftspeople worked for many small and medium-sized firms, these unions set up UMW-style multiemployer plans rather than UAW-style single-employer programs. In this design, employers made fixed contributions to a pension fund, typically a certain sum for each hour worked. A board of plan trustees, which the Taft-Hartley Act required to be appointed half by labor and half by management, would then set benefit, investment, and administrative policies. Negotiating and operating such multiemployer plans posed many more complications than a program set up within a single large firm. But the movement for multiemployer pension plans grew steadily over the 1950s.[51]

Neither management nor union negotiators seriously considered defined-contribution arrangements, such as the Teachers Insurance and Annuity Association that serves university faculties. The design simply did not address labor's immediate need — providing retirement income to the current cohort of elderly workers. Multiemployer plans, by crediting employees with benefit claims rather than monetary account balances, could readily recognize past service and provide adequate pensions to older workers. But perhaps the key advantage of the multiemployer design was its ability to distribute such "inequitable" benefits while remaining transparent to the labor market. Although older employees carried enormously higher actuarial price tags, all employers paid a uniform charge for each of their workers. By avoiding age-differentiated pension levies, the design avoided discrimination against the elderly, and exacerbation of the problem pensioning was designed to address. Nor did the program interfere with employment decisions: labor movements and employment relationships could proceed as before.[52]

On the issue of funding, however, neither labor traditions nor CIO examples provided clear guidance. Multiemployer plans, in clothing and coal, had been the first to appear in the CIO's drive for collectively bargained pensions. Like traditional union schemes, they had operated on a paygo basis. But the CIO's single-employer plans, set up after 1949, had followed labor's traditional dicta on corporate schemes and were funded in advance. AFL policy was largely set during the stormy years of the late 1940s, when the federation's leadership needed to justify itself in the face of the CIO's first pension successes. To differentiate itself from a reckless rival, the AFL had scorned the CIO's early paygo schemes and had insisted on the virtues of conservative funding. It claimed a high standard of soundness even though its multiemployer plans were hardly 100 percent funded; the assets were controlled in practice, if not in law, by labor trustees; and its programs were closer to the old union plans than to the sounder corporate schemes. But when the UAW and the rest of the CIO took a similar stand, funding became labor's general position. The unions looked to a pool of assets, as well as their bargaining power, to back up their pension programs.[53]

The AFL pension drive lasted through the 1950s and had largely run its course by the end of the decade. The Federation represented a wide variety of crafts, often organized on a local or regional rather than a national basis. So by the spring of 1960 there were eight hundred different multiemployer schemes in operation. Together with the CIO's single-employer programs, labor plans then covered 11 million workers, half of all participants in private arrangements. Coverage of the entire private pension institution had leaped from 19 percent of the workforce in 1945 to 40 percent in 1960, and this jump was almost entirely attributable to union initiatives.[54]

Although collectively bargained plans grew at a significantly slower rate after 1960, they remained a critical component of the larger pension edifice. In 1979, over thirty years since labor plans had burst on the scene, 80 percent of union members participated in a pension plan, and they still constituted half of the covered workforce. From a statistical perspective, union status was "probably the single strongest determinant of pension coverage." The union movement exerted even greater influence on pension development than is indicated by these statistics. In industries with union pension plans, employers were often forced to create programs for their nonunion workforce. And once in place, such programs had to keep benefits as good as those in the steadily liberalized union plans. The salaried staff in unionized establishments, and employees of unorganized competitors, thus were indirect beneficiaries of the labor programs.[55]

Using its right to bargain collectively, labor had created a private social welfare system comparable in coverage to that of corporate employers. Without union pressure, postwar business might never have provided production workers with significant pension benefits. Social Security alone may have satisfied management's basic need for blue-collar pensioning. The federal program had legitimated 65 as the national retirement age, and it guaranteed that all ex-workers, separated voluntarily or otherwise, would not go penniless. Management had little interest in expensive pension programs to develop career commitments among its production workers. But to union members approaching retirement, Social Security benefits that replaced just one-third of their pre-retirement incomes were hardly satisfactory. Older workers had significant moral and political influence within their unions, and they used this strength to give voice to their needs. Total compensation of the collective labor force was fixed at the bargaining table; there, older unionists shifted its composition from cash to pension benefits. Collectively bargained plans thereby raised total retirement income, including Social Security, to an adequate 50 percent of pre-retirement earnings.[56]

Collectively bargained pension programs were essentially social welfare schemes benefiting a specific needy class — the elderly union members. The population of young workers, who effectively financed the schemes, benefited only indirectly and secondarily. As active workers, they clearly profited from the reduction in labor supply created by retirements. Advance funding also provided some assurance that they would receive pensions. But most labor plans, though union leaders claimed the opposite, were notoriously underfunded. Union negotiators typically chose to liberalize benefits rather than rapidly accumulate assets to meet accrued liabilities. As in Social Security, young union workers relied more on an implicit intergenerational contract for the receipt of their benefits. If they were loyal to the union and fair to the aged of their generation, went the compact, the union would take care of them in their own old age. The equity accruing to the young and able, as in most social welfare systems, was more political than financial.

From the beginning, collectively bargained schemes had come under sharp criticism as mechanisms of social welfare. One of the leading actuaries of the day, Dorrance Bronson, faulted the labor plans organized by 1949 as "long on liberality and short on actuarial science." Rainard Robbins, another perceptive observer, wrote in 1952:

> The steel fact-finders wrote glibly about the responsibility of the employer to provide the "security" of prospective pensions. Yet not one of the major negotiated pension plans furnishes security to anyone who retires after the contract expires — and the longest agreement runs for a period of five years — and even if these contracts were renewed indefinitely, none of them provides real security for the worker who leaves, voluntarily or otherwise, the covered group before completing the age and service requirements for retirement income. Anyone who has given even casual attention to turnover statistics knows that a large majority of workers who have this presumed "security" will never qualify for the benefits so carelessly tossed about in discussion and so heatedly contended for as slogans in the labor dispute.[57]

This very insecurity of collectively bargained pension benefits, of course, served to tie workers to their unions. Only so long as the union maintained its bargaining strength would benefits flow and accumulated pension credits have value. Corporations had also used contingent welfare programs to enhance organizational attachment. But labor plans were more tenuous and binding. Benefits in employer plans depended primarily on the survival of the firm, and employees were rarely in a position to influence corporate viability. Collectively bargained benefits, however, depended on the continued strength of both the firm or industry (in the case of multiemployer schemes) and the union, and the success of the union often required significant personal commitment. Because of these dependencies, collectively bargained pension arrangements actually created a community of interest among workers, unions, and employers. And the implicit disciplinary effects were obvious to all.[58]

The realities of labor's pension arrangements, as Robbins had pointed out, conflicted rather sharply with their rhetoric of security. Corporations had finessed a similar fragility by calling pensions a free will gratuity. Employers had long protected this position, even to the point of funding pensions with corporate resources alone. Union leaders, however, had no such luxury. They had long insisted that pensions were deferred wages, not subject to managerial discretion. Benefits, moreover, now were clearly bought and paid for at the bargaining table; they reduced the cash wages of every worker under contract by a specific cents-per-hour. So union leaders had little choice but to recognize the claims of younger workers. From the beginning of the pension drive, leaders in both the AFL and the CIO listed vesting as a basic design objective. And in time they had to deliver. The CIO's single-employer plans — older, simpler, and more stable — were the first to provide younger workers with such rights. Within the area of union organization, especially that of CIO penetration, the pension thus was shifting from a corporate (or union) gratuity toward the status of a labor right. And rights in the system accrued to younger and younger participants. Because of organized labor's influence on corporate personnel policies, pensions began to be treated as deferred wages in ever wider portions of the economy.[59]

By 1960 unions had thus succeeded in establishing a large and viable pension edifice. Collective bargaining had given workers not only a vehicle for expressing their need for old age income but the means of providing it. Negotiated plans at the end of the 1950s covered as many people as corporate programs, and their influence had a major liberalizing effect on plan design. By successfully asserting claims of benefit entitlement, they helped legitimate and institutionalize private pensions as a fact of modern economic life.

The Tale of Two Classes

The rise of class-based pension plans, both the collectively bargained and those serving management, were adjustments to the quickening American state. With the federal government providing basic retirement income, private pensions became supplementary benefits. The older big-business programs continued, essentially to provide for their better-paid employees. Responding to the new environment created by the state, successful economic groups not covered by corporate plans saw fit to organize their own. This occurred in both the working and the entrepreneurial classes. Labor needed the New Deal's Wagner Act to advance its pension program, and its strategy adjusted with alacrity to changes in Social Security. America's business and professional people, in contrast, predicated their pension planning on the tax policies of a vigorous state.

The new class-based pension schemes varied quite radically from one another and to a lesser extent from the older corporate programs. The managerial plans emphasized asset accumulation and were often schemes for tax-sheltered savings as much as retirement income per se. They thus used the most sober of all instruments — the insured individual level-premium contract — and provided significant assurances that monies put in would ultimately come out. Labor plans stood at the opposite end. They were primarily welfare arrangements designed to provide adequate support to those in need. Even when collectively bargained schemes added vesting and optional survivor annuities, they were guided by the principle of adequacy, not equity. If the participant died prior to retirement, and thus no longer needed an old age pension, his or her heirs got nothing. And as union officials viewed their pension plans as continuing social instruments, they readily accepted the existence, if not permanence, of significant unfunded liabilities.

All pension plans are by nature long-run affairs, and it took time for the new schemes to emerge and the old plans to adjust. Pension planners had the necessary time because the larger society was stabilizing after two decades of depression and war. The radical stridency of the 1930s, rekindled for a moment after World War II, all but vanished in the 1950s. The CIO rejoined the AFL in 1955, and union leaders finally turned their attention from boundary expansion toward managing the gains of the past twenty years. Nor would officials in Eisenhower's Treasury Department launch crusades against tax avoidance or other wrongdoings of the rich. The entrepreneurial class could, within limits, shelter significant sums from taxation. And within the American enterprise, class lines softened and were in many cases smudged over by multitiered occupational ladders and the absorption of labor into managerial tasks.[60]

The private pension not only benefited from the new institutional stability but was also among its important supports. In the first instance, the second U.S. pension system was far more effective at providing retirement income than all that had come before. This assurance of income in old age removed a key source of employee discontent. Pension programs were also one of organized labor's most significant successes. But when the union movement established its own private welfare system, its passion for liberalizing Social Security subsided. The most vigorous element of the American working class no longer had a material interest in demanding the expansion of this key public welfare program. Pensions likewise became a favored tax-planning vehicle for the rich, allowing the entrepreneurial class to satisfy its need to accumulate. And corporate programs continued attaching career employees to the organization and then retiring them in a timely fashion.

In the second American pension system, the traditional corporate instrument attempted fewer things. The government and the unions usurped a good deal of its former turf, so the role of pensions in stabilizing *corporate* organizations declined. But the second U.S. pension system involved more players and mechanisms, and more important, created new communities of interest among business, labor, and government. In so doing the institution helped stabilize the larger society, and found for itself a significant new function.

Chapter 7

♦ ♦ ♦

The Pension Industry Reorganizes

As private pensioning expanded vigorously during and after World War II, the industry serving the institution passed through a tremendously turbulent period. The giant eastern insurance companies, which had created the business in the 1920s, had remained the dominant players through the dark years of the Great Depression. But in post–New Deal America, serious obstacles suddenly stymied the success of these firms. The carriers tried to respond to their difficulties, but they steadily lost their grip on the industry. Sponsors found it advantageous to assume a greater role in their pension programs, and especially to insure their own risks and to make basic decisions about design and investment. And instead of farming out the remaining work to large, integrated insurance companies, they turned increasingly to the harbinger of a new industrial era, a network of specialized professional service firms.[1]

The Decline of Insurance

Through the crisis of the 1930s, the insurance industry clearly held the initiative in the pension provision business. Its plans stood out like beacons of security, weathering both the Depression and the government's rapidly shifting social and economic policies. All insured benefits had been fully funded and their assets conservatively invested. When the crash arrived, the insurance companies were able to piece their way through the financial wreckage and make good on their pension promises. As the Depression dragged on and the search for security deepened, the carriers actually saw demand for their pension products explode. Insured plans had covered but 100,000 participants in 1930, 3.6 percent of total coverage. But the carriers took in 600,000 new employees during the 1930s, nearly half of all new plan participation. By 1940 insured plans covered 700,000 participants, a 16.3 percent market share.[2]

As late as 1938 the Metropolitan Life Insurance Company still dominated the pension insurance industry. The Met garnered over half of the nation's group annuity premiums, underwrote 34 percent of the 642 insured plans, and enrolled the same percentage of certificate holders. The Prudential with 22 percent of insured participants, the Equitable (NY) with 19 percent, and Aetna with 13 percent, were also significant players. Travelers, John Hancock, and Connecticut General rounded out the field of seven active American firms, and Sun Life, Canada's largest insurer, also competed in the U.S. market. These giant East Coast carriers together underwrote 606,000 of 615,000 insured participants. They had established the monopolistic "Group Association," under the auspices of the New York Insurance Department, to maintain order in the entire group insurance industry. Through their association, these carriers defined common rates and underwriting practices and thereby brought a measure of stability to their business.[3]

This is not to say that sponsors of insured pension programs serenely passed through the Great Depression. All expenditures unrelated to basic operations were especially trying in the 1930s, and hard-pressed employers typically saw their pension expense rise as their workforces aged. More critically, the cost of a deferred annuity for the average male employee nearly doubled in the decade as mortality and interest rates fell dramatically. In response to this unexpected cost increase, various insuring sponsors adopted "money purchase" arrangements. Employers and employees in such plans contributed a set percentage of pay, and the insurance company exchanged these sums for deferred annuities at the going rate. By fixing contribution rates, sponsors defined their cost as a set percentage of payroll. From the *personal* perspective of the high-level corporate executives who controlled plan design, money purchase was the least favorable method of defining pension benefits. Their incomes rose sharply as their careers progressed, and benefits based on final salary magnified the significance of these last few years of extraordinary earnings. Career-average formulas, another option, treated all years alike. But money purchase, reflecting the rising cost of annuities as the participant aged, yielded smaller benefits, at any given salary, for later years of service. That management adopted such programs demonstrates the *corporate* aversion to risk. That firms such as Standard Oil should do so showed the intensity of this aversion, and the concomitant attractions of insurance.[4]

The carriers faced greater problems than many of their corporate clients. They had written pension insurance contracts with specific mortality and interest-rate guarantees. But mortality fell below expectations and returns on twenty-year corporate bonds fell to 2.5 percent, far below the 4 percent typically guaranteed in the 1920s. And during the war the government pursued a cheap money policy that kept yields well below 3 percent. The insurers thus had to make up the financial difference between the actual and guaranteed rates of mortality and interest. While the insurance companies had captured the initiative in the pension business, unexpected longevity and the carriers' inability to reinvest at higher yields made this success unprofitable.[5]

A key characteristic of insurance company operations — when combined with this sharp fall in interest rates — created a powerful internal check on the expansion of the carriers' business. The insurance companies pictured all their assets standing behind all their liabilities. As such, they credited all contracts with a common rate of interest. As yields declined through the 1930s and 1940s, accepting new clients meant investing more money at the rates below the yield on the insurer's existing portfolio, which would reduce the income credited to existing policyholders. The yields on existing portfolios, however, were often less than the rates guaranteed on older group annuity contracts. New business would only widen the gap, with the carriers having to make up the deficit. Some of the most experienced companies in the group annuity business, with heavy loads of old contracts, shut the window on new pension business. Others limited sales to employers that purchased other group insurance products and discouraged new clients by quoting the Group Association's conservative 2 percent interest-rate guarantee.[6]

The caution imposed upon the pioneer carriers ironically developed just as pensions became the rage, in the high-tax, hothouse economy of World War II. The net effect of this exploding demand and hesitant supply was a moderate expansion of the carriers' business. Kenneth Black, author of an excellent 1955 study on group annuities, reported that the seven major eastern companies increased their business by 50 percent from the end of 1942 to the end of 1946 — from 1,108 to 1,654 contracts. Black's data also showed that the carriers responded quite differently to the anomalous situation. The Metropolitan, with the heaviest overhang of old business, raised its number of contracts by just 6 percent, to 290 from 274. But the Equitable, the most aggressive pension insurer in the late 1930s, continued pursuing business through the war years. The firm had actually pulled even with the Metropolitan by 1942, with the two companies each underwriting a quarter of all plans and enrolling similar proportions of all participants. But the Equitable then doubled its business through the end of 1946, underwriting 531 contracts compared to 268 four years earlier, and by the end of the conflict clearly dominated the nation's pension insurance business. Through 1953, the last year in Black's data series, the company handled over 30 percent of all insured plans, participants, and premium income. The conservative Metropolitan continued to lose market share, and by the end of 1953 underwrote just 12 percent of all plans. By then Aetna and Connecticut General, each specializing in small plans, had more contracts on their books; the Prudential, which focused on larger sponsors, enrolled more participants and collected more premium income.[7]

With many of the established companies content to pass business by, and more employers wanting group annuities, smaller, upstart insurers had a chance in the wartime pension boom. Among the first firms to respond to the new opportunity, and clearly the most successful, was Bankers Life of Iowa (now known as the Principal Financial Group). The company had carefully eyed the group insurance business since the late 1930s, making discreet inquiries in actuarial circles as to its profitability and prospects. The firm finally entered the business in 1941, and sold its first pension contract in July of that year. Five months later America was at war, and Bankers Life was processing plans — both group and individual trust — at a rate of one a day. As a midwestern company, the company found its natural market among smaller, regional employers. But the firm also pursued larger clients that typically had turned to Group Association members. To gain public notice and a foothold in the marketplace, Bankers offered a few prominent firms contracts guaranteeing a 2.5 percent interest rate — half a point more than that offered by the large eastern carriers. The firm also relaxed Group Association underwriting standards, and became known as a firm that would "issue any contract which could be soundly underwritten [and that was] willing to tailor the contract to fit the needs of the customer rather than force him into a ready-made suit complying with the Group Association rules."[8]

Bankers Life could offer custom plan design because its greatest strength was its first-class complement of actuaries. The company employed many of the best actuaries trained in the Midwest and gave them an unusually large role in the firm. But insurance companies do not grow large by custom-tailoring individual contracts; they do so by distributing relatively standard products across a broad marketplace. And Bankers Life became a major player by turning its actuarial talent to the design of an innovative new pension arrangement — the group permanent contract. Group permanent was essentially the individual retirement income contract (a level-premium product combining life insurance and a retirement annuity) written on a group basis. It offered the advantages of individual permanent plans — larger current tax deductions, portability, and attractive withdrawal and settlement options. At the same time the arrangement captured the economies of group insurance — low-cost marketing and limited adverse selection.[9]

Bankers Life sold its first major group permanent contract to the Marshall Field Company early in 1943. And as long as wartime tax rates obtained, group permanent won the firm a major piece of business and the general respect of the pension community. Indeed, the major carriers were soon offering group permanent contracts of their own. Bankers Life, conversely, used its new visibility to gain the attention of large employers and insurance brokers, and it moved briskly into the corporate group annuity market. By 1953 it was the eighth-largest pension insurer, with 157 group contracts in force and collecting over $12 million in premium income.[10]

By 1953 at least forty smaller insurance companies, in addition to Bankers Life, had entered the group pension business. They added breadth and energy, and according to Kenneth Black, underwrote 930 group annuity plans in 1953. This represented one-quarter of the 3,771 contracts Black discovered for that year, and was nearly 50 percent greater than the TNEC's universe of 642 insured plans in 1938. But the new carriers hardly compensated for the flagging vigor of the larger firms. These new companies found their greatest success among smaller employers, and they enrolled just 8 percent of group annuity certificate holders and 6 percent of all premium income. In terms of raw capital and labor, the seven major carriers still defined the industry's participation in the group pension institution. And the eastern giants failed to satisfy the surging demand for pension programs. Whereas a third of all new plans in the years 1948–1950 adopted traditional group annuities, between 1950 and 1952 that figure dropped to 26 percent and by 1953–54 to 15 percent. The rising tide of pension insurance, which had begun in the mid-1920s, thus came to a halt. The initiative in the business had moved decisively toward trusteed plans.[11]

The overwhelming wartime demand for pensions, coupled with the established insurers' hesitation, had opened up the market. When postwar prosperity and inflation finally lifted interest rates, reducing the cost of deferred annuities and comfortably covering contractual guarantees, the carriers all attacked the marketplace with renewed vigor. But pension insurance, and especially the group annuity contract, never regained its former preeminence. By the early 1960s fewer than one in ten conventional single-employer plans and practically no bargained programs used purely group annuity vehicles.[12]

The continued loss of business, in such a salubrious climate, indicated that the industry's earlier difficulties were not due solely to the anomalous macroeconomics and subpar investment yields of the 1930s and 1940s. It became clear over the course of the 1950s that the phenomenon grew out of two far more permanent issues. The decline of insurance was in part a response to the post–New Deal environment. It also involved a rejection of pension insurance per se and reflected the sponsors' cumulating experience in pension planning. If the carriers were to survive in the pension business, they would have to fundamentally restructure their products and services. The war had served as a catalyst, prying open the industry, and the pension business would thereafter change dramatically and permanently.

The New Deal reforms, which formed the stage for the second U.S. private pension system, provided the clearest shocks to the pension insurance business. The Wagner Act, the Revenue Act of 1942, and especially the establishment of Social Security, all diminished the appeal of commercial risk-bearing services. Ironically, these same New Deal reforms occasioned the tremendous postwar burst in private pensioning. Thus the very factors that sparked the growth of the institution also directed it away from its traditional commercial structures.

Social Security, of course, played the critical role in the pension picture. Before 1935 employees and employers alike had rallied to pension insurance as a secure third-party repository of accruing pension benefits. The underwriters were among the nation's most reputable financial institutions, and they promised benefits independent of an employer's solvency or personnel policies. But Social Security, by guaranteeing everyone a basic retirement income, provided even greater stability and independence than insurance company contracts. With this new security, workers could be less insistent on the reliability of their employer-based pensions. They could also afford to have their supplementary private plans pursue riskier investment strategies than those permitted to insurance companies. But Social Security also created significant *uninsurable* risks, for both sponsor and participant. An unexpected liberalization of Social Security benefits or a burst of inflation without a compensating rise in government allowances would throw any integrated, insured annuity plan totally out of kilter. Self-insurance, however, gave plans the necessary flexibility to supplement Social Security efficiently.

The New Deal's second great reform, the Wagner Act, further undercut the appeal of insured pension arrangements. With the establishment of statutory collective bargaining, labor would come to look to its unions, not to allocated insurance contracts, to secure its pension accruals. Indeed, it was a major victory for organized labor to tie pensions to the workplace, not a third-party carrier, and for the unions to use their institutional strength to enforce payment from the employer. The critical grant of past-service credits to older and retiring workers, and labor's increasingly complicated benefit packages, placed further strain on insurance company products. The large unfunded liabilities were tough and costly (in up-front cash), and each actuarially irregular wrinkle involved additional calculations, special reserves, and administrative overhead. Trusteed plans, by contrast, allowed far looser funding, costing, and bookkeeping arrangements. The establishment of a trusteed union plan often resulted in an insured pension program for the salaried staff. But because labor's benefit packages were widely mimicked in these and other nonunion plans, white-collar programs often shifted to a trusteed approach.[13]

Finally, the New Deal's Revenue Act of 1942 gave trusteed plans their clearest advantage in the postwar era. Congress had already exempted pension trusts from taxation in the 1920s without offering the carriers similar relief. Levies on insurance companies were not terribly exacting, as income earned on their substantial reserve accounts was exempt from taxation. Nevertheless insurance companies paid tax on the remaining portion of their investment earnings while pension trusts paid nothing, and the size of this expense was rising rapidly. In the early 1950s the levy lowered yields nearly 6 percent and, according to a respected industry executive, raised the cost of insurance by 5 percent. Before 1942, however, the carriers had a critical compensatory advantage. Corporations could deduct their entire pension insurance premium from taxable income. Self-insuring sponsors, in contrast, were limited to the current year's normal cost plus 10 percent of contributions retiring past-service liabilities. The Revenue Act of 1942 continued the disparate treatment of investment income, but it imposed a new and uniform upper limit on annual pension deductions: normal cost plus the 10 percent of initial past-service liabilities. In the Treasury's rush to raise wartime revenues and eliminate tax avoidance, the insurers lost a major competitive advantage, while trusteed plans gained additional relief through the simplification and expansion of past-service funding deductions.[14]

The sum total of these New Deal structural changes seriously undermined the appeal of pension insurance. With Social Security and a vigorous labor movement on the scene, insurance company guarantees suddenly lost much of their appeal. The Revenue Act of 1942 took a key tax-planning advantage away from the carriers. But sponsors in the 1950s moved away from insurance for reasons more basic than these institutional changes. The items the carriers would insure — essentially mortality, administrative expenses, nominal pension benefits, and interest rates — turned out to be relatively unimportant. The more significant variables — labor turnover, real benefits, and real interest rates — lay beyond the scope of insurance company protection. And the cost of the limited risk-bearing services that the carriers did offer was increasingly seen as excessive. Corporate managers had always resented sales commissions and having their money "sequestered," as John Lewis put it, in low-yielding reserve accounts.[15]

More important, the rigid inflexibility of pension insurance contracts drastically reduced their appeal to increasingly sophisticated corporate pension managers. This was displayed most graphically in the benefits paid out by the carriers. During the deflated and depressed 1930s, carriers had paid out sums far in excess of an employer's need. Sponsors had too much money in their plans and no way to get it out. During and after World War II, in contrast, inflation eroded the real value of pension benefits below any reasonable standard of adequacy. Sponsors now had too little in their plans, and they typically made up the deficit on an ad hoc basis. (If they did not, they reneged on their employees' real expectations and suffered the consequences.) In a world where nominal values gyrated wildly about their real counterparts, the standard group annuity contract provided arbitrary and inappropriate money benefits. It presented employers with an untenable "heads I win — tails you lose" proposition.[16]

Insurance failed to provide appropriate pension benefits for the very reason these contracts proved so attractive in the 1920s. The carriers paid fixed dollar amounts that were largely defined decades prior to retirement. The insurance industry served as a conduit, transferring nominal sums of money across long stretches of time and actuarial experience. But changes in the value of money were of such significance in the twentieth century that benefits had to move with inflation if they were to satisfy a plan's intentions. To keep benefits "real," sponsors increasingly pegged pensions to final average salary or otherwise indexed plan allowances. But such benefits were indeterminate in nominal terms, and thereby uninsurable. The carriers could provide annuities, not pensions, and the former could not substitute for the latter. It was the employer, more than his insurance company, that emerged as the real security behind benefit promises.[17]

The insurance of pension finance also turned out to be a flawed idea. Indeed, postwar sponsors most often explained the appeal of the trusteed approach on the basis of its superior financial characteristics. The Treasury allowed wide discretion in actuarial costing methods and assumptions and in the rate of amortizing past-service liabilities. And employers had important uses for this permitted flexibility. At times their shareholders, bankers, and other creditors would be screaming for higher earnings; at other times, management sought to bury mountains of cash in the pension fund. But to keep the plan on an even keel, and to prevent adverse financial selection, the carriers had to cut down the sponsors' discretion over funding. They established rigid premium schedules based on the specific costing method appropriate to the specific contract. This prevented employers from adjusting contributions to fit their tax planning or corporate financial needs, or from forcing funds on the insurer whenever the carrier's portfolio rate of interest exceeded the rates available in the market. To protect the plan and its retirees, the carriers also insisted upon the systematic reduction of past-service liabilities. And to facilitate the management of the underwriting process, the insurance companies relied on their own standard actuarial assumptions.[18]

In the realm of investments, employers lost their passion for security in the confident and inflationary postwar prosperity. Increasingly they focused on the returns generated by their pension fund portfolio and, when compared to the 1930s and 1940s, had far fewer hesitations about holding risky high-yielding investments. Indeed, equities came to be seen as the perfect hedge against inflation and the best way to participate in the blossoming postwar economy. Employers reasoned that they could lower their pension contributions, freeing up funds for use in the business, if only their plans reaped greater returns through common stock investments. But insurance companies were forbidden by law from holding more than trivial amounts of equities. Insurers were society's designated rocks of security, not its instruments of speculation. Nor could stocks serve as the basic asset base for contracts promising fixed-dollar benefits. All states therefore channeled insurance company investments into conservative, fixed-income securities. And while prosperity lifted the yields on such investments, the weight of an insurer's older, low-yielding assets dragged down its portfolio rate of return. Self-insurance was thus a sponsor's only path to superior investment performance.[19]

For carriers to write efficient contracts, interest rates had to be relatively stable and not too different from the returns on equities. Such conditions had prevailed when the insurers had entered the business, in the mid-1920s. But this moment of macroeconomic stability turned out to be anomalous. In the 1930s and 1940s, when interest rates had fallen dramatically, the carriers wanted out. Now, with the return of prosperity, it was the sponsors who wished to go elsewhere. And they increasingly went to the stock market, where insurance companies were forbidden to go.[20]

The Trusteed Pension Business

Although the insurance companies were the most active providers of pension services through the years of depression and war, the trusteed plan had hardly disappeared. Most of the nation's giant corporations continued operating their own plans with the aid of a consulting actuary, a bank trustee, and perhaps an investment advisor. Because of the size of these enterprises, trusteed plans had never covered less than three-quarters of total participation. And as the latest cohort of maturing big businesses began adopting pension programs — firms such as the auto makers and their suppliers — they naturally considered the trusteed approach. Once the war broke out, the trust companies, especially, began aggressively seeking out business. These major banks had served as custodians of pension fund investments, with Bankers Trust of New York having performed this function since 1927. With the acceleration in plan installations, firms such as Chase, and Mellon in Pittsburgh, and smaller trust companies around the nation, began vigorously pursuing this business. These banks added pension record-keeping and disbursement services and advertised their investment facilities in publications such as *Business Week* and the *Harvard Business Review*. Their primary claim, of course, was that they could generate superior investment earnings.[21]

The banks did not, however, offer extensive plan design and actuarial services. They referred their clients, instead, to specialized pension consulting firms. The case of the Ford Motor Company is instructive. In 1946 the firm had established a salaried-only group annuity plan with the Equitable; and of course it had agreed to set up and fund a plan for its hourly employees in 1949. But by the latter date the company had decided to use pension trusts to fund these plans. Ford was convinced that it could earn a higher return on assets purchased by a trust. Secondarily, it expected that a consulting actuary, using less conservative assumptions than the insurers, would allow it to lower its current contributions. Ford was large enough to do its own legal and administrative work, as well as carry its own risk. Through the 1950s the company also exercised substantial control over the investment decisions. Ford needed only a bank trustee and a first-class actuary to cost the plan, review its design, and keep the company informed of legislative and regulatory changes. Ford went to New York to set up its trusts and to inquire after a large, top-flight actuarial firm. One of its banks — probably Chase — directed Ford to George Buck and his now venerable firm.[22]

After establishing a reputation redesigning New York City's pension plans, George Buck developed a large consulting practice with other states and municipalities. Along the way, Buck also picked up business advising private sponsors. But the firm's big break into the burgeoning postwar marketplace came in 1949. In that year it convinced United States Steel to carry its own salaried plan, with Buck as consulting actuary, rather than place it with the Metropolitan. After this victory, the major New York City banks began flooding Buck with more clients than the firm could handle. Referrals from U.S. Steel then gave it much of the major Pittsburgh market, including giant firms like Alcoa and Gulf Oil. Buck added pension law and pension communications departments to satisfy its clients, but 90 percent of the firm's revenue came from pure actuarial analysis. Buck did not develop an aggressive marketing program, but as long as it consistently produced high-quality actuarial analysis, it had all the clients it wanted.[23]

Buck prospered not only because it did fine work but because for all intents and purposes it was the only independent, well-established, first-class New York pension actuary. There were relatively few actuaries in the country in 1945, and insurance companies had been practically the only market for their services. The function of the actuary is costing risk, and risk-bearing by its very nature is a function characterized by significant economies of scale. In typical insurance operations, marketing and administrative costs, as well as the expense of risk-bearing per se, show a marked tendency to fall as the size of the business rises. Thus independent actuaries could hardly conduct their own insurance operations, and the overwhelming majority were insurance company employees or consultants to the industry. But large pension plans, which presented sponsors with significant actuarial uncertainty, carried little in the way of insurable risk. Sponsors needed sophisticated risk-costing, rather than risk-bearing services. Buck, with its long and focused experience in pension planning, was quickly identified as the "Tiffany" of the pension consulting business.[24]

With the limited supply of independent pension actuaries, a second source of pension consultants came from the ranks of the insurance brokers. These middlemen between plan sponsor and insurance company had played an increasingly significant role. A broker typically sold a sponsor on the idea of a plan, and then placed the contract with a carrier. As more insurance companies entered the business, brokers grew more independent of the carriers and more closely aligned with the sponsors. They would often place a contract out to bid and analyze the carrier responses for their employer clients. And when sponsors moved away from insurance, the more aggressive of these brokers followed them and developed a general pension consulting practice.

Illustrative of the evolving role of insurance brokers is the history of Towers, Perrin, Forster & Crosby. The nation's largest pension insurance broker in 1950, TPF&C began as a prominent Philadelphia fire insurance and reinsurance broker in the early years of the twentieth century. It had entered the pension market ahead of the insurance carriers when, in 1917, it helped United Carbide and Carbon design a paygo pension plan. Led by Walter Forster, one of the great insurance salesmen of his day, TPF&C adapted quickly as insurance took the lead in pension planning. Forster sold his first major insurance contract in 1929, a group annuity plan to Eastman Kodak. This indeed was the first such plan sold to a major corporation, and it was placed with the Metropolitan. Through the 1930s and 1940s Forster and TPF&C developed an enormous pension business. The firm installed both group annuity and individual trust plans in corporations like International Harvester, General Foods, Pure Oil, and Lockheed, and by 1950 had over two hundred plans on the books paying in aggregate more than $200 million in annual premiums.[25]

TPF&C's size and influence had expanded steadily. Its staff grew from 26 in 1934 to 120 by 1951. And where Kodak had directed its contract to the Met in 1929, TPF&C increasingly won the confidence of employers and exercised significant influence over plan design and the carrier selected. By World War II the company typically laid out the plan, put it out to bid, and placed business with a smaller firm such as Bankers Life, Mutual Benefit Life, or Pacific Mutual. In the process, TPF&C drew even closer to the sponsor. While continuing to sell insured contracts and receiving insurance company commissions, the firm increasingly designed, managed, and marketed plans on a fee-for-service basis. As the sponsor-oriented, fee-for-service portion of its business expanded, TPF&C consciously cultivated a more professional image. It recruited a staff of accomplished college graduates and, in 1937, hired actuary John K. Dyer away from the Prudential. The firm published the TPF&C *Tax Manual* in 1943 (it contained the new requirements of the 1942 Revenue Act as well as all Internal Revenue Service rulings, regulations, and technical bulletins relating to pensions). The company then began issuing the *TPF&C Letter* on a periodic basis in 1945, and its publications soon won widespread acclaim. That the IRS issued the *Tax Manual* to each of its pension agents did wonders for the firm's reputation.[26]

Walter Forster never left the world of pension insurance. But others in the firm were eager to design and service trusteed plans. With an actuary on staff, they could offer their clients proper actuarial costing services. The firm added a few more actuaries by 1950, including Preston Basset, again from the Prudential. These actuaries, and other

TPF&C personnel from the brokerage business, were committed to the trust fund approach. And because of TPF&C's background in sales, the firm had a far more aggressive posture toward the marketplace than Buck's organization. So when the movement to trusteed plans took hold in the 1950s, the firm's actuarial and plan design units exploded. Indeed the firm did an excellent business shifting employers out of the insurance contracts that Forster had sold them in the 1930s and 1940s. And by 1960 the firm joined Buck as one of the elite pension actuarial and consulting firms to corporate sponsors.[27]

There were far more insurance brokers than consulting actuaries active in the pension business in 1940. And these brokers were by nature sensitive to the marketplace and flexible in the services they provided. Thus the growing ranks of pension consultants came primarily from firms following the TPF&C model. Most of the leading companies in the early 1960s had originated in insurance brokerage. They recruited strong actuarial staffs and moved into consulting during the 1940s, then rapidly expanded their practice and actuarial acumen during the 1950s. Two other firms, illustrative of the process and taking key roles in the emerging second U.S. private pension institution, are the Wyatt and Martin E. Segal companies.[28]

Birchard E. (Byrd) Wyatt, a young and charismatic insurance salesman, left TPF&C in 1943 to form his own pension and employee benefit consulting firm. A remarkable leader and strategist, Wyatt saw early on the rising significance of trusteed pension arrangements. Although not an actuary, he understood the new importance of actuarial consulting and vigorously courted such talent. It has been said that Wyatt's greatest sale was selling his brand-new firm to some of the finest actuaries in the nation. In three years Wyatt recruited a cadre of first-class actuaries, including former Social Security actuary Dorrance Bronson, one of the most highly regarded figures in the profession. Wyatt also established his head office in Washington, D.C., the source of the newly important Internal Revenue Service pronouncements, and quickly organized a series of four branch offices to provide clients with ready access to his consultants. These three strategic decisions — to recruit the best actuarial talent, to establish a listening post in Washington, and to get consultants close to their clients — were remarkably brilliant. All major pension consulting firms would in time adopt these measures. And although Wyatt died suddenly in 1946, at the age of 38, the firm bearing his name went on to join Buck and TPF&C as one of the three top pension consulting companies by the early 1960s.[29]

The Martin E. Segal Company provides a final example of a broker-age firm transformed into a consulting house. Segal had established a Metropolitan Life Insurance agency in 1939, just before the major expansion of employee benefits during World War II, and he worked with the New York City craft unions to set up group insurance and savings plans. Although legally the agent of the carriers, Segal developed a business practice that promoted the interests of his customers. By 1942 he challenged the identical group health insurance bids submitted by Group Association members. He demanded an itemized breakdown of their insurance and administrative charges and an estimate of the net price to the consumer — the premium less the projected year-end dividend. By the end of the decade Segal was often the agent of the customer, not the carrier. He charged many of his clients a consulting fee and returned the commissions on any insurance he placed. (This required the permission of the New York state authorities, for commission rebates were otherwise illegal.) Segal, by then, had successfully entered the pension business.[30]

Like Wyatt and TPF&C, Segal rode the great expansion of the pension institution in the 1950s. And like these other firms, it had to hire actuaries to do so. Jack Elkin left the Railroad Retirement Board for Segal in 1954, and the firm's pension business boomed in the last half of the decade. But while the major consulting firms aligned themselves with management and large corporate plans and had refused union business, Segal eagerly worked for labor and the labor-management boards mandated by the Taft-Hartley Act for multiemployer benefit plans. From the very beginning of his business, Martin Segal had worked with construction, hotel, and other union officials. When the AFL organizations began actively negotiating pension schemes, they naturally turned to his firm. As Segal had developed a close understanding of the labor costs and labor-relations dynamics in these industries, he soon gained the confidence of the employer trustees as well. He and his firm helped design their plans and develop a systematic funding program. The rapid spread of AFL multiemployer plans indeed owed much to the Segal Company and to Robert Tilove, perhaps its most creative consultant. Compared to corporate sponsors, the joint labor-management pension boards directing these plans lacked sophisticated staff and were highly dependent on diligent, competent, and politic advisors. The Segal Company grew to be a major pension consulting firm primarily by providing such services.[31]

The basic function provided by all pension consultants was to custom design a pension plan to suit the specific needs of the sponsor. They could readily tailor a benefit package to skew accruals to certain employee classes, base benefits on final salary, or integrate the plan with Social Security. While coverage and participation had to pass muster with the Treasury, a consultant could ignore an insurer's underwriting requirement that a minimum number of lives and a minimum percentage of the workforce participate in the plan. Custom vesting schedules and the full gamut of ancillary benefits, none of which had to be calculated and contracted for on an actuarial basis, could readily be written into the program.

Perhaps the most important area of custom design lay in funding policy. By selecting the appropriate actuarial costing method and set of assumptions, the consultant could tailor the funding pattern to the sponsor's specific tax and financial profile. The most flexible and by far the most popular costing method was "entry-age normal." This technique was essentially the level-premium costing method, with charges assumed to start at the beginning of an employee's career. Of all costing methods, entry-age normal pulled the greatest burden of pension cost into the earliest years of service. It thus generated the greatest past-service liability, and a large past-service liability was the key to funding flexibility. The Treasury allowed sponsors to amortize this liability in as little as ten years, so employers using entry-age normal could pile up very large current deductions and tax-favored asset accumulations. The government also allowed sponsors merely to "freeze" their past-service liabilities. Since entry-age normal produced the smallest stream of future normal costs, it could also minimize pension contributions. Thus the method typically allowed both the highest and lowest levels of current contributions.

The second area of financial flexibility lay in the set of assumptions used by the actuary. For any given costing method, the choice of assumptions dramatically influenced the distribution of contributions through time. To minimize current contributions, the actuary could assume a high rate of mortality and separation from service, no future salary increases, and a high rate of interest for discounting future liabilities and projecting the growth in plan assets. If the sponsor wanted to bury large sums in its pension plan, the actuary could assume the opposite — a rapid run-up in future salaries and low rates of mortality, turnover, disability, and interest. For each assumption there was a reasonable range of choice — a set of values acceptable both to the Internal Revenue and to the actuary's own sense of propriety. As pension schemes were very long-term affairs, shifting from one end of this range of assumptions to the other had a tremendous impact on cost projections. Actuarial valuations were most sensitive, through the 1950s, to interest-rate assumptions. But for any parameter, sliding up and down the range of acceptable values had a marked effect on current pension expenses. Taken together, a conservative valuation could easily produce a current cost estimate twice as large as a liberal one. As gaps developed between the actuary's projection and the plan's experience, a sponsor would of course have to modify its funding program. But these "actuarial gains and losses" would emerge far in the future, and even then could be amortized over many years.[32]

The insurance companies had offered none of this flexibility. The standard group annuity used the single-premium deferred annuity, or "unit credit," costing method; individual trust plans and group permanent contracts used level-premium deferred annuity funding, running from the participant's current attained age to the date of retirement. The carriers also used standard mortality, disability, and interest-rate guarantees in all their contracts and had no convenient way to fund benefits based on future salary increases. They allowed no discounts in advance for future turnover — a major item in reducing current costs — but merely refunded sums put away for nonvested, separating employees as they left the plan. By requiring the amortization of past-service liabilities, the carriers established a condition more onerous than those of the IRS, which only insisted that these liabilities be frozen.[33]

Most of these insurance company practices pushed current contributions higher, although the inability to fund future salary increases pulled them back down. In an expanding economy, and with managers pushed to show and retain profits, corporate sponsors generally sought to reduce their current pension contributions. In tax-minimization situations, the opposite was the case. But whatever the interest of the sponsor, pension consultants could develop benefit and funding policies suited to their client's specific labor and financial profile.

The decade of the 1950s was the most bitterly competitive in the entire history of the pension industry, as the carriers and consultants did battle. The insurers challenged the notion that equities could provide a secure asset base for retirement programs. And they cautioned against consultants who sacrificed soundness, using questionable assumptions and antiquated mortality tables, to reduce current pension contributions. The consultants, for their part, disparaged the carriers' investments as hopelessly stodgy, their actuaries as unimaginative, and their executives and salesmen as implacably avaricious. On a more objective, conceptual level, they came to reject

> the relatively narrow concept of fiscal soundness of the pension plan itself but [preferred] rather soundness in relation to the employer's total operation. Actually, there is a possible conflict between (1) actuarial supersoundness (or redundancy) applying to pensions and (2) the long-range welfare of the company and its employees ... Any course of action which leads to a stronger company, better able to weather occasional financial reverses, and to meet competition, may enhance the security of the employees as a whole, regardless of the current effect on the level of pension contributions ... within the framework of adequate assumptions, it is entirely proper to choose that actuarial cost method best suited to the company's long-range objectives.[34]

In this sea of contention, it became inordinately difficult to make complex pension decisions. And with reputable professionals all but calling each other charlatans, genuine charlatans easily slipped into the industry. To help sort things through and shed light on complex pension matters, several organizations emerged in the late 1940s and through the 1950s. The Council on Employee Benefits, a 1947 outgrowth of the U.S. Chamber of Commerce, provided a meeting ground for benefits managers from the nation's largest corporations. The Conference of Actuaries in Public Practice emerged in 1949 as a second-tier professional association, below the Society of Actuaries, serving those who serviced self-insured pension and employee benefit plan sponsors. The Industrial Relations Counselors created the American Pension Conference to serve as a forum for pension professionals of all persuasions. The Pension Research Council, established in 1952 at the Wharton School's renowned Insurance Department, became the source of pension texts and the focal point for academic research on the subject. And in the late 1950s a group of Milwaukee contractors formed what became the International Foundation of Employee Benefit Plans to help sort through the new multiemployer pension and welfare systems. The net result of all this activity was the greater comprehensibility, if not the outright advocacy, of trusteed pension plans.[35]

Insurance executives responded to their postwar problems with persistence and ingenuity, but not dispatch. The carriers were by nature large bureaucratic enterprises, and it took them two decades to fully respond to the postwar marketplace. But by the early 1960s they would significantly recast their environment, their contracts, and their way of doing business. Problems remained, stemming especially from their operation as big-business enterprises. But because of their adaptations, the insurance companies survived as major players in the pension business.

The industry's clearest objective was redressing its tax problem. Its accomplishment, however, would not be a simple exercise in congressional lobbying. Pensions were never an insurance company's primary line of business, so pension executives first had to convince top management to invest the firm's political resources in their campaign. They needed to show that more could be gained in pensions than in life, health, or property/casualty. Then the industry would have to be convinced. Insurance company taxation was a maze of special rules, reliefs, and regulations, and Congress, in its wisdom, picked a dollar amount of total revenues it wanted and gave the industry significant freedom in dividing up this collective obligation. So once a major pension insurer was convinced that it needed relief, it had to persuade the rest of the industry to shift taxes from pensions to other products. The process, not surprisingly, was slow. Pension investments held by insurance companies, but not those held by trust companies, were subject to federal income tax until 1961.[36]

The industry's main difficulty, however, lay in its products rather than its tax situation. The enormous trade literature that rehashed the insurance–trust fund debate focused on basic characteristics of insurance company contracts. Most criticism was directed at the group annuity, the industry's flagship program in the critical market for large corporate sponsors. The Metropolitan had developed the product in the 1920s, and it became the industry standard in the 1930s. The product owed its success, in this early period, to the tremendous demand for benefit security. But with Social Security, the enfranchisement of labor, and the onset of inflationary times, the group annuity clearly became an inflexible and overly expensive instrument. The demand for self-insurance, flexibility, and equity investments rose steadily over time, and these sponsor preferences proved far more resistant to change than the federal tax code. If insurance companies were to survive in the pension industry, they would have to market new products.[37]

In its first response to the new conditions, the insurance industry began marketing products that transferred far less risk from the sponsor to the carrier than did the old group annuity. The basic innovation was the "deposit administration" contract. Under deposit administration, the sponsor made contributions to a "deposit account" with the carrier. There it compounded at a guaranteed rate, sharing in any excess earnings through the carrier's normal dividend or experience rating policy. When employees retired, the plan used assets from this accumulation fund to buy them single-premium immediate annuities. As in the case of investment earnings, the carrier provided sponsors with guarantees on the cost of these annuities. But benefits and funding policies were determined outside of the deposit administration contract. The carriers insured only benefits in pay status and minimum interest and annuity purchase rates. The contract had been designed by the Equitable Life Assurance Company in 1929, the very year the firm sold its first pension contract. But the deposit administration concept had lain dormant through the Depression and war. As late as 1945 only twenty plans used the contract as a funding vehicle. But as sponsors then began demanding flexibility above security, deposit administration won an increasing number of adherents. There were 160 such plans in effect in 1950 and 990 by 1955. Six of the seven large insurers were offering deposit administration programs by 1953, and the arrangement was clearly the insurance company contract of choice for plans with more than 1,000 participants.[38]

The assurances still provided under deposit administration—nominal interest and annuity purchase rates—were nevertheless costly and cumbersome, and they provided only minimal protection. So in the early 1950s the industry developed the "immediate participation guarantee" deposit administration contract, which eliminated nearly all aspects of insurance. Under the IPG, sponsors bore their own investment and mortality risks for both active and retired lives. The retirees, however, remained secure in their benefits. Should the accumulation fund dip below a designated level, the carrier would terminate the scheme and purchase single-premium annuities to provide all pensions in pay status. But as long as the sponsor maintained a sufficient balance, there were no guarantees, no single-premium immediate annuity purchases, and all plan costs and benefits were "immediately" passed on to the sponsor. The IPG thus avoided the reserve accounts and pooling procedures that come with insurance. The carriers allowed only large sponsors, typically with two thousand or more lives, to elect the IPG contract. And only four of the seven big insurers offered the program in 1953, with one other considering adoption and two adamantly opposed. But it was the immediate participation guarantee, or the elimination of standard insurance protections, that allowed the carriers to come back into the marketplace.[39]

Deposit administration arrangements, including the IPG, were clearly far better suited to postwar conditions than the group annuity, and they became the basic insurance industry products for large pension clients. These contracts eliminated the risk-bearing services that sponsors showed little interest in purchasing. As there were no individual accounts allocated prior to retirement, and rarely employee contributions, they greatly reduced record-keeping and marketing expenses. But most important, deposit administration and immediate participation guarantee plans allowed great flexibility in plan design and funding. As the plan rather than the carrier bore the risk of fund insufficiency, sponsors could include those features that were uninsurable, or insurable only with great difficulty. These included Social Security integration, nonactuarial early retirement benefits, or pensions based on final average salary. And because sponsors did not transfer benefit obligations to a third-party insurer, only Treasury Department regulations limited their basic discretion over the flow of pension contributions. They could choose from any of the approved actuarial costing methods, discount future employee turnover in advance, and either freeze past-service liabilities at their initial level or amortize them at any rate allowed by law.[40]

By eliminating unwanted and expensive services, the deposit administration contract and its IPG variant were critically important in freeing the insurance industry to compete for pension business. These innovations, however, did not change the industry's investment offering — the carrier's "general account" with its portfolio of conservative fixed-income securities. Nor did it affect the risk-sharing practice of crediting all contracts with an interest rate based on the earnings of the firm's whole portfolio. Only the carrier's entire assembly of stodgy fixed-income assets, to paraphrase the industry adage, stood behind all its liabilities.

In a regime of steadily rising interest rates, sponsors had little reason to seek out an insurer's portfolio rate of interest. Current investment options were more attractive, and most sponsors expected this situation to continue. The carriers came to understand that sponsors would be far more willing to invest with an insurance company if their assets were credited at current market rates of return. Various firms in the industry, including the Aetna and Connecticut General, responded to this sentiment in the mid-1950s with the "investment year" method of allocating investment income. Although quite complicated in practical operation, the technique credited earnings much like a simple, single, investment account: new money, whether fresh contributions or reinvested earnings, nailed down the rates and durations of the carrier's new investments. Among larger pension contracts, the investment-year method quickly became the common arrangement. Insurance companies continued pooling results of investments made in a single period, typically a single year. But for sponsors electing the method, they no longer pooled their results with investments made in different periods.[41]

With the investment-year method in an immediate participation deposit administration contract, the insurance companies could offer clients a pension program that eliminated nearly all elements of insurance. Assets placed in such contracts behaved much as they would in a fixed-income investment trust or mutual fund. Because insurance companies typically had greater facility in mortgages and private placements, the industry could actually boast a higher rate of return on fixed-income investments than other fixed-income investors.

Dan McGill, in 1962, found that life insurance carriers credited 1961 "new money" interest at approximately 5.3 percent, while the trust companies averaged but 4.5 percent in dividends and realized capital gains. However, if the trust companies could include unrealized capital gains as "income," McGill concluded, then "the overall yield on trust funds (valued at cost) with substantial percentages of common stocks is likely to be higher — often much higher — than the return on the general investment account of the life insurer." The inability to invest in equities thus came to be a central barrier to insurance company success in the pension field.[42]

The insurance industry attacked this final regulatory hurdle at the end of the 1950s, and developed a means of offering equity investments for pension funds. In 1959 the Prudential won permission from the state of New Jersey to establish various independent funds, separate from the firm's general account, to be used by its pension clients. Each fund would accept assets from various plans and invest in a single class of securities; one of these classes was common stock. Plans large enough to achieve adequate diversification could establish their own separate accounts and, like a trust fund, could hold a variety of securities. John Hancock led the fight for separate accounts in Massachusetts, and the Equitable did so in the crucial state of New York; Hancock won its battle in 1960, and the Equitable succeeded in 1962. In winning the right to establish separate accounts, insurance companies had to over-come the vigorous opposition of their trust company competitors and also of one of their conservative brethren — the Metropolitan. They also had to convince the Securities and Exchange Commission to waive its exacting securities and investment company regulations. This issue was finally settled in January 1963, with the SEC's rule 3c-c. Thereafter carriers could establish separate accounts to receive, free from SEC oversight, employer (but not employee) contributions from qualified group plans (with twenty-five or more participants). The carriers in effect won trust powers within the pension institution, and could com-pete with trust companies on an equal footing. Within three years, eighteen of the largest carriers had 548 clients with separate accounts.[43]

With the creation of separate accounts, the insurance company could function as a pension fund investment company. For the first time in insurance company practice, assets were valued at market. And they could move freely, at market value, from one separate account to an-other or to another investment manager altogether. In such a system, the sponsor clearly controlled the basic allocation of its pension assets among the different investment options. The insurance companies were in effect operating a pure trust company business, and it was a strange new world for the carriers. But it was essential that the industry develop these instruments if it was to survive as a major player in the pension industry.[44]

By the early 1950s pensions had become a major business for the leading group annuity carriers. Among the fifteen leading insurers in 1953, pension reserves accounted for 30 percent of total reserves. At three of these firms they made up half of the total. A carrier with such a commitment to pensions was, as Black had noted, "as much an an-nuity company as a life insurance company," and had a great deal at stake in the pension business. The 1950s were clearly a difficult decade. But by the early 1960s the carriers had finished their adjustments to the second U.S. pension institution. They had won from Congress the same tax treatment accorded to pension trusts. The carriers competing for large corporate business had reorganized to give sponsors the design and investment flexibility they demanded. So the insurers looked to the future with optimism. Robert K. Trapp, director of group pension sales for John Hancock, predicted that "the insured plan will in the years ahead achieve a greater prominence as a medium of funding pension plans than existed even in the late 1930s and early 1940s." But the carriers understood that they would not be bearers of plan risks, but integrated providers of pension services. They had left the group annuity business to participate in the broader pension industry.[45]

The Professionalization of the Pension Industry

For large and mid-sized sponsors the transition to self-insurance was largely accomplished by the early 1960s. Employers now bore the key plan risks, even if they used an insurance company separate account or a deposit administration contract. This precipitated a major reorganization of the pension industry. The nation's giant insurance companies, vertically and horizontally integrated, had emerged as the dominant providers of pension products of the first U.S. private pension institution. Now that sponsors assumed their basic plan risks, the carriers had repositioned themselves as integrated providers of the remaining plan functions. Their competition, however, the consulting actuaries and bank trust companies, presented sponsors with a nonintegrated alternative. The consultants did not invest funds, while the trust companies never developed sophisticated actuarial or plan design capabilities. Early in the postwar period the carriers' competitors emphasized their broader investment opportunities. But by the early 1960s there was little separating the investment options of the two camps. The issue increasingly became a choice between an integrated and a nonintegrated solution to pension provision.[46]

The nation's major life insurance companies, before World War II, were uniquely qualified, and so recognized, to translate current contributions into streams of future retirement income. In delivering this service, the behemoth insurance organizations, along with their agents and brokers, had performed six subsidiary functions. They had designed the plan, calculated its costs, invested its assets, underwritten the risk, kept the books, and marketed the plan to employees. But in the second U.S. pension system, sponsors' demand for underwriting, bookkeeping, and employee marketing declined sharply. Their interest in design, costing, and investment services, meanwhile, expanded dramatically. The elimination of underwriting, coupled with the heightened intensity of demand for those services still needed, radically changed the industrial organization of the pension business.

Clearly, risk-bearing was the most important external service suffering a decline in demand. The risks generated by mortality, administrative expense, and real investment performance turned out to be surprisingly small. Even mid-sized employers, given enough lead time, could comfortably carry the load. And the carriers refused to underwrite the more volatile turnover and salary-scale factors or the key and potentially catastrophic risk of inflation. As for the two other externally supplied services in decline, record-keeping had flowed primarily from the carriers' function as a third-party guarantor, while employee marketing had been critical to the success of voluntary, contributory plans. In the postwar era, as participants and sponsors grew more secure, longevity increased, and new taxes on middle-class incomes discouraged after-tax employee contributions, funding became increasingly noncontributory and plan participation universal. With the transition to mandatory, noncontributory designs, plans no longer established carefully allocated individual accounts. And as corporate personnel systems computerized and grew more sophisticated, they increasingly tracked the data needed by the plan.[47]

While the demand for external insurance, administration, and marketing declined, that for design, actuarial, legal, and investment services climbed sharply. Developing the increasingly complex benefit packages, tailoring funding programs to the sponsor's overall business situation, while simultaneously complying with IRS regulations, involved a great deal of work. Investment management became far more intricate as the universe of acceptable pension assets expanded. The future of the pension industry thus lay in the efficient provision of high-quality design, actuarial, legal, and investment services. The insurance companies, which had to retreat from risk-bearing, record-keeping, and marketing activities, possessed well-developed design, actuarial, and investment facilities. And their optimism in the early 1960s was based on the continued demand for these services. The issue remaining was whether the large, vertically integrated insurance company would be the most efficient supplier.

When pension plans required six closely interconnected services, among them risk-bearing, the hierarchical, vertically integrated insurance organization had shown itself to be a most efficient provider. It encountered little difficulty supervising the various pension services, as each task was reasonably routine. Installing a typical group annuity program involved just standard modifications in plan design, actuarial evaluations, marketing, record-keeping, and underwriting services. With assets restricted to fixed-income securities, investments primarily required regular credit reviews. There were positive forces, as well, promoting central managerial coordination: an insurer needed to control key aspects of the plan if it were to bear any risk at all.

The central direction of six closely and simultaneously interacting services, moreover, saved time and avoided conflict and confusion. The complexity of a pension system and the guarantees it offered required transactions among the various specialists to proceed in a clear and consistent manner. Everyone, for example, could work more efficiently if plan designs were all of a type and modifications confined within reasonable bounds. A central authority could set such performance standards and provide coordination far more effectively than a collection of independent, self-interested suppliers. If there was a problem, say a discrepancy between an employer's legitimate dividend expectation and the sum actually recorded to his credit, the sponsor had one organization with which to deal. An insurance company manager could usually determine responsibility and arrange a remedy far more efficiently than negotiations among a half-dozen providers, or lengthy litigation before a courtroom judge.[48]

In the first U.S. pension institution, a provider integrated horizontally, as well as vertically, proved most efficient. Underwriting, by its very nature, displayed clear economies of scale. This is because risk — the expected variance from the expected value — declines monotonically as the number of cases rises. A large organization is also better equipped to bear the cost of adverse experience. The very necessity of offering six different specialized services, each at a significant level of competence, also meant that a carrier had to have a reasonably large pension staff and a comparably large pension business. This was especially true in group annuities, as opposed to individual trusts. The latter were essentially extensions of a carrier's ordinary individual life business, while group annuities were a separate product requiring a specialized staff. The insurance of large corporate pension plans was thus the province of a small number of giant carriers.

But the decline of risk-bearing in the 1950s, and the restructuring of the remaining pension services, undermined the value of both horizontal and vertical integration. Where sponsors bore the primary risks in a plan, economies of scale in risk-bearing no longer expanded the optimal size of service providers. And while the synchronization of six independent service providers required close managerial control, the same could not be said of the coordination of two or three. Providers of plan design and actuarial costing were in close and constant contact, and transactions between these services did benefit from organizational integration. The two functions were indeed performed most successfully when fused together in the role of the consulting actuary — the experienced number cruncher who met with clients and hammered out plan designs. But there were few connections between investment decisions and this design and costing cluster, and their interaction derived little benefit from direct coordination or integration into a common enterprise. Actuaries needed to know the size of the plan's assets and its rate of return, and the investment manager had to be informed of cash flows into and out of the pension fund. But this information could be communicated quickly and infrequently, and as a practical matter these interchanges never developed into protracted give-and-take negotiations.[49]

Just as positive forces had encouraged the integration of services in the first U.S. pension institution, the pressures for unbundling were powerful now. While plan design and costing were intimately tied together in the self-insurance regime, there were reasons to disassociate this cluster from the investment function. Sponsors clearly wanted the greater flexibility such a separation provided. Should an employer wish to change its investment manager, for example, it was far easier to accomplish if the sponsor had no continuing design and actuarial relationship with the firm. A second reason to use two-stop shopping was to avoid a conflict of interest inherent in the combination of services. An investment company, be it an insurer, a bank, or a mutual fund, was compensated according to the amount of assets it managed. But a sponsor's plan design and funding advisor largely defined the size and timing of pension contributions. As most sponsors wanted to minimize their current payments, they preferred not to use designers and actuaries employed by their investment firm. Sponsors of trusteed plans thus usually sought out an independent actuary, and the consulting firms chose not to enter the investment management business. Sponsors with deposit administration arrangements increasingly hired their own designers and actuaries rather than use insurance company personnel. Actuaries and trust companies naturally developed informal alliances and referral networks. But these ties did not lead to stronger associations, let alone mergers.[50]

There were also positive forces pushing to break up horizontal concentrations in the industry. The key factor was the enormous array of benefit and funding options opened up by the release from insurance company underwriting policies. All firms had idiosyncratic financial and personnel needs; this was because capital and labor flows had to fit the corporation's more basic, more logically constructed production and marketing program. As firms shifted their business strategies over time, their financial and personnel profiles, and thus their pension programs, had to adapt in response. Chief executive officers were also delegating pension policy to their personnel and financial officers — to managers who understood the intimate details of these functional areas. To make use of this expertise, to exploit the new freedoms available in plan design and investment management, and to conform to the constantly changing body of Internal Revenue Service regulations required careful, continuous, and custom attention. In the first U.S. pension institution, with its emphasis on security, it was best to fit the plan to the requirements of the insurance provider. But in second U.S. pension institution it was more advantageous to fit the plan to the needs of the sponsor.[51]

The advantages of a custom pension policy became especially clear as sponsors recognized the financial implications of self-insurance. Pension contributions and the yield on pension assets had a significant impact on a corporation's taxes, reported income, and basic financial position. Corporate chief financial officers soon recognized the pension plan as a manageable liability — as a source of funds, an investment outlet, and a general reservoir of balance sheet slack. Because the top financial officers held greater sway in the corporate hierarchy than the personnel directors, in the 1950s they took control of the major plan decisions. They could converse more fluently with their actuarial and investment consultants, and together they made pension planning a more customized endeavor. By the end of the 1950s James McNulty could describe the "sophisticated manifestations of the trend towards weaving pension affairs into the total financial strategy of the firm" and the intent to make pension finances "a function of the venture position of the sponsoring firm."[52]

By necessity, service organizations that could customize a corporate pension plan, that could deliver intensive "local processing," had to delegate a great deal of discretion to highly competent front-line personnel. The large, hierarchical insurance companies were not set up to motivate or monitor such field providers. Their most sophisticated expertise was concentrated at headquarters, where it focused on developing new financial products. So many of the industry's best pension actuaries quit, seeing better opportunities in the field. They joined the consulting firms that, as typical professional firms, used short managerial hierarchies, exercised limited control over the work process, and offered partnership opportunities. The key advantage of size in the consulting business lay in marketing and market visibility — a competitive edge in the murky and esoteric world of pension planning. Companies such as Wyatt that stuck most closely to the decentralized model expanded rapidly, through acquisitions and internal growth, and captured these scale economies. Firms pursuing a more centralized or more narrowly actuarial strategy — such as Buck — expanded at a slower pace than Wyatt, but otherwise did well. And a cottage industry of small pension consulting and actuarial shops, accounting firms, and insurance brokers sprang up all around the country to provide custom service to small and mid-sized sponsors.[53]

Investment management was the one area of the pension business where large-scale enterprise still prospered in 1960. Even the insurance companies had come to emphasize their investment, not their actuarial, prowess. Large asset pools could significantly reduce investment risk without reducing yield by diversifying. An investment fund could also employ the most competent, well-trained staff and spread the cost over a large asset base. With the growth of modern portfolio theory and other forms of sophisticated financial analysis, investing was becoming a science best applied by sophisticated full-time professionals. Such was the argument made for insurance company portfolio investments — whether through a traditional contract or a deposit administration arrangement. And indeed the carriers' proficiency in mortgages and direct placements resulted in consistently high yields in fixed-income investments. So too, trust company commingled funds, insurance company separate funds, and the increasingly popular mutual funds all claimed the advantages of pooled, managed investments.

But even in the area of investments the tide was turning against the large-scale service providers. As with their actuarial risks, the big plans generated asset pools large enough to capture much of the risk reduction available through portfolio diversification. Their pension funds were also sufficiently large to justify their own full-time management. And having captured the key economies of scale, such sponsors then sought to customize their portfolios. They often developed close relations with their bank trustees (or insurance company separate account managers) and directed plan investments to suit their own tastes, liquidity needs, or larger business strategies. Given the proper legal release from fiduciary responsibilities under state law, trustees were reasonably responsive to sponsor direction. If not, sponsors could find new trustees. And as with plan design, sponsors sought out increasingly sophisticated counselors to provide custom financial advice. Such professional advisors developed a pension investment program after analyzing the plan's liquidity requirements, the sponsor's risk tolerance, cash flow needs, and tax strategies. Such a workup required a great deal of time and discretion, and was best carried out by an experienced, independent professional. Whether operating their own companies or working in decentralized settings, these advisors quietly stole the march on bureaucratic investment operations that inevitably remained distant from particular plan sponsors.[54]

A comparable breakup was simultaneously developing in the area of pension investment per se. As long as pension plans had limited their investments to collateralized, fixed-income assets, selecting and monitoring securities had been a relatively routine activity. But common stock carried no collateral. It was a claim on a residual income stream and its value depended on a host of factors. As such, each equity investment required continuous and careful attention.

When plan managers first moved into equities, they either picked their own stocks or relied on their trust company's recommended list or its commingled common stock fund. But by the end of the 1950s stock picking had become unduly burdensome for busy corporate treasury departments; the activity also proved too treacherous for long-term, career officials. Investment counselors, in the meantime, were pressing pension managers to abandon the trust company's balanced equity position and adopt more aggressive financial strategies. As pension executives responded to this advice, they discovered a maze of independent, growth-oriented money managers and mutual fund operators. Each of these security market specialists tracked a specific investment strategy, focused on an individual industry or region, followed securities with particular financial characteristics, or offered a unique piece of financial engineering. All, of course, claimed above-average performance.[55]

Coupled with this promise of higher returns was higher risk, growing out of myopia and the limited diversification of these small money managers. Large plans found that they could eliminate much of this risk, while capturing the returns of specialization, by spreading their investments across many such managers. Mutual funds, trust companies, and special account departments in insurance companies could likewise capture the advantages of local processing by decentralizing their operations and giving a large number of front-line money managers far greater discretion. The investment industry remained concentrated, geographically, in the great financial marketplace of New York City. So the large trust companies and insurance companies could keep their expertise at headquarters and remain competitive. But as the pension funds and their financial intermediaries adopted this diversified local processing strategy, the business of pension investing became far more individualized and less integrated.[56]

The nation's large insurance companies had initially dominated the private pension business by selling sophisticated financial products that claimed to absorb the risks in a pension program. But as large corporate and multiemployer sponsors retained the responsibility for delivering future streams of old age income, they sought out sophisticated labor services from a variety of professional experts. By 1960 the actuarial consultants had largely taken charge of plan design, costing, and funding policy. The advantages of professional specialization in finance had been recognized, and the great growth of this business lay just ahead.

It was up to the sponsor to keep these providers honest and diligent and to blend their contributions into a coherent pension program. The task was not dissimilar to managing the sponsors' own employees, who also contracted to provide labor services. These outside professionals controlled the work process, of course. But sponsors needed mechanisms to assure good performance, and to get the benefits promised.[57]

The sponsor's relationship with the actuarial consultant was the most complex, and the control mechanism the least direct. Designing a custom plan, and keeping it up-to-date, involved close, continual, and confidential interactions. The complexity of the task made it difficult to evaluate the service received, or to compare it with work done by others in the field. As in other agency relationships suffering from high "monitoring" costs, sponsors pursued an "efficiency wage" strategy to keep their consultants loyal and energetic. Just as the nineteenth-century B&O Railroad had paid blue-collar workers premium wages, sponsors now offered high fees to establish a "gift exchange" with their consultants — they gave out premium pay and expected, in return, premium service. The arrangement also carried a stick. Should the sponsor become dissatisfied, the consultant stood to lose this stream of surplus compensation. The B&O had added pensions in 1880 only because its workers had needed a form of compensation other than wages; the B&O had provided insurance, and a routinized personnel system, to alleviate its employees' sense of insecurity. The sponsors did not give their consultants pensions; but the premium fees they paid functioned as a token in a "gift-exchange" (or dismissal threat) reminiscent of welfare capitalism.[58]

Sponsors developed different mechanisms to control their money managers, largely because of their superior ability to monitor performance. While employers could never specify precisely what they wanted from their actuaries, the basic investment outputs were simple, quantitative, and well defined; they wanted a good rate of return, given some specified liquidity and risk considerations. Sponsors had reason to prefer Smith if he earned 9 percent and Jones only 7. Extenuating circumstances always clouded the issue: Jones's industry was depressed, and he had the best performance of all money managers active in that area; Jones had outperformed Smith over the past five years; or Jones had steadily produced 7 percent while Smith's results varied substantially from one year to the next. But despite these complications, rates of return gave sponsors far superior measures of performance. And because of this monitoring ability, they built their agency relationships around periodic evaluations. Their best managers got more assets to invest, or higher fees; the others got less, or perhaps were replaced. As a money manager's income closely tracked these performance measures, the sponsors had good reason to believe they would work diligently and hard.

Compared to the long-term, highly compensated ties that sponsors developed with actuarial consultants, their relations with money managers were notoriously fickle. The sums they paid to particular managers were erratic, and often outrageously high. The tremendous fees were not so much an "efficiency wage," nor compensation for risk. They were, instead, what economists call "rents." They were payments for what sponsors perceived as a unique ability to manage money. Small differences mattered greatly when handling hundreds of millions or billions of dollars, and the best performers exacted their share of the difference.

If bank trust departments and insurance company separate account departments were to compete for pension investment business, they had to approximate this lucrative and volatile pattern of employment and compensation. Otherwise the best performers would join downtown investment boutiques, leaving only the mediocre behind. Elsewhere in the organization, banks and insurance companies cultivated stable, long-term career employment relationships. They used the pension, of course, as part of this effort. But money managers were a different kettle of fish. And lest traditional administrative and personnel systems interfere in their management, these banks and insurance companies had to isolate their investment departments and develop compensation and employment practices that mimicked the market.[59]

The ascent of the professional service firm, and its imitation in traditional corporations, represents a significant irony in pension history. The private pension had appeared as an instrument of giant enterprise, part of an ambitious program to tie labor to a stable, long-term relationship. This stability let corporate employers routinize operations and make massive, long-term investments. But no big business — neither the sponsors themselves nor the large integrated insurance companies — could service the institution as efficiently as the decentralized financial marketplace. The institution needed professional, not managerial, rationalization. It needed actuarial, investment, legal, and accounting expertise, not close and systematic coordination. The pension had emerged as a tool of labor management in mass-production, mass-distribution industries. But the industry it spawned after World War II used different managerial structures, and different instruments of control.

The shift was clearly advantageous from the standpoint of the sponsor. It offered far more flexibility in many key areas and access to much higher rates of return on pension investments. But from the standpoint of the employees and the government — the other two participants in the private pension institution — the decline of insurance was more ambiguous. No longer did a super-solvent guarantor stand behind the promised pension. As retirements extending a decade or more became the norm and not the exception, the private pension became a critical element in the nation's economic structure. With only the corporate sponsor and its amorphous network of advisors assuring payments far into the future, both employees and the government grew anxious over the strength of the new institution.

Chapter 8

◆ ◆ ◆

ERISA and the Reformation
of Pensions

The pension emerged as a huge economic institution in the third quarter of the twentieth century. On the liability side of the balance sheet, participation increased from 19 to 45 percent of the private-sector workforce between 1945 and 1970. On the asset side, private plans held 7 percent of U.S. financial claims in 1970, up from 2 percent in 1950; claims against the sponsor for unfunded liabilities and the value of government tax favors augmented pension assets to a significant but indeterminate extent. The pension, initially a mechanism for accommodating labor to the needs of employers, had become a pervasive and potent institution accommodating U.S. households to an economy of labor markets, capital markets, and production organized in separately incorporated enterprises.[1]

The quarter-century nevertheless culminated in a massive legislative overhaul of the private pension system. The Employee Retirement Income Security Act of 1974, ERISA, addressed all aspects of the institution and made the federal government a central player as regulator of plans and guarantor of benefits. This formidable intrusion was prompted initially by holes in the institution. In time, however, reform refocused on a new set of issues related to size. The pension had reached an awkward adolescent moment in the eyes of government. It was no longer just an occasional charitable exercise in need of policing. The government's huge and growing expenditure of pension tax favors, key policymakers argued, was where the institution had to make a significant contribution to the national agenda. If the private pension was to become a basic building block of the national economy, it had to pay benefits more reliably to a larger portion of the population. ERISA, in the end, was government's attempt to expand the private pension and fit it into the institutional structure of the U.S. economy. The institution's success, more than its failings, led to the new legislation.

Holes in the Institution

As insurers lost their place in the pension institution, they warned of hardships ahead. The carriers had entered the business in the 1920s to assure the soundness of corporate pension promises. With the eclipse of group annuity contracts, in the 1950s, executives like Ray Peterson of the Equitable again questioned the solidity of employer pension promises. The times were now quite different, of course, from the days following the 1923 collapse of the Morris Packing plan. Social Security had increased the nation's tolerance for risk, and the Revenue Act of 1942, IRS oversight, and the maturation of the pension service industry had put the institution on a much sounder footing. Nevertheless, the moneys pouring into corporate or union pension funds could be invested in risky or self-dealing ventures. Heavy past-service obligations or investment failures could render assets inadequate should payments suddenly come due, as in the Morris fiasco. Participants in noninsured schemes also held distinctly inferior withdrawal rights and legal claims to a benefit. For all these reasons, warned the defenders of insurance, the pension credits now accumulating so rapidly could suddenly turn to dust.

In the public mind, Jimmy Hoffa personified such troubles. He was president of the International Brotherhood of Teamsters and operated the best-known pension scheme of the postwar era — the Central and Southern States Pension Fund (CSPF). Hoffa's association with pensions was nevertheless surprising. He had shown little concern for the benefit over his long career in the labor movement, stretching back to the 1930s. Only in 1955 did he sign a contract calling for pensions, and he did so, according to Ralph and Estelle James, authors of the remarkable *Hoffa and the Teamsters,* because the lack of a plan had become an embarrassment in labor circles.[2]

Once Hoffa established his plan, the fact that it captured public attention is hardly surprising. Hoffa was a brilliant, tough-as-nails centralizer who took control of the over-the-road trucking industry, now the nation's basic freight transportation system, over the course of the

1950s. In practice, if not in mind, he conflated the success of himself and his friends with that of the Teamsters and labor writ large. He had no time for the legal and institutional niceties of the pension. He viewed the law, said the Jameses, as

> not something to respect, but rather a set of principles designed to perpetuate those already in power and something for others to "get around." Thus, Hoffa feels clear of conscience about his expertise in devising legal loop-holes and practicing legal brinkmanship . . . Hoffa rationalizes his "anything goes" philosophy on grounds that "life is a jungle" where one must constantly fight to survive. People who think primarily in terms of right and wrong are "naive"— Hoffa's favorite characterization of those with an approach to life different from his own.

So he used his power as a union chief to gain control of the newly established fund. He then used the fund to advance his larger agenda.[3]

To control the CSPF, Hoffa had to defeat Ben Miller, labor relations director of the American Trucking Associations and leader of the employers on the pension board. Miller relied on the loyalty of the five major employer associations, each of which had a representative on the board. But Hoffa insisted on a sixth trustee on either side, to give representation to the independent truckers. He also demanded straight majority votes, not the "unit rule" used by most multiemployer plans (where each side caucuses, then casts a single vote — a format requiring majorities on both sides of the table). At the critical meeting where the rules were set, Hoffa railed against the employers and threatened each trustee individually: " 'Ben Miller might run you, he ain't going to run us, God damn it. You want some strikes, you will have some strikes. It won't be overall; we'll pick out the selected carriers to go on strike. We will see God damn well whether that straightens it out or not.' " Hoffa's tenacity and threats succeeded: he got his way on these procedural matters. He thenceforth got his way on substance, for he commanded the absolute allegiance of all labor trustees and could always pick up a vote from the other side. The Jameses found this "hardly surprising given that one employer trustee was long delinquent in paying off a loan granted him by the Fund and all stand exposed to a possible Teamster strike."[4]

Pension trustees were legally bound by the "prudent man" standard: they were to act "with the care, skill, prudence, and diligence under the circumstances then prevailing that a prudent man acting in a like capacity and familiar with such matters would use in conducting an enterprise of like character and with like aims." They were, in simple terms, to maximize investment returns while staying within the generally accepted parameters of risk. But Hoffa had an altogether different program. "We are in this business to make friends," he confided to the Jameses. Thus, in the first two years of the plan's operation, he placed assets with the trust departments of hometown banks of union and management trustees. And he deposited the funds with orchestrated hoopla and publicity.[5]

Then Hoffa discovered the usefulness of lending direct, and by the mid-1960s commercial mortgages and similar loans absorbed 75 percent of CSPF assets. Prudence, however, remained in the back seat. "That non-financial considerations shape the allocation of Pension moneys is apparent as one observes a meeting of the trustees," wrote the Jameses. "Individual trustees, with Hoffa the leading example, and some non-trustee observers, promote loans for their friends, associates, and influential persons. The employer trustees have a long-standing agreement on this patronage approach, and the financial strength of the Fund has suffered as a result." The Jameses witnessed trustees actually demanding *reductions* in interest rates lest *their* borrowers get terms less advantageous than the CSPF norm. Hoffa and his associates, of course, got the biggest piece of the action. Mortgage loans to Morris (Moe) Dalitz and associates (Dalitz was the major owner of the Desert Inn and Stardust Hotels in Las Vegas) absorbed 5 percent of fund assets in the early 1960s. As principals or intermediaries in CSPF loans, Ben Dranow and associates took 12 percent. Where Dranow et al. served as intermediaries, they were accused of taking finders' fees ranging from 5 to 10 percent of the principal. Such exorbitant fees, and other income lost to the fund, may have gone to enrich Hoffa or his friends. The Jameses also pass on the speculation that Dranow and his cohorts were "funnels" — channels for illicit payments to politicians, journalists, judges, and crooks.[6]

The financial results were predictably bad, not surprising as finance was not the primary concern. The Jameses estimated that "a rational lender, demanding commercially competitive rates, could have charged 8 to 10 per cent instead of 6 to 6½ per cent on CSPF-type mortgages." Moreover, twenty loans, representing 18 percent of CSPF assets, were in "serious difficulty" by the mid-1960s. In one bizarre case, that of a loan to a runaway rubber plant relocating in Deming, New Mexico, Hoffa had to *organize the workforce,* preempting the more aggressive United Rubber Workers, in order to negotiate a labor contract that would *protect his investment!*[7]

Despite Hoffa's rising notoriety, he hardly represented typical practice. Some small multiemployer plans were dominated by criminal or borderline elements who helped themselves to pension fund assets. The United Mine Workers, on a somewhat less sinister note, effectively transferred pension fund income to the union treasury by depositing pension fund assets in a no-interest checking account at a union-owned bank. The Mine Workers also bought utility company stock with pension fund dollars to promote the sale of union coal. Business likewise used pension fund assets to finance itself, its customers, or its suppliers. But such fiduciary violations, while holes, never threatened the larger institution. Even within Hoffa's own International, the Western Conference of Teamsters beat back Hoffa's 1961 campaign to absorb its plan into the CSPF. While there were clearly other instances of self-dealing and corruption, most large multiemployer funds were known more for excessive caution and portfolios stuffed full of ultra-safe government bonds. Corporate trustees (banks and insurance companies) held the great bulk of the remaining pension fund assets. These they invested primarily in publicly traded securities, and secondarily in investment-grade real estate and private placements. Pension trustees for the most part focused on their manifest task — maximizing returns in a prudent fashion; self-dealing was peripheral and criminality more so.

More troublesome and nearly as dramatic was the hole that came to light in the spectacular Studebaker collapse of 1964. The United Auto Workers, which had negotiated the Studebaker plan, stood at the opposite pole from the Teamsters in union pension policy, and in many other ways as well. Walter Reuther's organization had helped create the new collectively bargained programs and continued to field the finest staff of pension experts in the labor movement. Along with the Steelworkers, the UAW had developed many of the more progressive features of the pension institution. Its 1955 contract with Ford, for example, vested involuntarily separated workers over age 40 in their pension benefits after ten years of service. The UAW also developed a joint-and-survivor annuity option in 1961, so that widows (or widowers) could continue to receive a pension after the primary beneficiary had died. So when the Studebaker plan collapsed, it signaled a more fundamental problem than Jimmy Hoffa's back-door casino loans.[8]

Studebaker, after a long struggle in the shadow of the "Big Three" automakers, withdrew from the U.S. auto market, closed its South Bend, Indiana, plant, and terminated its pension plan at the end of its labor contract, on November 1, 1964. The pension fund, however, was millions short. Despite the UAW's record as labor's champion of conservative funding and investing, the plan did not have enough assets to redeem all benefits promised. The UAW had struck Chrysler, in 1950, solely to establish the principle of funding. It had insisted, as a minimum, the program sanctioned by the actuarial community and modeled after insurance company practice: that Chrysler contribute an amount equal to the pension credits earned during the current contract period (the "normal" cost) and pay down, over a thirty-year period, the huge initial cost for benefits granted for service in the past (the "past service" or "accrued" liability). In negotiations with Ford and General Motors in 1950, the UAW also conceded control over investment policy in return for bargaining rights over benefits and funding.[9]

The Studebaker fiasco not only dramatized the weakness of the UAW's funding strategy but revealed a liquidation program that struck the public as shockingly inequitable. According to the terms of the plan, first claim to the carcass went to retirees and employees eligible to retire (those over 60 with ten years of service). These 3,600 at the head of the line — a third of the total — were entitled to benefits in full, and Studebaker spent $21.5 million of the fund's $24 million to buy lifetime annuities from the Aetna. These retirees would get no cost-of-living increases — a customary practice in UAW plans. But they otherwise emerged unscathed.

Next in line stood 4,080 participants too young to retire, but with vested rights to a pension. Each was at least 40 years old with ten or more years of service. On average they were 52 years of age, with twenty-three years with the firm. But as they stepped up to the table, the money ran out. The $2.5 million remaining came to 15 percent of the value of the group's vested benefits, sums so slight that each recipient got just a small lump of money, ranging from $200 to $1,600 and averaging $600. The final group of 2,900 participants — those who had not become vested — got nothing. A 1961 IRS ruling (made a regulation in 1962) required immediate vesting of all pension credits upon termination. But the terms of the plan put these workers at the back of the line, and nothing was left in the fund.[10]

Despite Studebaker's funding in accordance with accepted actuarial practice, the company's failure left 7,000 workers with little or nothing to show for their tenures with the firm. At the UAW's insistence, Studebaker had funded normal costs in full and was amortizing its past-service liabilities over a thirty-year period. The policy gave the appearance of securing current credits *first* and past-service credits *gradually*. This indeed was the case in insurance company schemes, which issued certificates for current service immediately and for past service only as funded. Just the reverse was true, however, for the self-insured plans of the second private pension institution. The past-service claims of retirees and older workers took precedence. The younger workers who accrued current credits would secure their benefits only after the senior obligations were met.

Had the amortization program proceeded as initially projected, however, Studebaker's plan would have terminated with a far healthier ratio of assets to liabilities. The company had been funding its "normal cost" and whittling away at its past-service liabilities for nearly fourteen years. But the plan, like other bargained schemes, was structured in a way that all but guaranteed a continual stream of benefit liberalizations. Allowances were defined in nominal terms — for example, $100 per month, integrated with Social Security, for thirty years of service — at a level bearing some relation to current wages. As inflation and productivity pushed wages up, pensions rose more or less in tandem; but this pushed up the plan's liabilities, counteracting the amortization program.

The UAW, moreover, also had negotiated bona fide liberalizations. It had lowered the early retirement age to 60, which meant longer and therefore costlier annuities, fewer years of contributions and of investment-income compounding to meet this cost, and more first-tier (retiree) claimants at Studebaker's termination. The UAW also negotiated ten-year vesting for workers over 40 years of age. This created a class of "vested-terminated" workers who drew benefits from Studebaker's pension fund before the termination, and lengthened the line of claimants when the program went bust. With each liberalization, moreover, Studebaker initiated a fresh thirty-year paydown schedule for the resulting increase in its unfunded liability. The company's labor force was steadily aging and its financial position eroding. But Studebaker and the UAW kept extending this heavy fixed-cost obligation further and further past the expected worklife of the plan participants, or even of the firm itself.[11]

At a 1966 congressional hearing on private pension plans, Representative Martha Griffiths suggested, and Studebaker vice president Clifford MacMillan concurred, that "the effect of extending the funding date was to permit you to pay greater benefits." "A new funding period was established," he explained, "so that the immediate cash outlay of the company did not increase dramatically, as it would have otherwise, because you pick up very substantial chunks of liability when you change these benefits patterns." But recalculating the past-service liability and restretching the amortization over the next thirty years kept the pension fund lean. The financing was indeed little better than a "terminal funding" scheme — the actuarially discredited program whereby sponsors simply purchase (or fund) annuities for retiring workers and active employees have no security at all. Studebaker's plan had but a 15 percent "advance" funding ratio: after satisfying retiree obligations, it had just fifteen cents in assets for each dollar of vested liabilities. Thus Studebaker's cash had flowed right through the fund to pay current benefits and secure retiree pensions with little accumulating to secure the credits of young active workers.[12]

Funding weakness was characteristic of collectively bargained plans, with UAW programs actually among the strongest and AFL multiemployer schemes the weakest. Richard Ippolito has estimated that bargained plans, as a group, had "true economic" funding ratios in the order of 60 percent, versus 90 percent for the nonbargained universe. Sponsors of single-employer plans, especially, could have funded more vigorously and actually lost valuable tax benefits by under-contributing. For firms on the ropes, like Studebaker, the reason for this deficiency is readily apparent. The company needed all the cash it could get, and it could get it from no other place. For firms like GM, Ford, and Chrysler, Ippolito offers a second and rather controversial explanation. Underfunding their plans, he says, helped management keep unions in check. Labor would precipitate a pension fiasco should it push too hard, for "future contributions" was the critical "asset" bringing union plans into balance. And "future contributions" depended on continuing corporate success. The funding arrangement made labor a corporate partner, continuing the pension's peace-keeping role it assumed in the 1949 contract negotiations. But as Studebaker showed, workers also became partners in failure.[13]

These holes on the asset side of the pension ledger and the failure of an underfunded plan aroused the loudest public alarms. The holes on the liability side of the pension ledger were different, however. Shortfalls in the accrual of claims were not aberrant events running counter to the intended workings of the program. Sponsors distributed benefits to maximize their labor-management value, and participants and critics found their methods inequitable. The holes in benefit accruals were also far less dramatic — with workers falling through the participation and vesting cracks quietly, steadily, and one by one. But their effects were far broader and resulted, the experts concurred, in a situation where most plan participants would never get a benefit.[14]

Worker claims to pensions were weak on two counts. First, employers asserted rights, increasingly disputed in the courts, to alter or abrogate benefits at will. Second, stringent vesting standards could deny pensions even to faithful long-service workers. In both instances, sponsors violated no law. In both, however, they transgressed common standards of equity.

Employers naturally wished to get the full personnel benefit from their plans, so they raised pension expectations in their brochures, pamphlets, and oral communications. Most fully intended to honor these promises. But pension commitments stretch far into the uncertain future, and employers, advised by their lawyers, limited their liability as best they could. Most plan documents thus presented pensions as gratuitous, free-will gifts. Under this construction, workers had no legal claims and employers could modify, reduce, or eliminate pensions at will.

But gratuitous pensions created their share of pain and offended public and judicial sensibilities. The courts typically had upheld the letter of the plan document through the first half of the century. Should a poor legal draftsman have failed to include the standard exculpatory boilerplate, the courts could enforce a participant's claim using the principle of *promissory estoppel:*

> *A promise* which the promisor should reasonably expect to induce action or forbearance of a definite or substantial character on the part of the promisee and which does induce such action or forbearance *is binding* if injustice can be avoided only by enforcement of the promise.

Most plan documents, however, had explicitly reserved the employer's right to alter or deny benefits. The principle of promissory estoppel thus had limited play in pension adjudication.[15]

Following World War II, shifts in the legal landscape substantially raised the status of participant claims. The Revenue Act of 1942 had insisted that plans be "permanent" undertakings in order to qualify for tax favors. As part of this permanence, the IRS forbade employers to reduce the value of an employee's vested credits. Lawyers for aggrieved participants, meanwhile, attacked the gratuity notion in court. They argued that pension plans should be viewed as "unilateral contracts" that gave employees contractual rights to their benefits. The issue was settled in common law fashion — gradually, sporadically, and with apparently contradictory rulings. Over time, however, the "contract" notion gained ground. All contracts had three parts — an offer, an acceptance, and a consideration given in exchange. In his 1961 survey of the scene Benjamin Aaron wrote, "there is now a respectable body of authority that the pension plan embodies an offer . . . which the employee accepts by remaining continuously on the job and rendering faithful service for the requisite period." The old age annuity is the consideration given in return. Thus "pension benefits, regarded originally as mere gratuities, are rapidly achieving the status of protected legal rights."[16]

Strengthened by this construction, pensions became part of a standard, bilateral contract in the collectively bargained plans that emerged after World War II. First the Inland Steel decision held that pensions were "other conditions of employment," not the employer's gratuitous gift, and therefore legally open to negotiation. Then unions "bought" their benefits at the bargaining table for a given reduction in wages. This practice soon made the "deferred wage" notion of pensions a commonplace. The notion had difficulties, for individual workers typically had no claim to a benefit, supposedly the deferral of their cash compensation, until they satisfied the specified vesting requirements. Nevertheless, collectively bargained pensions and the "deferred wage" notion strengthened participant claims elsewhere in the institution.

Most sponsors, however, were able to parry this assertion of liability. They did so by distinguishing claims against the plan from claims against themselves. Despite what they said or led workers to expect, the liability was (generally) only a claim against the plan; employees had no right to reach through the empty shell of a depleted pension fund to attach the assets of the corporate sponsor. Dan McGill, after surveying a great many plan documents, including the American Bar Association model, found, in general, that the plan document states in clear and unequivocal language that at normal retirement age the eligible participant shall receive a benefit of a stipulated type in an amount determined by a specified formula and commits the employer to contribute whatever sums that may be necessary, when supplemented by employee contributions, if any, to provide the benefits described in the plan. In later sections of the plan, however, the employer says, in effect, that, regardless of what he may have appeared to promise in earlier sections with respect to benefits and their financing, he reserves the right to discontinue his contributions at any time without further obligation to see that the benefits which his employees were led to expect will actually be paid. To further safeguard his right to abandon the plan without any residual obligations, the employer usually incorporates a specific disclaimer of any liability beyond the funds already contributed.[17]

McGill found the practice so common and effective that he reproached "the conventional pension plan" as a mere "declaration of intention" masquerading as something else entirely. Employers, at any point, could break off their participation and extinguish all further obligations as defined by the plan. Even vested benefits, or claims otherwise recognized by the courts as contractual liabilities, would have to make do with the assets in the pension fund. Jack L. Treynor, Patrick J. Regan, and William W. Priest later called this employer option the "pension put." It allowed Studebaker, after it shut down its South Bend plant and cut its pension plan adrift, to limp into Canada with a handful of assets and no further obligation to its former workers.[18]

The second way sponsors limited pension liabilities was through their vesting policies. Employers generally targeted benefits to specific groups — to long-service workers who had earned charitable treatment, to older workers clogging the works, or to middle-aged employees who could contribute careers. Many unions likewise focused benefits on their older, long-service members. For any sponsor, a vesting requirement of twenty or so years, if there was preretirement vesting, was usually a sufficient screen. During the great creation of plans in the 1940s and 1950s, the sponsor's older employees generally qualified for benefits. Most had been on the job during the long expansion from the depths of the Depression, and earned their pensions on the basis of past service. Those who had left prior to the establishment of the plan, of course, were never participants. But as the institution matured, this changed. Increasing numbers of current and former participants began to reach retirement age, with significant years of service, but failed to qualify for a pension.

In 1964 Merton Bernstein presented an exhaustive brief against current vesting standards in *The Future of Private Pensions*. Bernstein gave examples of workers arriving at retirement age with lengthy tenures, but not the twenty, twenty-five, or thirty years required for a pension. He documented cases where trivial technicalities, where a union or plant superintendent shifted an employee from one classification to another, created a disqualifying break in service. But the fundamental problem, Bernstein argued, was that the U.S. economy had become so volatile that workers could simply not expect to remain with a single employer for fifteen or twenty years. The ceaseless rise and fall of industrial and occupational employments guaranteed that few Americans would be the long-tenure workers that sponsors typically targeted for pensions. The incessantly shifting postwar demand for labor, claimed Bernstein, was the fundamental hole in the accrual of pension liabilities.[19]

By the early 1960s, when Bernstein's book was published, vesting deficiencies were joining fiduciary and funding failures as voluble public complaints. The "deferred wage" notion implied full and immediate vesting, as did the example of workers paying for benefits at the bargaining table. Arthur Corbin, Emeritus Professor of Law at Yale University, advanced beyond the "unilateral contract" argument to claim that employees held a legal right to a pension after rendering some "substantial" amount of service; a worker then would be in "substantial compliance" with the employer's unilateral contract. Such claims were of course stronger when employees were prevented from completing the required service through no fault of their own. There were examples and rumors of employers that dismissed older workers to dodge their pension liabilities. But far more common were the issues outlined by Bernstein — layoffs, plant closures, mergers, and the like, all employer decisions taken in response to external economic shocks.[20]

When the Metropolitan Life Insurance Company developed its first commercial pension products, in the 1920s, it could hold itself out as a sober and well-funded fiduciary. But before workers would sign up for its voluntary group annuity or packaged benefit programs, the Met had to satisfy worker notions of equity. Most important, the plans had to include withdrawal rights — payouts to participants who left the plan — that were "equitable" in the eyes of the workers. Vesting is precisely analogous. It is the "withdrawal right" from the trusteed, non-contributory plans of the second private pension institution. Vesting was not a concept of the 1920s; Murray Latimer, in his exhaustive 1932 survey of the institution, made no mention of it. But as insurers in the 1920s had to satisfy common notions of equity, the self-insured programs of the postwar era came under similar pressure to provide equitable standards of vesting.[21]

Expanding the Institution

Reform came slowly, however, for the pension lives largely beyond the pale of public awareness. Hoffa and Studebaker did make the nightly news and were absorbed into the common culture of the nation. But pensions assume a material form for retirees only. Pensions, even then, are what Frederick Herzberg calls "dissatisfiers." The retirees most exercised and attentive are those who *lack* an adequate allowance. Otherwise pensioners, like employers and active workers, focus their attention on more pressing or interesting matters.[22]

The provision of old age income had traditionally been a private affair, a matter of personal thrift or employer discretion. It became a burning public issue only in the 1930s, when a thoroughly "dissatisfied" elderly cohort forced a political fix to their desperate economic condition. With the establishment of Social Security, employer pensions assumed a subordinate role. Public attention focused on the extent of the government's largess, or the extent of individual thrift; the role of employer pensions remained firmly in the shadows.

Nor did the pension gain prominence during the strident debates over U.S. labor relations. Its "fringe" benefit status defined its place at the tail end of compensation disputes, and compensation itself was often peripheral to conflicts over labor representation and power. The one time bargaining did hinge on pensions, in 1949, only a handful grasped the magnitude of the bargain. Indeed, the public took ignorant comfort in the "noninflationary" nature of the settlement.

Nor did the institution capture the public's eye in finance. The institution's rapid accumulation of assets raised scattered alarms about a consolidation of economic power. It certainly magnified the demand for sophisticated Wall Street services. But concerns soon evaporated as the funds remained passive investors and showed no sign of becoming America's new corporate directorate.[23]

The reform movement thus could not emerge out of long-standing debates over the nature and purpose of employer pensions. There were none. Reform came instead in response to scandal. Fiduciary, vesting, and funding lapses kept appearing in the press, and the pain and injustice they caused generated public demands to shore up pension soundness. The pool of violated retirees also kept expanding, and these frustrated workers, with their families, friends, and neighbors, became ever more vocal in their demand for regulation. As the institution slid into government hands, however, another agenda came into play. Officials decided not just to solidify pension expectations but to turn the institution to public ends. Using the political energy generated by frustration and scandal, they would attempt to expand the institution and make private pensions a nearly universal source of old age support for middle-income America.

The movement for reform might properly be dated to the late 1950s, to congressional investigations of the "employee benefit" activities of Jimmy Hoffa and similar union chieftains. Hearings of the Senate Labor and Public Welfare Committee, led by Senators Paul Douglas and Irving Ives, and the Select Committee on Improper Activities in the Labor or Management Field, led by Senator John McClellan, spotlighted ripoffs in multiemployer "welfare" plans (union-run life, health, and disability insurance schemes). Multiemployer pension plans had just gotten off the ground, and Congress discovered scant evidence of wrongdoing there. But pensions were included in the reform legislation developed from these investigations — the Welfare and Pension Plan Disclosure Act of 1958.[24]

The statute, however, was a hopelessly limited law. It did name the U.S. Department of Labor, an advocate of the beneficiary, as the repository for the new fiduciary disclosures. But it required only rudimentary disclosures of trust fund activities and authorized no policing at all. More serious reform was stymied by a standoff between labor (which feared witch-hunts if the law focused exclusively on union-based plans) and business (which resisted regulation of the relatively clean corporate scene). President Eisenhower criticized the legislation but signed it into law because it "establishes a precedent of Federal responsibility in this area." The criticism was justified. Hoffa only *began* his real estate lending in 1958, and the Department of Labor was soon flooded with mail detailing horrors and begging for help. But the department was powerless to act.[25]

Of more importance than the statute, the congressional investigations of the late 1950s introduced John F. Kennedy, Eisenhower's successor, to pensions. Kennedy served diligently on the Senate Labor and Public Welfare Committee, chaired its subcommittee that prepared the reform legislation, and was its principal sponsor and Senate floor manager. His brother Robert had been counsel to Senator John McClellan's committee, where he developed a passionate distaste for the Teamster leader. So JFK, when he became President, stepped up the pursuit of pension reform, and Robert, his Attorney-General, intensified the Justice Department's pursuit of Hoffa. The President got Congress to toughen fiduciary standards, especially in the 1962 amendments to the 1958 Act. The legislation gave the Secretary of Labor power to force disclosures, check the accuracy of plan submissions, and institute criminal penalties for self-dealing, kickbacks, and embezzlement.[26]

Kennedy, however, had glimpsed a larger agenda. Government thitherto had viewed the pension quite narrowly, focusing on tax avoidance and now fiduciary misconduct. But in March 1962 Kennedy ordered a broad examination of the entire employee pension and welfare institution. He established a cabinet-level committee, chaired by the Secretary of Labor, to conduct "a review of the implications of the growing retirement and welfare funds for the *financial structure* of the economy, as well as a review of the role and character of the private pension and other retirement systems in the *economic security system* of the nation, and consideration of how they may contribute more effectively to efficient *manpower utilization and mobility.*" Kennedy asked this committee to submit legislative proposals by fall — in time for the upcoming 1963 congressional session.[27]

The cabinet committee duly submitted its report in November. It confined its comments to pensions, excluding welfare plans, citing a lack of time and the complexity of the assignment. In response to President Kennedy's queries, it recommended no new initiatives to regulate interactions with the capital or labor markets. But the role of private pensions in the nation's economic security system emerged as the committee's dominant focus. In its letter of transmittal to the president it declared: "the aim of the Committee was to explore the potentialities of private plans as part of the Nation's economic security system and to suggest ways and means by which these plans can play a more effective role as part of this system." This concern for old age income security would refocus government's legislative approach to pensions and would underlie a drive not just to shore up the institution but to expand it.[28]

In 1962 Social Security benefits stood at about the same level as in 1950, after Congress had restored allowances to the 1939 benchmark. The "average" benefit replaced 30 percent of the "average" U.S. wage — far below the 50 percent rule-of-thumb minimum and half the common 60 percent target for an adequate old age income. (For couples with nonworking spouses, adding the minimum spousal allowance brought the "average" household replacement rate to 45 percent.) Social Security actually replaced less than 30 (or 45) percent of *preretirement* income, as James Schulz would show in 1968: while Social Security based benefits on earnings across the beneficiary's entire workspan, workers typically earn above-average wages at the end of their careers. So while the U.S. economy was enjoying its long postwar expansion, and active workers were earning ever higher incomes, the old were fast becoming a notoriously poor population. Agitation for higher benefits began in earnest with the inauguration of a Democratic president in 1961. The movement would result in the enactment of Medicare in 1965 and in a major expansion of Social Security allowances, with benefits statutorily pegged to inflation, in 1972. This concern for old age income security informed the cabinet committee's approach and became its impetus for reform.[29]

The committee saw a need to expand private pensions, even if Social Security benefits were higher. "Even with significant future improvement in the public program there will still be ample room for supplementation," it declared, "especially among career employees with above-average earnings." Social Security was first and foremost a floor of protection. Its allowances never offered significant replacement toward the upper end of the wage base. And as the committee emphasized, the wage base had also slipped quite sharply; more than half of all male workers in 1961 had earnings above the Social Security wage base — up dramatically from 6 percent in 1935. These workers not only got the lowest replacement rates on the Social Security schedule, they also had income that the public program made no attempt to replace.[30]

Other industrial nations were at the time reworking their old age income systems in similar fashion. They were pushing for more adequate replacement rates for middle-income earners and enlisting the participation of private retirement schemes. Like their American counterparts, they hoped to shift income from the years of work to those of retirement, and they sought to do so gaining the benefits of private arrangements: greater flexibility in plan design, investment in the private sector, and reduced demands on the taxing power of the state.

Initiatives in Britain and Canada were most important to U.S. planners. They were the easiest to follow, for these nations were English-speaking, and they had similar political traditions. Both Britain and Canada had public plans that emerged out of means-tested welfare programs that paid low, flat benefits. In 1959 the British government proposed a graduated, earnings-related pension atop these flat allowances and allowed, indeed invited, employers to "contract out" of this upper, earnings-related supplement. (Champ Clark's unsuccessful amendment to the 1935 Social Security Act would have allowed employers to "contract out" of the entire public program.) The expansion of pensions in Britain thus formally absorbed private plans into a universal government-directed program. In Canada the Ontario government designed a program relying even more directly on private arrangements. Reminiscent of the Met's 1923 "American Pension Plan," which would have required universal participation in a privately insured program, Ontario's Committee on Portable Pensions, in August 1961, proposed a similar mandate. All organizations in the province employing fifteen or more workers would have to establish a plan with minimum vesting, funding, and benefit levels.[31]

Kennedy's cabinet committee knew of these initiatives, but had no mandate to pursue such ambitious political agendas. Nevertheless, income security for the elderly was the lens through which it viewed private pensions. In this the administration was well in advance of public opinion. National attention on the matter remained fixed on Social Security or on the reliability of private pension *expectations*— that workers get the "deferred wage" benefits for which they had "paid." The cabinet committee, by contrast, focused on the reliability of the private pension *institution*. It reasoned that government, too, had paid into the private system. Stanley Surrey, Assistant Secretary of the Treasury and that department's key representative on the cabinet committee, priced private plans at "a current revenue loss of $1 billion annually." This represented 1 percent of government receipts, and Kennedy's task force expected a comparable contribution to public welfare: "The basic justification for the indirect public subsidy involved in favored tax treatment must lie in the social purpose served by private pension plans. They constitute an important rounding out of the Nation's income maintenance programs for retired workers."[32]

The fundamental thrust of the committee's report was the need to expand the private pension institution. To justify the substantial cost to the Treasury, many more people would have to accrue claims. The institution's "liabilities" would have to expand, making private pensions nearly universal for middle-income Americans. The committee's central reform was thus mandatory vesting. Too few workers collected a pension because sponsors rewarded just managers and long-service workers, not leavers. By forcing employers to vest shorter-service workers, the committee would directly expand the number of participants who in fact got pensions. To get the principle on the table, the standard it proposed was "graded" and mild: tax-favored plans had to vest 50 percent of accrued pension credits after fifteen years of service, and the rest over the next ten years.[33]

The cabinet committee was also enamored with "portability," a broad and slippery term that included vesting as a special case. Portable arrangements allow workers to leave an employer and take pension credits with them. Social Security and multiemployer plans are highly portable schemes: workers earn credits according to a single schedule that covers a universe of employers. The accruals are uniform, continuous, and portable from firm to firm. So long as workers remain in the system, accruals from a previous employer are treated exactly like past accruals from their current employer. The private components of the Ontario and British schemes were also portable, but less so. Workers earned their credits according to schedules defined by their employer (above the mandated minimum rate). These credits were frozen in quasi-nominal terms upon termination: their purchasing power above the mandated minimum rate was not preserved against the ravages of inflation. Nor did it rise as the worker's wage increased; here portability is reduced to vesting. In both nations proposals also called for a central government agency to record all vested accruals and stand ready to assume the liability in exchange for an actuarially equivalent payment.[34]

The committee did not give details on its portability ideas, but no doubt had British- and Canadian-style programs in mind. What it proposed was a central government portability agency (perhaps the Social Security Administration) to record all accruals and offer to cumulate disparate pensions and pay retirees a single, aggregate benefit. The committee thought this facility had significant advantages beyond vesting alone: "The potential of private pension systems in supplementing OASDI benefits could be more fully achieved by arrangements to provide for *portability* of pension credits and permit credits earned with different employers to be combined in computing an individual's pension benefits."[35]

While expansion was the committee's overriding ambition, it could not ignore issues of "soundness." Congress and the public thought of such holes when thinking of pension reform, and their concerns had substance. Extending pension liabilities, the administration's objective, could be foolhardy so long as assets were short. So the cabinet committee proposed ways to shore up soundness. But lest it derail its central campaign for vesting, it did so in ways that avoided controversy.

Four strategies for bolstering the asset side of the pension balance sheet lay on the table: improved fiduciary conduct, faster funding of past-service obligations, making employers liable for pension benefits, and creating a pension insurance scheme. The committee picked only funding, the obvious, common-sense proposal. Fiduciary reform was obvious, but faced stiff resistance; the two other attacks, employer liability and insurance, represented new political initiatives.

Current law essentially guarded against excess funding. It protected the Treasury by setting upper limits on pension contributions. The government also set minimums to assure that a scheme was a permanent, bona fide employee benefit plan: each year sponsors had to pay in the currently accrued "normal cost" plus "interest" on the unfunded past-service liability (thus "freezing" the size of this deficit). Enormous past-service obligations were the primary source of financial insecurity in the postwar plans, and requiring sponsors to pay them down was the obvious reform. So the committee proposed the mandatory amortization of past-service obligations over a "reasonable period — such as the expected average years of service of plan participants, but in any case not more than 25 years." It would also require the amortization of liabilities created by plan amendments and/or losses in the pension fund "over an appropriate period of years." Pension obligations clearly had to be matched by assets other than vacuous "future contributions," and compared to the other approaches to soundness, funding was the least objectionable politically.[36]

Various writers, including Dan McGill, entertained the notion of making pensions a legal liability of the corporate sponsor. "Future contributions" currently balanced the pension plan books; could a formal bond or employer guarantee replace this informal "security"? Would it not be equitable, for the employer had promised the pensions and presumably had captured some benefit? In times of distress, should the employer be allowed to terminate the plan and hide its assets behind an empty pension fund shell?[37]

No matter where equity lay, however, sponsor liability was not a promising line of attack. Most insufficient terminations were accompanied by the bankruptcy or near-bankruptcy of the sponsor, so attaching its assets would rarely yield much. The threat of attachment could even precipitate the failure of a firm and its plan, by scaring away creditors. And then there was politics. So recognizing that an employer guarantee was "a far-reaching change in the character of the legal obligation involved, . . . [the cabinet committee does] not believe such a requirement is feasible at the present time."[38]

The committee also sidestepped aggressive fiduciary reform. It knew full well that the public and the Commission on Money and Credit (the ostensible stimulus to reform) thought of little else when thinking of pension failures. But a campaign for tougher regulations would rile the unions; nor would the administration target only labor, for it knew of corporations that appeared to be taking liberties with pension fund assets. Overseeing corporate plans, however, would ruffle business feathers. So the committee took the politically prudent path. It rejected the Commission on Money and Credit's assertion that "the problem is one of enforcing existing standards." The committee backed away from the need for a government agency to

> watch out for the collective interests of employees and their beneficiaries and, if necessary, to bring suit in behalf of plan participants. The Committee believes it is premature, short of a real test of the effectiveness of the disclosure approach as a means of enforcing standards of fiduciary responsibility, and in the absence of sufficient facts as to the prevalence of abuses, to make a recommendation for regulatory action of this kind at this time.

The committee indeed saw a rationale for loosening the standards of fiduciary conduct: "with minimal liquidity requirements and long-term investment objectives, private pension funds are especially well situated to be flexible and responsive to changing investment opportunities . . . The question is how to permit broad exercise of discretion on the part of trustees or plan managers but to hold them to the highest standards of fiduciary responsibility."[39]

A pension insurance scheme, the final means of shoring up pensions, had been suggested and pushed by the UAW. But insurance otherwise attracted scant attention and remained a nettlesome notion on the periphery of the pension debate. Any program would clearly be complicated, and few in business could be expected to view it with favor. The committee noted "very serious problems in designing any such insurance scheme," and only proposed "further study."[40]

The cabinet committee thus cleared the decks for vesting and portability, for expanding the institution, by avoiding other points of controversy. And to get expansion on the table, it kept its vesting and portability proposals unusually mild, especially compared to the radical initiatives going forward in Britain and Canada.

The response to the committee's report, however, was neither benign nor slow to develop. President Kennedy forwarded the document to his Labor-Management Advisory Committee, a sounding board of the nation's most powerful economic interests. The group included top corporate executives, union presidents, respected experts in labor-management relations, and (ex-officio) the secretaries of labor and commerce. The advisory committee received the cabinet report in January 1963, and pensions became its primary focus of attention for the rest of the year. The advisory committee's response, delivered in December, was hardly auspicious for the party of reform.[41]

A majority of the advisory committee supported the "soundness" agenda, although the margin was thin. It narrowly sanctioned stepped-up funding, but would set the standard at the commonly used thirty-year paydown rate. It endorsed stepped-up disclosures of "prohibited [party-at-interest] transactions" and even added a fiduciary control of its own — that investments in employer securities be limited to 10 percent of pension fund assets. But the barons of the advisory committee flatly rejected mandatory vesting, the cabinet committee's touchstone proposal. They would go part way with financial "soundness," but rejected "expansion" out of hand. Individual members had further complaints, and nine submitted critical written comments. Only two offered written statements of support.[42]

Five corporate executives submitted comments, all critical. They all saw their pension plans as private affairs and resented government intrusion. They warned that new regulations would be burdensome and costly, would stymie new plan formation, and thus contract, not expand, the institution. Several also objected quite pointedly to proposals that constrained their ability to design different compensation packages for different groups of workers. (Existing practice allowed flexibility so long as upper-income groups were not disproportionately advantaged.) They especially opposed regulations that could extend collectively bargained benefits to all employees. Thus Henry Ford II, chairman of Ford Motor Company, urged:

> The widest possible scope should be given to private decision-making in the design of private pension plans, consistent with the public interest in preventing abuses. The present Treasury regulations covering qualified pension plans already afford protection against abuses, and to my mind the Committee has not been presented with convincing evidence of the need to change them in the respects recommended in the report.
>
> The suggestion for changing the present Treasury rules so as to require the application of a generally similar pension plan to all classes of employes is particularly disturbing. The suggestion may seem innocuous, but it would in fact introduce a distortion in the collective bargaining process, and it also ignores the fundamental fact that a pension plan is but one part of total employe compensation . . . [and would] reduce needlessly the scope for adapting compensation to the differing needs, desires and circumstances of various employe groups.[43]

Somewhat surprisingly, to those unfamiliar with pensions, most labor leaders lined up alongside management to criticize the committee report. David Dubinsky of the International Garment Workers Union, Joseph Keenan of the International Brotherhood of Electrical Workers, W. Anthony Boyle of the United Mine Workers, all with multiemployer plans, plus George Meany, president of the reunified AFL-CIO, all attacked the administration's funding and vesting proposals. AFL multiemployer plans had by far the lowest levels of vesting and funding in the entire institution, and these AFL leaders saw no need to change. Participants could move from one covered employer to another without affecting their accruals, said the union chiefs, so they had little or no need for vesting. Dubinsky and Keenan objected to funding standards and wrote, in their comment, that "the likelihood of termination of such plans is farfetched" because their schemes covered entire industries.

Labor also objected to higher vesting and funding because they would force down benefits for any given level of employer contributions. Thus Boyle complained that "if we were to apply the recommended minimum funding requirements suggested in the report to many private pension plans such as the United Mine Workers Welfare and Retirement Fund, the reserve for accrued benefits would need to be increased by several times or, in the alternative, benefit levels would need to be slashed correspondingly, although no imperative need is shown for either." In sum, union leaders resisted comparison to the world of single-employer plans and pictured their schemes as little Social Securities — universal, portable, unfunded systems.[44]

The one labor leader to wholeheartedly support the committee's program was Walter Reuther. He endorsed mandatory vesting, echoing the administration's rationale:

> A private pension system which actually provides benefits to fewer persons as rapid technological change increases employee turnover, or a private pension system which impedes the necessary mobility of labor, does not contribute to the social objectives which the favorable tax treatment accorded pension plans is intended to achieve.

Reuther in fact recommended the stricter vesting standard used in UAW plans — full vesting after ten years of service. He argued that the increased cost "will not be substantial" and that

> if the end result may mean slightly lower benefits for persons who remain with the employer until retirement age, I believe that tax advantages should not be afforded to a program which, like a lottery, pays benefits to these fortunate few, but rather should be limited to pension plans which assure benefits at least to those employees who have been covered by the plan for at least 10 years.

And Reuther, long a champion of funding, argued that funding was "essential" if private plans were to "be financially able to meet their commitments."[45]

Reuther took these positions because he viewed the UAW as the leader of a larger labor struggle, and he saw these reforms as beneficial to workers in general. He also hoped to shore up the UAW's somewhat exposed position in pensions. Reuther's union was well ahead of the pack in securing old age benefits for its members. From the beginning it had insisted on funding and its 1955 pact with Ford had established ten-year vesting as the national "progressive" standard. These features cost money that could have gone to higher cash wages or to current pension allowances. By imposing similar standards on other plans, Reuther could dampen invidious comparisons to the fatter pay envelopes and benefit checks enjoyed by other union members.[46]

The general hostility of the advisory committee, however, came as a shock. The cabinet committee had developed its program in the spirit of American individualism and belief in progress. As it declared at the opening of its report, "one of the distinctive features of American life has been its concern for the individual. The welfare of the individual worker and his family after he has completed his working life has been steadily enhanced through major advances in both private and public policy." The administration now hoped to take another step forward. But the nation's economic powers, the organizations that employed or represented a major portion of the U.S. workforce, had smacked the reformers down. The policies of these organizations, of course, were the very targets of reform. And the barons had made their objections heard even before the cabinet had made its report public. The struggle thus was joined. At the beginning of 1964 the administration had to decide whether to stop or proceed; whether to let the issue die or to challenge this wall of organized opposition.[47]

Securing Expectations

That the Employee Retirement Income Security Act was ultimately enacted, in 1974, is far more remarkable than the time it took to win passage. Opposition by the leaders of American big business and labor, as represented on the Labor-Management Advisory Committee, was a powerful obstacle. So was the general ignorance of pensions among politicians and the public alike. Moreover, John F. Kennedy was dead. He had been assassinated in November 1963, even before the advisory committee had submitted its response. His successor, Lyndon Baines Johnson, had no personal interest in pensions, and without vigorous presidential leadership, the task of fashioning a workable consensus and pushing a bill through Congress would be enormously complicated. ERISA's passage could thus be nothing but long and tortuous.

Key administration officials were nevertheless committed to reform. They included the Secretary of Labor, Willard Wirtz; the Assistant Secretary of the Treasury, Stanley Surrey; and the chairman of the Securities

Exchange Commission, Manuel Cohen. So the mood in the administration had a feisty edge. In preparation for a key February 13 cabinet committee meeting, Walter Heller, the judicious and respected chairman of the Council of Economic Advisers, asked his aide Myron Joseph to survey the landscape. After discussing the situation with compatriots in other departments, Joseph put as good a face on the situation as possible. The advisory committee had concurred on the need to tighten funding and fiduciary standards, he wrote, despite the narrow margin and the written dissents. The barons opposed corporate liability for benefits and urged further study for insurance; and so did the administration. Joseph even cited the advisory committee's agreement in "principle" on the virtues of vesting. He concluded:

> The Cabinet Committee can accept the principal recommendations of the LMAC without too much loss. The vesting position is the major point of disagreement. The Cabinet Committee could make a strong statement supporting the principle of vesting — and recognize the need for further study of the costs of implementing the principle in different industrial situations.[48]

As it turned out, 1964 was a good year for the reformers. Merton Bernstein published *The Future of Private Pensions,* and his vigorous 300-page brief for mandatory vesting gave a jolt to the pension debate. Studebaker, however, was the blockbuster event of the year. The spectacle of 7,000 workers getting nothing or fifteen cents on the dollar became an instant national scandal and created an enormous call for reform. So the cabinet committee revised its report and stuck to mandatory vesting and the expansionist program. In January 1965, nearly three years after President Kennedy had set the process in motion, it finally published its report and the advisory committee's response.

The cabinet committee then proceeded to the task of drafting its bill. It hired as its consultant Dan McGill, the widely respected head of the Pension Research Council. It divided itself into small working groups, heard from a wide array of technical experts, and in 1966 renamed itself the "Inter-Agency Staff Committee" on private pensions. Treasury and Labor remained the lead agencies. They had experience, expertise, and responsibility for pensions, and they had programs of reform they wished to enact. Treasury focused on its traditional concerns — tax avoidance, discrimination, and coordination with other parts of the Revenue Code. Labor took up the newer issues of vesting, fiduciary regulation, and insurance. The two departments jointly addressed funding, and Labor continued giving overall direction. In each substantive area, rafts of sticky technicalities had to be tracked and nailed down, and maintaining coherence was a continual problem.

The group from the Treasury, led by Stanley Surrey, attacked the notoriously complex and interest-infested thicket of pension taxation. Here Surrey picked up where he had left off in 1942: the campaign to block abuse of pension tax favors and assure that benefits flowed down to the bona fide employee ranks. Thus Surrey drafted tighter requirements for participation, benefit accruals, and Social Security integration — all to deliver more benefits to lower-paid and shorter-service workers. He reintroduced the notion of caps on benefits and contributions, to limit tax relief to "middle-income" pensions. He also revised the treatment of lump-sum distributions, so plans could not serve so readily as investment tax shelters with minimal contribution to the government's objectives for old age income maintenance.

Although Labor had the clearer slate, even straightforward issues like vesting got thorny. How much work in a year, for example, was needed to qualify for the vesting requirement — 500 hours? 1,000 hours? 1,500 hours? How long must a break in service be before the employer could set the vesting clock back to zero — six months? two years? ten years? More critically, what vesting principle should the administration back? Should it stick with graded vesting, giving workers a partial claim after partial service? That approach promised to spread benefits most widely, but was administratively complex and rarely used in practice. Most plans had "cliff" vesting — giving workers a legal claim to *all* accrued credits when they crossed some milestone (typically years of service, or service plus age). Also on the table was the "Rule of X" — vesting all credits when the sum of a worker's age plus service equaled X (typically 40, 45, or 50) — which gave added weight to age. The administration, for the moment, stuck with the graded approach. It wanted to maximize the number of beneficiaries and was not especially bothered by complexity.[49]

While administration technicians chiseled away, the Congress began percolating with pension activity. Various committees turned to examine the subject, the most active being the Subcommittee on Fiscal Policy of the Joint Economic Committee, chaired by Martha Griffiths. Testimony from its 1966 hearings on private pension plans filled two volumes, and in 1967 it published a solid, six-volume compendium of papers on "old age income assurance." Meanwhile, members of Congress were filing their own bills and expanding the legislative agenda. The administration had focused on the liability side of the balance sheet, to extend pension claims widely. Congress directed its attention to the asset side — to controversial issues the committee had tried to finesse.

Fiduciary infidelity, that pension perennial, again reared its head in the summer of 1965. Senator John McClellan's committee uncovered still more egregious abuses that violated no existing statute. (The Disclosure Act, even after the 1962 amendments, essentially still demanded only disclosure.) McClellan asked the Labor Department to draft a remedial bill, which strengthened the hand of reformers who would put the issue back in play. Manuel Cohen, chairman of the Securities and Exchange Commission, was perhaps the strongest voice for fiduciary reform. He oversaw another fiduciary-beneficiary relationship at the SEC — that between the directors and the shareholders of joint stock corporations — and he brought this experience to the pension debate.[50]

In any institution, fiduciaries are agents of beneficiaries considered by law too ill-informed, ill-organized, or immature to protect their own interests. Governments impose standards of reporting and conduct to protect beneficiaries and thereby encourage the use of socially valuable fiduciary institutions. Congress already had developed special disclosure rules for pension trusts and would develop more in the future. Cohen now directed attention to conduct.

The common law of trusts demanded two things of pension fiduciaries: strict *loyalty* to the interests of plan beneficiaries, and *prudence,* or probity in all investment decisions. Adaptations were needed in each, however, as standard common law protections had failed miserably. This was so because pensions violated a key assumption of trust law: the existence of a community of interest between sponsors and workers. Trusts were presumably established by "grantors" to benefit the beneficiaries, and legal attention focused on controlling infidelity and mismanagement on the part of the fiduciary agent. But there was a great deal of conflict in employer-employee and union-worker relations, as labor law presumed. Almost all fiduciary breaches in pensions could be traced to actions taken by sponsors, not agents. As the grantors of the trust, they could write instructions into the basic trust agreement that gave them effective control of the assets. They could direct the trustees to buy company securities or invest in Las Vegas casinos, with the presumption that their interests and those of the beneficiaries coincided.

Congress had addressed the company securities problem in 1942 by requiring prior government permission for any purchase. The 1958 Act required disclosures of any "prohibited transaction," but had left it to the aggrieved beneficiaries and the courts to straighten things out. This strategy to control the broader conflicts had failed; the government ultimately had to convict Hoffa of mail fraud. So Cohen now insisted on a "prophylactic" approach. He would preempt grantor instructions and allow no "prohibited transaction" (aside from the 10 percent investment in sponsor securities — the limit proposed by the advisory committee) without prior governmental approval.[51]

The cabinet committee report had also urged a shift in the prudence standard. Under common law of trusts, each investment had to be individually "prudent." Cohen and others on the committee were aware of a sophisticated new approach to investments then being introduced on Wall Street. Diversification and the performance of the portfolio as a whole were the key ideas. Investments "imprudent" by themselves thus could increase the "prudence" of the entire fund. Put and call options, for example, could hedge a stock portfolio; a portfolio with volatile investments and low-risk securities could yield a standard investment-grade return at lower overall risk. Recognizing the fast-evolving pace of investment management, Cohen also resisted a statutory definition of prudence and instead required pension fiduciaries to keep up with thinking in the industry.

Congress soon opened a second contentious debate, which the administration had hoped to avoid, in response to the Studebaker failure. Faster funding was the cabinet committee's key proposal on the asset side of the ledger. But as Studebaker had shown, this mandate alone could not guarantee pension payments. Studebaker had been amortizing its past-service obligations on a thirty-year schedule when the company's business had hit the skids. Its workforce had shrunk as sales had declined, but its pension obligations had hardly budged. As had been revealed in the Great Depression, pension plan costs tend to be fixed, not variable; this is especially so for plans with large unfunded liabilities. Seniority practices lead employers to retain older workers who have higher "normal costs," and much higher "past-service" claims. As huge unfunded liabilities were endemic to the second U.S. private pension institution, and especially to negotiated plans, its costs became an added source of stress when a sponsor's business turned down. To make private pensions a reliable source of security, a base of financial support other than thirty-year paydowns clearly had to be found.

After Studebaker, the UAW initiated a determined campaign for insurance. At the instigation and with the help of the UAW, Senator Vance Hartke introduced a bill to establish a federal insurance program in August 1964. Hartke represented Indiana, home of Studebaker's South Bend plant, and he filed his bill in advance of the impending November termination. The proposal was rough and many issues were unaired. Hartke, for example, pegged premiums to the size of the plan's unfunded liability. But critics asked whether the insurer should accept the sponsor's calculation or must prescribe baseline actuarial methods and factors; either choice carried serious complications. Other critics asked whether the insurer should also gauge risks in the fund portfolio or weigh the sponsor's financial stability or funding commitment. What, moreover, constituted termination? Was the shutdown of a plant and a sponsor's declaration of a plan termination sufficient — as happened at Studebaker — or would the firm itself have to go bust? Could a viable firm simply terminate its plan and turn any unfunded liabilities over to the insurer? "As a first effort at formulating a complex problem," wrote McGill, Hartke's "bill was understandably drawn in very general terms and failed to come to grips with many of the technical problems that would be encountered in such an undertaking." It soon died in committee.[52]

But two months after the release of the cabinet committee report, in March 1965, Hartke reintroduced his measure. Administration officials had viewed insurance sympathetically, but had seen it as a difficult and controversial initiative. They sought to sidestep the issue for the moment. Their report had reiterated the call for "serious study" and had defined a set of fundamental questions that would have to be addressed: "Is the possibility of a plan's termination an insurable risk? What types of termination (bankruptcy, merger, etc.) could be included? Is experience available on which to set a premium? How would such an insurance arrangement be administered?" But Hartke and his allies in labor would not be put off and insisted that an insurance scheme be part of any reform package.[53]

The intensity of the UAW's post-Studebaker embrace of insurance is indicated best in a speech delivered by Howard Young, the union's actuarial consultant, in April 1965. Young based his argument on what was becoming the touchstone of pension reform — the rising volatility in the U.S. economy. Young said it sharply increased the likelihood of Studebaker-type terminations and made such events a matter of chance, not the outcome of union or management decisions. But in exchange for insurance premiums, a plan could solidify its balance sheet with a contingent claim on the insurance pool. The lucky firms that prospered would cover the unlucky ones caught and destroyed in the economic storms.[54]

The huge unfunded liabilities in collectively bargained plans, and their precarious dependence on "future contributions," made such risks politically untenable. Active workers paid for the system but bore all the risk. "If the private pension system is to survive," Young asserted, "a means must be developed to assure those currently providing money to pay benefits that their benefits will in fact be paid when they reach retirement age." Young's advocacy of insurance extended to the point that he saw it as an alternative to funding: "The goal is security of benefit expectations and a realistic recognition of costs. Funding is merely a means to that end; if other mechanisms — particularly the re-insurance proposed — can achieve the goal, then our present ideas about the need for funding must be reassessed." He entertained the notion that the combination of insurance and partial funding could be a permanent and preferable arrangement to the standard full-funding objective. Insurance could secure retirement benefits without "[tying] up a substantial amount of assets," and Young doubted there were enough investment-grade assets to support an expanded institution — an observation commonly made with regard to Social Security.[55]

Howard Young's pension system would not be so private. In addition to standard pension fund assets, a compulsory "insurance" mechanism — supported by the taxing power of the state — would stand behind private benefit promises. Private plans would thus be partly "social insurance" schemes (à la Social Security); they would lie halfway between their current straight-capitalist, advanced-funded status and the Railroad Retirement program — the totally socialized remains of the nation's first foray into occupational pensions.[56]

Needless to say, such lines of thinking attracted little support in business circles. Executives in the nation's most powerful firms saw little need for insurance, for their funds were full and their cash flows strong. Robert E. Royce, Secretary of the Benefits Committee of AT&T, characterized the fiasco at Studebaker as the outcome of a gamble taken —

and lost — by consenting adults: "The parties entered into an arrangement which would work well if Studebaker prospered, and which would not yield all of the hoped for results if Studebaker could not afford to continue it." The outcome of any federal "insurance" scheme would likely be a tax on the rich and prudent to bail out someone else. And the someone else would likely be aggressive unionized workers. Royce asked, rhetorically, "Was there anything anti-social or against sound public policy in [the] agreement between Studebaker and the UAW to run the risks which were inherent in their bargain? Should the parties who assume the risk of establishing a pension plan with large unfunded liabilities expect others to bail them out if things go wrong?"[57]

Business could also dismiss Studebaker's termination, though shocking and painful, as aberrant. A 1967 study of plan terminations, by Emerson Beier of the U.S. Bureau of Labor Statistics, found only *0.1 percent* of all participants affected each year. Many or most of these workers suffered little or no losses, he continued, because their pension funds were sufficient (or nearly so) or they were transferred to a successor plan. Beier had no information on workers who lost jobs and benefits prior to a plan's termination; the numbers in some instances were large, as with Packard Motors after the firm was merged with Studebaker. But his baseline figure — one-tenth of one percent per annum — was sufficiently small to comfort business. Beier's research, moreover, contradicted Young's claim that rising economic instability was causing an increase in plan terminations. Terminations were up, but so was the number of plans. "The *rate* of termination," Beier reported, "has consistently remained around 1 percent of active plans."[58]

The strongest argument against insurance was the threat of "moral hazard"— that the program would *increase* the incidence of insufficient terminations. By taking the sting out of catastrophe, critics charged, insurance actually encouraged "accident-prone" behavior. The U.S. Chamber of Commerce presented the case succinctly in Senate hearings on Hartke's bill:

A primary requisite of an insurable risk is that the occurrence of loss must be accidental or fortuitous. Ideally, this would preclude any possibility that the loss of claim would be under the control of the insured.

The liability involved in pension plans and the extent to which past service liabilities are funded are usually within the direct control of the employer. This poses the problem of pension insurance *causing* dis-incentives to funding, unrealistic benefits, and other possible abuses.

With the plan's financial condition and the decision to terminate largely controlled by the sponsor, the insurer had no clear way to limit coverage to cases of true "distress" terminations. Firms (or unions) on the edge, with cash flows stretched thin, could pay workers in *credits*, unfund their plans, and gamble with pension fund assets. The government insurer would inevitably be drawn not just into funding policy but into the pattern of benefit accruals and investment management as well.[59]

In many collectively bargained situations, insurance also presented employers with "moral hazard" threats. Insurance vitiated the discipli-nary value of an underfunded plan: if union exactions bankrupted the sponsor(s) and "future contributions" dematerialized, vested workers would still get their pensions. The cooperation business hoped to buy with a pension, and "secure" with an underfunded plan, would be put at risk.

Business executives essentially dismissed insurance as unworkable or an invitation to theft. They rejected Young's assertion that fate con-trolled the fortunes of a plan and that growing economic instability would generate a rising tide of "no-fault" plan terminations. (They also resented the implication that luck, and not hard work or talent, ex-plained their own success; and they repressed the uncomfortable im-plication that someday their firm could succumb to Young's incessant competitive pressure.) Business thus saw Studebaker's fiasco as the re-sult of decisions freely taken. Management bought loyalty, commit-ment, and retirements — at significant cost — because they contributed to the success of the firm. In collectively bargained situations, the pur-chase came in a risk-laden game. Insurance would radically change the rules, playing fast and loose with existing institutional boundaries and incentive schemes. Young's ambitious vision would do so in ways that especially threatened the current distribution of wealth and power.[60]

In February 1967, while the experts and interest groups were still struggling in a sea of technical detail and political trade-offs, Senator Jacob Javits, Republican of New York, shocked the process by intro-ducing his own comprehensive reform bill. Javits had already weighed into the pension debates in impressive fashion. He was the ranking minority member of the Senate Labor and Public Welfare Committee — the focal point of pensions in Congress. There he collaborated with the committee's minority counsel, Frank Cummins, who had worked for Studebaker and understood pensions from a practical point of view. Javits also served on Senator McClellan's investigatory committee (on "Government Operations") and had co-sponsored a fiduciary reform bill. He sat on Martha Griffith's subcommittee and, at its opening session in April 1966, laid out an ambitious legislative agenda that mirrored Canadian initiatives. He reported on developments in Ontario, where the provincial government had developed a comprehensive set of funding, vesting, and fiduciary regulations (adopted after Canada enacted a national public pension system, preempting Ontario's mandatory private pension scheme). Javits argued that the United States needed a similar approach. So in 1967 he introduced a bill calling for vesting, funding, insurance, fiduciary standards, a government-run portability scheme, and a central regulatory authority. Javits's contribution was not in the technical details, but in tying all issues together and bringing comprehensive reform to a head.[61]

On the key issues, Javits set reasonably centrist mandates. He called for vesting after fifteen years of service and the attainment of age 45. (He also allowed a graded schedule of half after ten years and the rest after twenty.) He would require sponsors to extinguish past-service liabilities within a thirty-year period. And his bill included insurance. (Unlike Hartke's scheme it insured only benefits; pension fund losses remained the sponsor's headache.)

Capping his proposal, and giving institutional form to his comprehensive vision, Javits proposed a central agency, an independent federal commission, to oversee private pensions as a whole. Javits saw the pension as a complex, dynamic institution. Only a single regulatory authority, he argued, could respond effectively to the inevitable shocks in its economic environment and shifts in the power, and interests, of its various constituents. Oversight currently was divided, primarily between the IRS Pension Trust Division in the Treasury and the Office of Labor-Management and Welfare Pension Reports in Labor, with officials in agencies ranging from the SEC to the Social Security Administration having authority over various secondary matters. Javits would subsume many of these functions in his pension authority and give it the added responsibility of operating a national pension portability scheme, accumulating the various bits of vested pension credits and assets into a single old age allowance.

The Javits bill, Michael Gordon reports, "startled the administration and galvanized the interagency task force into speeding along the drafting process." The Republican had offered an ambitious and fully integrated program. The administration now had to produce a "competitive" bill.[62]

Javits's institutional proposals — a central pension agency and a government repository for portable credits — were listed in the original cabinet committee reports. But the administration was rapidly backing away from both. As noted by McGill, the Canadians had authorized a portability program but had not set one up and the British had examined and rejected the notion. Ambitious schemes involved tremendous political and financial difficulties, even when restricted to vested credits. Inflation-proofing, for example, would be tough to implement and could favor terminated workers, perversely, over active employees. (Only they would get a government guarantee on the "real" economic value of their accrual.) A portability scheme that preserved just the nominal value of a vested credit, McGill observed, "would offer no advantage not currently available through the purchase of fixed or variable annuities from life insurers," and benefits that remained liabilities of trusteed plans would be protected by Javits's pension insurance scheme.[63]

The administration task force also nixed the central pension agency idea for political reasons. Stanley Surrey had reported to the group that Representative Wilbur Mills, the powerful chairman of the Ways and Means Committee, saw significant merit in business's various objections to pension reform. So Surrey, and the task force, saw considerable merit in avoiding Representative Mills. Attempts to absorb the IRS Pension Trust Division and its enforcement responsibilities into a pension megaagency would inevitably pass through Ways and Means. So the task force dropped the single agency idea and designed its proposal as a purely labor bill, to be administered by the Department of Labor and to come under the friendlier jurisdiction of the congressional labor committees.[64]

The administration made its bill "competitive" in the core funding and vesting requirements. The original cabinet committee had proposed rather mild standards. But pressed by Javits, the task force now pushed for tougher measures. It returned to its twenty-five-year amortization period for unfunded liabilities, where Javits had proposed a thirty-year paydown. It now demanded ten-year cliff vesting, where

Javits set the main hurdle at fifteen years of service plus forty-five years of age. These differences, in hindsight, do not seem significant.

A year after Javits introduced his bill, in early 1968, the debate was set to begin. Wirtz and his team finally had drafted their far more detailed proposals, and the Bureau of the Budget, the administration's central legislative gatekeeper, had given its green light. Congress was primed. Business, labor, and other interested parties were fine-tuning their positions and lining up lobbyists.

The prospects for reform were thin. There was the general hostility of organized business and much of organized labor. The CIO demanded insurance, but business abhorred the idea. And Javits's expanded vision pushed the reform initiative into regions dominated by congressional conservatives. The administration thus had lost control of the agenda. The campaign for pension reform had expanded beyond vesting and funding to accommodate fiduciary reform, insurance, portability, and administrative shifts. The issues grew sharper and more complex and involved an increasing number of fundamental interests. Nevertheless, with the administration actively campaigning, there was a chance a consensus could be fashioned in the give-and-take of Congress.

The Politics of Enactment

The Employee Retirement Income Security Act had originated as a presidential initiative in the Kennedy administration. The drafting was largely done in the executive branch during Lyndon Johnson's tenure in office. But before the congressional debate could commence, presidential politics intervened. At the very last minute Johnson himself pulled the plug. Rumor has it that Henry Ford II told the President, in no uncertain terms, that pension legislation was a litmus test. If Johnson went forward, Ford warned, he would forfeit all big-business support in his upcoming reelection campaign. Johnson then apparently contacted old Capitol Hill pals, congressional barons such as Wilbur Mills. They told him how intense business resistance on pensions could be, and that they would not touch the issue with a ten-foot pole. Johnson decided that this would be his policy too.[65]

Wirtz was incensed. He and his staff had spent years on the bill. Key constituents — the CIO and the liberal wing of the party — were primed and clamoring for action. So despite Johnson's instructions, in what was "widely believed to reflect an act of rebellion," he sent the bill to Congress in May 1968. It went to the Hill as the "Wirtz Bill"—a Labor Department initiative, not an administration proposal. A sympathetic Senator Ralph Yarborough of the Labor Committee held hearings and sponsored the bill, and Wirtz and several aides gave testimony. But without Johnson's backing its prospects were nil.[66]

Presidential politics then intervened again, and again against the cause of reform. Johnson, facing mounting opposition to the Vietnam war, the outbreak of ghetto riots, disarray in his party, and a stunning rebuke (though not an outright loss) in his contest with Eugene McCarthy in the New Hampshire presidential primary, abdicated the race for a second term. Hubert Humphrey, his liberal-minded successor, then lost the November elections to Richard Nixon, a moderately conservative Republican. Nixon had no interest in the expansive pension reforms originating in the liberal wing of his own party (the Javits bill), let alone the bills proposed by the liberal wing of the liberal party. His administration would go along with the ever-more-popular fiduciary reforms. It also would develop the "individual retirement account" program, which allowed workers not covered by an employer plan to save part of their annual compensation (the lesser of $1,500 or 15 percent of compensation) with the standard pension tax favors and withdrawal restrictions. But Nixon had little interest in advancing the central vesting, funding, and insurance initiatives for employer plans. With his election, all administrative wind left the sails of pension reform.[67]

On the face of it, ERISA should have died in 1968. Johnson's kibosh eliminated presidential support for this complex and contentious cause. Nixon's election then installed an administration that countered the reform agenda with minimalist alternatives. But the half-dozen years between the abdication of Johnson and that of Nixon, in 1974, were anything but a normal political season. A series of hurricanes washed across the Washington landscape. As they did, a skilled assault by the reformers finally brought ERISA to life, at the dawn of Gerald Ford's caretaker presidency.

Critical to ERISA's passage was the declining resistance to pension reform. The sharpest conflicts had been over vesting and insurance, and both proved less contentious with the passage of time. During the run-up to the aborted 1968 congressional battle, a blue-ribbon panel said, "the proposed injection of federal vesting standards into the regulation of private pension systems is the key issue in the current pension debate. This is apparent from the statements of both advocates and opponents of the proposal." Insurance was the fundamental demand of the CIO, the only powerful interest group that supported reform. Insurance was the primary benefit the CIO stood to gain from reform, and it could win such a safety net only from Congress. The business community, however, rejected insurance out of hand, viewing the notion as so out-landish that they gave it little serious consideration.[68]

While vesting took center stage in the Washington policy debate, real-world changes were undercutting the opposition to federal mandates. On its own, the pension institution was gravitating toward the proposed legislative targets. This was especially so for the collectively bargained plans that had emerged after World War II, claimed Jack Barbash, Robert Tilove, and other defenders of negotiated arrangements. These schemes initially had focused on supplementing the meager allowances Social Security paid out to currently retiring workers. After these plans had met this initial need, Barbash and Tilove argued, they could add more generous vesting provisions and build up their pension fund assets.[69]

Surveys conducted by Bankers Trust and the Bureau of Labor Statistics showed that vesting and funding had indeed reached their nadir in the mid-1950s, when the new collectively bargained plans had been established. Employer contributions, in many such schemes, were simply passed through the plans to pay benefits to current retirees. Liabilities for initial "past-service" obligations were typically huge, vastly exceeding the slim asset buildups, and such sponsors dared not expand their commitments by adding generous vesting provisions. It was then — in the late 1950s and early 1960s — that demands for reform grew loud and insistent. But vesting and funding both turned up over the course of the 1960s and, by the end of the decade, surveys conducted by Bankers Trust and the U.S. Bureau of Labor Statistics had picked up this trend toward "soundness." Convincing confirmation was provided by a long-awaited Pension Research Council study conducted by Frank Griffin and Charles Trowbridge, released in 1969. Vice presidents and actuaries at the Wyatt Company and Bankers Life, respectively, Griffin and Trowbridge had access to internal corporate and insurance company records covering 9 million participants. Their data showed about half were covered by a ten-year (or equivalent) vesting rule and 81 percent of all accrued benefits were vested. Assets, moreover, "were sufficient, on average, to cover 94.4 percent of all accrued benefits . . . [and] an even greater proportion of *vested* benefits." These vesting and funding levels were sharply higher than most had expected, and than the levels of a decade earlier.[70]

Griffin and Trowbridge likewise challenged the primary source of resistance to mandatory vesting: they showed it to be surprisingly cheap. Vesting benefits for terminated workers, with ten or more years of service, absorbed less than 2 percent of total plan expenses, they estimated. Howard Winklevoss and Dan McGill then confirmed this result in an elaborate simulation conducted under contract to the Senate Labor Committee. Their results, accounting for factors such as the replacement of vested workers with younger, less expensive workers, also arrived at extremely low cost figures. By the early 1970s sophisticated business circles thus viewed vesting and funding mandates as far less onerous than they had just a few years prior. The goals would be easy to reach, and not too burdensome to keep.[71]

A second PRC contribution, Dan McGill's slim 1970 volume *Guaranty Fund for Private Pension Obligations,* may have had an even greater impact on the passage of ERISA. A bill without insurance was a political impossibility, for the CIO absolutely insisted on the inclusion of a safety net. But business had refused to give the concept serious consideration. McGill neutralized much of this resistance, reports Michael Gordon, by creating a rough consensus among pension experts that insurance was both desirable and feasible.

McGill first showed the usefulness of insurance. "Insufficient terminations"—plan terminations with insufficient assets—could be intensely painful, as Studebaker had shown. So protection had value. The cost would also be low, if history was a guide. As Emerson Beier reported, fewer than one-tenth of one percent of all participants were affected each year. While this figure was not the best, it was low enough for McGill to conclude that the cost would be moderate. He also proposed a relatively tractable and unobtrusive method for calculating a plan's unfunded liability, which could serve as the basis of a risk-adjusted premium. In the event of some large unexpected shortfall, mandatory assessments against the universe of sponsors could augment these premiums, as in the federal insurance plan for bank deposits. In the rare event of a general crisis, such as a depression, McGill thought that the "government should assume an appropriate share of the total burden in recognition of the fundamental nature of the risk."[72]

In the business community moral hazard emerged as the central contentious issue. Would the existence of benefit insurance create a riskier system, and thus more terminations with insufficient assets? To control moral hazard, McGill would deny coverage to any benefit liberalization within five years of the plan's termination; floundering firms could not pay workers with benefits to be paid by other employers (via the insurance system). But McGill's primary defense was employer liability for benefit payments and making the failure of the firm, not its abandonment of the plan, the triggering event. Employer liability had been proposed in the past, by McGill and others, as an equitable extension of the employer's pension promise. Business, of course, was bitterly opposed and reformers recognized that sponsors in insufficient terminations were typically insolvent. So neither the cabinet committee nor mainstream bills had called for such claims against the sponsor. But now McGill gave employer liability a conservative, not liberal, purpose — to control moral hazard in a benefit insurance regime. He argued that such claims would induce typical sponsors, far from the brink of bankruptcy, to limit the risk in their plans. With business failure as the triggering event, there was no escape from any shortfall. Employers thus would be chary about giving excessive benefits or risking their pension fund assets.[73]

The growth of pension soundness, and the recognition that a viable insurance scheme was possible, led to a calming of business resistance during Nixon's years in the White House. But the reformers were not so quickly calmed. "Soundness" may have been rising, as vesting and funding advanced. But other indications were troubling. Increasing labor mobility meant vesting had to expand just to keep the level of benefit accruals constant. The size of the second U.S. private pension institution, moreover, was approaching its natural limits. Its noncontributory defined-benefit plans were adjuncts to big business and unions, and the significance of these large employment organizations was peaking. Thus, where coverage had grown from 19 to 41 percent of the workforce between 1945 and 1960, it grew to only 45 percent by 1970. Using carrots to extend the institution to smaller firms, with their impermanent workforces and tax-avoiding owners, was strikingly inefficient; a given gain in public welfare cost far more in forgone tax receipts than in the large corporate plans. And Surrey's group in the Treasury was actually tightening restrictions and reducing inducements in the small-business sector. Existing plans, moreover, already covered most of the middle- and upper-income earners who needed supplements to Social Security allowances. At one time or another, the great majority were included in the 45 percent of the workforce currently covered by the private pension institution. So the vesting mandates on the table seemed the best approach to expansion, and the *de minimis* requirements for making private pensions a part of the nation's old age income system.[74]

With a resistant Nixon in the White House, the initiative in the campaign for reform now shifted to the Congress. Various senators and representatives, such as Javits, Hartke, Yarborough, and John Dent (who sponsored the successor to the Wirtz bill) had staked out positions and were far too invested to quit. And as Michael Gordon points out, Congress was ascendant in the half-dozen years between the fall of Lyndon Johnson and that of Richard Nixon. Urban riots, strident antiwar protests, drugs, youth culture, feminism, gay liberation, and the oil shock of 1973 had turned the U.S. political landscape upside-down. The big losers, notes Gordon, were business, labor, and the President; the big winner was Congress. Responding to a vociferous nation, the 93rd Congress had the temerity to enact legislation ranging from the Clean Water Act to the War Powers Act, and then to force Richard Nixon from office.[75]

Pension reformers in the Nixon years also adopted a new political tack. In addition to legislative wrangling, they launched a concerted campaign to influence public opinion. Their message focused not on national old age income policy, an issue of no media value, but on "soundness" and scandal. They displayed case after case of violated expectations, which had tremendous audience appeal, not the probability that John Q. Public would get an adequate old age pension. Gordon and other reformers had accumulated a fat portfolio of "horror stories" while working at the Labor Department, and until now had been unable to do much about them. But the media had a "ravenous appetite," says Gordon, for stories of workers denied pensions because of vesting hurdles, breaks in "continuous" service due to a layoff, illness, job change, or the like, or terminations with insufficient assets due to funding deficiencies or fiduciary malfeasance. Gordon and his colleagues helped the CBS and NBC television networks produce one-hour prime-time specials on violated expectations. They also directed local newspapers and TV stations to workers in their communities who had suffered such wrenching denials. The number of frustrated claimants had been accumulating over the years, roughly in line with the rapid growth of private pensioners, and they now seemed to be in every locality, and available for the nightly news.[76]

The people who value a pension allowance most intensely are those who need one, thought they had one, but had it taken away. They are generally old and poor, and get short shrift in the normal political process. But the media, especially TV, brought their suffering and anger to the living rooms of a sympathetic public. Here they generated a political asset which, in the topsy-turvy of the Nixon presidency, helped the reformers outflank Washington's traditional interest-group politics. As in the campaigns in the 1930s for railroad retirement and Social Security, public opinion carried the battle and most elected officials were late to discover the intensity of grass-roots support for pensions.

At crucial junctures in the campaign for ERISA, the public's rising demand for reform proved decisive. When the House Labor Committee turned to the subject, in March 1972, it began with a series of hearings on termination insurance, which it conducted out in the field. There it discovered the breadth and intensity of support for reform, which helped convince John Dent (the Democratic chairman) and John Ehrlenborn (the ranking Republican) to go forward. In the Senate, in September 1972, the Senate Finance Committee demanded and received jurisdiction after the Senate Labor Committee had unanimously cleared the Javits-Williams pension bill. The Finance Committee totally gutted the measure. It eliminated the vesting, insurance, and funding provisions, eliciting an uncharacteristically vicious assault from Javits on the floor of the Senate. Congress then adjourned for the fall election campaigns, the Finance Committee senators no doubt eager to flee the "Jacobin" rhetoric on Capitol Hill. At home, however, they found similar opposition to their actions on pensions. On the stump, on the street, and in newspaper editorials, their constituents registered support for reform with surprising intensity. Soon after Congress reconvened, in December 1973, Gordon reports, the Senate Finance Committee proved suddenly cooperative. Indeed he credits their help in fashioning a far more precise and technically proficient bill.[77]

From 1973 through mid-1974, four congressional committees — the House and Senate labor and finance committees (in the House, the Ways and Means Committee) — worked diligently on ERISA's provisions and language. It was a mammoth piece of legislation. It addressed the full panoply of pension issues and needed to satisfy four congressional committees, each with its own turf and constituency. In line with government's traditional concerns, ERISA restricted discrimination in favor of owners and upper-income employees; it tightened Social Security integration allowances, capped benefit and contribution levels and benefits insured by the new Pension Benefit Guaranty Corporation. In line with traditional fiduciary concerns, ERISA broadened fiduciary obligations to cover all who made or influenced plan decisions, expanded the list of "prohibited transactions," and required prior approval from the Department of Labor for all exceptions.[78]

Congress also defined its new interest in funding, vesting, and benefit insurance. The funding of past-service liabilities was set at a thirty-year paydown rate. As academic studies showed the costs and benefits of the vesting proposals then on the table to be roughly equivalent (ten-year cliff, five- to fifteen-year graded, and rule of forty-five), the lawmakers compromised, included all three, and allowed sponsors to pick. Congress also hammered out the basic design of the insurance scheme. It included employer liability to control moral hazard, but limited this liability to 30 percent of corporate net worth, and allowed plan terminations without the failure of the firm. Congress set a non-risk-adjusted premium of $1 per head; the actuarial cost appeared so low that Congress adopted this patently unfair but simpler and administratively less expensive arrangement. Multiemployer plans got special treatment: looser vesting and funding requirements, a $.50 per head insurance premium, and postponement of any pronouncements on the contentious issue of employer liability. Various other matters also pushed their way in, now that pen had hit the paper. Congress made joint-and-survivor the default annuity form and required certification of the actuarial calculations by an actuary enrolled by a board that the Secretaries of Labor and Treasury would establish.[79]

ERISA'S passage then got a final push from external events. The oil shock of October 1973 sparked an unprecedented peacetime inflation and the sharpest economic downturn since the Great Depression. The disruption threatened the tenure of long-service workers and challenged the viability of various sponsors. It also undermined the solvency of a great many schemes. The stock market crashed, with the Dow Jones Industrial Average falling from over 1000 at the beginning of 1973 to 730 by August 1974; the inflation pushed up interest rates, eroding the value of fixed-income securities held in pension funds. Richard Ippolito's calculations of the critical "economic advanced funding ratio"—

the degree to which pension fund assets covered obligations to active workers — fell by a third. Much of the institution's progress toward soundness since the early 1960s thus had come undone. And congressmen received urgent messages from constituents who feared that they would lose their benefits if ERISA's vesting mandates and insurance scheme did not become law.[80]

Support for ERISA also benefited from Richard Nixon's final downfall, observes the attorney Steven J. Sacher. While four congressional committees were laboring away on pensions, the main show in Washington, in 1974, was the Watergate hearings, where Congress was methodically dissolving the Nixon presidency. ERISA had been locked in a House-Senate conference committee since March, with representatives and staff from all four committees ironing out details. Then, on August 8, Nixon resigned. There was a feeling, in the aftermath, that the U.S. political process had broken down. Washington needed something to demonstrate that this was not so, and Sacher believes that the congressional leadership, to reverse this sense of drift, accelerated ERISA's progress. The bill was reported out and passed by the House on August 20 and by the Senate on August 22. ERISA became the first major piece of legislation to land on the desk of Gerald Ford, the nation's new President, and he signed it into law on Labor Day, September 2, 1974.[81]

The Meaning of ERISA

ERISA was indeed an ambitious and a wide-reaching initiative. In response to public opinion, it policed the commitments made by big business and unions, the most powerful players in the American economy. The legislation also aimed at expanding this personnel instrument of private employers into an instrument of national social welfare. The bulk of Americans now worked as employees. They could expect to grow old, thanks to medical advances, and retire when they could no longer keep pace with a job. But employment generated no assets — aside from public and private pensions — that could sustain them when their years of work were done. Employers gave pensions in exchange for a specific labor contribution — loyal service, a career, or termination at an appointed age. Social Security gave pensions in exchange for essentially any wage labor. ERISA, using the leverage of federal tax favors, would turn the former into something more like the latter.

To broaden the distribution of adequate, well-secured employer al-lowances, Congress would expand the balance sheet of the private in-stitution. ERISA would increase liabilities through its coverage, parti-cipation, and vesting mandates. It bolstered the asset side of the ledger through stepped-up funding and the new benefit insurance scheme. Congress also specified a tougher fiduciary ethos, so that pension fund assets would be used more effectively to satisfy the institution's ex-panded obligations.

The private pension promise had always been an oddball financial instrument. Employees acquired their claims not with money but with labor of a specified form. The benefit was often bundled with other types of insurance, such as disability, life, and survivorship. Unlike stan-dard annuities, pensions typically carried inflation protection, even if implicit and partial. The ultimate value of the allowance also depended on a host of contingencies during both the accumulation and payout periods. And the institution's conversion of labor to old age income was accomplished over durations that far exceeded the lifespans of all but a handful of economic institutions.

After an experimental period in the nineteenth century, the noncon-tributory defined-benefit pension plan became standard in the first two decades of the twentieth century. The employer alone secured the pen-sion arrangement. The sponsor provided the opportunity for employees to work and accrue benefits, and paid allowances out of its operating budget on a pay-as-you-go basis. Growing awareness of the accruing nature of plan liabilities, and of the fragility of the worker's position, led to various restructurings in the 1920s. As employers recognized the accruing nature of their obligations, there was a brief vogue for "bal-ance-sheet reserves." The approach helped sponsors manage their plans in a more rational fashion. But the government refused to extend tax benefits to the "contributions" and "investment income" of balance-sheet programs, so the practice died out.

Insurance companies also entered the field in the 1920s, offering contributory, deferred-annuity contracts in lieu of the employer's pen-sion promise. These securities were government-regulated contracts. They had withdrawal rights and were backed by a portfolio of senior claims against solid economic entities, typically governments and blue chip corporations. But the financial performance of these instruments proved totally inadequate in the inflating and booming postwar era. Given continual shifts in employer needs, Social Security, and IRS regulations, their provisions were far too rigid. So for large and mid-sized sponsors, insured pension arrangements also died away.

The 1920s also saw the growth of advance-funded trusts, and by the third quarter of the twentieth century they had become the dominant medium of pension finance. Most of these early trusts were little more than extensions of the balance-sheet reserve. In the latter, pension obligations were balanced by a bookkeeping claim against the sponsor, typically a deduction from the "shareholder's equity" account. In advance-funded trusts, cash was taken from the asset side of the corporate ledger and transferred to the plan trustee; then the trustee bought securities, or claims against corporations or other entities, in the financial marketplace. In the 1920s and early 1930s, the cash in these trusts was often transferred right back to the sponsor in exchange for the employer's bond(s). As pension trusts could be revocable, the arrangement was often functionally equivalent to a balance-sheet reserve, but one that garnered tax benefits.

The government, however, tried to pry these trusts away from the sponsor. Congress gave tax breaks to private plans because they delivered socially beneficial old age allowances, and it wanted to solidify the delivery of such benefits. So in 1938 Congress denied tax advantages to revocable pension trusts. In 1942 it set a floor on funding, forbade the expansion of a plan's initial "unfunded" liability, and required prior approval for the purchase of employer securities. These initiatives clearly differentiated advance-funded trusts from balance-sheet reserves. They stimulated the accumulation of pension fund assets and placed them beyond the sponsor's grasp. Diversifying pension fund assets *away* from sponsor securities also broadened a plan's base of support. Benefit payments would derive not just from the employer's future cash flow but from cash that arrived from other organizations, via trust fund securities; it came from dividends, interest payments, rents, royalties, or the sale of these financial claims.[82]

To the extent that private pension funds held claims on the corporate sector, the institution as a whole could be viewed as a balance-sheet reserve for Corporate America. Each sponsor balanced its pension-plan liabilities by accumulating assets in a pension fund. The corporate stocks and bonds held in this trust, however, were liabilities on the books of other firms; while the financial obligation was transferred from the sponsor to another firm, and was transformed from a pension obligation into a debt or equity claim, it remained within the corporate sector.

Corporate stocks and bonds accounted for about two-thirds of private pension fund assets from 1960 forward. Significant unfunded liabilities incremented still further this private-pension dependence on corporate assets. Like a balance-sheet-reserve plan at the corporate level, the setup could be seen as a paygo affair managed in a more rational fashion. Pension allowances would be paid mainly out of Corporate America's current cash flow — out of employer contributions, dividend and interest payments, and PBGC transfers. The cash was passed to Corporate America's retired workforce, via the pension institution, from income generated in its various constituent parts.[83]

Even though this extended pension apparatus had not been created by the federal government, Congress defined the fiduciary ethos to direct the institution. From 1921 forward it had given its tax favors only to plans that acted for "exclusive benefit" of "some or all of the employees," and not for the sponsor. ERISA stiffened the exclusive-benefit rule with prophylactic loyalty, detaching plan investments more thoroughly from the sponsor's interests. The statute's new prudence standard emphasized diversification and the risk-return interactions of financial instruments, orientations that also distanced the pension investor from the enterprises receiving its funds. ERISA's "institutional man" standard thus conjured a clean, transparent fiduciary engine, one that maximized each plan's ability to deliver its specified benefits, given its assets, projected cash flow, and risk preference. The ethos would shift funds from declining to expanding sectors and from less to more effective management teams. It would keep the institution afloat in a fluid financial world, focused on fulfilling pension expectations, largely untethered to the world of concrete corporate enterprise.[84]

In pursuit of retirement income objectives, private pension fiduciaries invest about one-half of their assets in common stock and own about one-fifth of outstanding corporate equities. "Institutional man" investors bought stock for financial reasons, for their attractive risk-return trade-off given the pension fund's long-term perspective. (Pension funds have negligible liquidity constraints, so the volatility of equity values is largely irrelevant.) Substantial common stock ownership, however, involved the pension fund's "institutional man" investors in the sticky world of corporate ownership decisions. Should the firm do business in South Africa? How tough should the corporation be in dealing with labor, local communities, or the federal government? Should management be replaced? The accumulation of common stock in private pension funds made employees (in the guise of plan beneficiaries), or fiduciaries acting in their behalf, the principal owners of their corporate employers. It made the institution the overseer of the sponsors which had brought it to life. This irony, which Peter Drucker in 1976 called "the unseen revolution: how pension fund socialism came to America," grows roughly with the ratio of funded pension obligations to corporate equities outstanding.[85]

The independent role of the sponsor, however, would not be overwhelmed so quickly. Employers and unions remained special, for the plans were *their* incorporations, not those of the federal government. They originated the schemes voluntarily and could terminate them at will. The government might mandate that a worker vest after ten years of service. But the opportunity to labor ten years, let alone the time needed to earn an adequate old age allowance, required the sponsor's longevity and its decision to continue the plan. Congress could mandate prudent diversification. But the sponsors remained the institution's primary financial guarantor. Aside from bankruptcy, when the PBGC took over, sponsors were responsible for meeting unfunded liabilities, the actuarial miscalculations, pension fund losses, and bouts of unexpected inflation. Because of these responsibilities, Congress in 1974, like the UAW in 1950, explicitly allowed sponsors to select the plan trustees (almost always their own executives) and to set the mutually dependent contribution rate and the basic investment strategy. Congress restricted the sponsor's freedom. But the corporate employer retained the initiative, and ample discretion, in administrative and financial matters.[86]

What ERISA created was a far more complex institution, with the government joining employers and unions as an active and assertive participant. In the past, government had been reactive. It had accommodated pensions to its new income tax system; then it had policed the most egregious fiduciary breaches. With ERISA government took on a more ambitious agenda. It would turn private pension arrangements into a quasi-public, national institution.

Private pensions, a century after their arrival on the continent, had been established as a normal aspect of economic life. The institution had developed a life of its own and had come to be owned, in part, by many key players. ERISA tied private pensions even more tightly to the three basic institutional pillars of the U.S. economy: big business, big labor, and the federal government. It established an intricate institutional web through the nation's labor and financial markets. It routinized the agency relationships between the nation's households and its engines of corporate production — the employment relationship between management and labor and the investment relationship between beneficiaries and management. And the entire apparatus functioned, for itself and these institutional players, so long as it helped the average American traverse the modern industrial economy to a reasonably comfortable old age.

Epilogue

◆ ◆ ◆

Pensions and
Post-Industrial Capitalism

Old age pension institutions emerged in the United States, as in all industrial nations, in response to the rise of the rational factor-market economy. Households came to earn dramatically higher incomes by selling their labor to corporations, governments, or other extrafamilial employers that provided them with tools and materials, supervision, and tasks that greatly enhanced their productivity. But when this labor grew old, its productive power decayed and the inflow of wage and salary income ultimately came to an end. Clear-sighted households prepared for this eventuality by accumulating stocks, bonds, bank deposits, rental properties, and other income-producing assets. But in very few cases was the effort sufficient. So in all industrial nations, employers, unions, governments, and financial intermediaries stepped in to develop old age pension mechanisms — vehicles for transferring income from the years of employment to those of retirement, or from active to retired workers.[1]

The U.S. private pension institution appeared in the last quarter of the nineteenth century as large and long-lived employers, primarily railroad corporations, found reasons to offer their employees old age income benefits. The plans helped these firms get diligent service out of blue-collar workers, secure career commitments from white-collar workers, and facilitate retirements at a specified age. Pensions became a standard component of big-business personnel systems and spread across the industrial landscape in the first quarter of the twentieth century. In the second quarter the environment shifted. A segment of the U.S. business community developed the skills and facilities to manage

private pension arrangements; and the government established its massive Social Security pension program, legitimated collective bargaining,
and instituted a regime of broad and progressive income taxation. In
the third quarter of the twentieth century, on the basis of these structural changes, the institution renewed its expansion and came to approach ubiquity for the nation's middle- and upper-income households.
This expansion culminated in 1974, exactly one hundred years after the
first private plan had appeared on the North American continent, with
the passage of the omnibus Employee Retirement Income Security Act
(ERISA).

Congress enacted ERISA to secure and enlarge the institution and
build private pensions into the sinews of the U.S. economy. Through
the remaining years of the 1970s the effort was modestly successful.
Vesting, funding, and fiduciary conduct all improved, and the institution survived the decade's stagflation and the anemic performance of
the nation's securities markets. Participation, however, fell slightly —
from 39 percent of the private-sector workforce in 1975 to 38 percent
in 1980 — as ERISA's regulatory burdens and its restrictions on tax-
avoiding "top tier" schemes led to the termination of many small plans.

Despite ERISA's intent, the institution then began to weaken and
contract at a rather rapid pace. A dramatic runup in securities prices
after 1980 did push the value of pension fund assets, in many cases,
well above the value of plan liabilities. But huge financial shortfalls
emerged in critical sectors. And participation, the single most telling
measure of long-term institutional health, has fallen precipitously.
Whereas in 1980 38 percent of the private-sector workforce was enrolled in a plan, by 1987 that figure had fallen to 31 percent.[2]

The factors underlying this sharp decline, and its implications for
national well-being, are poorly understood. Some blame ERISA itself.
The law's regulatory burdens, hyper-rational standard of fiduciary conduct, and rising Pension Benefit Guaranty Corporation (PBGC) premiums clearly sped the contraction. Others cite the stagnant or declining real wages of much of the workforce. This sapped the vitality of
pension programs as workers, struggling to maintain consumption levels, increasingly opted for cash in lieu of pension compensation. But in
the argument sketched out below I find the primary source of decline
in the larger institutional setting. Private pensions, in the United States,
were creatures of big business, big labor, and big government. After
the passage of ERISA, and especially after 1980, all three either grew

weaker or became less interested in pensions. This erosion of structural support led to the first broad contraction of private pensioning in the history of the institution. From this perspective, ERISA neither solidified nor undermined the nation's private pension institution; it merely marked its high-water level.

The Decline of Organized Labor

Of the pension's three structural supports, organized labor has had the toughest time negotiating the final quarter of the twentieth century. The period has seen a huge expansion of the labor force — a 43 percent rise between 1974 and 1984, as the Baby Boom generation came of working age and more married women left the home for the workplace. This surge in the supply of labor put pressure on all compensation levels and work expectations, but especially on the structured employment arrangements found in collective-bargaining settings. The 1980s also began with the nastiest recessions since the Great Depression of the 1930s, and the U.S. economy has since been characterized by unusually high real interest rates and intense foreign competition. This hit the nation's manufacturers of mass-produced durable goods, the CIO's employers, especially hard. The AFL likewise has declined in importance as economic activity has shifted rapidly to nonunion occupations, regions, and industries. The rising employment of women undercut both branches of organized labor, for the unions traditionally represented men in male employments. The strength of U.S. unions thus dissipated rapidly. Membership stood at 21 million in 1979, representing 24 percent of the nation's workforce; but by 1985 unions represented only 17 million workers, 18 percent of the workforce. While total membership thereafter declined slowly — to 16.6 million by 1993 — the unionized share of the private-sector workforce continued to plummet: membership fell from 11.2 to 9.6 million between 1985 and 1994 — from 16.8 to 10.9 percent of the expanding private-sector workforce.[3]

This rapid union decline produced a sharp contraction on both the asset and liability sides of the pension ledger. In 1979 bargained plans accounted for more than half of all participants in the private pension institution. Three of four union workers were enrolled in a plan, versus one in four in the nonunion sector, and a portion of the latter got benefits only because their employers felt compelled to meet or match the union standard. The rapid decline in organized labor resulted in an absolute fall in enrollments in union plans. Between 1975 and 1987 participation in the AFL's multiemployer schemes fell by 1.8 million, or 26 percent; among industries organized by the CIO, coverage at the Big Three automakers fell by 210,000, or 22 percent. The U.S. labor force had meanwhile grown by some 30 percent. As a result, union members, in 1987, accounted for just one-third of the diminished share of private-sector workers accruing private pension claims.[4]

Sponsors find their pension obligations far more difficult to manage when profits vanish and employment contracts. Layoffs tend to eliminate younger, cheaper participants while stepped-up retirements — another response to the shrinking demand for labor — add to the payout burden. Unless the plans have been conservatively costed and funded (that is, on a level-premium-type method), pensions, unlike other payroll items, are more a fixed than a variable expense. So the charges become increasingly burdensome as a sponsor runs into economic trouble. The distress proved unusually sharp in the collectively bargained sector, for despite ERISA's funding mandates and CIO traditions, negotiated plans entered the final quarter of the century in an asset-deficient condition. So when the number of union members fell sharply, after 1980, the finances of many plans tipped radically out of balance.

Bargained plans, as we have seen, were funded in a way that all but guaranteed chronic asset shortfalls: labor contracts defined pension benefits as a specific dollar amount per year of service, not a percentage of the worker's projected final salary. This specified benefit per year of service rose, in each new contract, roughly in line with wages. As a result, the *value of* credits earned in the past — the plan's "past service" obligation — kept ratcheting up, ever ahead of the accumulating stock of pension fund assets. The inflation of the 1970s and early 1980s further aggravated these shortfalls by raising (nominal) benefit levels, and past-service obligations, at a pace far faster than anything seen in the past.[5]

The negotiated plans of the 1980s were further weakened by initiatives launched in the 1960s, in response to the unions' slowly eroding strength in the postwar U.S. economy. In 1945, at the dawn of the era of collectively bargained pensions, organized labor had represented 35 percent of the U.S. workforce. Through the 1950s unions continued to represent about one-third of all workers. But representation thereafter trended down, reaching 24 percent of the workforce in 1979, as employment grew faster than union membership. While the number of organized workers continued to rise, employers were substituting capital for high-cost union labor, and hiring disproportionately more non-union managerial, professional, technical, and administrative workers. Certain unions, notably the Steel Workers, had difficulty in the 1960s keeping their members employed. So they embraced a program of retirements — using generous early-retirement pension incentives, as the Mine Workers had done in the mid-1940s — to clear the market of excess union labor.[6]

The union campaign for retirements was facilitated, if not predicated, on the government's 1961 decision to allow men to retire at age 62 on a reduced Social Security allowance. (Women had been given the option in 1956, in part to allow them to retire at the same time as their presumably older husbands.) Labor contracts signed in the mid-1960s not only offered workers voluntary early-out pensions, they encouraged retirements by subsidizing the benefit: unlike Social Security, they lowered the early-out benefit by *less* than the "full actuarial reduction"— by less than the amount needed to offset the longer expected payout and the shorter time to accumulate contributions and investment income. These incentives proved ineffective, however, for benefits were low while the rewards from continued employment remained substantial. Even at age 65, CIO plans replaced just 15 percent of pre-retirement income and total replacement, with Social Security, approached just 30 percent. Remaining at work would not only pay over three times the cash, it would also raise the worker's old age pension benefit (by adding a year of service and by avoiding the early-retirement reduction on past-service credits; an additional year of work would lift Social Security allowances about 8 percent, and private pension benefits by a lesser amount). Such pension accruals ceased only at the "normal" retirement age; thereafter an additional year of labor meant the worker lost his pension payment without any increase in his future allowance. So after calculating their options, most workers decided to stay on the job to age 65, then retire.[7]

The union campaign to induce retirements succeeded with the contracts signed in the early 1970s, while ERISA was wending its way through Congress. Labor negotiators pushed private-pension replacement rates to about 30 percent of pre-retirement income. They also won "thirty-and-out," a contract provision allowing workers with thirty years of service to retire with unreduced benefits at a specified age (usually 62); workers who wanted to retire even earlier would usually see only modest reductions from these generous benefits and would get supplementary allowances until they became eligible for a government pension. After the Social Security increases of 1972, workers in these new union plans could retire at age 62 on about 50 percent of pre-retirement income. Staying on the job paid twice the cash, but required work, and work-related expenses, and would no longer increase the worker's future pension benefit. After calculating their options, union workers began retiring en masse between the ages of 59 and 62. Union negotiators thus turned the collectively bargained pension institution, initially an instrument for assuring workers a minimal old age income, into a high-cost tool for controlling the market for labor.[8]

This transformation exacerbated the problem of chronic asset short-falls in collectively bargained plans, as Robert C. Kryvicky has shown. The jump in benefits and the longer payouts raised the sponsors' obligations; "thirty-and-out" essentially guaranteed that past-service obligations would never be amortized on a thirty-year pay-down schedule. And as Kryvicky further has shown, the absolute drop in union employment after 1980 pushed many bargained plans even deeper into insolvency. The schemes now amassed barely enough assets to meet their expected obligations to current retirees. Like Studebaker's in 1964, their financial profile approximated "terminal funding"—a regime in which sponsors funded benefits as workers retired and set aside nothing for the active workforce. ERISA's funding mandates, based on "normal costs" and the gradual amortization of unfunded past-service obligations, rarely required larger contributions. And as the market value of blue-collar labor had begun its long decline, negotiators had less economic strength with which to fill the widening gap in plan finances. ERISA's benefit insurance program, moreover, protected worker benefits and dissuaded the unions from demanding more vigorous funding.[9]

The declining strength of organized labor means fewer blue-collar workers now earn private pension claims. Minorities and less-educated workers, who disproportionately earn their livelihoods through manual labor, have thus seen their access to a private pension narrow. Even union members with vested benefits now stand on shakier financial ground. In a terminal funding regime, plan viability relies on a continuing stream of sponsor contributions, or on the strength of the government's benefit guarantees. And in the 1980s, a difficult decade for blue-collar labor and its employing corporations, sponsors of negotiated plans increasingly chose, or were forced, to terminate their plans and put their unfunded obligations to the PBGC.

The Retrenchment of Government

The federal government, private pensioning's second structural pillar, has also seen its strength decline in the years since ERISA's enactment. Ronald Reagan, the primary figure in the retrenchment of the federal government, was elected President in 1980 explicitly promising to reduce the role of the state in the U.S. economy. Reagan oversaw a dramatic reduction in marginal tax rates and a reduction of Social Security and pension benefit guarantees. The tax reduction slashed the value of pension tax favors, sharply raising the after-tax cost of a plan. The Social Security reforms trimmed the massive federal program, weakening the foundation underlying the private institution's "supplementary" benefits. And the cutbacks in benefit guarantees — a response to the financial implosion under way in the negotiated pension sector — further trimmed the government's role in the provision of old age security.

Owing entirely to "insufficient" terminations of collectively bargained plans, claims against the Pension Benefit Guaranty Corporation more than quadrupled in the early 1980s. They had averaged $60 million (1986 dollars) per year in the 1970s — nearly double the experience assumed in the agency's initial premium of $1 per head. But in the 1980s, through June 1986, claims ran $275 million (1986 dollars) annually. And negotiated plans accounted for 95 percent of this expanded total, with the bulk of the claims arising from steel and auto plans that paid generous early retirement benefits. A PBGC ruling in the late 1970s had extended the government's guarantee to all benefits defined in the plan document. The agency thus covered the generous benefits for early retirees — and for even younger workers who lost their jobs in factory shutdowns — as defined in collectively bargained plans. This ruling pushed the PBGC into the difficult and expensive business of cushioning the shocks of a volatile industrial economy. This "industrial policy" use of the PBGC resulted in plans negotiated by the United Steel Workers accounting for 43 percent of the agency's mushrooming obligations, and United Auto Worker plans adding another 20 percent, through June 1986. When Chrysler and International Harvester teetered at the edge of bankruptcy in the late 1970s and in the recessions of the early 1980s, more than a little anxiety rippled through Congress and the PBGC. Then, in June 1986, LTV filed for Chapter 11 bankruptcy protection. It announced its intention to terminate four pension plans in its troubled steel operations and transfer $2 billion in unfunded obligations to the PBGC. LTV also intended to establish four "follow-on" pension plans that effectively continued the original schemes, but without the past-service deficit. If LTV's gambit succeeded, in a stroke it would double the size of the PBGC's outstanding obligations and invite other stressed employers to follow its example.[10]

The PBGC naturally defended itself against this rising tide of claims and issued regulations challenging what it saw as clear abuses of the benefit insurance scheme. In the view of many, both in and out of the agency, cash-strapped sponsors were "de-funding" their plans, or paying employees with pension promises in lieu of wages, then terminating their schemes and handing the bills to the PBGC. The agency issued regulations and went to court, as it did with LTV, to block terminations and "restore" insolvent plans to still-functional sponsors.[11]

But the beleaguered PBGC desperately needed legislative changes to shore up its insurance program. Congress, alarmed by the agency's battle with LTV, complied. It enacted the Single Employer Pension Plan Amendments Act in 1986 and the far more ambitious Pension Protection Act (PPA) in 1987. Through these laws, Congress codified sponsor "financial distress" as a necessary condition for the receipt of PBGC benefits. It raised PBGC premiums from $2.60 per head to $8.50 in 1986, and in 1987 to $16.00 plus a so-called risk-related premium pegged to the size of the plan's unfunded liability. To keep the agency's exposure (and these liabilities) in check, Congress delayed PBGC coverage of benefit liberalizations and banned liberalizations of severely underfunded plans. To assure the quality of the liability measures, Congress sharply narrowed the sponsor's discretion in selecting key actuarial parameters, such as the discount rate. The lawmakers also made sponsors fully liable for pension obligations, removing ERISA's 30-percent-of-net-worth limitation. Most important, perhaps, they accelerated the amortization of all financial shortfalls — from unfunded past-service obligations, to stock-market losses, to unexpected longevity among the retirees.[12]

Congress designed the new legislation primarily to protect the PBGC against sponsors (and unions) that abusively "gamed" the system. It hoped to prevent firms on the ropes from compensating workers with benefits likely to be provided by the PBGC. The reforms also reduced the government's role in backstopping and supervising the second U.S. private pension institution — a system that would approach solvency only over an extended period of time. This retrenchment is seen primarily in the PPA's faster funding requirements and in the unlimited sponsor liability for pension obligations. These provisions marked a clear rejection of Howard Young's notion that PBGC insurance could serve as a source of pension funding or as an instrument of industrial policy, easing the dislocations that arise in modern industrial economies. In cases where underfunding was the product of such distress, not wanton gaming of the insurance scheme, the higher "risk-adjusted" premiums and the unlimited sponsor liability actually penalized struggling sponsors and could even raise PBGC losses. The insurance surcharge and faster amortization schedules would tax the cash flow of such hard-pressed firms while the unlimited obligation impaired their ability to borrow. These stiffer financial requirements, moreover, no doubt discouraged potential sponsors from starting new plans.[13]

The high financial maneuverings around the government's benefit insurance scheme were full of drama. Perhaps more important for the future of private pensions, however, were cutbacks in Social Security and reductions in federal tax rates. In neither arena did policymakers especially concern themselves with the health of employer plans. But intended or not, these two developments intensified the pressure on the private institution.

Since its enactment in 1935, Social Security had absorbed much of the burden of caring for superannuated workers. Through the last quarter of the twentieth century, the government program provided 40 percent of the income of Americans 65 and older. Employers wishing to offer old age incomes as a token of corporate benevolence could readily add a supplementary allowance. Those seeking career attachments or voluntary terminations had to add more. But even here the government program significantly reduced the incremental cost of deploying old age pension incentives. Even in 1992 OASDI delivered twice as much income to the elderly as private pensions and annuities; only for the richest quintile of the elderly did Social Security deliver less than these private income sources.[14]

Social Security, however, ran into difficulties similar to those that befell the plans in the collectively bargained sector. In 1972, after a recent stretch of benefit expansions, Congress had raised Social Security allowances by 14 percent (real) and had tied future increases to the rate

of inflation. Before the decade ended, however, a consensus of experts
had come to agree that Social Security had fallen seriously out of balance. Rising longevity atop the expanding level of benefits had sharply
expanded the burdens on the system. Social Security's resources, meanwhile, were now projected to lag owing to a sharp deceleration in the
growth of aggregate labor income — the result of the slowdown in labor
force growth and the stagnation of per capita labor income, both factors
expected to continue into the future.[15]

Attempts to restore the system's finances led to an increase in the
payroll tax in 1977. Further attempts at reform, involving benefit
cutbacks, proved too hot for standard political wrangling. So Ronald
Reagan formed the bipartisan National Commission on Social Security Reform, under the chairmanship of the business economist Alan
Greenspan, with Robert J. Myers, longtime actuary of the system, as
executive director. The Commission report appeared in January 1983,
and Congress dutifully enacted its key recommendations. The effect of
these initiatives was to raise the payroll tax, with the combined OASI
levy on employer and employee rising from 8.75 percent of the Social
Security wage base in 1976 to 11.2 percent by 1990; the retirement
age was extended from 65 to 67, roughly one month a year, beginning
in 2003; and benefits flowing to households with more than a threshold
income level were taxed, with the proceeds credited back to the Social
Security program.[16]

The Commission's proposal also involved the temporary buildup of
surpluses in the Social Security trust fund, to be used to raise the level
of national investment and accelerate the growth of labor incomes. It
was hoped that this would ease both Social Security's real economic
burden and the growing crisis of confidence in the system's solidity and
fairness. Social Security is an intergenerational exchange. It taxes current labor income and hands out, in exchange, benefits backed by claims
on future labor income. The trade had been attractive in the past, even
for those not getting an initial windfall pension at the program's start.
But with the seemingly permanent decline in fertility since the 1930s,
the exchange suddenly seemed, to many, a dubious financial deal. Social
Security still provided valuable insurance against disability, future
downturns in household earnings, excess longevity when retired, and
inflation throughout the adult lifespan. The program also provided a
baseline old age income to the working poor. But with the expansion
of the labor force slowing to a crawl, only the growth of per capita

labor incomes could give each generation a viable "return" on its payroll tax "investment." The temporary Social Security surpluses, to be built up prior to the retirement of the Baby Boom, were primarily an attempt to speed up economic growth. The system would send its excess cash to the Treasury, in exchange for an IOU, with the expectation that this would offset the deficit on the federal operating budget and raise the national savings rate: payroll taxes, without balancing Social Security payments or government expenditures on current services, would cut consumption and boost the share of national output available for investment. If investment (by either the government or the private sector) rose and growth accelerated, the public's Social Security benefits, backed by claims against future labor income, might again be an attractive, equitable, and politically viable exchange for current payroll taxes.[17]

Whether Social Security surpluses have resulted in greater government saving, more investment, and faster economic growth is the subject of bitter debate. The retrenchment of the federal program, however, had more immediate effects on private pension planning. Higher payroll taxes cut into current labor incomes and thus, in turn, into the sums available to fund the employer institution. Social Security's rising retirement age also raised the cost to sponsors that hoped to keep retirement ages constant. As terminating employment relationships became an increasingly critical purpose of pension programs, and we have already seen this in union plans, the retrenchment of Social Security raised the cost of gaining a plan's most highly valued personnel-management benefit. And in integrated plans, this shift of the burden from public to private was automatic.

But perhaps the most immediate impact of the declining role of government in the U.S. economy came from shifts in tax policy. The value of federal tax favors, according to Emil Sunley's rule of thumb, is roughly equal to the value of an interest-free loan of the deferred tax amount — from the time the taxes would have been due to the time they are paid in retirement. As a result of cutting the top personal tax rate from 70 to 50 percent, as was done in 1981, the value of the tax benefit for employees in this income class fell by 28 percent; lowering the rate to 34 percent, as was done in 1986, cut the federal subsidy for this top income group by another 34 percent. A Congressional Budget Office study estimates that the 1986 Act alone cut the 1991 federal tax expenditure on retirement income plans — primarily pensions — by $18 billion, or 25 percent. Since there were about 42 million participants in all these programs, and perhaps 60 million including vested nonparticipants, this meant about a $300 per capita fall in the annual federal subsidy from the 1986 Act alone. As with cutbacks in Social Security and the retrenchment of the PBGC, this shift in federal tax policy was a major transfer of responsibility from the public back to the private sector.[18]

The 1981 cuts in federal taxes also were not matched by cuts in government spending, resulting in an unprecedented peacetime expansion of the federal deficit. For the remaining years of the century, closing this shortfall became the central issue in fiscal policy. And as the pension institution lost out when Congress slashed tax rates in 1981, it also lost out when Congress, in response to the deficit, sought to trim expenditures. Thus the 1982 Tax Equity and Fiscal Responsibility Act sharply reduced the federal tax expenditures on pensions. The law cut the maximum allowable benefit in a tax-favored plan and reduced the maximum contribution that could go into an employer's tax-favored retirement savings account. These cutbacks reduced the pension's appeal to top-tier owners and executives; indeed the legislation established a whole new regulatory concept — the "topheavy" plan — to be subjected to new and more onerous rules. These new limitations and burdens, when combined with the rise in the cost of a plan after taxes and Social Security changes and the rise in PBGC premiums, sharply reduced the appeal of a plan to self-interested business owners and executives. The government's offer of tax favors in exchange for a bona fide employee-benefit pension plan, in other words, lost much of its market appeal.[19]

Big Business Reorganizes

As the economic influence of government and organized labor declined, the U.S. private pension institution became far more dependent, as it had been before the New Deal reforms, on the strength of big business and its interest in providing old age benefits. The giant enterprise did negotiate the late-twentieth-century economy far better than the unions or the federal government. The Dow Jones Industrial Average actually stood at six times its (nominal) 1975 level; the Gross Domestic Product, by comparison, was up just four and one-half times. There were, however, signs of erosion and change. Giant firms employed a smaller share of the private-sector workers: a Department of Commerce survey found that firms with over 10,000 workers employed 24.5 percent of a very large sample of the workforce in 1987, versus 28.7 percent a decade earlier. For almost the first time since the rise of big business, U.S. giants also faced overseas competitors of equal or greater commercial prowess in the last quarter of the century. And dynamic new technologies, primarily in information processing, created volatile new industries, fast-growing firms, and new modes of business that challenged traditional practices at the nation's old-line corporate enterprises. These competitive and technical shocks tended to disrupt the long-term employment stability that fostered private pensioning. And ERISA's hyper-rational standard of fiduciary conduct tended to reward — and accelerate — corporate accommodations to these shocks, regardless of the long-term effects on the continuity of the corporate pension institution.[20]

Pensions had long been a standard component of corporate compensation packages, and the decline of big business as an employer of U.S. labor contributed to the contraction of private pensioning. As the economists Daniel Beller and Helen Lawrence of the U.S. Department of Labor's Pension and Welfare Administration put it, "the decrease in the average size of new plans, together with the decrease in employees covered under old DB [defined-benefit] plans, accounts for roughly half of the total decline in DB plan coverage from 40 percent in the early 1970s to 31 percent in 1987." Part of this decline reflected the receding role of big business in the nation's labor markets. Of potentially greater importance, however, was the waning of corporate interest in providing old age pensions — a development emerging from changes in the nature of the giant American enterprise, and in its relationships with employees.[21]

Business in America became huge in order to produce and distribute massive flows of standardized goods and services. In rail transport; steel and autos; gas, electric, and telephone service; insurance and banking; and packaged consumer products, commercial behemoths captured economies of scale through the use of huge blast furnaces, risk pools, distribution networks, and the like. They organized themselves into large functional departments and subdepartments and assigned each subunit and rank-and-file worker a narrow, well-defined task. They then achieved tremendous efficiencies by closely planning and coordinating a high-speed, high-volume productive process and closely supervising each link in this complex economic chain, from purchasing through production to national marketing and distribution. They achieved these administrative efficiencies by establishing elaborate supervisory hierarchies. First were foremen and section heads, then managers above them, then managers above the managers, and so on up through the functional departments, like pyramidal smokestacks, up to the top of the firm or division.

For firms that used this industrial system, the pension delivered a host of benefits related to personnel management. The old age allowances were part of the gift exchange that employers sought to establish with workers; they were tokens of concern for employee welfare, given in the hope of soliciting employee concern for the good of the corporation. Pensions also served as compensation for long and dutiful service, and for investments in skills and relationships useful to the firm, but not to outside employers. Pensions also allowed management to retire the superannuated or excessively compensated older worker. With the rise of collective bargaining, pensions also served as tokens of benevolence in a gift exchange with unions; in the standard underfunded plan, they served as a bonding device, making labor dependent for its old age security on the continued success of the firm.

What posed a fundamental threat to corporate pensions was management's growing dissatisfaction with the traditional mass production model. The powerful competitive and technical shocks of the final quarter of the twentieth century challenged the wisdom of building and operating long-lived mass production facilities, especially in the United States, where blue-collar labor was especially expensive. The nation's labor force meanwhile had become far more highly educated since the end of World War II, and firms needed new organizational structures and personnel policies to tap this pool of professional and technical skills. The primary corporate response to these new economic challenges and opportunities, deployed increasingly after 1980, was to flatten and splinter the organization, or at least a good deal of it, into small units or teams that focused on specific products or projects. The large corporation, thus transformed, found it could respond more quickly to technical and competitive shocks, and it could expand the contributions made by the nation's educated workers. Most large enterprises continued to operate mass production and mass distribution technologies in certain parts of the firm. But the most critical operations, in the nation's most successful big businesses, increasingly developed flat organizational structures.

The very function of the corporation has changed in the process. These flat organizations do not exist to coordinate a complex mass-production, mass-distribution operation. Some are "intensive organizations"—to use James Thompson's term. They supply funds, buildings, equipment, marketing, and other support services to front-line managers and professionals who deliver highly focused, highly localized products and services; the large actuarial consulting and investment management firms in the pension industry, which displaced the integrated insurance carriers in the large-plan market, serve as examples. A second form of flat organization has emerged in manufacturing and other mainstream sectors of the big-business economy. Here corporations reorganized to capture dynamic, as opposed to static, efficiencies; here they thrive by supervising and coordinating complex chains of *sequential investment,* not complex chains of *continuous production.* This is the case in firms driven by research and development, which survive by bringing to market complex and sophisticated innovations. It is also the case for firms whose productive process is highly dependent on rapidly changing technologies (in the last quarter of the twentieth century, this primarily has meant information processing technologies), for they must continually absorb and integrate clusters of innovative products and services. Once such innovations are developed or absorbed, the large firm can still engage in mass production and mass distribution using the traditional supervisory hierarchies. But the dynamic side of the enterprise is flat and splintered into small project teams and business units.[22]

Within these flat organizations, firms develop new employment relationships that make far less use of old age pensions as a form of employee compensation. Employers seek workers with "generic" human capital—skills and contacts acquired in schools and universities, at professional or industrial meetings, through journals and associations, or in dealings with other firms. This differs substantially from the traditional corporate model. In the case of generic human capital, the firm has no incentive to finance the human-capital investment and offer an old age pension, for there is no company-specific gain to capture. Since generic human capital is valuable to other employers, the firm must pay the market rate, which approximates the worker's productivity. The employer, in effect, rents the employee's human capital and has little to gain from a compensation package that defers payment past the end of the worker's active career.

Flat organizations also ask individual workers to make far different contributions from those required by traditional mass-production, mass-distribution firms. Their small teams and work units need judgment, skill, and creativity. These are contributions far more valuable, individual, and intimate than the traditional demands of punctuality, good behavior, and a solid day's labor. The employees who deliver, in turn, feel ownership of what they produce. They want to participate in the success they created as a matter of *equity*— a notion of distributive justice quite different from sentiments found in mass production settings. It is a sense of equity grounded in performance outcomes, not in honest effort, group solidarity, and seniority rights.[23]

As a matter of equity, as well as a direct performance incentive, flat corporations develop compensation packages that closely track a worker's current performance. The pattern is especially clear in intensive organizations, where the work is highly localized. The large actuarial consulting firms, and many large medical, educational, engineering, and legal firms, typically use a modified fee-for-service model; large investment management firms emphasize performance-based bonuses. In dynamic corporations, the continuing need for close coordination limits the utility and precision of individual performance measures. But the ubiquitous process of job reassignments, occasioned by the continual completion of projects or changes in products, provides a critically important form of performance-based compensation. Workers are reassigned periodically to new teams or units, and how they move — up, down, or sideways — is largely based on their performance on the just-completed assignment. When employees move up, moreover, they rarely take their boss's job, supervise former co-workers, or even become full-time managers. As Tracy Kidder wrote of a minicomputer firm in *The Soul of a New Machine,* the winners get to play again, but on a bigger stage. As their skills are largely generic, they periodically scan the market to see if that larger stage is with another firm; employers likewise scan the market not just for entry-level talent but for seasoned contributors. Career paths in flat organizations thus tend to be lateral and professional, not vertical and managerial, and they often lead workers out of the firm.[24]

The classic old age pension conflicts with this new employment model in various ways. As a reward for long and dutiful service, it violates the performance-based sense of distributional equity; by spending company resources on reliable but unexceptional workers, old age allowances run the risk of demotivating key contributors. Pensions also limit an employer's flexibility in hiring and firing mid-career workers. Because pension costs rise sharply with age, adding senior contributors becomes an expensive affair. Dismissing older employees also adds a significant pension loss to the shock of unemployment; such workers lose the opportunity to earn any more pension credits, as well as to increase the value of credits earned with future salary increases. As technical and competitive shocks increase the risk of layoffs, plant closings, and corporate "downsizings," surviving in service to collect an old age pension becomes something of a lottery. The existence of a pension plan thus could actually undermine the employee's sense of working in a fair and rational setting.

Large and mid-sized employers have responded to these drawbacks in traditional pension arrangements in two different ways. First, they redesigned their plans, making them instruments for defining an abbreviated employment relationship. By offering generous early retirement incentives, they encouraged workers to stay through their years of peak productivity, then leave. The employers' second response was far more radical: the replacement of corporate pensions — in whole or in part — with individually allocated retirement savings plans. While these savings schemes are commonly called "defined-contribution *pension* plans," the use of the term "pension" is erroneous. "Pension" means "payment," and these plans involve no obligation by a fiduciary to make periodic *payments* over a participant's retirement years. They are traditional corporate thrift plans given new tax favors and weighty responsibilities. And this lack of a pension fiduciary has dramatic implications for the provision of old age security.[25]

Large corporate employers began offering generous pension incentives for early retirement in the early 1970s, soon after the unions had introduced similar measures in their pension programs. The employers, of course, have quite different reasons. The unions hope to keep wage rates *up* by reducing the supply of homogeneous blue-collar workers — employees who do much the same work, for much the same pay, regardless of age. Corporate employers, in contrast, seek to *lower* unit labor costs and boost productivity by shortening corporate careers.[26]

As access to generic human capital becomes more critical to competitive success, and as giant enterprise flattens its supervisory hierarchies, older, long-service workers have less to contribute. The value of their company-specific knowledge and contacts declines and, according

to a sample of top corporate executives, their productivity begins to fall
at about age 55. Salaries in large corporations meanwhile tend to rise
monotonically, regardless of worker performance. So while older employees typically deliver sub-par performances in a given job, they earn
more than their younger co-workers. The inducements to early retirement thus kick in when this pay-performance gap begins to widen, at
about age 55. Like the Pennsylvania Railroad in 1900, sponsors offer
older workers a piece of this excess compensation — a portion of the
difference between their wage and their productive contribution — if
they leave the organization. But the offer now comes at the end of
middle age, ten to fifteen years earlier than the traditionally targeted
retirement age. Thus it focuses more on workers who are not truly
superannuated but who run afoul of the employer's internal wage and
labor-assignment systems.[27]

In the 1980s, the use of pensions as a severance device became especially important. Congress banned compulsory retirement prior to
age 70 in 1978, and prohibited the practice altogether in 1986. The
financial incentives imbedded in corporate pension plans have thus become the employer's primary device for terminating corporate careers.
Firms in the mid-1980s also began opening special early retirement
"windows," limited-time pension offers aimed at luring specific groups
of workers out of their jobs and into retirement. If the targets were too
young to retire, sponsors added a number of years to their age for
pension purposes; as the standard benefits were typically too low to
induce retirements, sponsors added years-of-service to boost the allowance. Financially speaking, these early retirement pensions were similar
to the pensions offered by the Pennsylvania in 1900: the expense was
the *price* the employer paid to sever uneconomic employment relationships, not the *cost,* ultimately borne by labor, of an old age income. To
the degree that these early retirement practices are institutionalized,
however, their additional expense will be absorbed into the cost of labor
compensation.[28]

How long pensions will serve this aggressive severance function is
hard to say. The special early retirement windows were in some ways
the product of specific circumstances. Big business, in the late 1980s
and early 1990s, was paring back its supervisory hierarchies and had a
one-time need for white-collar severances. These programs also benefited from the dramatic and hard-to-repeat runup in security prices,
which pushed pension fund assets far above standard measures of plan

liabilities. After Congress, in 1986, placed an onerous tax on the "re-version" of excess assets to the sponsor, these early retirement windows became an especially attractive use of these "excess" pension fund assets. Looking to the future, however, Congress is examining ways sponsors could access these "excess" accumulations for general corporate pur-poses. Inducements to early retirement also have significant hurdles to jump. As the Social Security retirement age rises, maintaining the cur-rent severance incentives will grow more expensive to both union and corporate sponsors. And as the publicly defined "normal" retirement age slides out, such sponsors may also see an end to the public acqui-escence in the use of government tax favors and benefit guarantees sup-porting payments to middle-aged, not elderly, recipients. More impor-tant, the need to buy workers out of their jobs relies on the expectation of a career employment relationship, whose violation would damage the employer's standing in the community and its "gift exchange" with workers. If expectations about employment tenures change, firms will not need expensive old age pension incentives to sever relationships.[29]

The employers' second pension adjustment to the new employment relationships is to replace the corporate plan, in whole or in part, with retirement savings schemes. In this, sponsors were greatly helped by changes in tax law, completed in 1982, that in effect created the 401(k) savings institution. The newly sanctioned programs let employees make voluntary contributions, which employers may match, to individually allocated retirement savings accounts. These schemes enjoy the standard array of pension tax favors: contributions and investment income are tax exempt, and taxes are due only on payouts. Like many employer-based retirement savings arrangements, 401(k)s are also far more flex-ible than Individual Retirement Accounts (IRAs), the employers' main competitor as a retirement saving vehicle: the government allows work-ers to contribute significantly larger amounts to their employer-based accounts, and also lets the employees borrow the money back out.[30]

Few sponsors have actually terminated traditional pension plans and substituted retirement savings programs. A great many offer "supple-mentary" 401(k)s, and by 1987 about half of all workers enrolled in a pension plan also contributed to a retirement savings account. These saving schemes, however, quickly became the overwhelming choice among employers starting old age income programs. And because of the rapid growth of these saving plans, overall participation in em-ployer-based retirement programs held steady between 1980 and 1987, at about 46 percent of the private nonagricultural workforce (or 52 percent of full-time workers). In 1987 about 10.5 percent of the private-sector workforce was enrolled in a collectively bargained pension plan; about 20.5 percent participated in a conventional corporate plan, with perhaps more than half also contributing to a retirement savings account. For 15 percent of the workforce, however, a savings plan was now their only employer-based retirement income program.[31]

The appeal of these retirement savings plans does not derive from advantages they offer top management. Compared to a traditional pension plan, funding is "front loaded." Far more employer funds flow to the young, the low-paid, and to those who will leave the firm. These plans also do little or nothing to condition employment tenures. Employee and usually also employer contributions are vested immediately, so the participant's account balance is essentially unaffected by quits, dismissals, or early retirements. But retirement savings programs do serve as a token of concern for employee welfare — part of the employer's gift exchange with workers. The gift is also relatively inexpensive, for much of the money comes from the participants themselves. Employers typically pay the operating expenses and a partial match, costing about 2 to 3 percent of payroll. A pension plan, by contrast, often runs 7 to 8 percent of payroll, plus the hefty financial risk.[32]

Despite their limited cost to employers, retirement savings schemes are quite popular with workers. They come with generous government tax benefits as well as the sponsor's contribution, and the accumulating balances appear large when measured against almost any employee benchmark. By contrast, the value of an old age pension had always been hard for employees to grasp. Sponsoring retirement saving schemes thus helps employers assemble a thrifty and sober workforce. And they allow employers to discharge a responsibility they assumed long ago but no longer have an interest in meeting.

The Household Economy

The nation's households at the end of the twentieth century still rely on the factor-market economy that emerged at the end of the nineteenth century. Most still earn the bulk of their income by selling labor to external employers, and this dependence has grown with the general entry of married women into the market for labor. And workers still retire from active employment years before they die. This period of rest at the end of the lifespan has grown substantially over the course of the twentieth century, while the period of work has contracted. Americans now enter the labor force after far more years of schooling, and most now retire by the end of their sixty-second year. Households thus must accumulate enough assets over forty-some years of labor to support retirements lasting roughly half as long. Providing an income over this final stretch of life has become a critical task of the federal government and, through the private pension institution, of the nation's employers, unions, and financial intermediaries. But with the contraction of the public and private pension institutions after 1980, a greater share of the responsibility has, by default, fallen to households.

The private pension institution is hardly moribund. Nearly one-third of all private-sector workers — over 28 million in 1987 — still participate in a private pension program. As the Revenue Act of 1986 tightened vesting requirements (a five-year cliff became the new standard), most could expect to gain a vested right to an old age pension. And as workers move in and out of pension-covered employment over the course of their working careers, far more will earn a claim to an old age pension than the number enrolled at any one time.[33]

Nevertheless, the decline in participation means a great many households will rely on nonpension assets to support their old age. And the mobility of the U.S. workforce, which Merton Bernstein identified in 1964 as the Achilles heel of the pension institution, became even more troublesome after 1980. The movement in and out of pension-covered employment, which expands the number of beneficiaries, also means fewer than 31 percent will spend twenty years or more with a single employer and retire on a long-service pension. The rising number of involuntary permanent separations — due to plant closings, "downsizings," or simple dismissals — suggests more breaks in pension-covered service. And the value of benefits from former employers decays quite rapidly at even moderate rates of inflation; if prices rise at just 3.5 percent per year, a benefit set when a worker is 45 loses half its value by age 65 — when payments begin.[34]

More corrosive than any increase in general labor market turbulence has been the deteriorating labor market position of workers over 50 years of age. Pension credits are especially valuable when earned at the end of a working career. Salaries tend to be high, especially in nominal terms, and the time to retirement short. Older workers, however, have become increasingly vulnerable as employers have flattened their supervisory hierarchies and as generic human capital has displaced company-specific skills at the top of the employer's hierarchy of needs. Older educated white males — hitherto the prime beneficiaries of the private pension institution — are especially threatened. Those who leave on a generous early-out pension clearly still get excellent value from the pension institution, though a portion of their benefits should be properly viewed as severance pay and inflation will somewhat erode the value of their allowance before they grow old. Those terminated involuntarily — and the number rose sharply after 1980 — typically leave without a pension, or with a benefit frozen in nominal terms, payable at age 65. Such workers then have difficulty finding a job with pension benefits; jobs become increasingly difficult to find for workers over 50, and employers sponsoring a pension plan generally have age-related career tracks, at least informally, and tend to promote from within. For all these reasons, pension participation among workers over 50 fell sharply in the 1980s.[35]

Further diminishing the contribution of private pensions to old age security is the increased longevity of the elderly, along with their rising need for health care. Life expectancy at age 65 rose from 14.4 to 16.4 years between 1960 and 1980. Few sponsors fully or contractually index benefits to inflation, and the postinflation size of their ad hoc adjustments declined in the 1980s, especially toward the end of the decade. Beneficiaries thus see the real value of their allowances fall as they age, as their health care and nursing care risks increase. The government's Medicare and Medicaid programs have absorbed a significant portion of these costs, and Social Security indexes its benefits to inflation. But private pensions deliver a diminishing share of support at the end of a participant's life; this is especially so for widows living on a survivor's half-pension benefit.[36]

The rapid growth of retirement savings plans signals the emergence of a major new employer-based vehicle for providing old age income. These programs are far better suited than a standard pension plan to the increased levels of job mobility, which could explain a good deal of their popularity. Assuming all firms offer a 401(k) or similar scheme, a worker's account balance would be unaffected by a change of employers. Even among participants in traditional pension plans, about half contribute to a retirement savings program offered by their employer. Because of the increased disruption of job tenures after the age of 50, it is hard to say which plan — the pension or the savings account — will make the greater contribution to their old age income.[37]

Retirement savings accounts, despite these advantages, have serious limitations as a source of old age security. Workers have to save early, vigorously, and well if they are to accumulate a sufficient sum by the time they retire. They actually have to save more than pension sponsors, for those who survive to retirement do not "inherit" the sums put aside for workers who leave the firm or die prematurely. Even though workers have a steeper hill to climb, the young often fail to participate, with married women often out of the workforce when young; middle-aged and older workers often contribute insufficient sums; and most participants are notoriously conservative investors. Only equities generate high enough yields to make retirement income programs work. They returned 7.5 percent, after inflation, over the middle years of the twentieth century, versus 1 percent or less for all forms of debt. Employer pension funds took advantage of these returns and placed half of their assets in stock. Some households moved their retirement savings aggressively into the equity markets and enjoyed the tremendous stock market gains. But most households put the bulk of their funds in low-yielding fixed-income securities.[38]

Behind this conservatism lie the significant financial risks households face when relying on savings accounts for retirement income. Should an investment executive or corporate manager violate their fiduciary trust, or should an investment drop sharply in value, the household absorbs the entire blow. Even a large and well-diversified portfolio could fail to protect the household should financial markets crumble or inflation surge — both of which happened as recently as the 1970s. Because the yields households earn on conservative investments are inherently low, they face a further dilemma. This strategy produces a relatively modest sum at retirement, which generates a correspondingly modest income. The elderly either have to consume just this income or eat into their principal and risk outliving their assets. Commercial annuities offer some advantage. But marketing costs, extended longevity, and adverse selection make annuities expensive and the risk of inflation limits their value. Savings portfolios can never offer the insurance protections provided by government or employer programs. So members of households with only a retirement savings account can hardly look forward to a secure and comfortable retirement.[39]

The dramatic inflow of funds into retirement savings accounts, more-over, overstates the contributions these programs make to old age income security. These plans are but one of a number of available household savings vehicles, and portions of the contributions flowing into them are not true additions to total saving; they include assets transferred from taxable bank and brokerage accounts, or saving redirected from after-tax vehicles to these pretax programs. Social Security and private pension plans also act as substitutes — as well as supplements — to other types of household saving. But contributions to these employer plans are even more likely to be tax-driven shuffles. Households can readily channel funds to their employer accounts, whereas they can only indirectly offset their lumpy and contingent pension claims. And because households can also access the funds, they have far more incentive to accumulate assets via these "retirement" savings programs. Participants can withdraw funds without penalty at age 59½; at earlier ages, sums can be borrowed or home mortgages taken or extended, and these loans repaid when the participant turns 59½. As corporate pension plans are in some sense integral parts of a larger corporate balance sheet, retirement savings plans are part of a larger household balance sheet, not a separate, segregated fund that can provide only old age income.[40]

Upon entering the workforce, members of most households make buying a house their primary financial objective. From the middle years of employment through the period approaching retirement, establishing the children in life — paying their tuitions and helping them with house down payments — rivals old age security as the household's primary financial responsibility. These intergenerational transfers became more expensive after 1980, as tuitions, house prices, and real interest rates rose faster than household incomes. These transfers also became more valuable. Education, the primary form of generic human capital, is the critical factor in labor incomes; communities increasingly sort themselves by income and wealthier communities, with costlier housing, offer more amenities and stronger educations for the subsequent generation.[41]

The division of wealth between the generations has thus become an increasingly important, risky, and anxiety-laden task for all but the wealthiest households. As children must borrow to pay tuitions, they raise the likelihood of future financial stress. But as parents absorb these costs, they eat into the provision for their own old age and increase the risk of outliving their assets. Public education programs, Social Security, and the private pension institution pooled and reduced these risks, facilitating the expansion of both human-capital investments and old age security. When these public programs retrenched, after 1980, these financial tasks fell, by default, back to the households.[42]

American households, however, appear ill-prepared for their new financial role. In the mid-1990s the median wealth of households headed by someone in his or her fifties, exclusive of pensions and human capital, is about $135,000. Social Security wealth is of comparable size, and the present value of employer retirement plans adds about $80,000. This is a substantial accumulation, and a larger sum than held by households in the past. But the distribution of nonpension wealth is very uneven; health, income, inheritance, and the number of offspring, among other factors, create a heterogeneous pattern. For most U.S. households approaching retirement, the bulk of this nonpension wealth is home equity and household furnishings. The median household headed by someone in his or her fifties has less than $17,000 in financial assets that can generate cash income. Inheritances will augment this sum; children now inherit relatively late in life as parents live longer and typically transfer their assets first to their surviving spouses and only then to the next generation. But the nonpension wealth of elderly households is even more concentrated and must survive treacherous medical and nursing care lotteries before it can pass to the next generation. So postmortem bequests are not expected to significantly improve the financial position of most U.S. households as they enter old age. With this financial profile, converting real estate equity becomes the primary option households have for replacing their receding public and private pension incomes.[43]

The response by employers, financial intermediaries, and government officials has been to exhort employees and households to save earlier and more out of their current incomes, and to invest in riskier but higher-yielding assets. A presidential commission at the end of the Carter administration, in 1981, issued a call for a "minimum universal pension system" (MUPS). Reminiscent of the Metropolitan Life Insurance Company's 1923 "American Pension Plan," MUPS was a compulsory old age income program run through the private sector. In design, however, it adopted the TIAA-CREF model, with participants accumulating balances, in equities as well as fixed-income securities, that became an annuity in retirement. But MUPS got little support, like the Met's proposal, and died with the election of Ronald Reagan.[44]

What is clear from both the MUPS balloon and the exhortations of the policy elites is where they look for solutions to the nation's old age income problem. They do not ask for significant new commitments, as ERISA did, from employers and their private pension programs. The future of business and that of old age are increasingly viewed as separate affairs.

The Future

Old age income programs have been giant ships at sea. By design they connect the basic elements of the rational factor-market economy — households, enterprises, government, and financial intermediaries — in intricate and exceedingly complex ways. They have been built for durability, for they have to transfer credits to dependent populations across large spans of history. So these ships change momentum and direction but slowly, and need long stretches of time to adjust to inevitable shocks. Many of the vessels launched in the 1880s, the 1900s, the 1920s, the 1950s, and the 1970s went aground at some point or another. We refloated these hulks, built new ships along more contemporary lines, and again put out to sea.

The current contraction of private pensioning reflects the weakening of key institutions — labor unions, governments, and giant corporations — and the pension's declining value in the labor market resulting from the decay of the career employment model. The contraction of public pensioning reflects both Social Security's financial difficulties and the generally declining role of the federal government. In response, the nation has turned to household savings arrangements for its latest old age income programs. This greater reliance on household assets offers a bold experiment in simplicity. With the current generation of older Americans reasonably served with public and private pensions, the younger generation, for the first time in the history of the factor-market economy, could finance its own old age via household savings vehicles. If the trend toward household responsibility continues and succeeds, the prior history of private and public pensioning may prove to have been largely transitional, a makeshift bridge carrying the elderly across the historic shift from household to capitalist production.

But the end may not be in sight. In the new programs, the household with its savings account stands alone. Government provision for the elderly poor is threatened. The investment performance of a household savings program built on fixed-income securities could well be far inferior to that of corporate pension plans or even Social Security. Most important, there are no strong fiduciaries in the new programs that offer critical long-term guarantees. There are no insurance companies, no employers, no unions, and no government assurances. The success of the new initiative would thus seem to depend on an economy far more tranquil, and households far more prescient, than any seen in the past. The history of pensions in the factor-market economy has been one of shock, accretion, and change. The solutions devised have always been partly financial, partly political, and they have always been partial solutions at best. Considering the difficulty of the endeavor, and the critical interests at stake, it is hard to see how things in the future can be much different.

Notes

◆ ◆ ◆

Introduction

1. "Private Trusteed Pension Assets Reach $2.5 Trillion by End of Third Quarter 1993," *EBRI Notes* 15:2 (Feb. 1994), Employee Benefit Research Institute, Washington, pp. 5–6. The $1.5 trillion figure excludes the $1 trillion in assets held in retirement savings accounts, such as profit-sharing and salary-reduction 401(k) plans. Mark Warshawsky, "Financial Accounting and the Funding Status of Pensions," in John A. Turner and Daniel J. Beller, eds., *Trends in Pensions 1992* (Washington: GPO, 1992), p. 502. Pension liability estimates vary tremendously, depending on the actuarial method and assumptions used, but the best estimates show liabilities generally exceeding pension fund assets. The financial balance also worsens dramatically whenever asset prices and (real) interest rates drop. (An interest rate decline explodes the present value of distant pension obligations.) Economic slumps, which depress the demand for funds and the price of corporate securities, thus place untimely burdens on pension plan sponsors. A large enough slump — such as a repeat of the Great Depression — would put tremendous pressure on the private pension institution and could precipitate an open-ended expansion of government into the private economy.

1. Pensions and Capitalism

1. W. Andrew Achenbaum, *Old Age in the New Land: The American Experience since 1790* (Baltimore: Johns Hopkins University Press, 1978), table 4.7, p. 67, also see pp. 179–81; Jackson Turner Main to author; Lee Welling Squier, *Old Age Dependency in the United States: A Complete Survey of the Pension Method* (New York: Macmillan, 1912), p. 12; J. R. Kearl and Clayne L. Pope, "The Life Cycle in Economic History," *Journal of Economic History* 43 (1983), p. 153.

2. See Carol Haber, *Beyond Sixty-Five: The Dilemma of Old Age in America's Past* (Cambridge: Cambridge University Press, 1983), pp. 8–27.

3. Gilbert Ghoz and Gary Becker, *The Allocation of Time and Goods over the Life Cycle* (New York: National Bureau of Economic Research, 1975); real estate had been an investment craze since the settlement of Jamestown, and landed property has always constituted the largest and most broadly based portion of tangible American wealth. Real estate investments, moreover, could yield a handsome income. Thus decent farmland in the American South commanded, at the end of the nineteenth century, a rent fully equal to the tenant's share of the harvest. See Stephen J. DeCanio, *Agriculture in the Post-Bellum South: The Economics of Production and Supply* (Cambridge, Mass.: MIT Press, 1974); Thomas C. Cochran, *200 Years of American Business* (New York: Basic Books, 1977), p. 29; for population figures, see Series A 1–3, U.S. Bureau of the Census and the Social Science Research Council, *Historical Statistics of the United States, Colonial Times to 1957* (Washington, 1960), p. 7 [hereafter *Historical Statistics*]; for national income figures, see "Value Added by Selected Industries, and Value of Output of Fixed Capital, in Current and 1879 Prices: 1839 to 1899," ibid., Series F 10–21, p. 139.

4. Jackson Turner Main, "Standards of Living and the Life Cycle in Colonial Connecticut," *Journal of Economic History* 43 (1983), pp. 159–65; Kearl and Pope, "Life Cycle," pp. 149–58; Achenbaum, *Old Age,* p. 29.

5. Achenbaum, *Old Age,* pp. 3–6.

6. William H. Glasson, *Federal Military Pensions in the United States* (New York: Oxford University Press, 1918); Carol Haber, *Beyond Sixty-Five,* 110–113; Henry Pritchett, *The Social Philosophy of Pensions with a Review of Existing Pension Systems for Professional Groups, Carnegie Foundation for the Advancement of Teaching Bulletin* 25 (New York, 1930), p. 55.

7. See Alfred D. Chandler Jr., *The Visible Hand* (Cambridge, Mass.: Harvard University Press, 1977); Ralph L. Nelson, *Merger Movements in American Industry, 1895–1956* (Princeton: Princeton University Press for the National Bureau of Economic Research, 1959).

8. "Life Insurance Companies and Life Insurance in Force in the United States, by Type: 1759–1957," *Historical Statistics,* Series X 435–40, p. 672; "All Banks — Number of Banks and Principal Assets and Liabilities: 1834 to 1957," ibid., Series X 20–41, p. 624; "National Wealth, by Type of Asset, in Current Prices: 1850 to 1956," ibid., Series F 197–221, p. 151; David Montgomery, "Labor in the Industrial Era," in Richard B. Morris, ed., *The American Worker* (Washington: U.S. Department of Labor, 1976), p. 109. In 1910, average hourly earnings in non-farm employments were $630, while 13,555,000 farm workers (proprietors, working family members, and hired hands) divided $4,703,000,000, or $345 on average. "Average Annual Earnings in All Industries and in Selected Occupations: 1890 to 1926," *Historical Statistics,* Series D 603–17, p. 91; "Farm Employment, Wages, and Man-Hours Used in Farmwork: 1866–1957," ibid., Series K 73–82, p. 280;

"Farm Cash Receipts and Income, and Indexes of Prices Received and Paid by Farmers, and Parity Ratio: 1910 to 1957," ibid., Series K 122–38, p. 283.

9. Robert A. Margo, "The Labor Force Participation of Older Americans in 1900: Further Results," National Bureau of Economic Research Working Paper Series on Historical Factors in Long Run Growth, no. 27 (1991), pp. 5–10 and figs. 1 and 2.

10. Squier, *Old Age Dependency,* pp. 12ff, 260. Squier cites Professor R. C. Chapin, of the Russell Sage Foundation, with the observation that saving "is relatively infrequent" among households with incomes less than $800 annually, and Scott Nearing's report, in *Wages in the United States,* that 60 percent of wage earners made less than $600 a year, pp. 248ff; David Parks Fackler, "Report for the U.S.A. on the Growth and Progress of Institutions and Conditions Requiring Actuarial Advice," *Proceedings of the Fourth International Congress of Actuaries* (New York: Actuarial Society of America, 1904), I, p. 716; European lives made up three-fourths of the annuity business of American insurance companies in the 1890s; Arthur Hunter, "Mortality Experience among Annuitants Resident in the U.S.A. and Canada," ibid., I, pp. 433–35.

11. At the end of the nineteenth century, males aged 65 had a life expectancy of 11.1 years; L. J. Seargeant, "Superannuation of Railroad Employes," *World Railway Congress* (Chicago, 1893), p. 184. Richard A. Ippolito, using post–World War II data, finds the real rate of return on investments less than or equal to the real rate of increase in a worker's wage (due to productivity gains and personal advancement), which ran at about 3 percent a year; *Pensions, Economics, and Public Policy* (Homewood, Ill.: Dow Jones-Irwin, for the Pension Research Council, 1986); if this was also true at the turn of the century, then anyone retiring at age 65, who had entered the labor force at age 15, would have had to put aside about 10 percent of his earnings each year to provide, in retirement, half the income he enjoyed at the end of his career. The personal saving rate in the United States in 1900 was 6.4 percent. While this figure is net of dissaving done by retirees, understating the potential available for retirement, saving had purposes other than retirement, and accumulations were highly concentrated in the upper-income families. An adequate retirement-income savings program would therefore have entailed a dramatic jump in the thriftiness of the American population and the development of institutions to pool mortality, disability, and investment risks both before and after retirement. "National Saving, by Major Saver Groups, in Current Prices: 1897 to 1945," *Historical Statistics,* Series F 304–15, p. 155; "Net National Product, National Income, Personal Income, and Disposable Income, in Current Prices: 1897 to 1957," ibid., Series F 6–9, p. 139. For the relatively low rates of "retirement" through the nineteenth century, see Jon Moen, "Essays on the Labor Force and Labor Force Participation Rates: The United States from 1860 through 1950" (Ph.D. diss., University of Chicago, 1987); for a different perspective see Roger L. Ransom and Richard Sutch, "The Labor of Older Americans: Retirement of Men On and Off

the Job, 1870–1937," *Journal of Economic History* 46 (1986), pp. 1–30. But see Jon Moen, "The Labor of Older Americans: Comment," *Journal of Economic History* 47 (1987), pp. 761–67, and "From Gainful Employment to Labor Force: Definitions and a New Estimate of Work Rates of American Males, 1860–1980," *Historical Methods* 21 (1988), pp. 149–59; and Margo, "Labor Force Participation." For the history of the concept "unemployment," see John A. Garraty, *Unemployment in History: Economic Thought and Public Policy* (New York, 1978), pp. 108–9, 121; and Michael Piore, "Historical Perspectives and the Interpretation of Unemployment," *Journal of Economic Literature* 25 (1987), pp. 1834–50.

12. "Short-term Interest Rates — Open Market Rates in New York City and Federal Reserve Bank Discount Rate: 1890 to 1957," *Historical Statistics,* Series X 305–13, p. 654; "Bank Suspensions — Number and Deposits of Suspended Banks: 1864 to 1933," ibid., Series X 165–79, p. 636; "Cost-of-Living Indexes (Federal Reserve Bank of N.Y., Burgess, Douglas, Rees): 1820 to 1926," ibid., Series E 157–60, p. 127.

13. Achenbaum, *Old Age,* pp. 85, 85nn44–45, 114ff; Murray Webb Latimer, *Industrial Pension Systems in the United States and Canada* (New York: Industrial Relations Counselors, 1932), p. 18.

14. Barbara M. Tucker, "The Family and Industrial Discipline in Ante-Bellum New England," *Labor History* 21 (1979–80), pp. 55–74; Charlotte Erickson, *American Industry and the European Immigrant, 1860–1885* (Cambridge: Harvard University Press, 1957), pp. 190–91; Harry Jerome, *Migration and Business Cycles* (New York: National Bureau of Economic Research, 1926), pp. 33–40; David Brody, *Steelworkers in America: The Nonunion Era* (Cambridge, Mass.: Harvard University Press, 1960), pp. 96–111; Gerald N. Grob, *Workers and Utopia: A Study of Ideological Conflict in the American Labor Movement, 1865–1900* (Evanston: Northwestern University Press, 1961); Arthur M. Schlesinger Jr., *The Age of Jackson* (Boston: Little, Brown, 1945); Edward Pessen, "The Working Men's Movement of the Jacksonian Era," *Mississippi Valley Historical Review* 43 (1956), pp. 428–43.

15. Achenbaum, *Old Age,* pp. 65, 68–75, 83–86; "Population by Sex, Residence, and Color: 1790 to 1950," *Historical Statistics,* Series A 34–60, p. 9.

16. Achenbaum, *Old Age,* 74; Jon Moen, "The Shifting Structure of Occupations and the Effect on the Labor Force Participation Rate of American Males, 1860–1980," Federal Reserve Bank of Atlanta Working Paper 88–3, May 1988.

17. Carole Haber and Brian Gratton, *Old Age and the Search for Security: An American Social History* (Bloomington and Indianapolis: Indiana University Press, 1994), p. 44; John Bodnar, *Worker's World: Kinship, Community, and Protest in an Industrial Society, 1900–1940* (Baltimore: Johns Hopkins University Press, 1982); Mark Stern, *Society and Family Strategy: Erie County, New York, 1850–1920* (Albany: State University of New York Press, 1987); also see Haber and Gratton, *Old Age,* pp. 72–80, for a more optimistic reading of the cohabitation relationship.

18. Achenbaum, *Old Age,* pp. 80–82; Carol Haber, *After Sixty-Five,* pp. 82–107.

19. Glasson, *Pensions,* pp. 233–235, 258–261, 269–273; Squier, *Old Age,* p. 6; "Estimated Population, by Sex, Color, and Age: 1900 to 1957," *Historical Statistics,* Series A 22–33, p. 8; "Summary of Federal Government Finances: 1789 to 1957," ibid., Series Y 254–57, p. 711; Theda Skocpol, *Protecting Soldiers and Mothers: The Political Origins of Social Policy in the United States* (Cambridge, Mass.: Belknap Press of Harvard University Press, 1992).

20. Glasson, *Pensions,* p. 273; Robert Wiebe, *The Search for Order, 1877–1920* (New York: Hill and Wang, 1967), p. 11.

21. Max Riebenack, "Railway Provident Institutions," address before the National Civic Federation, 14 Nov. 1904, Archives of the Pennsylvania Railroad, Personnel Records, Voluntary Relief Department (Insurance) 1920–51, Eleutherian Mills Historical Library, Greeneville, Delaware [hereafter PRR Archives], p. 17; also see Latimer, *Industrial Pension Systems,* pp. 17–19.

22. See Philip Taft, "Violence in American Labor Disputes," *Annals of the American Academy of Arts and Sciences* 364 (1966), pp. 127–38.

23. Stuart D. Brandes, *American Welfare Capitalism: 1880–1940* (Chicago: University of Chicago Press, 1970), p. 103.

24. Testimony of Charles J. Harrah, *Report of the Industrial Commission on the Relations and Conditions of Capital and Labor Employed in Manufactures and General Business* (Washington: GPO, 1901), vol. 14, p. 352.

25. Ibid.

26. Brandes, *Welfare Capitalism,* p. 103. Dolge and Solvay Process were controlled by Europeans who adopted welfare mechanisms that conformed with continental practice. They operated formal, welfare-based pension plans that posted account balances in passbooks held by individual workmen. Ad hoc arrangements — the vast majority of American welfare capitalist "pensioning"— did nothing to establish and safeguard individual equities. Monroe, "Dolge," pp. 507–8; Nicholas P. Gilman, *A Dividend to Labor* (Boston, 1899), p. 287.

27. *Dolge v. Dolge* (New York Supreme Court, Appellate Division, 1902), 70 App. Div. 517, 518, quoted in Latimer, *Industrial Pension Systems,* p. 686.

28. Brandes, *Welfare Capitalism,* p. 83.

29. Paul Monroe, "An American System of Labor Pensions and Insurance," *American Journal of Sociology* 2 (1897), pp. 506–8, 510–11; Alfred Dolge, *The Just Distribution of Earnings, so-called "Profit-Sharing"* (New York, 1889); Alfred Dolge, *Practical Application of Economic Theories in the Factories of Alfred Dolge and Son* (Dolgeville, N.Y., 1896); I. W. Howerth, "Profit-Sharing at Ivorydale," *American Journal of Sociology* 2 (1897), p. 49. Nor could workmen place much faith in a pension promised by a traditional family enterprise, even if pledged in writing. While nineteenth-century family firms had grown in size and durability, they still

lacked the stability needed to make reliable commitments so far into the future. Thus when Dolge went bankrupt, in 1898, all pension claims fell worthless.

2. Business Finds an Interest

1. The Grand Trunk organized its 1873 insurance program into an "Accident Insurance Association." Emory R. Johnson, "Railway Departments for the Relief and Insurance of Employes," *Annals of the American Academy of Political and Social Science* 6 (1895), p. 430; L. J. Seargeant, "Superannuation of Railroad Employes," *World's Railway Commercial Congress* (Chicago, 1893), p. 182.

2. Johnson, "Departments for Relief," pp. 444–45; Seargeant, "Superannuation," pp. 182–83; Murray Webb Latimer, *Industrial Pension Systems in the United States and Canada* (New York: Industrial Relations Counselors, 1932), p. 44. Participation in the plan was compulsory for all employees under the age of 37 and unavailable for those entering at an age over 37. When the plan was established, however, all workers were given the opportunity to join regardless of age; employees withdrawing from the plan, by leaving prior to retirement, had the following rights: heirs of members dying in service received a refund of the employee's contributions; workers disabled after contributing ten or more years received a pension as determined by a management committee; members honorably discharged, resigning after five years of service, or becoming disabled before five years of service received back half of their contributions; Leslie Hannah, "The Early Spread of Pension Schemes (to circa 1925)," Pension Working Paper no. 2, Business History Unit, London School of Economics, pp. 27–28; Leslie Hannah, *Inventing Retirement: The Development of Occupational Pensions in Britain* (Cambridge: Cambridge University Press, 1986), pp. 9–11.

3. For contemporary analyses of the relation of pensions to career employment, see Edward P. Lazear, "Why Is There Mandatory Retirement?" *Journal of Political Economy* 87 (1979), pp. 1261–84 (for a model that emphasizes monitoring problems) and Gary Becker, "Investment in Human Capital: A Theoretical Analysis," *Journal of Political Economy* 70 (1962), pp. 9–49; Masanori Hashimoto, "Firm-Specific Human Capital as a Shared Investment," *American Economic Review* 71 (1981), pp. 475–82 (for models that emphasize the investment in human capital); Hannah, "Spread of Pensions," pp. 17–18; Stuart D. Brandes, *American Welfare Capitalism: 1880–1940* (Chicago: University of Chicago Press, 1970), p. 103; Nicholas P. Gilman, *A Dividend to Labor* (Boston, 1899), p. 287.

4. See Marios Raphael, *Pensions and Public Servants: A Study of the Origins of the British System* (Paris: Mouton, 1964).

5. Walter W. Skeat, *A Concise Etymological Dictionary of the English Language,* s.v. "career"; *Oxford English Dictionary,* s.v. "career."

6. G. D. Gilling-Smith, *The Complete Guide to Pensions and Superannuation* (Middlesex, England: Penguin, 1967); Michael Pilch and Victor Wood, *Pension*

Schemes (Westmead, England: Gower Press, 1979), p. 3; Hannah, "Spread of Pensions," pp. 17–21; Hannah, *Inventing Retirement,* pp. 9–10; Raphael, *Pensions and Public Servants.*

7. Seargeant, "Superannuation," p. 175. Company pension schemes clearly reduced an employee's financial vulnerability. By substituting one risk for another — by replacing an employee's fear of future destitution with anxiety over his tenure at the firm — the enterprise gained as well.

8. Seargeant, "Superannuation," p. 182; Walter M. Licht, *Working for the Railroad* (Princeton: Princeton University Press, 1983), pp. 147–55.

9. Seargeant, "Superannuation," p. 174.

10. Minutes of the Executive Committee of the American Express Company, 16 Nov. 1875. American Express was an essential part of the railroad industry, though not an operator of track and trains. American Express and similar enterprises developed highly intricate and bureaucratic distribution networks that alternately served and competed with services offered by railroad companies proper. Max Riebenack's 1904 survey included a discussion of the American Express pension plan as well as the welfare activities of others in the freight-forwarding business: Riebenack, *Railroad Provident Institutions in English-Speaking Countries* (Philadelphia, 1905), pp. 338–39; and Riebenack, "On the Question of Provident Institutions," *Bulletin of the International Railway Congress* 12 (Dec. 1904), pp. 182–85.

While American Express originally declared half-pay as the maximum pension benefit, the company seems to have set all allowances at this level. Minutes of the Executive Committee of the American Express Company, 28 March 1876, 21 April 1876; a 1893 company document actually refers to the pension as a "half pay allowance"; President [Jas. C. Fargo] to Chas. Fargo and H. S. Julier, 24 June 1893; "General Rules Governing the Allowing of Pensions to Employees of the American Express Company," 10 Dec. 1902; all in the Archives of the American Express Company [hereafter Amex Archives].

Pension expense at American Express remained rather low. In 1876, the first full year of operation, the company spent $3,465, or 0.18 percent of total payroll, and costs remained less than 1 percent of payroll throughout the nineteenth century. Despite their radically different approaches to pension provision, the American Express and Grand Trunk programs expensed somewhat similar sums: American Express expensed $290,076 between 1875 and 1892. (Figures from W. E. Powelson, Comptroller, to F. F. Flagg, Second Vice-President, 12 May 1902, Amex Archives.) Seargeant gives "total amount received" by the Grand Trunk fund between 1874 and 1892, eighteen years, as $389,682, and net after "payments of refunds and other outgoings" as $357,719 ("Superannuation," p. 182). Assuming that the first figure represents matching employee and employer contributions, and that employees and employers share equally in the "payments of refunds and other outgoings," Grand Trunk expenditures to 1892 would be $178,860; the company, in fact, received most "payments of refunds and other outgoings" upon employee withdrawal — all accrued interest and a refund of its own and some part of employee principal. Crediting two-thirds of "payments of refunds and other outgoings" to the company would bring the Grand Trunk's pension bill to $157,551. The two company amounts, of course, were spread over different numbers of workers. In 1903 the American Express pension plan included all of its 16,800 workers. The Grand Trunk, with a labor force of 27,520, restricted participation to approximately 5,250 officers, agents, clerks, telegraph operators, and other stationmen. Of this subset, only 1,350 were members of the association. American Express thus expensed nearly twice as much as the Grand Trunk, but perhaps as little as 15 percent as much per participant. Figures for 1903 given in Riebenack, "On the Question of Provident Institutions," pp. 123–24, 182, 183; the 5,250 figure assumes that Riebenack's enumeration of "other officers" includes foremen and inspectors, who were eligible to participate in the Grand Trunk plan.

11. See Johnson, "Departments for Relief," p. 429; Samuel R. Barr, "Protection and Improvement of Employes," *World's Railway Commerce Congress* (Chicago, 1893), pp. 209–13.

12. Licht, *Working for the Railroad,* pp. 269, 77, 93–124; also see Robert V. Bruce, *1877: Year of Violence* (Indianapolis: Bobbs-Merrill, 1959). The role of organized labor in the development of corporate plans remains an interesting subject for future research.

13. Trainmen, who made up 20 percent of railroad employment, were most exposed to accident and suffered by far the majority of deaths and injuries. Licht, *Working for the Railroad,* pp. 190–97; also see Johnson, "Departments for Relief," p. 429; George A. Akerlof, "Labor Contracts as Partial Gift Exchanges," *Quarterly Journal of Economics* 92 (1982), pp. 543–69.

14. R. F. Smith, "Relief of Railway Employes," *World's Railway Commerce Congress,* pp. 216, 215; W. T. Barnard, "The Relations of Railway Managers and Their Employes," quoted by Barr, "Protection and Improvement," p. 211. Barnard continued: "Constantly confronted with the history and with comparisons of the grievances of his fellow members and without motive of cause for attachment to his employers, perhaps unconsciously feelings of discontent and ill-will will arise, and naturally he meets any reduction of wages or suspension from labor with outraged feeling and often with violent actions, born of long though secret hostility where there should have been but fraternity and good fellowship of affiliated interests." Working-class welfare organizations were far stronger in England, where unions and mutual insurance associations both supported reputable pension schemes. English railroad companies therefore faced stiff competition in the provision of employee benefits. Barnard was well acquainted with foreign practice and knew that American business history often recapitulated British. Thus he set up the B&O relief association not only to provide needed services and remove arbitrary power from the hands of minor officials, but to preempt independent labor organizations from

taking over this aspect of the industry. Johnson, "Departments for Relief," 427–30; Hannah, "Spread of Pensions," 6–12.

15. Smith, "Relief," p. 216. Smith continued that even with the high level of administrative control as achieved by the railroads, sickness insurance was "feasible or safe . . . to a limited extent only, and under thorough safeguards." *Fifth Annual Report of the Massachusetts Board of Railroad Commissioners (1880)* (Boston, 1881), p. 58; Johnson, "Departments for Relief," p. 430; Riebenack, "On the Question of Provident Institutions," p. 69; Neal Owen Higgins, "Early Pension Plans of the Baltimore and Ohio and the Pennsylvania Railroads, 1880–1937" (Ph.D. diss., University of Nebraska, 1974), pp. 23–24.

16. *Carnegie Foundation for the Advancement of Teaching, Thirteenth Annual Report* (New York: CFAT, 1918), pp. 110–11; calculations of pension benefits, asset accumulations, and interest streams made by the author, assuming interest at 5 percent (the figure used by the Grand Trunk Railway in 1893, and readily available in the United States); a 2 percent annual increase in salary to age 40, and no increase thereafter. Figures for those entering the service at different ages are not radically different: A worker joining the B&O and its relief association at age 30 would get only 20 percent of his final salary; however, this pension then matched the interest generated by the fund his contributions created. An employee entering the plan at age 37, the age limit established by the Grand Trunk, would get 16 percent of his final salary, but that was 10 percent greater than the annual interest payment on the accumulated fund.

17. Johnson, "Departments for Relief," pp. 457–58, 460–61; labor demanded, for example, that life insurance cash values not evaporate upon separation from the firm; so Barnard allowed ex-employees to continue their policies. Although Samuel R. Barr of the B&O claimed that "no objection on the part of any organized body of labor has ever come to my attention since this institution was organized," Johnson provided ample evidence of such objections. Barr, letter to Johnson, Aug. 10, 1895, quoted by Johnson, p. 461.

18. See Johnson, "Departments for Relief," pp. 436, 446; *Railway Gazette* 31 (1899), p. 78, 32(1900), p. 130; in the nine months between 1 September 1891 and 30 June 1892, for example, 201 B&O pensioners received only $22,381, which amounted to $29,841 on an annualized basis, or $148.46 per pensioner. The American Express Company, by contrast, gave its pensioners $42,787 in 1892. As the B&O had a workforce of 55,688 in 1903 while American Express employed 16,800, it is also probable that American Express supported far fewer pensioners with nearly 50 percent more money. Riebenack, "On the Question of Provident Institutions," pp. 59, 182.

The B&O pension depended primarily on an employee's relief association classification, which in turn depended on his earnings. Contributions and benefits were directly proportional; and both increased with earnings, although not in a linear fashion. Thus employees at the bottom of the third classification, earning $600 a year, bore the heaviest burden and received the highest level of protection; they paid $36 a year to the relief association (6 percent of their income) but could retire on a pension of $234 a year (39 percent of their income). Other employees contributed a lower percentage of their incomes, and their retirement allowances replaced a lower percentage of their preretirement earnings.

19. See Brian Gratton, " 'A Triumph of Modern Philanthropy': Age Criteria in Labor Management at the Pennsylvania Railroad, 1975–1930," *Business History Review* 64 (1990), pp. 630–56; Alfred D. Chandler, *The Visible Hand: The Managerial Revolution in American Business* (Cambridge, Mass.: Harvard University Press, 1977), pp. 176–85; Riebenack, "Railway Provident Institutions," address before the National Civic Federation, 14 Nov. 1904, pp. 12–15, PRR Archives.

20. Adam Smith, *An Inquiry into the Nature and Causes of the Wealth of Nations* (New York: Random House, 1937), pp. 4–5; Chandler, *Visible Hand,* esp. pp. 79–187; *Travellers Official Guide,* appended to Powelson to Flagg.

21. See William Graebner, *A History of Retirement: The Meaning and Function of an American Institution, 1885–1978* (New Haven: Yale University Press, 1980), esp. pp. 3–187.

22. Chandler, *Visible Hand,* p. 167; all union contracts included formal seniority rules, while in the managerial ranks an informal seniority system also gained influence; Dan Mater, "The Development and Operation of the Railroad Seniority System," *Journal of Business of the University of Chicago* 13 (1940) esp. p. 412; Murray W. Latimer and Everett D. Hawkins, "Railroad Retirement Systems in the United States" (mimeo, 1938) Heubner Library, Wharton School, University of Pennsylvania, pp. 16–19, 24–30, and literature cited, esp. William W. Bennett, "Railroad Enginemen Brotherhoods and Collective Bargaining" (Ph.D. diss., Princeton University, 1932); Burnham N. Dell, "The Railway Shopcraft Unions to 1920" (Ph.D. diss., Princeton University, 1933), Charles Harold Howard, "Systems of Promotion and Tenure in Typical American Trade Unions" (Masters essay, Johns Hopkins University, 1926); Licht, *Working for the Railroad,* pp. 131–32, 155, 171; Stuart Morris, "Stalled Professionalism: The Recruitment of Railway Officials in the United States, 1885–1940," *Business History Review* 48 (1973), pp. 330–32; Riebenack, "On the Question of Provident Institutions," pp. 113–14.

23. Smith, "Relief," pp. 221, 220; Johnson, "Departments for Relief," p. 438; William B. Wilson's *History of the Pennsylvania Railroad Company,* commenting on Anderson, also noted the "benevolent trend of his mind" (Philadelphia: Henry T. Coates, 1899), vol. II, p. 167; Max Riebenack to John P. Green in E. B. Hunt to Mr. Felton, 21 Jan. 1926, p. 4, PRR Archives; while the B&O initiative formally offered pension benefits before accumulating an earmarked pension endowment, it too was building a fund. The formal offer, however, seems to have made a significant difference. The B&O spent $34,457 on pensions in 1894 while the Pennsylvania Railroad, with three times the number of employees, paid pensioners $31,627;

likewise, American Express expensed $45,341 that year while the Philadelphia and Reading Railroad, with an informal plan, paid only $6,800. Johnson, "Departments for Relief," p. 438n, Powelson to Flagg, 12 May 1902; *Carnegie Foundation, Thirteenth Annual Report,* p. 112; Riebenack, "On the Question of Provident Institutions," pp. 59, 64. This lack of a formal pension promise at the Pennsylvania Railroad may have been due to its decision to make membership in the relief association voluntary. The company was thus under less pressure to sweeten the pot to gain labor's acceptance. A pension benefit offered by a voluntary relief association could also induce the enrollment of those most likely to use it — the old and infirm — making the plan quite costly and undermining its "insurance" characteristics.

24. The B&O, after enduring nearly a decade of turmoil with its employee association, also found the Pennsylvania's strategy quite attractive. And after the financial reorganization of the parent company and Maryland's revocation of the benefit association charter, both in 1888, the company shifted its welfare activities to an internal department of the firm in 1889. See esp. Johnson, "Departments for Relief," pp. 430–31; Chandler, *Visible Hand,* p. 171.

25. Riebenack, "On the Question of Provident Institutions," p. 41; Minutes of the Pennsylvania Railroad Board of Directors, 1 Oct. 1887, quoted by Johnson, "Departments for Relief," p. 438; Riebenack, "Railway Provident Institutions," pp. 12–14; Smith, "Relief," pp. 217–18; the B&O gave essentially the same allowances to a man with forty years' tenure with the firm as to one with ten, assuming equal participation in the benefit program; the Pennsylvania's pensions would be in the ratio of four to one.

26. Barr, "Relief," pp. 211–13; Farr and his list had influence beyond Superintendent Barr. In 1895 Emory Johnson used language strikingly similar to the Englishman's, but placed even greater stress on efficiency considerations: "Quite aside from any humanitarian motives, the advantage a wise plan of pensioning employes brings to a railway company in the increased efficiency of its staff justifies the company in aiding their employes in maintaining a pension fund. Pensioning employes gives good servants greater inducement to remain in the service; it tends to make workingmen and officials more faithful and efficient; and makes it possible for a company to retire its old servants from its service in such a way as not to reduce them to a disgraceful dependence when age shall have rendered them incapable of doing their work well." Johnson, "Departments for Relief," p. 443; Johnson also declared that "no system of relief . . . can be considered complete unless it makes provision for employes whom sickness or old age permanently disqualifies for labor" (pp. 442–43).

27. Graebner, *History of Retirement,* p. 14; Kurt Wetzel, "Railroad Management's Response to Operating Employees' Accidents, 1890–1913," *Labor History* 21, no. 3 (summer 1980): 351–68. Walter Licht gives 3 percent as the number of railroad workers living in Philadelphia over the age of 55; *Working for the Railroad,* p. 220. In 1877 Robert Harris, president of the Chicago, Burlington, and Quincy, also

remarked that there were few old people in railroading; ibid., pp. 213, 216–17. By 1903, however, the Pennsylvania Railroad (East and West) pension plan had supported 2,134 men over 70 or otherwise aged and incapacitated. This represented 1.3 percent of the company's labor force of 158,248; Riebenack, "On the Question of Provident Institutions," p. 64.

28. Hunt to Felton, p. 4; Wentzel, "Employee's Accidents"; Licht, *Working for the Railroad,* p. 194; *Travellers Official Guide,* Jan. 1900, appended to W. E. Powelson to F. F. Flagg, 8 Jan. 1900; Leslie Hannah, "Terms and Conditions in Early Pension Schemes (to circa 1925)," Pension Working Paper no. 3, Business History Unit, London School of Economics, p. 60; Hannah, *Inventing Retirement,* pp. 134–35; Michael Kremer, "The O-Ring Theory of Economic Development," *Quarterly Journal of Economics* 108 (1993), pp. 551–75; Lazear, "Why Is There Mandatory Retirement?"

29. Powelson to Flagg, 8 Jan. 1900; Hunt to Felton, pp. 4–5; C. G. DuBois to the Directors of the Western Electric, 2 Feb. 1906, Box 75, Archives of the American Telephone and Telegraph Company [hereafter AT&T Archives], p. 10. Nor was the relief department's pension fund transferred to the new Pension Department. Instead, it was immediately put to use to pay small supplementary pension allowances to relief association members; with the requirement of thirty years of service and a practical upper bound of fifty years with the company, pensions were set between 30 percent and 50 percent of final ten-year salary. This would usually be somewhat less than the same percentage of final salary, because of promotions and inflation.

30. Riebenack, "On the Question of Provident Institutions," p. 17–18, 129.

31. Riebenack quoted in DuBois, p. 10; Riebenack, "On the Question of Provident Institutions," p. 130. In 1900 the Pennsylvania Railroad set $230,000 as its maximum pension expenditure. The sum was far greater than the $45,000 it spent in 1899 on its informal pension program. *Pennsylvania Railroad Annual Report, 1899,* p. 31, gives $44,500 as the amount spent by the relief department on benefits to those exceeding the 52-week coverage period; this completely disappeared in the 1900 annual report while actual pension expense was $194,359, $35,000 below the liability limit and four times its pension expense of 1899; *Pennsylvania Railroad Annual Report 1900,* p. 18. Should pension benefits have exceeded the limit, the company reserved the right to reduce allowances; Riebenack, "On the Question of Provident Institutions," p. 131. Demographics meanwhile pushed the B&O to a similar position. The company appropriated $31,000 for its pension fund in 1900, but the fund paid pensioners $49,026; although the company increased its contribution in 1901, pension expenses caught up in 1906 and by 1913 had totally exhausted the fund. *Carnegie Foundation for the Advancement of Teaching Annual Report* 13 (1918), p. 113; Hannah, "Terms and Conditions," pp. 12n2, 37, 46; Hannah, "Spread of Pensions," pp. 3, 29–30; Hannah, *Inventing Retirement,* p. 136.

32. Hunt to Felton, p. 4.

33. The first cohort of Pennsylvania Railroad retirees included John A. Anderson, who left his post at the Voluntary Relief Department after fifty years with the firm. Hunt to Felton, p. 4; *Pennsylvania Railroad Annual Report 1900*, p. 20.

3. The Logic of Pension Expansion

1. A listing of private pension plans in the United States and Canada, with various characteristics detailed, can be gathered from Murray Webb Latimer, *Industrial Pension Systems in the United States and Canada* (New York: Industrial Relations Counselors, 1932); *Industrial Pensions in the United States* (New York: National Industrial Conference Board, 1925); and a survey by the American Telephone and Telegraph Company, Walter S. Allen, "Provision for Employes," attached to J. D. Ellsworth to Theodore N. Vail, 25 July 1910, AT&T Archives, Box 75; also see Ellsworth to Vail, 6 April 1910, AT&T Archives, Box 75, and the list of plans in Samuel Williamson, "U.S. and Canadian Pensions before 1930: A Historical Perspective," in John A. Turner and Daniel J. Beller, eds., *Trends in Pensions 1992* (Washington: GPO, 1992), pp. 35ff.

2. Latimer, *Industrial Pension Systems*, table 1, pp. 26–27. Latimer's figures are taken from U.S. Interstate Commerce Commission, *Annual Report on the Statistics of Railways in the United States for the Year Ending Dec. 31, 1925* (Washington, 1927), p. civ, and *for the Year Ending Dec. 31, 1927* (Washington, 1928), p. lxxv, unpublished reports to the ICC, and questionnaire returns to Industrial Relations Counselors, Inc.

3. Max Riebenack, *Railroad Provident Institutions in English-Speaking Countries* (Philadelphia, 1905), and Riebenack, "On the Question of Provident Institutions," *Bulletin of the International Railway Congress* 12 (Dec. 1904 and Jan. 1905). Only five of the thirty-seven railroad plans established between 1900 and 1919 relied on voluntary retirement, and Murray Latimer, a careful student of North American pension plans, considered railroad "discretionary" retirement provisions as functionally equivalent to a mandatory separation; Latimer, *Industrial Pension Systems*, p. 8. The major railroads seem to have done a good deal of independent analysis on the pension idea and not merely followed the Pennsylvania in blind imitation. See W. A. Gardner to C. G. DuBois, quoted in DuBois to the Directors of the Western Electric, 2 Feb. 1906, pp. 9–10, Box 75, AT&T Archives. Twentieth-century railroad pension plans differed from the Pennsylvania design primarily by granting allowances to employees with fewer years of service.

4. "Pensioning or Retiring Employees," President [Jas. C. Fargo] to H. S. Julier, A. Antisdel, and J. W. Hutt, 31 Dec. 1901, p. 46, italics in original. Latimer recorded voluntary retirement at the B&O, *Industrial Pension Systems*, pp. 20–23, but Riebenack indicated compulsory retirement in 1903, Riebenack, *Provident Institutions*, p. 1749, as did AT&T's Allen in 1910. Allen, however, may have taken his information from Riebenack.

5. *Travelers Official Guide,* appended to W. E. Powelson to F. F. Flagg, 12 May 1902, Amex Archives; DuBois to Board of Directors of the Western Electric Company, 1 Feb. 1906, p. 9.

6. See the sources listed in note 1. Plans with a compulsory retirement feature were classified as "compulsory," those with voluntary but not compulsory retirement as "voluntary," and those with only discretionary retirement as "discretionary." "Discretionary" retirement is difficult to interpret, for it always involves the consent of management but sometimes also that of the employee. Benefits were classified "high" or "low" somewhat arbitrarily, based on a cut-off point of a 1.5 percent benefit factor (per year of service), taking into account specified maximum and minimum allowances. Benefits not figured on a "percentage of base salary times years of service" formula were translated into this form assuming thirty years of service and retirement at age 65. Thus a benefit of 50 percent of final salary yielded a pro forma 1.67 percent coefficient and was classified as "high"; a 40 percent benefit, yielding a pro forma 1.33 percent, would be "low." The maxima/minima cut-off points were $900 and 45 percent of salary base. So formulas with a benefit factor less than 1.5 percent *or* a maximum less than $900 *or* 45 percent of the salary base were classified as "low." A formula with a benefit factor higher than 1.5 percent *or* a minimum benefit greater than $900 or 45 percent of salary base *and* no maximum less than $900 or 45 percent of salary was classified as high. Formulas using a 1.5 percent coefficient or maxima/minima of $900 or 45 percent were not classified.

7. Stuart D. Brandes, *American Welfare Capitalism: 1880–1940* (Chicago: University of Chicago Press, 1970), pp. 103ff.

8. Joseph F. Wall, *Andrew Carnegie* (New York: Oxford University Press, 1970), p. 870; John A. Fitch, "The United States Steel Corporation and Labor," *Annals of the American Academy of Arts and Sciences* 42 (1912), pp. 15ff.

9. Robert Ozanne, *A Century of Labor-Management Relations at McCormick and International Harvester* (Madison: University of Wisconsin Press, 1967).

10. Homer J. Hagedorn, "A Note on the Motivation of Personnel Management: Industrial Welfare 1885–1910," *Explorations in Entrepreneurial History* 10 (1957–58), p. 137; Riebenack, *Provident Institutions.* By 1900 the railroad labor system included defined wage scales, working conditions, and employee benefits; recognized labor brotherhoods; the exclusion of more radical organizations; and government regulation in a few specific areas. While not all features were optimal from the point of view of management, the institutional structure stabilized the railroad labor supply and created a context for other policy initiatives. John Pencavel, "Work Effort, On-the-Job-Screening, and Alternative Methods of Remuneration," in Roland Ehrenberg, ed., *Research in Labor Economics,* vol. 1 (Greenwich, Conn.: JAI Press, 1977), p. 226; also see George A. Akerlof, "Labor Contracts as Partial Gift Exchanges," *Quarterly Journal of Economics* 92 (1982), pp. 543–69.

11. Philip Taft, "Violence in American Labor Disputes," *Annals of the American*

Academy of Arts and Sciences 364 (1966), p. 134. The Boston Elevated also had a bitter walkout in the early 1910s. See Cyrus S. Ching, *Review and Reflection: A Half Century of Labor Relations* (New York: B. C. Forbes, 1953); Hagedorn, "Motivation of Personnel Management," p. 135. Licht identified a similar dependence on labor, especially the problem of retaining good employees, as a primary impetus to welfare practices in the late nineteenth-century railroad industry. Walter M. Licht, *Working for the Railroad* (Princeton: Princeton University Press, 1983), pp. 124–27, 142–50; Latimer, *Industrial Pension Systems,* p. 36.

12. George W. Perkins, "The Underlying Principle of the Profit-Sharing, Benefit and Pension Plans of the International Harvester Company," paper presented before the National Civic Federation, 23 Nov. 1909, pp. 1, 2; David Brody, *Steelworkers in America: The Nonunion Era* (Cambridge, Mass.: Harvard University Press, 1960), esp. pp. 147–79; Ozanne, *Harvester,* pp. 71–73, 109. Many of these big firms also exercised monopoly power in their product markets, a situation which augmented their bargaining position vis-à-vis labor but opened opportunities for "rent sharing" as well.

13. John Brooks, *Telephone: The First Hundred Years* (New York: Harper and Row, 1975), pp. 127, 128, 131–33, 148, 169; H. J. Brandt, "The History of the Employees' Benefit Plan," read at the Bell Systems Benefit Secretaries' Conference, 23–28 March 1925, AT&T Archives, Box 75, p. 2.

14. Allen, "Provision," p. 1; Brandt, "Benefit Plan," p. 2; DuBois to Board of Directors of the Western Electric Company, 1 Feb. 1906. AT&T's new president as of 1907, Theodore N. Vail, set up a special committee of his chief lieutenants to design the company's comprehensive welfare program. Vail's employee benefit committee included H. B. Thayer, vice-president and the Vail's closest associate within the company, N. C. Kingsbury, vice-president and another trusted officer, and C. G. DuBois, comptroller — an office to which Vail assigned much responsibility. Walter S. Gifford, company statistician and Vail protégé, worked closely with the committee and conducted the first census of the company workforce as part of his duties. Thayer and then Gifford would succeed Vail as president of AT&T. Brandt, "Employees' Benefit Plan," p. 7.

15. Allen, "Provision," pp. 1–2, 5; Brandes, *Welfare Capitalism,* pp. 83–91; also see Ellsworth to Vail, 25 July 1910, pp. 12–13.

16. Brandes, *Welfare Capitalism,* pp. 119ff; Raymond B. Fosdick, *John D. Rockefeller, Jr.: A Portrait* (New York: Harper and Brothers, 1956), pp. 145–210; R. MacGregor Dawson, *William Lyon Mackenzie King: A Political Biography, 1874–1923,* vol. 1 of 3 (Toronto: University of Toronto Press, 1959), pp. 227–47.

17. The original members of the Special Conference Committee, also known as the Cowdrick Committee after its secretary, E. S. Cowdrick, were Standard Oil (N.J.), Bethlehem Steel, Du Pont, General Electric, General Motors, Goodyear, International Harvester, Irving Trust, U.S. Rubber, and Westinghouse; AT&T joined in 1925 and U.S. Steel in 1934. By 1920 the Rockefeller interests, eight of

the ten Special Committee firms, and many smaller enterprises had installed company unions. Ozanne, *Harvester,* pp. 156–73; Brandes, *Welfare Capitalism,* pp. 119ff. Rockefeller also created America's first labor relations consulting group, the Industrial Relations Counselors, in the aftermath of the Ludlow tragedy; Fosdick, *Rockefeller,* pp. 169ff; the IRC produced several major investigations of employee benefit programs including Murray Latimer's classic 1932 investigation of industrial pension systems. Also see Clarence J. Hicks, *My Life in Industrial Relations* (New York: Harper, 1941), and George Sweet Gibb and Evelyn Knowlton, *The Resurgent Years, 1911–1927,* History of the Standard Oil Company (New Jersey), vol. 2 (New York: Business History Foundation, 1956), pp. 135–52, 570–77.

18. Brandes, *Welfare Capitalism,* pp. 129ff.

19. While few middle-aged officials leave their organizations voluntarily, those who do are often the most talented and energetic personnel of the age cohort. Henry Pritchett, president of the Massachusetts Institute of Technology and the first president of Carnegie's foundation, was especially concerned about keeping the ablest and most energetic scholars in the universities and out of business employment. Abraham Flexner, *Henry S. Pritchett: A Biography* (New York: Columbia University Press, 1943), pp. 137ff. Production lost in the departure and replacement of such white-collar workers was typically much greater than in the case of manual workers. Ergo the greater interest in keeping them in harness.

20. Frank Vanderlip, "Insurance for Working-Men," *North American Review* 12 (1905), p. 932; Leslie Hannah, "The Early Spread of Pension Schemes (to circa 1925)," Pension Working Paper no. 2, Business History Unit, London School of Economics, p. 34n3.

21. Latimer, *Industrial Pension Systems,* pp. 36–37, 44–48. Grand Trunk scheme was also distinguished by a maximum pension benefit defined as a percentage of salary. This maximum was clearly intended to prevent retired workers from drawing incomes too close to their active pay, a problem not encountered by firms setting allowances at 1 percent of salary for each year of service. High-benefit plans often did include such a percentage maximum, as a mechanism for further defining the organizational career. Low-benefit plans, by contrast, would define maximum (and minimum) benefits in terms of dollar figures — in keeping with the welfare tradition of insuring workers against destitution in case of disability.

22. Perkins, "Underlying Principle," p. 4; Allen, "Provision," p. 4.

23. Even plans designed primarily for wage workers gradually became associated with the salaried staff. At AT&T, for example, the top 0.7 percent of pensioners absorbed 8.5 percent of all pension payments in 1934. Federal Accounting Department [Walker Commission], "Telephone Investigation, Special Investigation Docket No. 1: Report on the Bell Telephone System Pension Plan: Service Pensions," p. v. Allen had suspected that such a pattern would develop when he designed the plan in 1910. If the six railroads with "discretionary" retirement allowed employees no discretion over their separation from the firm — as Murray Latimer

suggested — then a clear majority of the decade's pension schemes vested the decision to terminate the employment relationship solely with the company.

24. William Miller, "The Business Elite in Business Bureaucracies: Careers of Top Executives in the Early Twentieth Century," in William Miller, ed., *Men in Business* (Cambridge, Mass.: Harvard University Press, 1952), p. 291. Law, accounting, and other professional service firms at the pinnacle of the U.S. business system also remained partnerships.

25. William Graebner, *A History of Retirement: The Meaning and Function of an American Institution, 1885–1978* (New Haven: Yale University Press, 1980), pp. 57–87, 133; Frederick W. Taylor, *Shop Management* (New York, 1911).

26. Chandler has shown that tight coordination in manufacturing enterprise varied with the precision and speed with which power machinery could process the inputs to an industry. As technology processed raw stock faster and within ever narrower epsilons, the smooth flow of goods through plant and distribution channels became the key factor in profitability. The manipulation of metal had reached the critical level at the turn of the century, so metal and machinery manufacturers now needed rational business control over the flows within their organizations. This "scientific" management standardized job classifications, creating superannuation, and then compelled retirement, eliminating the waste that rationalization produced.

27. See Daniel Nelson, *Managers and Workers* (Madison: University of Wisconsin Press, 1975), and Hugh Aitken, *Taylorism at Watertown Arsenal: Scientific Management in Action, 1908–1915* (Cambridge, Mass.: Harvard University Press, 1960), for treatments of the scientific management movement; Graebner, *History of Retirement,* pp. 31–40; Robert F. Hoxie, *Scientific Management and Labor* (New York: D. Appleton, 1915), p. 97; Roderic Olzendam, "What Industry Is Doing with the Older Worker," in *The Older Worker in Industry* (New York: National Association of Manufacturers, 1929), pp. 5–11.

28. Graebner, *History of Retirement,* pp. 45–46; see Alfred D. Chandler Jr., *Strategy and Structure* (Cambridge, Mass.: MIT Press, 1962), for the predominance of the centralized, functionally organized firm in U.S. big business through the 1950s — a structure ill-suited to continuous change.

29. Andrew Carnegie to the Trustees of the Carnegie Teachers Pension Fund, [1905], quoted in Wall, *Carnegie,* p. 872; Graebner *History of Retirement,* pp. 88–119, esp. 102–04, 111–12.

30. Graebner, *History of Retirement,* pp. 7, 100.

31. Louis Galambos, in Alexandra Oleson and John Voss, eds., *The Organization of Knowledge in Modern America, 1860–1920* (Baltimore: Johns Hopkins University Press, 1976).

32. Chandler, *Strategy and Structure,* pp. 164–85, esp. 180; all oil companies in the Rockefeller group copied the Standard of New Jersey plan, no doubt influenced by John D. Rockefeller Jr.

33. Thayer, DuBois, and Kingsbury to Vail, 8 Oct. 1912, Brandt to Driver, 17 July 1913, Devereaux to [Thayer], 26 Jan. 1914, Box 75, AT&T Archives. Theodore N. Vail, president of AT&T, was a vigorous 68 in 1913, when the company pension plan went into effect, and he retired in 1919, at the age of 74. Clearly he was not affected by the compulsory retirement order. AT&T, while not facing a large number of older employees in 1913, was expecting a rapid increase in the near future. Thayer et al. to Vail, 8 Oct. 1912; Perkins, "Underlying Principle," p. 6.

34. Reinhard Hohaus, "The Function and Future of Industrial Retirement Plans," address before the Casualty Actuarial Society, 21 May 1926, Hohaus file, Archives of the Metropolitan Life Insurance Company [hereafter MetLife Archives], p. 5.

35. Latimer, *Industrial Pension Systems,* pp. 45, 752ff.

36. Ibid., pp. 893–952.

4. The Hard Actuarial Realities

1. Arthur D. Cloud, *Pensions in Modern Industry* (Chicago: Hawkins and Loomis, 1925), pp. 253–66, 281–94, 311–22; Murray Webb Latimer, *Industrial Pension Systems in the United States and Canada* (New York: Industrial Relations Counselors, 1932), pp. 690–93.

2. The court's decision in the Morris case was consistent with rulings since *McNevin v. Solvay Process Company,* 32 App. Div. (New York, 1898) 610, the fountainhead of American pension law. The McNevin case, decided in 1892, interpreted the plan as a strict contractual arrangement with the terms laid down in the formal plan document. If the document anointed the company's Pension Board as the final arbiter of all disputes, as was the case at Solvay, the court gracefully withdrew, merely supporting the Board's authority. If the plan document characterized the benefit as a free-will gratuity, as at Dolge, the court accepted the judgment. *Dolge v. Dolge,* New York Supp., 1902, 386. It did not, in other words, delve into the equities or the public's interest in pensions. It did not ask if the company in fact provided the benefit as payment for some consideration from labor, making it not a free-will gratuity but a contractual responsibility. Both *Solvay* and *Dolge* were decided in the nineteenth century, before the start of the American pension movement. As such they were not part of the public consciousness when the Morris ruling came down. As Cloud pointed out, the court could have ruled differently in 1923. In *Heinze v. National Bank of St. Louis,* adjudicated in 1916, 8th Circuit Court of Appeals, 1916, 237 Fed., 942–43, a stockholder (Heinze) sued to forbid the bank from offering pension benefits. Heinze claimed that the plan was a charitable exercise outside the corporation's chartered profit-making purpose. (Heinze had a right to be especially aggrieved over management's right to pay — and receive — pensions: the only award actually granted by the bank had gone to the company's

president.) The court, however, held for the bank. It said the firm indeed received a valuable consideration in return for the pension benefit. The Internal Revenue Bureau agreed, ruling pension costs a legitimate, deductible business expense. Because Morris Packing received valuable labor services in response to its pension promise, Cloud reasoned, the employees could have been granted an equitable claim against the company assets no matter what the plan document said. But the only consistent thread in the early judicial history of the pension was the constant triumph of management's position. Cloud, *Pensions in Industry,* pp. 253–66, 281–94, 311–22; Latimer, *Industrial Pension Systems,* p. 697; also see Edwin W. Patterson, *Legal Protection of Private Pension Expectations* (Homewood, Ill.: Irwin, 1960), and Benjamin Aaron, *Legal Status of Employee Benefit Rights under Private Pension Plans* (Homewood, Ill.: Irwin, 1961).

3. Latimer called the Morris plan "probably as generous as any pension plan ever formulated by a private corporation in America." Latimer, *Industrial Pension Systems,* p. 690. John Merrill, president of All-America Cables, Inc., refers to "rumors [that] came to me of the possible inadequacy of the pension funds of several large corporations and in one instance of a large corporation being forced to discontinue payments to pensioners." Merrill to Ingalls Kimball, 9 Nov. 1926, MetLife Archives.

4. E. B. Hunt to Mr. Felton, 21 Jan. 1927, PRR Archives; also see the various reports of the actuarial firm, Fackler and Breiby, esp. "Report on Pension Plan of the Pennsylvania Railroad Company, 20 March 1933," PRR Archives.

5. Max Riebenack, *Railway Gazette* 31 (18 April 1899), p. 878.

6. See Murray W. Latimer and Everett D. Hawkins, "Railroad Retirement Systems in the United States" (mimeo, 1938, Huebner Library, Wharton School, University of Pennsylvania).

7. Ibid.

8. E. B. Hunt to G. L. Peck, 2 Dec. 1925, 1, PRR Archives; A. J. County to G.L.P[eck] and M.C.K., 4 Dec. 1925, PRR Archives; Irving Bernstein, *The Lean Years: A History of the American Worker 1920–1933* (Boston: Houghton Mifflin, 1960), pp. 157, 217.

9. Latimer, *Industrial Pension Systems,* p. 898; Louis D. Brandeis, "Our New Peonage: Discretionary Pensions," *The Independent* 73 (25 July 1912), pp. 187–91.

10. See, for example, Henry C. Pritchett, "Industrial Pensions," *Annual Report of the Carnegie Foundation for the Advancement of Teaching* 18 (1923), pp. 110–11; Latimer, *Industrial Pension Systems,* pp. 232ff.

11. Rainard B. Robbins, "Pension Planning in the United States," ed. William C. Greenough, typescript (New York: Teachers Insurance and Annuity Association of America, [1952]), pp. 13–61; Paul Studenski, *Teachers' Pension Systems in the United States* (New York: Appleton, 1920).

12. Margaret Allen Burt, *George B. Buck, Consulting Actuaries, Inc.: The First*

Twenty-Five Years (privately printed, 1976), pp. 12, 7–26. The "nucleus of Mr. Buck's pension library," according to Burt, included the 1910 *Report of the Departmental Committee on Railway Superannuation* (British); *Report, 1912, on the Establishment of a Superannuation Fund for the Whole of the Government Services, including the Municipal and Shire Services* (New South Wales); and *Report(s) on New Zealand Teachers', Public Service and Railway Pension Finds, 1912–13*, as well as the writings of Manley and King. For a review of the early actuarial literature, see Arnold Frank Shapiro, "A General Model of Expected Pension Costs" (Ph.D. diss., University of Pennsylvania, 1975), pp. 13–40. The (U.S.) Society of Actuaries at the time required no knowledge of pensions in its professional examinations, and when pensions did appear, in the 1920s, the recommended readings were primarily British in origin. Interviews with Margaret Burt, Murray Latimer, Ray M. Peterson.

13. Burt, *Buck*, pp. 54, 8–25, 36; George B. Buck, "Valuation of Pension Funds, With Special Reference to the Work of the New York City Pension Commission," *Proceedings of the Casualty Actuarial Society* 2 (1915–16).

14. Robbins, *Pension Planning*, p. 68, emphasis added; also see pp. 62–78; Henry C. Pritchett, "A Comprehensive Plan of Insurance and Annuities for College Teachers," *Carnegie Foundation for the Advancement of Teaching Bulletin* 9 (1918); James A. Hamilton and Dorrance C. Bronson, *Pensions* (New York: McGraw-Hill, 1958), p. 342.

15. As large numbers of institutions joined TIAA — 139 by 1928 — and because professors could transport their pension credits as they traveled from institution to institution, TIAA overcame the common criticism that private pension schemes restricted labor mobility. William C. Greenough and Francis P. King, *Pension Plans and Public Policy* (New York: Columbia University Press, 1976), p. 56.

16. Burt, *Buck*, pp. 36–37; see Henry C. Pritchett, *Annual Report of the Carnegie Foundation for the Advancement of Teaching* 11 (1916), p. 117; Latimer, *Industrial Pension Systems*, pp. 351, 429–30.

17. "Proposed Report to W. W. Atterbury," attached to F. J. Fell Jr. to Judge Heiserman, Mr. County, and Mr. Beasy, 16 Jan. 1934; C. B. Heiserman To Mr. Clement, Mr. County, and Mr. F. J. Fell, 27 April 1933; "Assets of the Pennsylvania Railroad" [1932?], PRR Archives; the company's actuary was Fackler and Breiby.

18. Henry C. Pritchett, "Present Day Pension Problems," *Annual Report of the Carnegie Foundation for the Advancement of Teaching* 13 (1918), pp. 109–10.

19. Ingalls Kimball, "Industrial Pensions," *Annals of the American Academy of Political and Social Science* (1932), p. 3.

20. J. D. Craig, "Memorandum of a Conference on Industrial Pensions Held at the Office of the Metropolitan Life Insurance Company of New York on Tuesday, April 3rd, 1923," MetLife Archives, pp. 6, 11, 14, 18–21, 23–25; statement by Ingalls Kimball, p. 23.

21. The New York Insurance Department of course regulated only carriers doing business in the state. But because it required such firms to abide by its regulations

in all of their operations, it became in essence the national arbiter of insurance practice. For the effect of state regulation on pension contracts and an insurance company's adjustments, see Hohaus, "Group Annuities," *Record of the American Institute of Actuaries* 18 (1929), p. 61.

22. Metropolitan Life Insurance Company, *Pensions: The Metropolitan's Old Age Pension Bond Plan for Employers and Employees* (New York, [1920?]), MetLife Archives, p. 21. Pension bond premiums ranged from $8.52 for a 15-year-old male to $95.53 for one aged 65. The figures for females were $10.20 to $109.14. The Metropolitan also offered a "refund pension bond" that guaranteed at least ten annuity payments or a return of the premiums paid in case of death prior to retirement. Costs for this contract ranged from $15.40 to $122.48 for males and $17.57 to $132.80 for females. Ibid., pp. 5–7.

23. Ibid., p. 18. Although the Met claimed its plan to be the soundest available, the other designs had strong points as well. Buck's plan, basing benefits on final salaries, ensured a retirement income most likely to fit individual needs. TIAA allowed flexibility with retirement dates and contribution amounts.

24. Ibid. Pritchett, citing a British "monumental report on pensions," offered the estimate that an adequate pension during this period required an annual contribution of 10 percent of salary. Henry C. Pritchett, "Pension Theory," *Annual Report of the Carnegie Foundation for the Advancement of Teaching* 14 (1919), pp. 71, 78, citing W. J. Whittal, Sir William Collins, and Harry L. Hopkinson, *Pensions for Hospital Officers and Staffs* (London: King Edward's Hospital Fund, 1919). With the nation's wage bill running at 60 percent of national income, if insurers handled pension arrangements paying adequate half-pay pensions for half the workforce, 3 percent of national income would annually be transferred to insurance industry management. Pension allowances paid out would eventually approximate contributions and investment interest taken in, but pension assets under insurance company management would be enormous, at a level determined by various demographic and economic factors. "Percent Distribution of Aggregate Payments, by Type of Income, in Current Prices, 1870–1948," *Historical Statistics,* Series F62, p. 141.

25. "Memorandum of Conference," p. 75 and passim; the 1927 Old Age Pension Conference of the National Civic Federation was held at the Metropolitan's New York Headquarters; *Old Age Pension Conference* (New York: National Civic Federation, 1927); James E. Kavanaugh, "Industrial Pensions," address to the Chamber of Commerce of the United States, 6 May 1924; Ingalls Kimball, "The Administration of the Industrial Pension Plans by an Insurance Company," address to the Associated Industries of Massachusetts, 17 Oct. 1928; all in MetLife Archives.

26. Mills, "Memorandum of Conference," pp. 74, 78; Hicks, p. 76. The firms present at the Metropolitan's pension conferences together employed more than 1.5 million workers; ibid., pp. 1–2, 16, 23, 70–71. The attendees at the 1923 Metropolitan Life Insurance Company Pension Conference were American Rolling

Mill; Bethlehem Steel; Brooklyn Edison; Central Hudson Gas and Electric; Cheney Brothers; Consolidated Gas; Curtis Publishing; Deering; Milliken; DuPont; General Electric; General Motors; R. H. Macy; New York Central Railroad; New York Telephone; Otis Elevator; Public Service Corporation of New Jersey; Stanley Rule and Level; Sears, Roebuck; Standard Oil (N.J.); St. Joseph Lead; Union Carbide and Carbon; U.S. Rubber; U.S. Steel; Virginia Railway and Power; Western Electric; Western Union; and R. D. Wood.

27. Hohaus, "Group Annuities," p. 54.

28. Henry C. Pritchett, "Industrial Pensions," *Annual Report of the Carnegie Foundation for the Advancement of Teaching* 15 (1920), p. 108.

29. "Memorandum of Conference," pp. 55–57. One-third of participant premiums, however, represented the additional cost of a death benefit over and above a straight pension annuity: should an employee die prior to retirement his heirs would receive a return of his contributions, while after retirement he or his heirs were guaranteed at least ten pension payments; ibid., pp. 61–62. As employer payments for each individual employee were "back-loaded," or expended at older ages, they would be made with dollars less valuable than those expended by the employee. The Met also recommended a minimum service requirement for plan participation to eliminate short-service workers.

30. Hohaus, "Group Annuities," p. 54; E. C. Roth, "Western Clock Income and Pension Plan," National Civic Federation, *Old Age Pensions Conference,* p. 16. Western Clock defined the contribution it made for each employee on the basis of service, and thus the size of any "pension" varied according to the employee's entry and retirement age, length of service, and sex. Roth, the secretary of company, gave the following schedule of Western Clock "pension" *contributions* in 1927: for 3–5 years of service, $7.50; for 6–10 years, $15.00; for 11–25 years, $45.00 for women and $60.00 for men; for 26+ years, $75.00 for women and $90.00 for men. The NCF conference highlighted the problem of actuarial soundness and gave special attention to insured plans. The session was conducted, fittingly enough, at the Metropolitan's building. Roth reports that his company had solicited the advice of the Met, the Equitable, the Carnegie Foundation, Gorton James of Harvard, and the Merchants Association of New York and developed its own plan before any insurance company offered the precise contract. Ibid., pp. 10, 18.

31. Rainard B. Robbins, "Teachers' Pensions and Our More General Old Age Problem," *Transactions of the Actuarial Society of America* 31 (1932), pp. 240–48; R. M. Peterson, "Written Discussion," and Robbins, "Author's Review of Discussion," ibid., pp. 133–35, 138–40; Pritchett, "Industrial Pensions," p. 109; Hohaus, "Group Annuities," p. 56; Roth, "Western Clock," p. 18; Latimer, *Industrial Pension Systems,* pp. 920–21, 934–36. Most thought it unlikely that employees could afford to permanently tie their money to a pension plan while they faced emergency needs for cash and critical unemployment risks. With special withdrawal provisions in the plans, macroeconomic stability, and effective unemployment insurance, these

analysts thought that employees could assume the burden of financing their own old age using something akin to the Metropolitan's pension bond scheme. The pension could then be in fact a "deferred wage."

32. All interest earned by the insurance company over and above the contractual rate — between 3.5 and 4 percent in the 1920s — was "declared as dividends to the employer, not to the individual holder, precisely the same as holdings [*sic*] are declared on group life insurance contract[s]." Kimball, "Memorandum of Conference," p. 70. This policy helped the Met overcome its basic problem — getting sponsors to sign up.

33. Hohaus, "Group Annuities," pp. 56–59. Employee contributions in the new contracts still took the form of an LPDA with employers paying a differential premium; withdrawals remained essentially unchanged, although cash withdrawals increasingly included interest on employee contributions. The use of salary classes allowed sponsors to further skew their contributions toward more valued employees. Those promoted into higher-paying positions could purchase annuities without any upward adjustment for their presumedly higher ages. A company's pension funds would therefore be heavily absorbed by upper-level employees.

34. Ibid., pp. 57–58.

35. Ibid., p. 72; Latimer, *Industrial Pension Systems*, pp. 446–62, 904–21, 960. Hohaus's figures and Latimer's do not correspond: Hohaus reported that the Met alone underwrote more insured pension contracts in 1927 than Latimer found in 1929.

36. Hohaus, "Group Annuities," p. 72.

37. Ingalls Kimball, "The Problem of the Superannuated Employee" (1932), MetLife Archives.

38. Latimer, *Industrial Pension Systems*, table 6, p. 50; table 7, pp. 52–53.

39. C. G DuBois to the Directors of the Western Electric, 2 Feb. 1906, Box 75, AT&T Archives, p. 15. AT&T had its own actuary probably not only because it was the nation's largest employer but because the division of the Bell system into subsidiary companies, all regulated by various state and federal agencies, added enormously to its demand for actuarial information. AT&T's president in the 1920s, Walter S. Gifford, had also worked as a statistician — first cousin to the actuary — in the design of the original 1913 Bell plan.

40. C. S. Ching, discussion of Edward S. Cowdrick, *Pensions: A Problem of Management*, Annual Convention Series no. 75 (New York: American Management Association, 1928), p. 36. Management wanted assets of the bankrupt firm to go to creditors, not pensioners, so that the firm, when facing a financial crisis, would be more "credible" to creditors.

41. Latimer, *Industrial Pension Systems*, pp. 348–51. Actuaries also estimated the growth of company payroll and fixed pension contributions as a level percentage of that anticipated payroll. Management could thus routinize pension expense charges into the flow of corporate finance. This procedure usually led to faster

funding, as level premium methods smoothed the higher costs of maturity into current periods. As consulting actuaries usually developed funding schedules taking withdrawal credits in advance but using this level percent of payroll method, funding could proceed either faster or slower than under insurance. Management, however, felt more comfortable adjusting pension finance to corporate finance than vice versa. Ibid., pp. 279–81, 339, 426.

42. Ibid., pp. 351, 429–30. Contemporary estimates have final-salary formulas costing 25 percent more than average-salary formulas with the same percentage benefit per year of service. Managers were by no means unaware that their own allowances benefited the most from this additional expense.

43. Pritchett, "Industrial Pensions," *Annual Report of the Carnegie Foundation for the Advancement of Teaching* 14 (1919), pp. 79–81; Robbins, "Teachers' Pensions," pp. 233–34, 238, and discussion; Joseph H. Woodward, "Industrial Retirement Systems based on the Money Purchase Principle," *Economic World*, 3 and 10 Dec. 1921.

44. Stanley P. Farwell, comment on Cowdrick, *Pensions*, p. 33; Latimer, *Industrial Pension Systems*, pp. 275–354; table 24, pp. 954–55; table 28, p. 960.

45. Chairman, Board of Pension Officers, to W. W. Atterbury, 21 March 1929, PRR Archives. The Pension Department figured the firm's obligation to current retirees, at the end of 1924, at a staggering $32 million — about six times the firm's paygo expenditure; also see T. O. Edwards, "Pension Accounting," *Annual Report, Railroad Accounting Officers Association* (1930), pp. 67–68; Hunt to Peck, 2 Dec. 1925; T. O. Edwards, "Presidential Address," *Annual Report, Railroad Accounting Officers Association* (1930), pp. 5–6. The ICC went far further than the railroads had intended: in the interest of uniform railroad accounting, an important regulatory goal, the commissioners began inquiring whether a contractual, funded pension right ought to be required of all carriers. As business had reacted to the Metropolitan's similar proposal of 1923, the railroads at once rejected the idea. They claimed their plans to have unique characteristics, largely due to varied demography, to be purely discretionary, and that the proposed obligation would be unnecessarily burdensome. The ICC then retreated to its original, voluntary set of accrual conditions.

46. E. B. Hunt to R. V. Massey, 12 Sept. 1928, pp. 1–2, PRR Archives; Edwards, "Pension Accounting," p. 67; Latimer, *Industrial Pension Systems*, table 47, pp. 238–39; note the specification of the model; the general shape of actual expense curves follows the hypothetical pattern. See "Annual Charges into Operating Expenses for Pensions, Under Four Methods of Cost Accounting, One Selected Company, 1965 to Peak Year (Combined Annuity Mortality, 4 Per Cent Interest)," pp. 254–55; Latimer's sample firm seems to be the Pennsylvania Railroad. In 1929, while paygo outlays ran to $6.6 million, Hunt estimated the SPIA expense at $7.9 million. As the company would still pay existing pensioners should it decide to fund new benefits as awarded, total expenditures under a new SPIA funding program

would be $13.8 million. (This figure is *not* a sum of paygo and SPIA expense as both costs include payments to those retired in the current year.) Company officials estimated that in twenty years a funding program would result in charges to operating expenses 20 percent less than paygo. Chairman to Atterbury, p. 2.

47. "Pensions," Box 75, AT&T Archives, pp. 2–3. The AT&T-ICC settlement reflected the railroad lawyers' views by distinguishing between liability for present pensioners and liability for future pensioners. The comparable *actuarial* distinction is between the current year's pension expense accrual and the "past service," or "accrued" liability — pension credits previously accrued by plan participants but not funded by the firm. Accrued liability in a young and fast-growing enterprise, such as AT&T, is a smaller burden than in an old and stagnant firm such as a railroad. The telephone company thus had relatively little difficulty assuming this responsibility.

48. Edwards, "Pension Accounting," p. 67; Latimer, *Industrial Pension Systems,* pp. 677, 651–60; Chairman to Atterbury, p. 2. The regulators were probably relieved that no railroad took up its accrual option and that pension accounting remained uniform in the industry.

49. Latimer, *Industrial Pension Systems,* table 72, p. 577; table XXXIV, pp. 968–71; table 75, p. 593; and p. 596.

50. Ibid., pp. 596, 741–46, 1022.

51. Ibid., pp. 741–46, 1022.

52. Ibid., pp. 596–615, table 76, p. 604; table XXIV, pp. 954–55; "Gross National Product, Total and Per Capita, in Current and 1929 Prices: 1869 to 1957," *Historical Statistics,* Series F 1–5, p. 139; "National Balance Sheet, in Current Prices: 1900 to 1955," ibid., Series F 158–196, p. 150. AT&T funded its plan entirely with special-issue company securities from the initiation of trust funding in 1927. It changed this policy for retirees in 1933 and for the plan as a whole in 1938, in each instance prescribing securities approved for life insurance companies by New York State. Statement by Donald P. Harrington, "Pensions Today and Tomorrow," *1989 Centennial Celebration Proceedings of the Actuarial Profession in North America, June 12–14, 1989* (Schaumburg, Ill.: Society of Actuaries, 1989), vol. 1, p. 147; Albert Handy, writing in 1939, reported that over 80 percent of Standard Oil's pension fund investments were in company securities. Albert Handy, *Private Pension Plans and the Federal Revenue Act,* Contemporary Law Pamphlets Series 1, #15 (New York: New York University School of Law, 1939), p. 15.

53. T. A. E. Layborn, "Pensions — the Past and the Future," *Policy Holder,* 24 Feb. 1966, p. 242.

5. The Public Character of Private Pensions

1. "National Income by Type of Income, in Current Prices: 1929 to 1957," *Historical Statistics,* Series F 49–54, p. 141; "Unemployment: 1900 to 1957," ibid.,

Series D 46–47, p. 73; "Bond and Stock Yields: 1857–1957," ibid., Series X 330–342, p. 656; "Basic Yields of Corporate Bonds, By Term to Maturity: 1900–1957," ibid., Series X 343–347, p. 657; "Expectation of Life at Specified Ages, by Sex, 1850–1956," ibid., Series B 76–91, p. 24; Murray Webb Latimer, *Industrial Pension Systems in the United States and Canada* (New York: Industrial Relations Counselors, 1932), pp. 383–84, 868, 938–41.

2. Latimer, *Industrial Pension Systems,* p. 874; *Investigation of Concentration of Economic Power Hearings before the Temporary National Economic Committee,* part 10: *Life Insurance* (1939, 76th Cong., 1st Sess.); see esp. testimony of E. E. Cammack, pp. 4154–4224, esp. 4206; also see "Total Group Annuity Business in Force, End of Year — 1934–1938," p. 4716.

3. Latimer, *Industrial Pension Systems,* pp. 844–47, 872; interview with Arthur Brown.

4. Latimer, *Industrial* Pension Systems, pp. 843, 848, 850, 854, 856; Murray W. Latimer and Karl Tufel, *Trends in Industrial Pension Plans* (New York: Industrial Relations Counselors, 1940), pp. 32–33, table 21, p. 75.

5. W. Andrew Achenbaum, *Old Age in the New Land: The American Experience since 1790,* table 5.1, pp. 91, 128.

6. Roy Lubove, *The Struggle for Social Security 1900–1935* (Cambridge, Mass.: Harvard University Press, 1968), pp. 113–43; Achenbaum, *Old Age,* pp. 122–23.

7. Murray W. Latimer and Everett D. Hawkins, "Railroad Retirement Systems in the United States," (mimeo, 1938, Huebner Library, Wharton School, University of Pennsylvania), pp. 4a, 8a, 31, 61a, 1–13, 31–32, 61–69; William Graebner, *A History of Retirement: The Meaning and Function of an American Institution, 1885–1978* (New Haven: Yale University Press, 1980), p. 154; Jack Elkin to author, 20 Nov. 1985.

8. Latimer and Hawkins, "Railroad Retirement," pp. 49–55; Walter M. Licht, *Working for the Railroad* (Princeton: Princeton University Press, 1983), pp. 255–57.

9. Latimer and Hawkins, "Railroad Retirement," pp. 78–133; for each year of service, up to a maximum of thirty, RENPA proposed a monthly pension of 2 percent for the first $50 of average monthly income, 1.5 percent on the next $100, 1 percent on the next $150, and nothing for average monthly income above $300. For two interpretations of the purposes behind the RENPA initiatives, see William C. Greenough and Francis P. King, *Pension Plans and Public Policy* (New York: Columbia University Press, 1976), pp. 38–40, and excerpts of a letter from Latimer to Greenough and King, dated 24 Jan. 1975, quoted on pp. 285–88, nn31–32.

10. Latimer and Hawkins, "Railroad Retirement," pp. 78–133.

11. Ibid., pp. 181–271.

12. Ibid., p. 81; William E. Leuchtenburg, *Franklin D. Roosevelt and the New Deal* (New York: Harper and Row, 1963), pp. 104–06.

13. Edwin Witte quoted in Lubove, *Struggle for Social Security,* p. 175. The

monthly benefit formula was 1/2 percent of the first $3,000 of *cumulative* earnings; 1/12 percent of the next $42,000; and 1/24 percent of the next $84,000; Alicia H. Munnell, *The Future of Social Security* (Washington: Brookings Institution, 1977), table A-5, p. 170. Contributions were 1 percent of payroll on both employee and employer on income below $3,000; ibid., table A-12, pp. 182–83. On the comparability of benefits see Paul H. Douglas, *Social Security in the United States: An Analysis and Appraisal of the Federal Social Security Act* (New York: McGraw-Hill, 1936), pp. 151–84, 278–79. The program's allowances, approximately 1.3 percent of average pay for each year of service, were comparable to benefits paid by corporate programs for all but the higher-paid staff. The Act included a separate relief program, distinct from its social insurance core, to provide temporary relief to the elderly without sufficient income and who had not earned a sufficient Social Security benefit; see Theron F. Schlaback, *Edwin E. Witte: Cautious Reformer* (Madison: University of Wisconsin Press, 1969), p. 100; Arthur J. Altmeyer, *The Formative Years of Social Security* (Madison: University of Wisconsin Press, 1966); Edwin E. Witte, *Development of the Social Security Act* (Madison: University of Wisconsin Press, 1962); Lubove, *Struggle for Social Security;* Douglas, *Social Security;* Joseph A. Pechman et al., *Social Security: Perspectives for Reform* (Washington: Brookings Institution, 1968), pp. 31–33; Achenbaum, *Old Age,* pp. 128–141. Louis Brandeis had designed a voluntary state annuity program for Massachusetts during the Progressive era, but it had failed to attract subscribers. The original CES bill had provisions for such voluntary supplementary government annuities, but this feature was seen as an intrusion on private enterprise and failed to clear Congress; Schlaback, *Witte*, p. 148; Leuchtenburg, *Roosevelt and New Deal,* pp. 131–32.

14. Douglas, *Social Security,* pp. 271–91; [H. Walter Forster], *The Story of Towers, Perrin, Forster and Crosby* (Philadelphia: privately printed, 1951), pp. 107–08; Schlaback, *Witte,* pp. 150–51; Martha Derthick, *Policymaking for Social Security* (Washington: Brookings Institution, 1979), p. 18.

15. C. Arthur Kulp, "Discussion" of Rainard B. Robbins, "The Effect of Social Security Legislation on Private Pension Plans," *Journal of the American Association of University Teachers of Insurance* 5 (1938), p. 56; the sponsors could see that their pension costs would rise, for with the enactment of Social Security they would support leavers as well as stayers. But as their competitors would likewise be saddled with this labor cost, their *relative, competitive* position would improve. Douglas, *Social Security,* pp. 271–91, and *Hearing on Private Pensions,* Subcommittee of the Committee on Finance, U.S. Senate, and Committee on Ways and Means, House of Representatives, 1936; for reasons of practicality, not policy, Social Security was originally not extended to everyone in the private workforce. Only railroad workers, protected by the Railroad Retirement Act, were excluded by design. In time, however, the great bulk of the private workforce was absorbed into the Social Security system.

Even as Congress debated the CES proposal, corporate sponsors began viewing their programs as supplements to Social Security. See Industrial Relations Counselors, "Memorandum to Clients: Company Pension Plans and the Economic Security Bill," 1 Feb. 1935, archives of the Industrial Relations Counselors, Rockefeller Center, New York; full committee hearings on the Clark Amendment, promised by FDR in order to win passage of the Social Security Act, were never held.

16. M. Albert Linton quoted in Schlaback, *Witte*, p. 164.

17. In an odd marriage of the American political left with the American political right, the Metropolitan actually helped finance Epstein's campaign for "adequacy" in Social Security. Schlaback, *Witte*, p. 170.

18. While the lower investment yields resulting from funding Social Security would have made pension plans more costly, corporate profits would have benefited from the lower cost of capital. While firms could thus have been in a better position to pay for private plans, the higher cost of funding benefits in advance would have probably discouraged the development of a sound corporate pensioning system. Munnell, *Future of Social Security*, pp. 113–133.

19. Latimer and Tufel, *Trends*, p. 17.

20. Ibid., pp. 7–9.

21. Ibid., pp. 26–27; with the government program providing a secure base of retirement income, some sponsors began abandoning insurance to base benefits on final average salaries. With the public program providing pensions to lower-income workers, these employees would be more likely to leave a pension sponsor; but this allowed the company to direct its money to its career employees.

22. Ibid., table 20, p. 73. Sponsors developed two methods of integrating pension plans. Employer interests were generally better served by the "envelope" or "offset" technique that defined a benefit in traditional fashion and paid the difference between this figure and the retiree's Social Security allowance. This method allowed employers to skew benefits from their plan away from noncareer personnel, whose low wages reflected their limited contribution to the corporation. These workers received little from the firm as their Social Security allowances made up a significant portion of their target benefit. Envelope integration also accommodated Social Security design changes, and reaped full value from future increases in the level of public benefits. Employers who controlled plan design — the large sponsors of noncontributory, self-managed programs — thus adopted the envelope approach. But firms with the newer insured, contributory designs could not use a simple Social Security offset. Insurance companies could not insure its indefinite allowances. Nor would lower-rank employees, who contributed a standard portion of their wages to the plan, accept substandard corporate pensions. Sponsors thus integrated such plans by establishing two equitable rates of participation, with salaries above the Social Security wage base paying, and in turn receiving benefits, at a higher rate. But this arrangement could neither adjust quickly to changes in the government

program nor award pensions on the basis of final salary. Nor could this two-tier program easily capture benefit from future liberalizations of Social Security. But because of the large number of contributory, reinsured plans in existence, it became by far the most common form of integration. For more on integration see Nancy Altman Lupu, "Rethinking Retirement Income Policies: Nondiscrimination, Integration and the Quest for Worker Security," manuscript.

23. Leuchtenburg, *Roosevelt and New Deal,* pp. 150–54.

24. Sponsors had clearly responded to the combination of tax relief and the new interest in soundness. Assets in tax-benefited trust funds more than doubled between 1928 and 1932, while balance sheet reserves increased by only 60 percent. Latimer, *Industrial Pension Systems,* pp. 873–84. In the days when the cost of funds was low, the requirement that deductions for past-service contributions be spread over ten years was not particularly onerous. With the cost of capital in 1928 at roughly 4 percent, the present value of the deduction was thereby reduced by less than 20 percent.

25. *Hearings Before the Joint Committee on Evasion and Avoidance* (75th Cong., 1st Sess., 1937), pp. 290–304. At least three manuals outlining the tax treatment of pension trusts appeared in the late 1930s: C. Morton Winslow and K. Raymond Clark, *Profit Sharing and Pension Plans (Their Creation and Tax Effect)* (Chicago: Commerce Clearing House, 1939); Meyer Goldstein, *Stock-Bonus, Profit-Sharing, and Pension Trusts* (New York: Pension Planning Company, 1941); and Albert Handy, "Private Pensions and the Federal Revenue Act," *New York University Law Quarterly* 16 (1939), pp. 408–34.

26. IRS Regulations, Article 23(p) Reg. 94, quoted in Charles T. Russell, written statement in *Hearings on Evasion and Avoidance,* p. 294. For sophisticated discussions of the "reasonableness" test, see Rainard B. Robbins, *Impact of Taxes on Industrial Pension Plans* (New York: Industrial Relations Counselors, 1949), pp. 11–13, 16–19; Erwin D. Griswold, "New Light on 'A Reasonable Allowance for Salaries,'" *Harvard Law Review,* Dec. 1945, pp. 287, 290; Winslow and Clark, *Pension Plans,* pp. 37, 143.

27. *Hearings on Evasion and Avoidance,* p. 32.

28. Ibid., pp. 290–304. A device for shifting corporate income away from years of high tax exposure should have had great appeal to corporate treasurers of the day, as the tax code had not yet provided for tax losses to be carried forward or back.

29. Robbins, *Impact of Taxes;* Winslow and Clark, *Pension Plans;* the courts had allowed the 1921 tax reliefs to pension funds held separate from corporate assets, even if not held by trustees. The 1938 Revenue Act, however, limited benefits to funds placed in trust or with an insurance company. A copy of the trust indenture, along with the plan document and the relevant actuarial schedules, had to be submitted to the IRS. The sponsors were also required to communicate the main features of the plan to their employees. Although Congress made pension trusts

irrevocable, it allowed sponsors to recapture the assets of terminated plans that remained after the satisfaction of all plan liabilities.

30. Article 165–1(a), Winslow and Clark, *Pension Plans,* p. 126; for the Albert W. Harris case, see 8 BTA Mem Dec P 39.472 (1939). The IRS also clearly declared employers to be ineligible participants in tax-exempt pension trusts, because "an employer cannot be his own employee" and that if the employer were included as a beneficiary, "the trust would not operate for the 'exclusive' benefit of his employees as required by Section 165"; Winslow and Clark, *Pension Plans,* p. 127. Scuttlebutt at the IRS in the mid-1940s actually supported the industry's position that Congress had sanctioned top-tier plans in 1921. Congress had done so, according to these Revenue officials, to stimulate managerial effort during a sharp economic depression; interview with Isadore Goodman.

31. Robbins, *Impact of Taxes,* pp. 11-15. The government's investigation of AT&T in the late 1930s, which reviewed the company's pension plan in great detail, vividly demonstrated how a program that included all employees, and that had been established as part of a welfare-capitalist campaign, in fact skewed benefits sharply toward management. The lack of vesting led to an overrepresentation of management among plan beneficiaries; the scheme's benefit formula based on final average salary resulted in their getting much higher allowances; *House Ways and Means Committee Hearings on Revenue Revision of 1942* v. 3 (77th Cong., 2d Sess.), testimony of Randolph Paul, pp. 2405–2406.

32. Robbins, *Impact of Taxes,* pp. 76–79.

33. *Hearings of 1942,* testimony of Randolph Paul, pp. 2405–2406.

34. *Hearings of 1942*: see testimony of Keith S. McHugh, pp. 2416–18; James L. O'Neill, pp. 2411–12; H. Walter Forster, pp. 2436–44; Arthur S. Hansen, pp. 2476–80. See Robert A. Taft, "Pension Trusts and Welfare Funds," *Journal of Commerce,* 29 May 1946.

35. Taft, "Pension Trusts"; testimony of Paul, p. 2406, testimony of Forster, p. 2441; testimony of Hansen, p. 2478; Robbins, *Impact of Taxes,* pp. 20–27, 76–77.

36. Robbins, *Impact of Taxes,* pp. 20–27, 76–78; testimony of Paul, p. 2406, testimony of Forster, p. 2442; testimony of Hansen, p. 2478; testimony of McHugh, pp. 2416–18.

37. Latimer and Tufel, *Trends,* pp. 32–33 and table 21, p. 75; *Hearings of 1942,* testimony of Paul, pp. 2406–07, testimony of Forster, p. 2439; testimony of Hansen, pp. 2478–80; Robbins, *Impact of Taxes,* pp. 76–79.

38. Interviews with Ray Peterson and Murray W. Latimer; Robbins, *Impact of Taxes,* pp. 76–79; U.S. Treasury Department, Division of Tax Research, *The Income Tax Treatment of Pensions and Annuities* (Washington: GPO, 1947); Arnold Frank Shapiro, "A General Model of Expected Pension Costs" (Ph.D. diss., University of Pennsylvania, 1975), p. 26.

39. Robbins, *Impact of Taxes,* pp. 21–27, 77–79.

40. Revenue Act of 1942, Section 23(p), quoted in Robbins, *Impact of Taxes,* p. 78.

41. Interview with Goodman; for regulations on integration, see Treasury Department 5278, Conforming Regulations 103 to Section 162 of the Revenue Act of 1942 and Treasury Department Mimeograph No. 5539.

42. Interviews with Goodman and Christopher O'Flinn, Mobil Corporation.

6. A Tale of Two Classes

1. Alicia Munnell gives a replacement ratio of .292 for "average" workers in 1940. Replacement rates for rank-and-file pension plan participants would no doubt differ from this figure. Plan sponsors typically paid higher-than-average wages and, as James Schulz has observed, retiring employees earn more than their younger co-workers. Both factors would reduce the relevant replacement ratio below .292. Rank-and-file workers, however, earn less than the firm's average income and the Schulz effect was probably less pronounced in 1940 than now, when many more workers are on professional, technical, or managerial career paths. Alicia H. Munnell, *The Economics of Private Pensions* (Washington: Brookings Institution, 1982), table 2–3, p. 20; James H. Schulz, "Assessing the Adequacy of Pension Income," testimony before the President's Commission on Pension Policy, 11 Jan. 1980.

2. Murray W. Latimer and Karl Tufel, *Trends in Industrial Pension Plans* (New York: Industrial Relations Counselors, 1940), pp. 22–27, 28–30. For more on integration methods, see note 22 of the previous chapter, and "Significant Developments in Pension Plans," National Industrial Conference Board *Management Record,* May 1948, table 1, p. 279 (data prepared by the Bureau of Internal Revenue); I am grateful to James Wooten for providing me with this source.

3. Kenneth Black Jr., *Group Annuities* (Philadelphia: University of Pennsylvania Press, 1955), pp. 65–67; Walter Couper and Roger Vaughn, *Pension Planning: Experience and Trends* (New York: Industrial Relations Counselors, 1954), p. 67. The 1939 amendments threw a monkey wrench into the simple and popular excess method of integration. This technique, whereby the plan differentiated between earnings above and below the wage base, now tended to discriminate against middle-income earners or to become an actuarial nightmare. Excess plans generally became far too discriminatory, complicated, and open to managerial manipulation to be accepted by labor. After 1939 the offset method of integration thus became more popular while excess designs grew fuzzier, less discriminatory, and largely confined to salaried-only arrangements.

4. Couper and Vaughn, *Pension Planning,* pp. 47–48. Insurance companies typically required fifty lives and the participation of at least 75 percent of the workforce to qualify for group rates. Premiums on life insurance and annuity contracts both rose with age, but they did so for different reasons: steadily rising mortality

drove up life insurance; the cost of annuities rose because of the diminishing time to accumulate investment income and for policy holders to die prior to retirement. Holding annuity contracts in a trust, as opposed to distributing the policies directly to the plan participants, also gave the sponsor some control of the policy and its cash value should the employee withdraw from the program. In any case, the Revenue Act of 1942 made a trust mandatory for individual annuity plans to qualify for tax relief; see Dan McGill, *The Fundamentals of Private Pensions*, 2nd ed. (Homewood, Ill.: Richard D. Irwin for the Pension Research Council, 1964), pp. 111–28.

5. McGill, *Fundamentals*, 2nd ed., pp. 122–23, 145–47, 292–98. Gross loadings overstate the administrative charges on both individual trust and group annuity contracts as these costs were typically reduced by dividends. On group annuity contracts, insurance companies also held additional contingency reserves.

6. Because premiums rose dramatically with age, pure final average benefit formulas proved very expensive. Where sponsor and beneficiary were the same party — where tax avoidance motivated the program — this was just a problem in cash management. But where the sponsor intended to trade pensions for managerial careers, benefit formulas typically controlled cost by ignoring salary raises in the last ten years of service.

7. Couper and Vaughn, *Pension Planning*, p. 48.

8. McGill, *Fundamentals*, 2nd ed., pp. 112–28. Employers could not supply employees with individual life insurance on a tax-favored basis — the benefit was considered taxable income to the plan participant. Thus there was no tax advantage in funding such protection on a noncontributory basis. So despite the tax-avoiding intent in managerial plans, many of these schemes kept the contributory format. They salvaged a goodly tax benefit by specifying that employee contributions paid for the life insurance while employer funds went primarily toward the pension benefit. The contributory format also allowed firms to exclude, from both a practical and legal standpoint, those employees with little interest in the plan. The indifferent simply would not put up their money. And while the 1942 Revenue Act required that noncontributory plans cover 70 percent to become tax-qualified, contributory plans needed a participation rate of but 56 percent: a minimum of 70 percent of those eligible had to participate, with at least 80 percent of the workforce eligible.

Some plans added insurance coverage greater than $1,000 for each $10 in monthly income before the IRS restricted such insurance to an "incidental" element of tax-favored pension programs. The inclusion of life insurance also raised the cost of these contracts by involving medical examinations of the plan participants.

9. James A. Hamilton and Dorrance C. Bronson, *Pensions* (New York: McGraw-Hill, 1958), pp. 81–84.

10. Richard Goode, *The Individual Income Tax* (Washington: Brookings Institution, 1964), pp. 2–4; John T. Dunlop, "Appraisal of Wage Stabilization Policies," *Problems and Policies of Dispute Settlements and Wage Stabilization during World*

War II, U.S. Department of Labor, Bureau of Labor Statistics, Bulletin 1009 (Washington: GPO, 1950). Assessing the inflationary impact of pension expenditures is a tricky subject. Clearly, a firm that funded its accruing pension liabilities incurred an additional cost of production which would almost inevitably raise prices. The price increase would primarily depend on the elasticity of demand for the firm's products and, in the wartime setting, on the rulings of the Office of Price Administration. But as the pension contribution was probably invested by the funding agent in U.S. government bonds, rather than spent by the worker or invested by the firm, it reduced aggregate demand and tended to lower prices in other portions of the economy.

11. F. Beatrice Brower, Conference Board Reports, Studies in Personnel Policy #61 (New York: National Industrial Conference Board, 1944), p. 13; F. Beatrice Brower, *Company Group Insurance Plans* (New York: National Industrial Conference Board, 1951); National Industrial Conference Board, *Company Pension Plans and the Social Security Act* (New York: National Industrial Conference Board, 1939), p. 24; "Significant Developments," National Industrial Conference Board *Management Record,* May 1948, p. 279; "Insured Pension Plans in the United States in Force with Life Insurance Companies," in Morgan H. Alvord, "Insured Pension Plans in the United States and Canada," *Transactions of the Fifteenth International Congress of Actuaries* (New York: Mallon, 1957), p. 188; Black, *Group Annuities,* 15–23; also see Reinhart A. Hohaus, speech before United States Chamber of Commerce, quoted in *Eastern Underwriter,* 21 Jan. 1944, p. 3; Dorrance Bronson, "Pensions — 1949," *Transactions of the Society of Actuaries* 1 (1949), p. 226.

12. Brower, *Trends in Company Pensions;* Latimer and Tufel, *Trends,* pp. 3, 9.

13. See Charles L. Dearing, *Industrial Pensions* (Washington: Brookings Institution, 1954), p. 38.

14. U.S. Bureau of Economic Analysis, *Long Term Economic Growth: 1860–1970* (Washington: GPO, 1973), Series B65, B69, B70, pp. 222–23; Munnell, *Private Pensions,* p. 20.

15. Martha Derthick, *Policymaking for Social Security* (Washington: Brookings Institution, 1979), pp. 273–74.

16. International Association of Machinists, *Report of the Grand Lodge Officers to the 18th Convention* (Washington, 1928), p. 66.

17. In the earliest days, old age homes and commutations of death benefits — into either a lump sum payment or a life annuity — had been quite common forms of support. But homes had been expensive and unpopular with the membership while the value of a commuted death benefit had been far too low to support a worker, let alone a couple, in retirement. (That individual policy plans using retirement income insurance contracts had to have a "side fund" to finance pension benefits demonstrated this inadequacy.) Unions thus gravitated toward pensions as the old age benefit of choice. By the 1920s annuities had far surpassed the other two forms of old age protection; see note 20 below for more on union motivation.

18. Union plans also based benefits on years of work because they had records of union membership but not of earnings; because benefits were supported by annual union dues; and because the variation of earnings within a craft was actually quite small. Social Security, especially after the 1939 amendments, had a quasi-flat benefit formula that reflected strong welfare considerations.

19. Dearing, *Industrial Pensions,* pp. 30–32; Murray W. Latimer, *Trade Union Pension Systems and Other Superannuation and Permanent and Total Disability Benefits in the United States and Canada* (New York: Industrial Relations Counselors, 1932), pp. 8ff, 126. The Railroad Brotherhood programs had been little more than individual savings plans, with a single premium immediate annuity kicker added at retirement, supplementing employer defined-benefit plans. Thus they will not be included in the subsequent discussion of union pension plans. The typographers, faced with a serious automation problem, likewise set up a pension plan with unusual characteristics. All unions were aware that retiring older workers reduced the supply of labor, thereby strengthening their bargaining position. But because of technological changes in typesetting, the demand for labor, and especially for substandard older labor, declined especially rapidly. Thus the typographers, far more than other unions, tied their pensions to a "retirement" program; see William Graebner, *A History of Retirement* (New Haven: Yale University Press, 1980), pp. 21–27, 135–39.

20. Latimer, *Union Pension Systems,* pp. 93ff.; Dearing, *Industrial Pensions,* pp. 32–33.

21. Dearing, *Industrial Pensions,* pp. 31–35.

22. E. K. Goodman, *National Union Benefit Plans, 1947-1967* (Washington: U.S. Department of Labor, 1970), p. 31.

23. Herbert J. Harris, *Labor's Civil War* (New York: Knopf, 1940); Florence Peterson, *American Labor Unions: What They Are and How They Work* (New York: Harper and Brothers, 1945), p. 56; *Handbook of Labor Statistics* (Washington: U.S. Bureau of Labor Statistics, 1980), p. 420; *Employment and Earnings* (Washington: U.S. Bureau of Labor Statistics, 1988), p. 43.

24. B. M. Selekman, S. K. Selekman, and S. H. Fuller, *Problems in Labor Relations* (New York: McGraw-Hill, 1950), p. 6; see Elizabeth Fones-Jones, "Industrial Recreation, the Second World War, and the Revival of Welfare Capitalism," *Business History Review* 60 (1986), pp. 232–57; Nelson Lichtenstein, *Labor's War at Home: The CIO in World War II* (New York, 1982).

25. Congress of Industrial Organizations, "Resolutions," CIO NEWS, 25 Nov. 1946, pp. 14–17, rpt. in E. Wright Bakke and Clark Kerr, eds., *Unions, Management, and the Public* (New York: Harcourt, Brace, 1948), pp. 224–25; compare with the American Federation of Labor, "The Federation's Postwar Program," *American Federationist,* May 1944, p. 32, rpt. ibid., pp. 224–25.

26. Selekman, *Labor Relations,* pp. 554, 555n1, 341–42; U.S. Bureau of Labor Statistics, "Work Stoppages in the United States, 1916–1946," *Monthly Labor Re-*

view 60:5 and 8 (May and Aug. 1947); also see Howell J. Harris, *The Right to Manage: Industrial Relations Policies of American Business in the 1940s* (Madison: University of Wisconsin Press, 1982).

27. See Jack Barbash, "The Structure and Evolution of Union Interest in Pensions," in U.S. Joint Economic Committee, *Old Age Income Assurance,* part 4: *Employment Aspects of Pension Plans,* 90th Cong., 1st Sess. (1967), pp. 64ff.

28. By 1955 the UMW Welfare and Retirement Fund supported 60,000 pensioners, nearly one-fourth of the industry's active workforce and over one-third of the workforce reduction over the previous decade. Louis S. Reed, report submitted to U.S. Senate, Committee on Labor and Public Welfare, *Welfare and Pension Plans Investigation Hearings before a Subcommittee of the Committee on Labor and Public Welfare,* 84th Cong., 1st Sess. (1955), pp. 1027, 1019; International Ladies Garment Workers and the Amalgamated Clothing Workers, both founding CIO unions, had set up programs during the conflict, but these earlier programs, largely based in New York City, had none of the national drama and impact of the UMW success. See Adolph Held, "Health and Welfare Funds in the Needle Trades," *Industrial and Labor Relations Review* (1948); Barbash, "Union Interest in Pensions," pp. 61, 72; also see Robert Tilove, "Income for the Elderly through Work-life Extension, Asset Conversion, and Pension Improvements," *Old Age Income Assurance,* part 4, pp. 31–42.

29. Lewis wanted sole union management of pension and welfare funds, as existed in most union schemes, including those of the New York City needle trades that received employer contributions. Krug, however, refused. This experience led Congress to prohibit, in Section 302 of the 1947 Taft-Hartley Act, sole union control over employer contributions to welfare funds. The union nevertheless dominated the pension fund. William C. Greenough and Francis P. King, *Pension Plans and Public Policy* (New York: Columbia University Press, 1976), pp. 44, 65; Joseph E. Finley, *The Corrupt Kingdom* (New York: Simon and Schuster, 1972), pp. 159–204; and three papers presented at the Ninth Annual Conference on Labor of New York University, June 6–8, 1956: Martin E. Segal, "Self-Insured vs. Insured Pension and Welfare Programs," Robert Tilove, "Welfare and Pension Funds in Multi-Employer Bargaining," and Jack M. Elkin, "Costs in Pension Planning."

30. Statement by John L. Lewis to Senate Committee on Labor and Welfare, *Welfare and Pension Investigation,* p. 1050. Lewis also saw no need "for our insurance companies to build up these huge reserves on the basis they are now being built, and concentrate money in the hands of the comparatively few . . . They are the people who are seeking to dominate American industry" (p. 1051). Traditional group annuity insurance contracts would require the plan to "sequester" the actuarial present value of all *vested* pension accruals, not just those in pay status. The UMW, however, did not have to use insurance companies but could have funded its plan in advance using a pension trust.

31. Barbash, "Union Interest in Pensions," p. 63.

32. To plan UAW welfare programs and to help influence national social insurance and welfare policy, Reuther set up a "Social Security" department within his union soon after World War II. This group, which included an actuary on staff, quickly made the UAW the union with the most sophistication in the area of worker benefits. The auto workers have maintained this leadership role to the present day; interview with Willard Solenberger. For the influence of the UAW on CIO pension design, see Charles Dearing, *Industrial Pensions,* p. 52.

33. Quotation from Selekman et al., *Labor Relations,* pp. 303, 288–89; for a colorful, if biased, account of UAW politics, see Irving Howe and B. J. Widick, *The UAW and Walter Reuther* (New York: Random House, 1949).

34. Selekman et al., *Labor Relations,* pp. 289, 300–301; 1946 UAW–Ford Motor Company Agreement, Article V, quoted on pp. 296, 299–301.

35. Ibid., pp. 299–301.

36. The tentative agreement on the pension plan was actually announced four days before Taft Hartley was passed; ibid., pp., 296, 308–309; also see *Time* (29 Sept. 1947), p. 84; *Business Week* (27 Sept. 1947), p. 98.

37. Selekman et al., *Labor Relations,* pp. 310, 313n1, 318–22. Before the 1948 negotiations broke up, the parties agreed to establish separate committees to study the pension issue. There was a general understanding that pensions would reappear in the negotiations of the following year.

38. The NLRB took a "forward" position in the Inland Steel decision, going far beyond the arguments made by either management or labor: after Inland reinstated compulsory retirement in 1946, the United Steel Workers complained that this unilateral action violated a previously negotiated separation policy. Inland claimed that retirement policy was part of its pension plan, and thus beyond the purview of collective bargaining. Rather than narrowly uphold labor's position, the NLRB ruled that all "emoluments of value, like pensions and insurance benefits" were "wages"; and that "matters affecting tenure of employment, like the . . . retirement rule," were "conditions of employment." Pension plans in their entirety therefore lay "within the statutory scope of collective bargaining." *Inland Steel Company v. United Steelworkers of America (CIO),* 77 NLRB 4 (1948); see Dearing, *Industrial Pensions,* pp. 42–45; Report of the Joint Committee on Labor-Management Relations, 80th Cong., 2nd Sess., 1948, pp. 94–95; also see Selekman et al., *Labor Relations,* pp. 326n1, 340–46, 577–78; Howe and Widick, *The UAW and Reuther;* Walter P. Reuther, "Too Old to Work; Too Young to Die," in Walter P. Reuther, *Selected Papers,* ed. Henry M. Christman (New York: MacMillan, 1961), pp. 36–40.

39. Clark Kerr. "Social and Economic Implications of Private Pension Plans," *Commercial and Financial Chronicle* 1 (1949); reprint no. 16, University of California Institute of Industrial Relations, Berkeley, pp. 4, 8. The steel companies were quite agitated over government involvement in labor negotiations and at first opposed Truman's Steel Industry Board. They much preferred the fact-finding com-

missions mandated by the Taft-Hartley Act that had no power to make recommendations. But as the strike deadline approached, they decided to go along with the President's initiative. Selekman et al., *Labor Relations,* pp. 335, 556, 572.

40. In coal, the miners had gone on a slowdown strike to weaken management's bargaining position, and some operators retaliated by halting pension and welfare contributions. This pushed the UMW's fragile paygo plan into insolvency, and on Sept. 19 Lewis called a general walkout. See Barbash, "Union Interest in Pensions," and Selekman et al., *Labor Relations,* for the situation in autos.

41. Steel Industry Board, *Report to the President of the United States on the Labor Dispute in the Basic Steel Industry* (Washington: GPO, 1949), pp. 7–8. Carol R. Daugherty, Chairman of the Steel Industry Board, later answered the question "What does a board . . . think about as it sits in on a dispute? It tries to serve the public. It tries to define the public interest. There are several aspects of public interest that a board of this sort must take into consideration. In the first place, the board must try to make recommendations that are consistent with the economic welfare of the country. Second — and a matter which may or may not be in conflict with the first — the board must endeavor to eliminate the threat of a work stoppage. That is its main function." Daugherty quoted in Dearing, *Industrial Pensions,* p. 63.

42. Steel Industry Board, *Report,* p. 64. The Steel Board used the accounting concept of depreciation imprecisely. Depreciation is neither a measure of an asset's falling productivity nor a charge used to accumulate replacement costs. Rather, depreciation matches the expense of a durable asset with the value it delivers: it spreads an asset's cost over its useful life. The depreciation concept could justify pensions as a form of lifetime income spreading. It would spread the total economic cost of the worker — his or her income — over his or her life. It justified pensions by recognizing that labor's true cost is not just its cost while at work but across an entire lifetime. The "human depreciation" school, however, did not advance such arguments. It simply kept demanding compensation for the erosion of productive power. What remains unclear, using either approach, was how depreciation theory justified employer-pay-all financing. A retirement income program could just as logically be funded and managed by the individual worker.

U.S. Steel's Enders Voorhees not only provided the Steel Board with an orthodox criticism of the "human depreciation" argument, but he also argued that pensions ought to be an individual responsibility: "U.S. Steel takes care of and replenishes its materials and machinery because it owns them . . . Machines are not paid current wages which they can freely elect to spend or to save. U.S. Steel does not own its employees; they are free men, each entitled to the respect of the other as such. U.S. Steel 'cares for'— cooperates with — its employees by paying money to them representing the full value of services rendered, as judged by the public as customers." Statement by Enders M. Voorhees before the Presidential Steel Board, quoted in Dearing, *Industrial Pensions,* pp. 61–62. For a traditional statement of labor's view of pensions as "fringe" benefits, see William Green, "Pensions and the American Economy: A Series," *Pensions and Profit Sharing Report* (19 May 1950), p. 2, quoted in Dearing, *Industrial Pensions,* p. 52; for the UAW position, which supported the SIB, see UAW-CIO, *Collective Bargaining Handbook for Workers Security Programs* (Oct. 1949), p. 18, quoted in Dearing, *Industrial Pensions,* p. 224.

43. Solenberger interview. As Walter Reuther testified, "We fought for a non-contributory pension plan in industry because we knew that that was the key to getting action at the Federal level. We said, 'If we can fight to establish pension plans in private industry through collective bargaining on the principle that the employer must pay the total cost of such private pension plans, then the employer will have an incentive to go down to Washington and fight with us to get the Government to meet this problem because in the Federal program the employee pays part of the cost.'" Testimony of Walter Reuther, *Social Security Revision,* Hearings before the Senate Finance Committee, 81st Cong., 2nd Sess. (1950), pt. 3, p. 1908, quoted in Dearing, *Industrial Pensions,* p. 47n16. An increase in Social Security benefits would lower a firm's private pension expense while raising pension costs for competitors with no corporate plan of their own. (Firms with pension plans, however, would also pay higher Social Security taxes — without a compensating reduction in their private pension expense — for those workers who left prior to vesting, which in these early plans usually occurred at retirement.) Congress did raise Social Security benefits dramatically in 1950 — increasing the maximum allowance from $46 to $80. The maximum Steel Industry Board corporate pension would thereby fall 63 percent, from $54 to $20.

44. Statement by Voorhees before the Steel Board; Selekman et al., *Labor Relations,* pp. 571, 574–76.

45. The previous "rounds" of labor negotiations were in 1946, 1947, and 1948; Dearing, *Industrial Pensions,* p. 83. Ford agreed to the $.10 per hour social insurance figure established by the Steel Industry Board. But, claiming that it already offered more welfare benefits than U.S. Steel, in an amount equaling $.0125 per hour, the company would only pay $.0875 more. Ford further insisted that this entire amount go into the pension fund, far more than the minimum needed to satisfy the IRS (annual normal cost plus interest on the past service liability). Thinking a settlement costing $.10 per hour in welfare benefits inevitable, Ford thus chose an allocation that minimized current benefits and reduced future expenses. Ford also insisted on controlling the investment of the resulting fund. To win its pension plan, Reuther acceded to these demands and the membership overwhelmingly ratified the contract.

Bethlehem Steel, like most U.S. steel firms, had a preexisting pension plan. Most blue-collar workers, however, had been "integrated out" of any significant benefit: Philip Murray, USW president, testified before the Steel Industry Board that the average steelworker retired from U.S. Steel with a company pension of $5 monthly. The 1949 agreements raised the monthly minimum to $100, integrated with Social

Security. Blue-collar pensions thus jumped more than tenfold in 1949, from this $5 figure to over $50 monthly.

46. Hamilton and Bronson, *Pensions,* pp. 294–311.

47. Ibid., pp. 300–301. For a defense of defining both benefits and contributions for the relatively short period covered by a collective bargaining contract, see Solomon Barkin, "Labor's View on Actuarial Requirements for Pension Plans," *Proceedings of Panel Meeting Jointly Sponsored by the American Statistical Society and Others,* Chicago, Dec. 1952, quoted in Hamilton and Bronson, *Pensions,* p. 301. The United Mineworkers' program, like the Ford-UAW scheme, defined both contributions and benefits: employers paid a fixed contribution based on tonnage while the plan promised workers a specific benefit of $100 monthly. Because the plan was on a paygo basis, it had even greater difficulty staying in balance. Indeed, contributions had to rise substantially and benefits decline for the program to continue. As the key collectively bargained pension programs of the early 1950s were single-employer plans, the Ford-UAW experience, not that of the UMW, was more influential.

48. Hamilton and Bronson, *Pensions,* pp. 299–302. Ford also adopted the GM design.

49. Ibid., pp. 299–303.

50. Bureau of Labor Statistics, *Multiemployer Pension Plans under Collective Bargaining, Spring 1960,* Bulletin 1326, June 1962, p. 4.; also see H. Robert Bartell Jr. and Elizabeth T. Simpson, *Pension Funds of Multiemployer Industrial Groups, Unions, and Nonprofit Organizations,* National Bureau of Economic Research Occasional Paper 105 (New York: NBER, 1968); Robert Tilove, "Funds in Multi-Employer Bargaining."

51. Bureau of Labor Statistics, *Multiemployer Plans.* The institutional setup of multi-employer plans varied quite a bit. Sometimes a union would deal with a unified employer association; sometimes only some employers would bargain with the union and others would merely accept the terms of the contract so negotiated; sometimes an association of unions in one locality would organize a multi-employer plan for their combined membership; Tilove, "Funds in Multi-Employer Bargaining," p. 36.

52. Tilove, "Funds in Multi-Employer Bargaining," pp. 35–40. The multiemployer plan's nonactuarial charges encouraged firms with older employees to join the program and those with younger employees to leave. As plan participation was typically part of a larger collective bargaining agreement, firms rarely took such action. But to reduce such selection, and to facilitate entry into the plan (and to a lesser extent, movement out of the plan), the more sophisticated plans clearly specified the financial implications of entry and exit. Ibid., pp. 46–51.

53. Barbash, "Union Interest in Pensions," pp. 66, 79–83; Congress of Industrial Organizations, "Resolutions"; American Federation of Labor, "The Federation's Postwar Program."

54. Alfred M. Skolnik, "Private Pension Plans, 1950–74," *Social Security Bulletin* 39 (June 1976), p. 4; Bureau of Labor Statistics, *Multiemployer Plans*, p. 1; Bartell and Simpson, *Multiemployer Funds*, p. 6; David T. Ellwood, "Pensions and the Labor Market: A Starting Point (The Mouse Can Roar)," in David A. Wise, ed., *Pensions, Labor, and Individual Choice* (Chicago: University of Chicago Press for NBER, 1985), pp. 23–24.

55. Ellwood, "Pensions and the Labor Market," p. 23. Ellwood asserts that industry characteristics, not competitive emulation, explain the high pension coverage among nonunion employees in industries with high union coverage; this issue could bear further research.

56. Skolnik, "Pension Plans, 1950–74," pp. 4–5; Bureau of Labor Statistics, *Multiemployer Plans;* State of New York Department of Labor, Division of Research and Statistics, *Pensions: Larger Plans in New York State — 1957* (New York, July 1957), and Bankers Trust Company of New York, *1960 Study of Industrial Retirement Plans* (New York, 1960), pp. 19–21, both cited in Robert Tilove, "Social and Economic Implications of Private Pensions," *Industrial Labor Review* 14 (1960), pp. 27–28. For a fine analysis of "voice" in union policymaking, and its effect on pension planning, see Richard B. Freeman, "Unions, Pensions, and Union Pension Funds," in Wise, *Pensions, Labor, and Choice,* pp. 89–122. As long as the compensation package with pension benefits was sufficiently attractive to younger workers an employer wanted to hire, management would abide by the union's distribution of total compensation.

57. Bronson, "Pensions — 1949," pp. 231, 237; Rainard B. Robbins, "Pension Planning in the United States," mss. (1952), p. 143; Dearing, *Industrial Pensions,* p. 226.

58. For an analytical albeit controversial discussion of the connection between plan insecurity and organizational attachment, see Richard A. Ippolito, *Pensions, Economics, and Public Policy* (Homewood, Ill.: Dow Jones-Irwin for the Pension Research Council, 1986), pp. 193ff; for the periodic liberalization of pension benefits at contract renegotiation sessions and its dilutive effect on funded status, see Robert C. Kryvicky, "The Funding of Negotiated Pension Plans," *Transactions of the Society of Actuaries* 33 (1981), pp. 405–59.

59. Barbash, "Union Interest in Pensions," pp. 75–79; Tilove, "Income for the Elderly," pp. 31–42. Union activities were clearly not the only factor leading to the increasing acceptance of pensions as deferred wages. Such had been the direction of change since the Morris fiasco of 1923, as seen in the resulting popularity of secure and contractual insured pension arrangements; IRS pressures, requiring various indicia that a plan was a bona fide employee benefit scheme, also served to strengthen participant claims to pension benefits; for official union policy supporting vesting in 1950, see Harry Becker, "Organized Labor and Social Security," The Quest for Economic Security, a Symposium, University of Michigan, 2 Aug. 1950.

60. See Samuel Lubell, *The Future of American Politics,* 3rd ed. (New York:

Harper Colophon, 1965), pp. 174–75; Richard C. Edwards, *Contested Terrain: The Transformation of the Workplace in the Twentieth Century* (New York: Basic Books, 1979).

7. The Pension Industry Reorganizes

1. This chapter owes much to discussions and readings in works of Dan McGill, the leading observer of the U.S. pension scene in the postwar period. McGill directs the Pension Research Council, which supported my research. Kenneth Black Jr.'s *Group Annuities* (Philadelphia: University of Pennsylvania Press, 1955) and James E. McNulty Jr.'s *Decision and Influence Processes in Private Pension Plans* (Philadelphia: University of Pennsylvania Press, 1961), both written under the editorship of Dan McGill, were also extremely helpful. Finally, I learned a great deal about the U.S. situation from Leslie Hannah's brilliant study of the British pension institution, *Inventing Retirement: The Development of Occupational Pensions in Britain* (Cambridge: Cambridge University Press, 1986), and his set of insightful preliminary working papers.

2. "Number of Persons Covered by Major Pension and Retirement Programs in the United States," *Pension Facts 1974* (Washington: American Council on Life Insurance, 1974), p. 12; Morgan H. Alvord, "Insured Pension Plans in the United States and Canada," *Transactions of the International Congress of Actuaries* (New York: Mallon, 1957), p. 188. Alvord estimates the number of insured plans in 1940 at 1,500. For insurance company finances in the Depression, see Harold F. Williamson and Orange A. Smalley, *Northwestern Mutual Life: A Century of Trusteeship* (Evanston, Ill.: Northwestern University Press, 1957), pp. 258–74; R. Carlyle Buley, *The Equitable Life Assurance Society of the United States, 1859–1964* (New York: Appleton-Century-Crofts, 1967), pp. 992–1043; and Joseph Frazier Wall, *Policies and People: The First Hundred Years of the Bankers Life* (Englewood Cliffs, N.J.: Prentice-Hall, 1979), pp. 78–87.

3. The Equitable entered the pension business in 1927, the Prudential in 1928, and Aetna in 1931. Other than the carriers listed, the only companies issuing group annuity contracts in 1938 were the Minnesota Mutual Life Insurance Company (a Group Association member with but two small contracts) and Occidental Life Insurance of Raleigh, N.C. (which underwrote one large contract and was the only firm in the business not in the Group Association); "Total Group Annuity Business in Force, End of Year — 1934–1938," Temporary National Economic Committee, *Investigation of Concentration of Economic Power Hearings before the Temporary National Economic Committee,* part 10: *Life Insurance* (1939, 76th Cong., 1st Sess.), p. 4716. The New York Insurance Department endorsed the Group Association as its rules helped assure sound underwriting standards as well as control competitive behavior. Also see testimony of E. E. Cammack, pp. 4187ff.

4. See Black, *Group Annuities,* p. 236. After the initial economic collapse and

massive layoffs of 1929–1933, labor turnover declined sharply. For this reason, and because corporations seriously slowed their hiring programs, active workforces aged dramatically. Both phenomena raised employer group annuity costs: accruals grew increasingly expensive as the participant aged, and as employee contributions typically remained constant, the employer assumed the sharply rising incremental expense. Declining turnover also raised sponsor costs, as fewer terminations meant more retirements. Interest rates on twenty-year corporate bonds fell from 4.57 percent in 1929 to 2.65 percent in 1939; *Historical Statistics,* Series X 343–347, p. 657. Mortality rates also fell dramatically through the first half of the twentieth century. One study of group insurance policyholders during the 1940s showed an annual decline of 4.6 percent among white males age 25–34, and declines ranging from 2.6 to 1.3 percent for other age groups; Dan McGill, *Fundamentals of Private Pensions,* 1st ed. (Homewood, Ill.: Irwin, 1955), p. 163, and Appendix D, pp. 218–22; W. A. Jenkins and E. A. Lew, "A New Mortality Basis for Annuities," *Transactions of the Society of Actuaries* 1 (1949), pp. 369–466; Ray Peterson, "Group Annuity Mortality," *Transactions of the Society of Actuaries* 4 (1952), pp. 246–307. Standard Oil installed its money purchase pension plan on 1 Jan. 1936. The program was paired with a savings plan and employees had a choice, within limits, of selecting either the pension or savings option. As the large majority of employees elected the maximum savings plan contribution, and the company maintained its interest in supporting a rich retirement income program, Standard Oil shifted back to more a conventional arrangement after the war; interview with Arthur Brown.

5. *Historical Statistics,* Series X 343–347, p. 657; Black, *Group Annuities,* Appendix D, p. 236. The insurance companies significantly reduced the strength of their interest rate guarantees in contracts written after 1935. Earlier agreements guaranteed lifetime annuity purchase rates to each participant for the first five years of the plan and thereafter adjusted the lifetime rate guarantee annually for new employees. After 1935, however, the carriers guaranteed annuity rates only on money coming into the plan, with a rate minimum initially locked in for five years and thereafter revised annually; McGill, *Fundamentals,* 1st ed., pp. 94–95, 100.

6. Interviews with Dan McGill, Meyer Melnikoff, and Ray Peterson; see Darrison Silesky, "Past and Future Dynamics of North American Retirement Systems," *Transactions of the Society of Actuaries* 14, pt. 2 (1972), pp. D3–4. An analyst today might argue that carriers should have "marked their portfolios to market." As interest rates fell, they should have recognized the capital gain in the value of their bond portfolios and passed these gains along to their policyholders. *Then* they should have credited these policyholders with the current market rate of interest. Past policyholders thus would have captured all the benefit of the falling rates and adding new clients would not have diluted their position. But the insurers did not operate this way. Indeed one of their basic functions was to shield their clients from such shocks to asset values.

7. Black, *Group Annuities,* Appendix C:2, pp. 232–35; also see Appendix C:1, pp. 225–32.

8. Dennis N. Warters, "Early History of Bankers Life Department," quoted in Wall, *Policies and People,* pp. 106, 100–06.

9. McGill, *Fundamentals,* 1st ed., pp. 75–84; Wall, *Policies and People,* pp. 107–10.

10. Black, *Group Annuities,* Appendix A, p. 221; McGill, *Fundamentals,* 2nd ed., pp. 128–37. Group permanent grew out of a Bankers Life prototype product designed to provide group life insurance on a permanent rather than term basis. The specific purpose was to extend life insurance protection to retired participants of a group life plan. The product was funded while the employee was actively at work, developing cash values that would provide the continuing coverage. The Bankers Life actuaries quickly realized that such an accumulation could support an annuity, as well as a death benefit, and the group permanent pension contract was born. (An annuity large enough to serve as a pension allowance, however, required a significantly larger sum than the cash value created under the proposed permanent life insurance plan.)

The actuaries at Bankers Life gave the firm not only the technical ability to develop group permanent but the impetus to enter the group insurance business. The sales manager bitterly opposed the group insurance initiative, as he and his department were totally devoted to individual sales and group business clearly required a separate sales force. Bankers went ahead primarily because actuaries controlled the firm. Insurance companies dominated by sales departments, the typical case, developed far less interest in group insurance; Wall, *Policies and People,* pp. 102–04.

11. Black gives data on fifty-six carriers in 1953, while the TNEC lists only ten in 1938; TNEC, "Life Insurance," p. 4716; also see Black, *Group Annuities,* p. 40, and Appendix A, p. 233; for a similar trend, see *A Study of Industrial Retirement Plans [1960]* (New York: Bankers Trust Company, 1960) [hereafter *Bankers Trust Survey 19xx*], p. 26.

12. *Bankers Trust Survey 1965,* p. 30; Black, *Group Annuities,* Appendix C, pp. 225–231.

13. Union leaders had reasons of their own to avoid insurance: by tying benefits to the continuing strength of the union, they reinforced worker loyalty to the organization. Multi-employer plans were in many cases controlled by union trustees, moreover, some of whom wanted to use pension funds for purposes ranging from personal enrichment to promoting the broader interests of labor. The establishment of a pension program for the salaried staff was more likely to follow the creation of a single-employer than a multi-employer plan. This point was made by an anonymous critic from the Pension Research Council. For insurance company interest in bargained plans, see Buley, *Equitable,* p. 1242. For the growing complexity of pension benefits, see *Bankers Trust Survey 1956,* p. 18.

14. The reduction in net yield due to federal income tax on interest earnings computed from Black, *Group Annuities,* table 15, p. 168; for the increased net cost of insurance, see the statement by D. N. Warters before the Subcommittee on the Taxation of Life Insurance Companies of the Committee on Ways and Means, House of Representatives, 82nd Congress, pp. 2–3; see Buley, *Equitable,* pp. 1145–56; interview with Ray M. Peterson; U.S. Senate Finance Committee, *Life Insurance Company Income Tax Act of 1959: Report Together with Supplemental Views of the Committee on Finance, United States Senate* (86th Cong., 1st Sess., 1959). Before 1942 sponsors using trust funds could deduct 10 percent of *each* past service contribution, and do so for ten years. The procedure was designed to accommodate the transfer of large balance sheet reserves to pension trusts. But the method was extremely awkward for the far more common circumstance of a sponsor paying down a past-service liability over many years. The 1942 Act allowed sponsors to deduct their entire past service *contribution,* but limited that contribution to 10 percent of the initial liability. Deductions for any contributions above this figure would have to be carried forward to future tax years. In 1964 twenty-four states also levied a premium tax on contributions paid to pension insurers. And while the major industrial states were not among the seventeen, premium tax collections consistently absorbed nearly 1 percent of the carriers' total pension revenues; McGill, *Fundamentals,* 2nd ed., p. 295; Robert K. Trapp, "The Three Ages of Insured Pension Plans," *Pension and Welfare News,* April 1967, p. 13.

15. While sponsors complained about insurance's marketing, administrative, and risk-bearing expenses, these costs existed, either implicitly or explicitly, in self-insured arrangements. Specialized insurance carriers actually provided many of these services more efficiently than the sponsors.

Most organizations established plans to benefit retiring and soon-to-retire employees, as evidenced by the fact that the earliest plans were straight paygo affairs. Insurance company products, however, were not designed to provide pensions for this cohort. Insured pension arrangements operated on a strict accrual basis, charging "normal cost" and crediting employees with the pension credit earned that year. Past-service liabilities — which made up nearly the entire benefit of older employees — were handled separately. Insured pension programs thus allocated resources to the future while sponsors began programs thinking of the present. Aside from plans motivated simply by tax avoidance, sponsors in the wave of plan formations which began in World War II focused on the current need for retirement income.

16. In a study of 550 major corporations, with 38 percent responding, 75 percent added supplementary pensions or made special additional payments to retirees. "Extra Pension Payments," Industrial Relations Memorandum #103, 9 Nov. 1948, Archives of Industrial Relations Counselors, New York, p. 2.

17. For the steadily increasing popularity of final-average plans or periodic indexing of average-salary plans to account for inflation, see *Bankers Trust Survey 1956,* p. 18; *Bankers Trust Survey 1960,* p. 20; *Bankers Trust Survey 1965,* pp. 25–26, 29–

30; also see Howard E. Hennington, discussion in "Pension Plans in Perspective," *Transactions of the Society of Actuaries* 14 (1972), pp. D573–579. Benefit formulas based on final average salary tied a retiree's initial pension benefit to inflation. But once a pension goes into pay status, the sponsor and participant are back in a nominal annuity contract. Sponsors hardly ever provided formal indexing of pension benefits, and ad hoc improvements rarely equaled the rate of inflation. Thus the real values of pension payments tended to decay over time. Key factors determining this rate of decline were the pace of inflation and the sponsor's free will policy toward ad hoc benefit improvements. But sponsors lose interest in retirees as they age, both because personal attachments weaken with time and because older pensioners exert far less influence on the active workforce than those recently retired.

18. Interviews with Melnikoff, Peterson, and Charles Trowbridge.

19. Remembering interest rates in the recent past of less than 2 percent, the carriers refused to offer interest guarantees of any significance. See James A. Hamilton and Dorrance Bronson, *Pensions* (New York: McGraw-Hill, 1958), p. 157; Walter Couper and Roger Vaughn, *Pension Planning: Experience and Trends* (New York: Industrial Relations Counselors, 1954), pp. 45–46.

20. See McGill, *Fundamentals,* 2nd ed., p. 165.

21. Interview with George Cowles; McNulty, *Decision Processes,* pp. 69–70. At first the bank trustees did little more than provide custodial services with the sponsor actually directing investment policy. Thus, from 1927 when the trust was established to the late 1930s, American Telephone and Telegraph instructed Bankers' Trust to invest in specific AT&T securities. The sponsor then reversed this policy and instructed its trustee to purchase a diversified portfolio of other companies' securities. In general, the sponsors exercised a significant measure of control over their trustees' investment policy.

22. McNulty, *Decision Processes;* interviews with Harry Zebrowitz and George Swick.

23. Margaret Allen Burt, *George B. Buck, Consulting Actuaries, Inc.: The First Twenty-Five Years* ([New York]: 1976); Buck Consultants, Inc., *Buck: Review and Outlook 1982* (New York, 1982), p. 2; interviews with Margaret Allen Burt and George Swick.

24. Interview with Harry Zebrowitz; A. S. Hansen — another consulting actuarial firm with pension experience — assumed a leading position in its native Chicago.

25. On the basis of its work on United Carbide and Carbon's 1917 plan, TPF&C claims to be the second-oldest pension consulting firm, presumably after Buck. [H. Walter Forster], *The Story of the Towers, Perrin, Forster, and Crosby, Inc.* (Philadelphia, 1951), pp. 15–18, 67–68, 110, 113, 118; interview with Preston Basset.

26. Forster, *Towers, Perrin,* pp. 45–58, 138, 148, 163–64.

27. Interview with Preston Basset.

28. That more market-sensitive insurance brokers than technically based actuarial firms entered the pension consulting business parallels the experience of the textile industrial revolution: merchants, not craftsmen, developed the major firms in the industry.

29. Frank L. Griffen Jr., *WYCO: The Building of a Professional Actuarial and Consulting Organization: The Wyatt Company* (1979); interview with Herbert Osterman.

30. Interviews with Martin E. Segal, Robert Paul, and Robert Krinsky.

31. Interviews with Martin E. Segal, Robert Paul, and Robert Krinsky; McNulty, *Decision Processes,* pp. 57–63.

32. Interview with Preston Basset.

33. The group annuity's SPDA costing method pushed most plan costs into the future, reducing the significance of this requirement. All carriers, however, required that the past-service liability associated with each employee be paid off by the time the employee retired. Deviations from the carrier's standard projections were passed on to the sponsor though the insurance company's dividend policy or experience-rating program. But these adjustments — in effect the degree of self-insurance — were both partial and gradual.

34. Statement by Frank L. Griffin Jr., "Panel Discussion: Security of Private Pension Expectations," *Transactions of the Society of Actuaries* 15 (1973), pp. D284–85; also see statements by Ray M. Peterson, pp. D278–79, D298–99; Gilbert W. Fitzhugh, p. 304; and Richard Daskais, p. 306; D. N. Warters and J. Rae, "The Risks in Equity Investments of Pension Funds," *Transactions of the Society of Actuaries* 11 (1969), pp. 132ff; R. M. Peterson, "Group Annuity Mortality," *Transactions of the Society of Actuaries* 4 (1952), p. 265; R. M. Peterson, "Future Mortality Rates and Pension Costs" (privately printed); interview with Ray M. Peterson; Martin S. House, *Private Employee Benefit Plans — A Public Trust* (Albany: State of New York Insurance Department, 1956).

35. Interviews with Dan McGill, Robert Vaughn, Robert Collier, and Preston Basset; "The Conference of Actuaries in Private Practice," *Pension and Welfare News,* Sept. 1967, p. 32.

36. Interview with Ray M. Peterson; U.S. Senate Finance Committee, *Life Insurance Company Income Tax Act of 1959.*

37. Interviews with Dan McGill, Preston Bassett.

38. McGill, *Fundamentals,* 2nd ed., pp. 155ff; Black, *Group Annuities,* pp. 92 ff; *Bankers Trust Survey 1956,* p. 21; Thomas E. Meany, "Recent Trends in Retirement Plan Provisions," Equitable Life Assurance Society of the United States, *Proceedings of the Equitable Society Pension Forum* (New York, 1952), pp. 33–34; *1957 Life Insurance Fact Book* (New York: Institute of Life Insurance, 1957), p. 32. While the Equitable had developed the deposit administration concept in 1929, its contract only won approval from the New York State Insurance Department in 1932; Buley, *Equitable,* pp. 909–10.

39. McGill, *Fundamentals,* 1st ed., pp. 101–09; Black, *Group Annuities,* pp. 102–03, 109–10; interviews with George Swick and Sherman Sass.

40. McGill, *Fundamentals,* 1st ed., pp. 109–13, 202–05; Black, *Group Annuities,* pp. 105–10.

41. Buley, *Equitable,* pp. 1314–15, 1317–18; interviews with C. Lambert Trowbridge, Dan McGill, William C. Prouty, Pembroke Minster; for a full treatment, see Dan McGill in collaboration with Donald S. Grubbs Jr., *Fundamentals of Private Pensions,* 4th ed. (Homewood, Ill.: Richard D. Irwin for the Pension Research Council, 1979), pp. 282–89; Malcolm D. MacKinnon, discussion on "Design and Mechanics of Pension Plans," *Transactions of the Society of Actuaries* 19 (1967), pp. D527ff.

42. McGill, *Fundamentals,* 2nd ed., pp. 288–91; John M. Hines, "The Responsibility in Pension Funding," *Proceedings, Equitable Pension Forum,* pp. 16–17. The insurance companies faced a similar divergence of portfolio and market interest rates in the 1930s and 1940s, with the portfolio rate then standing well above the market. The carriers could have preserved the earning power of older contracts and moved aggressively after the exploding pension business had they adopted investment-year accounting. Although the idea was considered at least at one firm, it was not adopted. The threat of the loss of business in the 1950s, rather than the desire to safeguard the earning power of the existing policyholders or to capture new business, led the insurance companies to drop this traditional practice of inter-year investment pooling.

Because trust companies invested in equities, which carried higher risk and higher returns than bonds, these firms and their clients would tend to hedge or blend their positions with lower-risk/lower-return fixed-income securities. Insurance companies, denied access to equities, would gravitate toward the higher-risk/higher-return fixed-income issues. These structural biases, as well as the insurers' special facilities for mortgages and private placements, help explain the disparity noted by Hines and McGill.

43. See, generally, McGill, *Fundamentals,* 4th ed., pp. 207–24, 294–97; Buley, *Equitable,* pp. 1314–19; "Delay Action on Trustee Role for Life Companies, Met Asks," *National Underwriter,* 31 Jan. 1959, p. 5; interview with Ray M. Peterson; for the growth of separate accounts to 1966, see MacKinnon, "Design and Mechanics," p. D527. In some states, including New York, separate accounts were subject to restrictions on the quality of permissible investments; Buley, *Equitable,* p. 1318n28; McGill, *Fundamentals,* 4th ed., p. 295.

An early effort at providing equity investments in an insured context was the Teachers' Insurance and Annuity Association's 1952 "variable annuity" plan — the College Retirement Equity Fund. During the years of accumulation, the CREF variable annuity was essentially an individually allocated mutual fund account; in retirement, it became an individual annuity. But instead of paying out a benefit denominated in dollars, CREF defined its allowance as a set number of mutual fund units, and pension payments thus reflected the value of the underlying securities. TIAA specifically established CREF to assure participants that their pension benefits would keep up with inflation and the rising standard of living. The program's experience over its first fifteen years, 1952 to 1967, was nothing short of fabulous. Whereas the yield on thirty-year corporate bonds averaged 3.9 percent over the period, CREF registered an average annual return of 11 percent. But despite this success, and the great deal of publicity CREF received, the variable annuity failed to become a significant instrument outside of the college market. Such an individually allocated, common-stock-based pension program was seen as inherently too risky. TIAA itself restricted CREF investments to 50 percent of a participant's contributions (increased to a maximum of 75 percent of contributions in 1967 and 100 percent in 1972), and most other variable annuities were restricted to a similarly supplementary role. "Basic Yields of 30-Year Corporate Bonds," U.S. Bureau of Economic Analysis, *Long Term Economic Growth, 1860–1970* (Washington, 1973), pp. 224–25; William C. Greenough, "CREF and the Variable Annuity's First 15 Years," *Pension and Welfare News,* 8 March 1967, pp. 17–20; William C. Greenough, *A New Approach to Retirement Income* (New York: Teachers Insurance and Annuity Association, 1952); also see Robert M. Duncan, "A Retirement System Granting Unit Annuities and Investing in Equities," *Transactions of the Society of Actuaries* 4 (1952), pp. 317–44; George E. Johnson, "Variable Annuities — The Courts, Laws, and Regulations," *Pension and Welfare News,* Nov. 1964, pp. 21–24; Maximilian Wallach, "Variable Annuity Contracts — Fifteen or So Years Later," *Proceedings of the Conference of Actuaries in Public Practice* 20 (1970–71), pp. 406–19. For the limited role of variable annuities, see *Bankers Trust Survey 1965,* p. 27, and *Bankers Trust Survey 1970,* p. 30. Variable annuities and other individually allocated equity-linked pension arrangements do come under SEC securities and investment company regulations. They were, however, able to avoid the most burdensome requirements; McGill, *Fundamentals,* 4th ed., pp. 216, 296.

44. Interview with Margaret Del Tufo of the Equitable Life Assurance Company.

45. Black, *Group Annuities,* table 22, p. 216; Trapp, "Three Ages of Insured Pension Plans," p. 15; Ray M. Peterson, "Security of Pension Plan Expectations," *Transactions of the Society of Actuaries* 15 (1973), p. 279; "Fitzhugh Reviews Role of Life Companies in Pension Field," *The Standard,* 18 Oct. 1963, MetLife Archives.

46. This section owes much to James McNulty's remarkable and subtle *Decision Processes,* to the work of Oliver Williamson and Jay Galbraith, and to modern managerial agency theory as explicated in John W. Pratt and Richard J. Zeckhauser, eds., *Principals and Agents: The Structure of Business* (Cambridge, Mass.: Harvard Business School Press, 1985), esp. Pratt and Zeckhauser, "Principals and Agents: An Overview," pp. 1–35.

47. McNulty, *Decision Processes,* pp. 23–24; Couper and Vaughn, *Pension Planning,* pp. 6ff.

48. See George V. Thompson, "Intercompany Technical Standardization in the

Early American Automobile Industry," *Journal of Economic History* 14, no. 1 (1954): 1–20; Jay Galbraith, *Designing Complex Organizations* (Reading, Mass.: Addison Wesley, 1973); Oliver Williamson, *Markets and Hierarchies* (New York: Free Press, 1975).

49. McNulty, *Decision Processes,* pp. 94, 101. McNulty thought that there ought to be more contact, as the actuaries rarely communicated even payout projections to the investment managers.

50. Ibid., pp. 11, 66.

51. Ibid., pp. 8–15.

52. Ibid., pp. 48, 49, 14–16, 36–40.

53. Ibid., p. 66; Buttrick, "Intercompany Standardization"; Williamson,*Markets and Hierarchies;* David Maister, "Balancing the Professional Service Firm," *Sloan Management Review* 24, no. 1 (Fall 1982). The Equitable would actually abandon the actuarial consulting business in the early 1980s; interviews with Harrison Givens and Sherman Sass.

54. Interviews with McGill and Zebrowitz. Investment counselors generally encouraged their clients to move into equities; McNulty, *Decision Processes,* pp. 41, 73ff.

55. Interview with Zebrowitz; McNulty, *Decision Processes,* pp. 41–43, 46, 75.

56. McNulty, *Decision Processes,* pp. 74, 78–79; interview with George Cowles.

57. See Pratt and Zeckhauser, "Principals and Agents."

58. Interview with Preston Bassett; McNulty, *Decision Processes,* p. 98; also see George A. Akerlof, "Labor Contracts as Partial Gift Exchanges," *Quarterly Journal of Economics* 92 (1982), pp. 543–69; Joseph E. Stiglitz, "The Causes and Consequences of the Dependence of Quality on Price," *Journal of Economic Literature* 25 (1987), pp. 1–48.

59. Interview with Cowles.

8. ERISA and the Reformation of Pensions

1. This chapter is especially indebted to the writings and personal comments of Professor Dan McGill, who has been my mentor and guide to the development of the pension institution throughout the writing of this book. It also leans heavily on discussions with and articles by Michael Gordon, including "Overview: Why Was ERISA Enacted?" in *The Employee Retirement Income Security Act of 1974: The First Decade,* An Information Paper of the U.S. Senate Special Committee on Aging, 98th Cong., 2nd Sess., 1984 (Washington: GPO, 1984); "Introduction: The Social Policy Origins of ERISA," in Steven J. Sucher, Jeffrey L. Gibbs, and Howard Shapiro, eds., *Employee Benefits Law* (Washington: Bureau of National Affairs, 1991), pp. lxiii–lxxvii; and "ERISA, ESOPs, and Senator Javits: The Mind of a Reformer," *American Journal of Tax Policy* 3 (1988), pp. 3–30. "Share of Total Financial Assets held by Pension Plans, 1950–1989," table 16.3 in Arnold J. Hoffman and John P.

Mondejar, "Pension Funds and Financial Markets, 1950–1989," in John A. Turner and Daniel J. Beller, *Trends in Pensions 1992* (Washington: GPO, 1992); Alfred M. Skolnik, "Private Pension Plans, 1950–74," *Social Security Bulletin* 39 (June 1976), p. 4.

2. Ralph C. James and Estelle Dinerstein James, *Hoffa and the Teamsters* (Princeton: Van Nostrand, 1965), p. 216.

3. Ibid., p. 68.

4. Ibid., p. 220, quoted from CSPF transcripts. One of the Jameses was also present at this meeting; p. 35.

5. Dan McGill, in collaboration with Donald S. Grubbs Jr., *Fundamentals of Private Pensions,* 4th ed. (Homewood, Ill.: Richard D. Irwin for the Pension Research Council, 1979), pp. 54–55; James and James, *Hoffa,* pp. 227–33.

6. James and James, *Hoffa,* p. 35.

7. Ibid., pp. 295, 292–95.

8. See Dan McGill, *Preservation of Pension Benefit Rights* (Homewood, Ill.: Richard D. Irwin for the Pension Research Council, 1972), p. 107. Much to the chagrin of well-meaning officials in the UAW's social security department, few union members elected the voluntary joint-and-survivor option; Willard Solenberger interview.

9. Studebaker was hardly the first negotiated plan to terminate with insufficient funds, nor even the first negotiated by the UAW. Indeed, Studebaker itself had terminated the Packard Motor Company's plan in 1958, after absorbing the firm in 1954. Packard's plan involved a comparable number of workers (the firm employed 10,250 at the end of 1953) and had a substantial asset shortfall. (Retirees took a 15 percent hit; those over 60 and thus eligible for early retirement, but who remained in the active workforce, took a more substantial hit; those under 60 got nothing.) But only 625 workers were on hand for the final bustup, of whom 434 were over 60 and received a payout; 9,000 had been laid off for over two years. When the Studebaker plan went bust, 7,000 workers were thrown into the streets at once, and their pensions put at risk; Merton Bernstein, *The Future of Private Pensions* (New York: Free Press of Glencoe, 1964), pp. 94–95; testimony of Willard Solenberger, Hearings before the Subcommittee on Fiscal Policy of the Joint Economic Committee, 89th Cong., 2nd Sess., pt. 1 (1966), p. 125.

10. Solenberger testimony, Subcommittee on Fiscal Policy, pp. 125–26; Clifford M. MacMillan testimony, ibid., p. 109; Rev. Rul. 61-157, pt. 5, (c) (2), 1961–2 Cum. Bull. 67, 87, superseded by Treas. Reg. PP 1.401–6, 28 Fed. Reg. 10115, 10120–21.

11. C. M. MacMillan to H. E. Churchill, 16 April 1959 and 2 Sept. 1959, in "Negotiations 1959" Notebook, "Correspondence" Tab, as cited in James Wooten, "'The Infamous Studebaker Case': The Studebaker-Packard Corporation, the United Auto Workers, and the Origins of ERISA," MSS, dated 16 Nov. 1994.

12. MacMillan testimony, Subcommittee on Fiscal Policy, p. 107.

13. Richard A. Ippolito, *Pensions, Economics, and Public Policy* (Homewood, Ill.: Dow Jones–Irwin for the Pension Research Council, 1986), pp. 177ff. The "pension bond," of course, also tied young workers to the union organization.

14. McGill, *Preservation of Pension Benefit Rights.*

15. *Restatement, Contracts* (St. Paul: American Law Institute, 1932), sec. 90, quoted in Benjamin Aaron, *Legal Status of Employee Benefit Rights under Private Pension Plans* (Homewood, Ill.: Richard D. Irwin for the Pension Research Council, 1961), p. 9; italics added. Aaron cited two cases invoking the principle of promissory estoppel—*Hunter v. Sparling,* 87 Cal. App. 2nd 711, 197 P.2d 807 (1948) (alternative holding) and *Langer v. Superior Steel Corp.,* 105 Pa. Super. 570, 161, Atl. 571 (1932) (alternative holding), p. 9n13.

16. Aaron, *Legal Status,* pp. 10, 119; Dan McGill, *Fulfilling Pension Expectations* (Homewood, Ill.: Richard D. Irwin for the Pension Research Council, 1962), pp. 83, 164.

17. McGill, *Fulfilling Pension Expectations,* pp. 88, 63–93. A handful of corporations, primarily in the insurance and petroleum industries, voluntarily guaranteed employee pension benefits with their full faith and credit. See Dan McGill, *Employer Guarantee of Pension Benefits* (Homewood, Ill.: Richard D. Irwin for the Pension Research Council, 1974), p. 22.

18. McGill, *Fulfilling Pension Expectations,* p. 88; Jack L. Treynor, Patrick J. Regan, and William W. Priest, *The Financial Reality of Pension Funding under ERISA* (Homewood, Ill.: Dow Jones–Irwin, 1976), p. 50.

19. Bernstein, *The Future of Private Pensions.*

20. Corbin, *Contracts* (St. Paul: West Publishing, 1958) vol. 1, sec. 153, quoted in Aaron, *Legal Status,* p. 14.

21. I am indebted to Dan McGill for the observation that Latimer's text made no mention of vesting.

22. The remainder of this chapter, especially, owes much to the work of Michael Gordon.

23. See esp. Paul P. Harbrecht, *Pension Funds and Economic Power* (New York: Twentieth Century Fund, 1959).

24. 29 U.S.C. Secs. 301 et seq.

25. Eisenhower quoted in Aaron, *Legal Status,* p. 106. Aaron's own comment on the 1958 legislation bears repetition: "only an administrator of extraordinary contumaciousness and persistence could manage to bring himself within the scope of the criminal sanctions of the Act. Moreover, it is doubtful that the law presents formidable impediments to continued skullduggery of the more flagrant variety which investigations have revealed in the administration of some health and welfare plans" ibid., p. 107. In early drafts of the Welfare and Pension Plan Disclosure Act, the Senate Subcommittee on Welfare and Pension Funds recommended that the Securities and Exchange Commission, not the Department of Labor, oversee plan disclosures. The SEC in the 1950s had developed the best statistical series on pen-

sion financials and had great experience overseeing reporting to corporate shareholders. Labor won jurisdiction because the SEC demurred and because pension
beneficiaries were the Department's constituents and the governance of plans was
tied inextricably to the employment and collective-bargaining relationship. Interview with Michael Gordon; Harbrecht, *Funds and Power,* p. 146. Also see Senate
Committee on Labor and Public Welfare, *Welfare and Pension Plan Disclosure Acts,*
Senate Report no. 1440, 85th Cong., 2nd Sess. (1958), and Subcommittee on
Welfare and Pension Funds, Senate Committee on Labor and Public Welfare, *Welfare and Pension Plan Investigation,* Senate Report no. 1734, 84th Cong., 2nd Sess.,
(1956).

  26. James and James, *Hoffa,* p. 20; Bernstein, *Future of Private Pensions,* 47, 120;
see Robert F. Kennedy, *The Enemy Within* (New York: Harper and Row, 1960);
McGill, *Fundamentals,* 4th ed., p. 33.

  27. Memorandum from President Kennedy constituting the Cabinet Committee
on Corporate Pension Funds and Other Private Retirement and Welfare Programs,
28 March 1962, rpt. as Appendix C in *Public Policy and Private Pension Programs:
A Report to the President on Private Employee Retirement Plans* (Washington: GPO,
Jan. 1965). Kennedy, in his *1962 Economic Report of the President,* cited the "Commission on Money and Credit" as inspiring his review of the pension institution.
This smacks of political courtesy, however, more than honest reportage. The Commission on Money and Credit had been created by the Committee for Economic
Development and the Ford Foundation — powerful and respected organs of the
corporate establishment. It was to survey the *entire* U.S. financial apparatus, from
fiscal stabilization policies to local credit unions, and asked Victor Andrews, of MIT,
to study the role of corporate, state, and local pension plans. Andrews's report was
published in Irwin Friend, Hyman P. Minsky, and Victor L. Andrews, *Private Capital Markets* (Englewood Cliffs, N.J.: Prentice-Hall, 1964), pp. 381–531. Andrews's
study was solid but hardly raised disturbing questions of national import. And in
the Commission's overall report, the section on pensions occupied less than two
pages and recommended little beyond the need for tighter fiduciary standards su-
pervised by "an appropriate regulatory body." The Commission thus produced
nothing to inspire Kennedy's sweeping institutional charge to his Cabinet Committee. See *Money and Credit* (Englewood Cliffs, N.J.: Prentice-Hall, 1961),
pp. 175–77; "Provisional Report to the President," typescript, dated 15 Nov. 1962,
received 11 Nov. 1962, White House Central Subject File FG 645/FG 165, Box
199, Committee on Corporate Pension Funds and Other Private Retirement and
Welfare Programs, Kennedy Archives, John F. Kennedy Library, Boston.

  28. The Cabinet committee saw pensions as a beneficial source of saving and a
mild impediment to labor mobility. In neither situation did it call for legislative
intervention. Much of this material appears in the final published report, President's
Committee on Pensions, *Policy and Pensions* (Washington: GPO, 1965), pp. 27–
32, 70–72.

29. Merton Bernstein gives 60 percent as the target replacement rate; *Future of Private Pensions,* p. 145. The House Ways and Means Committee targeted a replacement rate of 50 percent for a couple; *Social Security Amendments of 1967: Report of the Committee on Ways and Means,* House Report 544, 90th Cong., 1st Sess. (Washington: GPO, 1967), cited in James H. Schulz et al., *Providing Adequate Retirement Income* (Hanover, N.H.: University Press of New England for Brandeis University Press, 1974), p. 299; James H. Schulz, *The Economic Status of the Retired Aged in 1980: Simulation Projections,* Research Report 24, U.S. Social Security Administration, Office of Research and Statistics (Washington: GPO, 1968).

30. President's Committee on Pensions, "Provisional Report," pp. 18, 16, 14–20. In its final 1965 report the Committee pictured the average full-time worker, earning $5,400 a year, getting a Social Security benefit equal to 30 percent of that figure (45 percent for married couples after including the spousal benefit); workers earning $7,500 a year got a benefit replacing only 20 percent (30 percent for couples); President's Committee on Pensions, *Policy and Pensions,* p. 22. While Social Security kept the elderly out of destitution, its critical Depression-era objective, retirement presented a rude economic shock. Raising the Social Security wage base, thus spreading more earnings to the future (or, more precisely, to current retirees with the assumption that future generations would transfer the same), became a primary goal of Social Security reformers; Martha Derthick, *Policymaking for Social Security* (Washington: Brookings Institution, 1979), pp. 283–87.

31. The Provincial Ontario legislature enacted the plan presented by its Committee on Portable Pensions in March 1963. Implementation was preempted, however, by the passage of an expanded nationwide program, the "Canada Pension Plan," in 1964. See McGill, *Preservation of Pension Benefit Rights,* pp. 238–321, esp. 241–51, 259–64, and 341; *Second Report of the Ontario Committee on Portable Pensions* (Toronto: Queen's Printer, Aug. 1961); Leslie Hannah, *Inventing Retirement: The Development of Occupational Pensions in Britain* (Cambridge: Cambridge University Press, 1986), pp. 46–65.

32. President's Committee on Pensions, "Provisional Report," pp. 2, 19. The current revenue loss could overstate the subsidy because the tax revenues are deferred, not lost. The subsidy amounts to the tax-free use of the monies otherwise paid in tax, and the lower rate of taxation typically paid by retirees. The magnitude of these favors, versus current taxation, is nevertheless still substantial; see Emil M. Sunley Jr., "Employee Benefits and Tax Payments," in Joseph A. Peckman, ed., *Comprehensive Income Taxation* (Washington: Brookings Institution, 1977), p. 77n. Some more inclusive calculations show the cost to the Treasury as about the same as the simple current revenue loss figures; see Alicia H. Munnell, "Current Taxation of Qualified Pension Plans: Has the Time Come?" *New England Economic Review* (March-April 1992), pp. 13–14. For arguments that pension plans enjoy common law tax treatment and no special tax subsidy, see Raymond Goetz, *Tax Treatment of Pension Plans: Preferential or Normal?* (Washington: American Enterprise Insti-

tute, 1969). The Cabinet Committee was aware that its approach to pensions was broader than the public's concern with soundness. Dan McGill had just published *Fulfilling Pension Expectations,* the capstone volume of a major Pension Research Council survey of the public's key concern. In a reference with a distinction, the committee entitled chapter 4 of its report "Fulfilling the Promise of the Private Pension System," which it defined as "fulfilling the promise of the private pension system . . . as a supplement to the basic public system for old-age security"; President's Committee on Pensions, "Provisional Report," p. 26.

33. President's Committee on Pensions, "Provisional Report," pp. 28–29; see McGill, *Preservation of Pension Benefit Rights,* pp. 72, 322–25, 338–41. The Ontario government task force, prior to settling on mandatory plans with mandatory vesting, had recommended mandatory vesting standards for the province's voluntary plans; see McGill, *Preservation of Pension Benefit Rights,* 241–42; and *A Summary Report of the Ontario Committee on Portable Pensions* (Toronto: Queen's Printer, Feb. 1961). In the United States, the IRS made vesting a de facto prerequisite for tax qualification (except for collectively bargained plans): only by vesting shorter-service workers, the agnecy held, could plans avoid a clearly discriminatory distribution of benefits. The de facto standard, however, was at about twenty years of service. See also Hugh Folk, "Private Pension Plans and Manpower Policy," BLS Bulletin no. 1359 (Washington: Bureau of Labor Statistics, 1963), and Walter Kolodrubetz, "Labor Mobility and Private Pension Plans," BLS Bulletin no. 1407 (Washington: Bureau of Labor Statistics, 1964).

34. Social Security offset the effects of inflation by basing benefits on "real" career average earnings; in multiemployer plans, the plan trustees or the negotiators at the bargaining table placed a dollar value on the accrued pension credits at the time they were paid.

35. President's Committee on Pensions, "Provisional Report," p. 32. The committee also proposed extending the portable Social Security system so that employers, primarily smaller employers, could "make voluntary contributions to a special OASDI fund which would entitle their employees to supplementary benefits," p. 33. See also Bernstein, *Future of Private Pensions,* pp. 264–96.

36. President's Committee on Pensions, "Provisional Report," pp. 28–29.

37. McGill, *Fulfilling Pension Expectations,* pp. 275–78.

38. President's Committee on Pensions, "Provisional Report," p. 34.

39. Ibid., p. 43.

40. Ibid., p. 34.

41. The corporate members of the advisory committee, all chairman of their respective corporations, were Elliott V. Bell of McGraw-Hill Publishing Company; Joseph L. Block of Inland Steel; Henry Ford II of Ford Motor Company; John M. Franklin of United States Lines Company; Richard S. Reynolds of Reynolds Metals Company; Stuart T. Saunders of the Pennsylvania Railroad; and Thomas J. Watson of International Business Machines Corporation. The Labor members, all presi-

dent, chief executive, or international secretary of their unions, were W. Anthony Boyle of the United Mine Workers of America; David Dubinsky of the International Garment Workers Union; George M. Harrison of the Brotherhood of Railway and Steamship Clerks, Freight Handlers, Express and Station Employees; Joseph Keenan of the International Brotherhood of Electrical Workers; David J. McDonald of the United Steelworkers of America; George Meany, president of the reunified AFL-CIO, and Walter Reuther of the International Union of Automobile, Aerospace, and Agricultural Implement Workers of America. The public members were W. Willard Wirtz (ex-officio), Secretary of Labor; Luther H. Hodges (ex-officio), Secretary of Commerce; Arthur F. Burns, president of the National Bureau of Economic Research; David L. Cole, attorney and arbitrator; Clark Kerr, president of the University of California; Ralph E. McGill, publisher of the *Atlanta Constitution;* and George W. Taylor, professor of industrial relations at the Wharton School of Finance and Commerce, University of Pennsylvania.

42. The report and individual comments were appended to President's Committee on Pensions, *Policy and Pensions.*

43. President's Advisory Committee, *Report,* pp. 14–15.

44. Ibid., pp. 14–15, 12.

45. Ibid., pp. 16–17.

46. Among the "public" members of the advisory committee, George Taylor and Arthur Burns registered criticisms. Taylor would let organized capital and labor divvy up compensation and pensions; Burns was particularly concerned about the cost of vesting. The only "public" member to write in support of the committee was Clark Kerr. Ibid., pp. 13–14, 15, 18–19.

47. President's Committee on Pensions, "Provisional Report," p. 1. The reference to American individualism was dropped from the opening of the published 1965 version of the Cabinet committee report in favor of "the welfare of the worker and his family, during and after he has completed his working life, has been steadily enhanced through major advances in private and public policy."

48. Myron L. Joseph to Walter Heller, "Briefing note for the Feb. 13 meeting of the Cabinet Committee on Corporate Benefits," 7 Feb. 1964, Walter J. Heller Papers, Box 41, Kennedy Archives, John F. Kennedy Library.

49. President's Committee on Pensions, *Policy and Pensions,* pp. 42–43.

50. Interview with Michael Gordon. The parallel between fiduciary issues in pensions and joint-stock corporations had not escaped prior attention. The Senate Subcommittee on Welfare and Pension Funds, in early drafts of the Disclosure Act of 1958, had recommended that the SEC oversee plan disclosures; Harbrecht, *Funds and Power,* p. 146.

51. James Wooten brought to my attention the 1942 prior-approval requirement for the purchase of company securities. Fiduciary infidelity violated the "exclusive benefit" requirement in existing pension tax law. But the only sanction available to the IRS was plan disqualification, which would precipitate a messy and ruinous

retroactive tax claim against all plan participants. IRS officials were understandably leery of adding to the insult and injury caused by the disloyal trustees. As a result, they hardly ever took action.

52. Dan McGill, *Guaranty Fund for Private Pension Obligations* (Homewood, Ill.: Richard D. Irwin for the Pension Research Council, 1970), p. 103. Hartke also proposed insuring plans against "the shrinkage of assets occasioned by the forced sale of investments to pay benefits," a largely unnecessary and confusing complication that could open an entirely unhealthy new line of government involvement in pensions; pp. 108–09. The UAW's *internal* interest in a pension insurance scheme dates from the Packard termination of 1958; see Wooten, "Infamous Studebaker Case."

53. President's Committee on Pensions, "Provisional Report," p. 34.

54. Howard Young, "Federal Reinsurance of Private Pension Plans," presented before the Chicago Actuarial Club, 19 April 1965; rpt. in McGill, *Guaranty Fund,* pp. 143–49; also see pp. 102–03. James Wooten makes the point that Young's advocacy of insurance also served a political purpose — it reduced the division between the CIO and the AFL on pension funding.

55. Young, "Federal Reinsurance," p. 149; Nelson McClung, economist to the Subcommittee on Fiscal Policy of the Joint Economic Committee and coordinator of its Old Age Income Assurance survey, claimed that insurance could provide benefits at lower contribution levels — an argument true in the short run but not in the long run.

56. Young's scheme resembled AFL multiemployer plans in that funding was low, contributions were as much assessment as savings, and benefits were backed by claims against "all" employers. It also resembled the French system of government-backed, industry-wide multiemployer plans. See McGill, *Preservation of Pension Benefit Rights,* pp. 283–94.

57. Robert E. Royce, at Nineteenth Annual Conference on Labor, New York University, 19 April 1966, quoted in American Enterprise Institute, *The Debate on Private Pensions* (Washington, March 1968), p. 43.

58. Emerson Beier, "Terminations of Pension Plans: 11 Years' Experience," *Monthly Labor Review* 80 (June 1967), p. 6, italics added.

59. Statement of the Chamber of Commerce of the United States, Senate Committee on Finance, *Hearings on S. 1575, Federal Reinsurance of Private Pension Plans,* 89th Cong., 2nd Sess., p. 105, italics added. Other critics of insurance claimed that Hartke's bill, which set premiums in proportion to a plan's unfunded liability, would discourage the creation of past-service credits, an essential element of defined-benefit plans and a key government objective, providing more income for the elderly.

60. An exasperated Young chastised his professional colleagues for ignoring the problem of plan terminations, saying that "actuaries and others should work toward the development of a sound solution, rather than expending energy on denying the

problem"; Young, "Federal Reinsurance," p. 149. The dismissive approach to insurance taken by business all but assured its lack of thoughtful input on the scheme finally established in ERISA.

61. Opening statement of Jacob K. Javits, "Private Pension Plans," Hearings before the Subcommittee on Fiscal Policy of the Joint Economic Committee, 89th Cong., 2nd Sess., pt. 1, pp. 4–27; see, generally, Michael S. Gordon, "ERISA, ESOPs and Senator Javits: The Mind of a Reformer," *American Journal of Tax Policy* 7 (1988), pp. 3–30. Javits had also participated in New York State investigations of private pensions in the mid-1950s while he served as Attorney General; see *Private Employee Benefit Plans—A Public Trust,* A Report on Welfare and Pension Funds in New York State submitted to the State of New York Insurance Department by Martin S. House, Special Counsel (31 Jan. 1956).

62. Gordon, "Why Was ERISA Enacted?" p. 23.

63. McGill, *Preservation of Pension Benefit Rights,* p. 336. Extremely ambitious portability, such as allowing the value of credits to rise with the terminated worker's subsequent earnings, was politically, if not financially, impossible.

64. Interview with Gordon.

65. Ibid.

66. Gordon, "Why Was ERISA Enacted?" p. 24; interview with Gordon. Rumor has it that Wirtz had his own Donnybrook with Johnson over the Vietnam war. The two, it was said, were sucked into a vitriolic shouting match and never spoke thereafter. If true, Wirtz's anger and isolation from Johnson helped bring the interagency bill to Capitol Hill, but cost it all hope of success.

67. The "individual retirement account" was similar to H.R. 10, or "Keogh" plans, for self-employed workers and their employees. H.R. 10 had been a congressional perennial since 1951, when Rep. Keogh introduced the bill, and was enacted into law in 1962; Harbrecht, *Funds and Power,* p. 133 and n27.

68. American Enterprise Institute, *Debate on Private Pensions,* p. 13. While requiring other plans to raise their vesting and funding standards would reduce the CIO's exposed forward position on pensions, and thus the burden on its employers, it also would reduce the distinctiveness of CIO compensation arrangements.

69. Jack Barbash, "The Structure and Evolution of Union Interest in Pensions," in *Old Age Income Assurance,* pt. 4, *Employment Aspects of Pension Plans,* 90th Cong., 1st Sess. (1967), pp. 64ff; Robert Tilove, "Income for the Elderly through Work-Life Extension, Asset Conversion, and Pension Improvements," ibid., p. 37. Michael Pilch and Victor Wood, writing on the British pension scene, also reported a growing interest in vesting on the part of corporate management. Firms wanted to ease the exit of middle-aged workers of middling performance or workers in declining sectors of the business; the lack of vested benefits made such separations difficult. Such an interest also may have encouraged the expansion of early vesting in U.S. corporate plans. Michael Pilch and Victor Wood, *New Trends in Pensions* (London: Hutchinson, 1960), p. 159.

70. Frank L. Griffin Jr. and Charles L. Trowbridge, *Status of Funding under Private Pension Plans* (Homewood, Ill.: Richard D. Irwin for the Pension Research Council, 1969), p. 77.

71. Ibid.; Dan M. McGill and Howard E. Winklevoss, "A Quantitative Analysis of Actuarial Cost Methods for Pension Plans," *Proceedings of the Conference of Actuaries in Public Practice* 23 (1974), pp. 212–43; McGill, *Preservation of Pension Benefit Rights,* pp. 141–76, 354–76.

72. McGill, *Guaranty Fund,* pp. 89, 16–22, 72–89. Premiums and assessments could not be raised to the point where large numbers of healthy sponsors would abandon their plans. This would weaken the system and could even reduce the receipts to the insurance scheme. The federal government at that point would have to back up the system, or see an agency it had created destroy the private pension edifice.

73. Ibid., pp. 48–54, 79–81.

74. Participation data from Alfred M. Skolnik, "Private Pension Plans, 1950–74," *Social Security Bulletin* 39 (June 1976), p. 4.

75. Gordon, "Why Was ERISA Enacted?"; interview with Gordon. As the initiative for reform shifted from the administration to Congress, long-time reformers shifted as well. Gordon, for example, left a job as a Department of Labor lawyer to work for Senator Javits.

76. Gordon, "Why Was ERISA Enacted?" pp. 24ff; interview with Gordon; also see Ralph Nader and Kate Blackwell, *You and Your Pension* (New York: Grossman, 1973).

77. Gordon, "Why Was ERISA Enacted?" pp. 33ff; interview with Gordon.

78. See McGill, *Fundamentals,* 4th ed., pp. 37–40.

79. The five- to fifteen-year graded vesting standard called for 25 percent vesting after five years, 5 percent a year for the next five, and 10 percent a year for the final five; the rule of forty-five called for 50 percent vesting when age plus service equaled forty-five (with a minimum of five years of service) and 10 percent a year for the next five years. Ibid., p. 141. For the $1 PBGC premium see Richard A. Ippolito, *The Economics of Pension Insurance* (Homewood, Ill., and Boston: Irwin for the Pension Research Council, 1989), pp. 50–52.

80. Ippolito, *Pensions, Economics, and Policy,* pp. 222–23. Inflation lowered the value of existing pensions, for sponsors typically raised allowances at a slower pace than the increase in prices. Higher interest rates would lower the value of future liabilities, counteracting the effect of declining pension fund assets. But this would be the case only if the increase was not just nominal but "real" (after accounting for inflation). "Real" interest rates, however, actually fell sharply in the 1970s, further exacerbating the stress on private pension plans. Interview with Gordon.

81. Conversation with Steven J. Sacher. Sacher says the rising pressure on Nixon through the spring and summer of 1974 also accelerated ERISA's progress. Impeachment was growing increasingly likely, and those working on the bill under-

stood that this would totally occupy the time and attention of Congress. If they were to enact as complex and ambitious a bill as ERISA, they would have to do it quickly, before any impeachment proceedings began. So they worked extra hours and cut necessary deals and got the bill into decent shape. Then, on August 8, everything changed, and ERISA's progress was accelerated for the reasons stated in the text.

82. The debates over Social Security in the late 1930s rejected, in parallel fashion, the notion that a "funded" plan, holding only "sponsor" securities, offered anything more than a balance-sheet reserve. With a "funded" Social Security program, the government's books would show an "asset" in its pension account — a government bond — to offset its accruing obligation. But the books would also show an equivalent liability in its "general" account — the very same bond. The government's obligations under either arrangement thus were identical and would have to be satisfied out of future tax revenues. The "unfunded" approach (paygo with or without a balance-sheet accounting entry) used the Social Security payroll tax, at the time the only mass tax in the nation, to satisfy claims. The "funded" arrangement, through its use of Treasury bonds, accessed the government's "general revenues" — cash that was raised from the more narrowly based income tax and from peripheral levies such as the tariff. See Harbrecht, *Funds and Power.*

83. A plan's unfunded liability — obligations without countervailing trust-fund assets — had been an official book-entry notation since 1948 (when the American Institute of Certified Public Accountants required the sponsor to disclose the figure in a footnote to its financial statements) and a straight balance-sheet item since 1989 (at the insistence of the Financial Accounting Standards Board); after the passage of ERISA, a plan's unfunded liability also became the potential obligation of all pension sponsors, via the Pension Benefit Guaranty Corporation. William D. Hall and David L. Landsittel, *A New Look at Accounting for Pension Costs* (Homewood, Ill.: Richard D. Irwin for the Pension Research Council, 1977); asset figures from "Pension Portfolios, Selected Years, 1950–89," Hoffman and Mondejar, "Pension Funds and Financial Markets," table 16.9, p. 438.

84. For a somewhat different perspective, see Daniel Fischel and John H. Langbein, "ERISA's Fundamental Contradiction: The Exclusive Benefit Rule," *University of Chicago Law Review* 55 (Fall 1988), pp. 1105–60.

85. Peter Drucker, *The Unseen Revolution: How Pension Fund Socialism Came to America* (New York: Harper and Row, 1976).

86. See Fischel and Langbein, "ERISA's Fundamental Contradiction."

Epilogue

1. Some of the arguments in this chapter have appeared in Steven Sass, "Crisis in Pensions," *Federal Reserve Bank of Boston Regional Review* (Spring 1993), pp. 13–18, and Steven Sass, "The Heyday of U.S. Collectively Bargained Pension Arrange-

ments," in Paul Johnson, Christoph Conrad, and David Thomson, eds., *Workers Versus Pensioners: Intergenerational Justice in an Aging World* (Manchester and New York: Manchester University Press in association with the Centre for Economic Policy Research, 1989), pp. 92–112.

2. John A. Turner and Daniel J. Beller, *Trends in Pensions 1992* (Washington: GPO, 1992), table 4.12, p. 88.

3. U.S. Bureau of Labor Statistics, Current Population Survey; while private-sector union membership fell by 1.6 million in the decade 1985–1994, public-sector membership rose by 1.2 million.

4. Participation figures estimated from Daniel J. Beller and Helen H. Lawrence, "Trends in Private Pension Plan Coverage," in Turner and Beller, *Trends in Pensions 1992,* table 4.5, p. 79. The U.S. Bureau of Labor Statistics gives 10.8 million as the number of unionized private-sector workers in 1987. The Bureau does not have private-sector figures prior to 1983, but assuming public sector membership held steady between 1979 and 1983, private-sector membership in 1979 would be about 15.3 million. Data supplied by Michael Cimini, U.S. Bureau of Labor Statistics; Beller and Lawrence, "Trends in Plan Coverage," table 4.12, p. 88. The labor force grew 43 percent between 1974 and 1994, from 91.2 to 130.6 million; it rose 30 percent between 1975 and 1987, from 93.1 to 118.8 million; U.S. Bureau of Labor Statistics.

5. Robert C. Kryvicky, "The Funding of Negotiated Pension Plans," *Transactions of the Society of Actuaries* 33 (1981). The IRS, in its effort to minimize tax avoidance, aggravated this funding problem. It insisted that sponsors' funding programs target the benefits specified in the formal plan document. Standard corporate plans defined their benefits, and thus their funding programs, in terms of projected final salaries, which incorporated estimates of future inflation and productivity increases during a participant's active years of employment. As collectively bargained plans defined benefits in terms of nominal dollar amounts per year of service — sums implicitly expected to rise in the future, owing to inflation and productivity increases — the IRS all but *mandated* chronic underfunding.

6. U.S. Bureau of Labor Statistics, Current Population Survey.

7. Kryvicky, "Funding Negotiated Plans," pp. 411–17, esp. table 2, p. 413; Bankers Trust, *1965 Study of Industrial Retirement Plans* (New York, 1965), pp. 11, 13; A. M. Skolnik, "Private Pension Plans, 1950–74," *Social Security Bulletin* 39 (1976), pp. 4–8. For married union workers, Social Security raised household replacement rates where the worker's wife (most union workers being male) had earned less than her husband, even if the wife had never worked for wages. This is because Social Security replaced a greater share of preretirement income for lower-income workers, and paid retirees the greater of their own earned benefit or one-half of their spouse's benefit. Legislation passed in 1986 required most private pension plans to continue the benefit accruals past the "normal retirement age";

Olivia Mitchell, "Trends in Pension Benefit Formulas and Retirement Provisions," in Turner and Beller, *Trends in Pensions 1992*, p. 180. Congress likewise has extended the accrual process for Social Security; see William M. Mercer, *Guide to Social Security and Medicare* (Louisville, 1993).

8. Kryvicky, "Funding Negotiated Plans," pp. 418–23; Bankers Trust, *1975 Study of Industrial Retirement Plans* (New York, 1975), pp. 10–14; Victor Zink, "1970 General Motors Settlement," address given to American Pension Conference, 1971; Olivia Mitchell and Rebecca Luzadis, "Changes in Pension Incentives through Time," *Industrial and Labor Relations Review* 42 (1988), pp. 100–08; Richard A. Ippolito, "Towards Explaining Earlier Retirement after 1970," *Industrial and Labor Relations Review* 44 (1990), pp. 556–69. The improvement in nominal replacement rates in the early 1970s actually understates the growth of retirees' real incomes. Rising Social Security payroll taxes and federal and state income taxes, for example, absorbed an ever greater share of *pre*-retirement income, while pension allowances either escaped these levies or paid at a lower rate. Increasing asset ownership — of homes, household property, and financial instruments — also provided retirees with significantly more nonpension income than they had had in the past. The unions also negotiated increases in existing pensions whenever raising allowances for new retirees. So all pensioners shared in benefit hikes resulting from plan liberalization, inflation, or rising productivity.

9. Kryvicky, "Funding Negotiated Plans."

10. Richard A. Ippolito, *The Economics of Pension Insurance* (Homewood, Ill., and Boston: Irwin for the Pension Research Council, 1989), pp. 41–65.

11. Ibid., pp. 69–80.

12. The PBGC premium went from the initial $1 per capita to $2.60 in 1978 as the early experience indicated $1.75 to be closer to the "correct" premium level and the insurance fund needed a still higher premium to make up its accumulated shortfall. The Pension Protection Act of 1987 pushed the per capita premium to $16 and added a $6 charge for every $1,000 of unfunded liability — with the total premium capped at $50 per capita. The Act also banned benefit increases for plans less than 60 percent funded; required sponsors to value their plan liabilities using a discount rate between 90 and 110 percent of the rate on thirty-year Treasury bonds; and sped the amortization period for unfunded past-service liabilities to eighteen years, for asset losses to five years, for actuarial losses to ten years, for IRS funding waivers to five years, for shutdown benefits to seven years, and for new past service to a rate dependent on the plan's funding ratio. Ippolito, *Pension Insurance*, pp. 69–104, 132–54.

13. See Richard Randall, "Safeguarding the Banking System from Financial Cycles," in Richard Randall, ed., *Safeguarding the Banking System in an Environment of Financial Cycles* (Boston: Federal Reserve Bank of Boston, 1993), pp. 17–64, for the analogy in banking regulation.

14. Paul Yakobowski and Celia Silverman, "Baby Boomers in Retirement: What Are Their Prospects?" *EBRI Special Report and Issue Brief* 151, appendix table 8, p. 53.

15. Congress pegged benefits to prices, not wages as a conservative gesture, reasoning that wages rose faster as they reflected productivity growth as well as inflation. W. Andrew Achenbaum, "The Elderly's Social Security Entitlements as a Measure of Modern American Life," *Old Age in a Bureaucratic Society* (New York: Greenwood Press, 1986), pp. 156–92; Robert M. Ball, "Social Security Amendments of 1972," *Social Security Bulletin* 36 (March 1973), pp. 3–25; Daniel N. Price and Robert O. Brunner, "Automatic Adjustment of OASDHI Cash Benefits," *Social Security Bulletin* 33 (May 1973), pp. 1-12; Robert J. Myers, *Indexation of Pension and Other Benefits* (Homewood, Ill.: Richard D. Irwin for the Pension Research Council, 1978), pp. 25–57; Michael Boskin, ed., *The Crisis in Social Security* (San Francisco: Institute for Contemporary Studies, 1977); Robert S. Kaplan, *The Financial Crisis in the Social Security System* (Washington: American Enterprise Institute, 1976); A. Haeworth Robertson, *The Coming Revolution in Social Security* (McLean, Va.: Security Press, 1981); A. Haeworth Robertson, "Fiscal Basis of the OASDI Program, Including Long-Range Cost Projections," in Dan M. McGill, ed., *Social Security and Private Pension Plans: Competitive or Complementary?* (Homewood, Ill.: Richard D. Irwin for the Pension Research Council, 1977), pp. 41–56; Robert J. Myers, "Concepts of Balance between OASDI and Private Pension Benefits: A Partnership or, Instead, the Lion's Share for OASDI?" in McGill, *Social Security and Private Pension Plans,* pp. 94–109.

16. Geoff Kollmann, "Social Security," in *Retirement Income for An Aging Population,* Committee on Ways and Means, U.S. House of Representatives, report prepared by the Congressional Research Service, Library of Congress, with analytic support from the Congressional Budget Office, 25 Aug. 1987 (Washington: GPO, 1987), p. 319; Alicia H. Munnell, *The Future of Social Security* (Washington: Brookings Institution, Brookings Studies in Social Economics, 1977), pp. 84–112. Expenditures on Medicare for the elderly were rising even faster and presented an even greater crisis than the Old Age and Survivors Insurance program.

17. See Rudolph G. Penner, *Social Security and National Saving* (New York: Committee for Economic Development, 1989); Alicia H. Munnell and Lynn E. Blais, "Do We Want Large Social Security Surpluses?" *New England Economic Review* (Oct.-Nov. 1984), pp. 14–15; Kollmann, "Social Security," pp. 328–41; Francis M. Bator, "On Deficit Cutting," *Federal Reserve Bank of Boston Regional Review* (Summer 1995), pp. 24–26. Building up Treasury IOUs also expanded the system's funding base to include general government revenues — that is, until rising payment obligations would deplete the stock of government bonds in the middle of the twenty-first century.

18. Emil M. Sunley Jr., "Employee Benefits and Transfer Payments," in Joseph A. Pechman, ed., *Comprehensive Income Taxation* (Washington: Brookings Institu-

tion, 1977), p. 77n; Pearl Richardson, *The Effects of Tax Reform on Tax Expenditures* (Washington: Congressional Budget Office, 1988), summary table 1, p. ix; also see Stuart Dorsey, "Taxation of Pensions," in Turner and Beller, *Trends in Pensions 1992,* pp. 577–587.

19. See Dan McGill, "Post-ERISA Legislation," U.S. Senate Special Committee on Aging, *The Employee Retirement Income Security Act of 1974: The First Decade* (Washington: GPO, 1984), pp. 65–70.

20. For profits' share in corporate output, see *Economic Report of the President, 1991* ((Washington: GPO, 1991), table B-13, p. 301; for the declining role of big business in the labor market, see U.S. Bureau of the Census, *General Report on Industrial Organization* (Washington: Bureau of the Census, 1977), table 3, and "Company Statistics by Employment Size," Enterprise Statistics, *Company Summary* (Washington: Bureau of the Census, 1987).

21. Beller and Lawrence, "Trends in Plan Coverage," in Turner and Beller, *Trends in Pensions 1992,* p. 69.

22. Steven Sass, "Dynamic Enterprise: A New Concept of the Corporation," *Federal Reserve Bank of Boston Regional Review* (Winter 1994), pp. 19–24; "New Firms on the Block," *Federal Reserve Bank of Boston Regional Review* (Spring 1991), pp. 6–12; James D. Thompson, *Organizations in Action* (New York: McGraw Hill, 1967); Michael Piore and Charles Sabel, *The Second Industrial Divide* (New York: Basic Books, 1984); Rosabeth Moss Kanter, *When Giants Learn to Dance* (New York: Simon and Schuster, 1990). Research and development expenditures went from 8 to 12 percent of total business investment (plant, equipment, plus R&D) between 1980 and 1991; expenditures on hyper-dynamic information processing equipment went from 15 to 20 percent; and expenditures on the two combined went from 23 to 33 percent; in 1991 expenditures on everything else — structures, transport, industrial, and other equipment — absorbed only two-thirds of U.S. business investment.

23. Steven Sass, "Just Compensation: Performance-Based Pay for Non-Supervisory Workers," *Federal Reserve Bank of Boston Regional Review* (Winter 1995), pp. 12–17; also see George A. Akerlof, "Labor Contracts as Partial Gift Exchanges," *Quarterly Journal of Economics* 92 (1982), pp. 543–69, and Charles Heckscher, *White-Collar Blues: Management Loyalties in an Age of Corporate Restructuring* (New York: Basic Books, 1995).

24. Sass, "Just Compensation"; Tracy Kidder, *The Soul of a New Machine* (Boston: Little, Brown, 1981). Flat corporations can tie compensation to individual performance because contributions are far more visible in small project teams and business units than in a mass-production setting; note also that giving supervisors more discretion over salaries, overturning older notions of "equitable" compensation, increases the risk of managerial myopia and downright favoritism.

25. See Ernest Weekley, *An Etymological Dictionary of Modern English* (London: John Murray, 1921); Mitchell, "Trends in Benefit Formulas," pp. 177–216.

26. Daniel Bell and William Marclay, "Trends in Retirement Eligibility and Pension Benefits," *Monthly Labor Review* 110:4 (April 1987), pp. 18–25.

27. Lazear has shown that the value of early retirement benefits varies with salary and tenure — the likely correlates of excess compensation. Older workers with less tenure with the firm, and presumably less (or no) discrepancy between their pay and performance, get lower early retirement "subsidies." Edward P. Lazear, "Pensions as Severance Pay," in Zvi Bodie and John B. Shoven, *Financial Aspects of the United States Pension System* (Chicago: University of Chicago Press for the National Bureau of Economic Research, 1983), pp. 57–89. For the continuing value of the pension in extending tenures (prior to eligibility for early retirement) see Richard A. Ippolito, "Encouraging Long-Term Tenure: Wage Tilt or Pensions?" *Industrial and Labor Relations Review* 44 (1991), pp. 520–35; for employee responsiveness to early retirement incentives in specific plans, see Laurence Kotlikoff and David Wise, "Employee Retirement and a Firm's Pension Plan," in David Wise, ed., *The Economics of Aging* (Chicago: University of Chicago Press for the National Bureau of Economic Research, 1989), pp. 279–330; Olivia Mitchell and Gary Fields, "The Economics of Retirement Behavior," *Journal of Labor Economics* 2 (1984), pp. 84–105; for the view of declining productivity after age 55, see *U.S. Retirement Policy: The Sleeping Giant Awakens* (n.p.: Wyatt Company [now Watson-Wyatt Worldwide], 1994); for the variance between pay and performance ratings for older workers, see Katharine Abraham and James Medoff, "Experience, Performance, and Earnings," *Quarterly Journal of Economics* 95 (1980), pp. 703–36.

28. Mitchell, "Trends in Benefit Formulas," p. 180; interview with Charles Commander of Watson-Wyatt.

29. Michael J. Alderson and Jack L. VanDerhai, "Pension Asset Reversions," in Turner and Beller, *Trends in Pensions 1992,* pp. 531–42; interview with Charles Commander; "Democrats Lose Bid to Block Pension Withdrawals," *Boston Globe,* 20 Sept. 1995, p. 14.

30. Emily S. Andrews, "The Growth and Distribution of 401(k) Plans," in Turner and Beller, *Trends in Pensions 1992,* pp. 149–76; Paul Yakobowski and Annmarie Reilly, "Salary Reduction Plans and Individual Saving for Retirement," *EBRI Issue Brief* (Nov. 1994), Employee Benefit Research Institute, Washington, pp. 11–16.

31. Participation figures as estimated in note 4 above; Beller and Lawrence, "Trends in Plan Coverage," table 4.7, pp. 80–81.

32. Mitchell and Luzadis, "Changes in Pension Incentives through Time."

33. Mitchell, "Trends in Benefit Formulas," p. 184. Social Security will still provide a reasonable replacement income to a portion of the workforce that does not participate in the private institution.

34. Merton Bernstein, *The Future of Private Pensions* (New York: Free Press of Glencoe, 1964). Whether or not labor market disruptions in the 1980s and 1990s resulted in more breaks in tenure is the subject of debate. What seems clear is the

sharp reduction in the proportion of workers with twenty-plus years of service with any one employer. See Howard Wial and Kenneth Swinnerton, "Is Job Stability Declining in the U.S. Economy?" U.S. Department of Labor Discussion Paper 42, 1993, esp. table 1; David E. Marcotte, "Evidence of a Decline in the Stability of Employment in the United States," MSS, Northern Illinois University, 1995; Henry S. Farber, "The Incidence and Costs of Job Loss: 1982–1991," *Brookings Papers on Economic Activity: Microeconomics 1993* (Washington: Brookings Institution, 1993), pp. 73–119.

35. The unfavorable reemployment prospects of workers over 50, and thereby the reduced access of dislocated older workers to employer-based pension benefits, is reminiscent of the situation Margo found in 1900. For an individual older worker, then as now, the key is keeping, not finding, a job. Robert Margo, "The Labor Force Participation of Older Americans in 1900: Further Results," *Explorations in Economic History* 30 (1993), pp. 409–23; Andrew M. Sum and Neal W. Fogg, "Profile of the Labor Market for Older Workers," in Peter Doeringer, ed., *Bridges to Retirement: Older Workers in a Challenging Labor Market* (Ithaca, N.Y.: ILR Press, 1990); Andrew M. Sum and Neal W. Fogg, "Labor Market Turbulence and the Older Worker: Implications for Future Workforce Preparedness," MSS, Center for Labor Market Studies, Northeastern University; Christopher Ruhm, "The Work and Retirement Patterns of Older Americans," *EBRI Issue Brief* 121, Dec. 1991; for the decline in pension participation among older workers, see John R. Woods, "Pension Coverage among Private Wage and Salary Workers," *Social Security Bulletin* 54 (1989), p. 17. Woods' figures actually understate the decline in participation among older workers because they include contributors to retirement savings accounts, which were a far more significant factor in 1988. Older workers are far more likely to contribute to such plans than other covered workers; their contributions often substitute rather than augment other forms of household saving; and participation in a retirement savings program, at this late age, produces far less old age income than participation in a traditional pension plan.

The market position of workers over fifty could deteriorate further after 1996, when the front edge of the huge baby boom generation (born between 1946 and 1964) turns 50. The unique contribution of older workers — maturity, experience, and company-specific skills — would then, and for the foreseeable future, be readily and cheaply available. This notion, of tougher times in the future, assumes that the services provided by older workers complement those provided by younger workers — that Indians need chiefs. If the two groups are more competitive than complementary, then the relative decline in the number of competitive younger workers should improve the market value of older labor.

36. Steven G. Allen, Robert L. Clark, and Ann A. McDermed, "Post-Retirement Benefit Increases in the 1980s," in Turner and Beller, *Trends in Pensions 1992*, pp. 319–39; Alan L. Gustman and Thomas L. Steinmeier, "Pension COLAS," National Bureau of Economic Research Working Paper 3908, Nov. 1991; Jeanne E.

Griffith, "Demographics and the Aging Population," in *Retirement Income for an Aging Population,* Committee on Ways and Means, U.S. House of Representatives, p. 104.

37. See note 31 above.

38. "New Evidence That Employees Choose Conservative Investments for Their Retirement Funds," *Employee Benefit Notes* 13:2 (Feb. 1992), Employee Benefit Research Institute; Alicia H. Munnell, "The Pitfalls of Social Investing," *New England Economic Review* (Sept.-Oct. 1983), p. 26. Yakobowski and Reilly offer some indications that participants in retirement savings plans may be becoming more aggressive investors; "Salary Reduction Plans," p. 18.

39. Standard defined-benefit pension plans handle many of these risks far better than the new retirement savings plans. The pension institution has developed an elaborate governance system to oversee investment and corporate managers. It pools, and thereby reduces, financial and mortality risks. And these risks are borne by parties better able than individual households to absorb any shocks — employers and the PBGC.

40. See, e.g., Martin Feldstein, "The Welfare Costs of Social Security's Impact on Private Saving," in Michael Boskin, ed., *Modern Developments in Public Finance* (New York and Oxford: Blackwell, 1987), pp. 1-13; Alicia H. Munnell, "Social Security, Private Pensions, and Saving," *New England Economic Review* (May-June 1980), pp. 31–47. The empirical measurements of the net additional saving attributable to employer-based retirement savings plans are still coming in; see Eric M. Engen, William G. Gale, and John Karl Scholz, "Do Saving Incentives Work?" *Brookings Papers on Economic Activity* 1 (1994), pp. 85–180; James M. Poterba, Steven F. Venti, and David A. Wise, "Do 401(k) Contributions Crowd Out Other Personal Saving?" National Bureau of Economic Research Working Paper 4391, June 1993; Steven F. Venti and David A. Wise, "Government Policy and Personal Retirement Saving," in James M. Poterba, ed., *Tax Policy and the Economy* (Cambridge, Mass.: MIT Press for the National Bureau of Economic Research, 1992).

41. Mark E. Schweitzer, "Accounting for Earnings Inequality in a Diverse Workforce," Working Paper 9314, Federal Reserve Bank of Cleveland, 1993; John Campbell, "The Richest Crop," *Federal Reserve Bank of Boston Regional Review* (Summer 1994), pp. 6–12; Christopher Mayer and Gary V. Englehardt, "Gifts for Home Purchase and Housing Behavior," *New England Economic Review* (May-June 1994), pp. 47–58.

42. See Steven Sass, "Passing the Buck: The Intergenerational Transmission of Wealth," *Federal Reserve Bank of Boston Regional Review* (Summer 1995), pp.12–17.

43. James P. Smith, "Unequal Wealth and Incentives to Save," manuscript, RAND Documented Briefing, pp. 7, 10, 12–26. Financial assets of families are still only $53,000 for 70th-percentile white households, and $5,000 and $3,000 for 70th-percentile black and Hispanic households; Smith, "Unequal Wealth," p. 10; James P. Smith, "Wealth Inequality among Older Americans," RAND DRU-

989-NIA, Labor and Population Program Working Paper 95–06, 1995; Carole Shammas, Marylynn Salmon, and Michel Dahlin, *Inheritance in America* (New Brunswick and London: Rutgers University Press, 1987); Yakobowski and Silverman, "Boomers in Retirement," p. 41.

44. President's Commission on Pension Policy, *Coming of Age: Toward a National Retirement Income Policy* (Washington: GPO, 1981).

Index

♦ ♦ ♦

Aaron, Benjamin, 188
accrued liability. *See* "past service"; pension expense
actuarial assumptions, 160–161; government regulation of, 234
actuarial consultants, 77, 80, 86, 155ff; competitive position, 156ff, 303n53; "enrolled" actuary status, 220
actuarial costing methods, 153, 161, 277n41; entry age normal, 160; level premium deferred annuity (LPDA), 64, 73; single premium deferred annuity (SPDA), 69, 74, 63, 300n33; single premium immediate annuity (SPIA), 81–83, 108–109; government regulation of, 234
actuarial gains and losses, 161
actuarial valuation, 66; tax treatment, 108–110; government regulation of, 77, 108–109, 234, 238
adverse selection, 74, 96, 149, 293n52
Aetna, 148, 166, 184, 295n3
agency relationships, 19–23, 48, 50, 66, 226, 302n46
aging, 4, 27, 33, 35, 40, 90, 92, 129, 140, 185, 194, 247, 295n4, 298n15, employment opportunities, 8, 10, 15, 23, 51, 59, 122, 247, 272n33, 318n34, 319n35
Akerlof, George, 24
Albert W. Harris plan, 105
Alcoa, 156
Alfred Dolge. *See* Dolge Company
All-America Cables, Inc., 273n3
Allen, Walter S., 44–45

Altmeyer, Arthur J., 95
Amalgamated Clothing Workers, 289n28
American Bar Association, 188
American Express Company, 23, 39–40, 261n10, 265n23
American Federation of Labor (AFL), 124, 229, 230, 309n4; on craft skill, 125, 137–139; reunited with CIO, 143; multiemployer schemes of, 186
American Federation of Labor–Congress of Industrial Organizations (AFL-CIO), 143, 200
American Pension Conference, 162
"American Pension Plan," 71, 96, 195, 251
American Rolling Mills, 275–276n26
American Telephone and Telegraph Company (AT&T), 43, 44–45, 53, 54, 77, 83, 85, 107, 269–270n17, 277n39, 299n21; benefits committee of, 208–209; pension department of, 266n29; government investigation of, 284n31
American Trucking Association, 181
Analysis of Industrial Pension Systems (Conant), 71
Anderson, John A., 30
Andrews, Victor, 306n27
annuities, 26, 115, 154. *See also* actuarial costing methods; joint-and-survivor annuity
APBM program, 109
Associated Industries of Massachusetts, 71
AT&T. *See* American Telephone and Telegraph Company
Atterbury, W. W., 60

baby boom generation, 229, 319n35; and Social Security surpluses, 237

balance sheet reserve, 77, 85, 222

Baltimore & Ohio Railroad, 23–24, 27, 31, 36–37, 39, 122, 127, 176; pension plan of, 263–264n18, 264n28, 265n24

Bankers Life of Iowa, 148–149, 157, 215–216, 297n10

Bankers Trust of New York, 83, 155, 215, 299n21

Barbash, Jack, 215

Barnard, W. T., 25–27, 30, 42, 262–263n14

Barr, Samuel R., 32, 263n17

Basset, Preston, 157, 299n27

Beier, Emerson, 209, 216

Bell, Elliott V., 308n41

Beller, Daniel, 239

Bernstein, Merton, 190, 203, 247

Bethlehem Steel, 136, 269n17, 276n26, 292n45

big business, 18, 38–55, 168–178, 199–200, 213, 238–246

Black, Kenneth, Jr., 147–148, 149, 167, 295n1

Block, Joseph L., 308n41

Board of Tax Appeals, 105

Boyle, W. Anthony, 200, 201, 309n41

Brandeis, Louis, 61, 95

Brandes, Stuart, 16–17, 41, 46

British Federated Universities Superannuation Scheme, 65

British National Telephone Company, 44

Bronson, Dorrance, 141, 158

Brooklyn Edison, 276n26

Brooks, John, 44

Brotherhood of Railway and Steamship Clerks, Freight Handlers, Express and Station Employees, 309n41

Brown, Herbert D., 63

Buck, George B., 63–67, 68, 70, 77, 155–156, 158, 173, 275n23

Bureau of the Budget, 213

Burns, Arthur F., 309nn41,46

Burt, Margaret Allen, 63, 273n12

Business Research Corporation, 80

Business Week, 155

Cabinet Committee on Corporate Pension Funds and Other Private Retirement and Welfare Programs, 193–202, 306n27

career employment, 10, 13–14, 19–23, 34, 48, 49, 52–54, 260nn3,5

Carnegie, Andrew, 41, 52

Carnegie Foundation for the Advancement of Teaching, 47, 52, 58, 64, 65–67, 276n30

Carnegie Steel, 41

Carter, Jimmy, administration of, 251

Central and Southern States Pension Fund (CSPF), 180–183

Central Hudson Gas and Electric, 276n26

Chandler, Alfred, 28, 29, 271n26

charity, 11, 120

Chase Bank, 155

Cheney Brothers, 276n26

Ching, C. S., 78, 80, 277n40

Chrysler, 130, 186, 233; and UAW, 136, 184

CIO. *See* Congress of Industrial Organizations

civil service, 19–21

Clark, Bennett, 95–96

Clark Amendment, 95–96, 100, 195

Clean Water Act, 218

Cloud, Arthur D., 272nn1,2

Cohen, Manuel, 203, 205–206

Cole, David L., 309n41

collective bargaining and collectively bargained plans, 29, 92, 125–126, 139–142, 185, 186, 188, 200, 215, 230, 314n5. *See also* multiemployer plans; unions

College Retirement Equity Fund (CREF), 301n43

Colorado Fuel and Iron, 45

Commission on Money and Credit, 198, 306n27

Committee for Economic Development, 306n27

Committee on Economic Security, 95

Committee on Portable Pensions (Canada), 195, 307n31

Commons, John R., 95

Conant, Luther, 71

Conference on Actuaries in Public Practice, 162

Congress (U.S.): and RENPA, 92–94; and IRS, 102, 104–105, 106; and increased tax rates, 118; on employer responsibilities, 134; raises Social Security benefits, 136, 235–236; and insurance industry, 163; bans compulsory retirement, 244; on excess pension fund assets, 245

Congressional Budget Office, 237–238

Congress of Industrial Organizations (CIO), 124–139, 213, 229, 230, 231; rejoins AFL, 143; on insurance reform, 215
Connecticut General, 146, 148, 166
Consolidated Gas, 276n26
contracting out, 95–96, 195
contributions: employee, 19, 21, 48, 57, 64, 131, 135, 245, 263n18, 286n8; employer, 19, 138, 238; "noncontributory" plans, 35, 40. *See also* funding
Corbin, Arthur, 190
corporate governance. *See* fiduciary management
Council of Economic Advisors, 203
Council on Employee Benefits, 162
County, A. J., 60
Couper, Walter, 115
Cowdrick, E. S., 269n17, 277n40
Cowdrick Committee, 269n17. *See also* Special Conference Committee
Cowles, George, 299n21
Craig, J. D., 68
Cummins, Frank, 211
Curtis Publishing Company, 276n26

Dalitz, Morris, 182
Daugherty, Carol R., 291n41
Dearing, Charles, 122
Deering Milliken, 276n26
"deferred wage" theory, 79, 188, 190
defined-benefit plans, 239
defined-contribution plans, 136, 242. *See also* profit-sharing; retirement savings plans; thrift plans
Dent, John, 218, 219
Depression of 1873–1879, 24
Depression of 1893–1896, 4, 11
disclosure, 57, 75, 192, 305n25
Disclosure Act. *See* Welfare and Pension Plan Disclosure Act of 1958
discrimination, tax treatment, 105, 107, 220, government regulation of, 110, 203. *See also* plan participation
Dolge Company, 16–17, 259n26
Dolge v. Dolge, 272n2
Douglas, Paul, 192
Dow-Jones Industrial Average, 220, 238
Dranow, Ben, 182
Drucker, Peter, 225
Dubinsky, David, 200, 309n41

DuBois, C. G., 40, 269n14, 277n39
DuPont, 269n17, 276n26
Dyer, John K., 157

Eastman Kodak, 85, 157
economies of scale, 7, 156
Edwards, T. O., 83, 84
Efficiency Commission, 63
efficiency movement, 28–37, 39, 49–52
efficiency wage, 14, 24, 127. *See also* pensions: as a "gift exchange"
Ehrlenborn, John, 219
Eisenhower, Dwight D., 192–193
Elkin, Jack, 159
employee demand for pensions, 74, 92, 124, 138, 246
employee relief associations, 22, 25, 41–42, 83, 263n18, 265n23
employee representation plans (company unions), 45–46, 60
Employee Retirement Income Security Act of 1974 (ERISA), 179–226; provisions, 219–220
employer pension obligations, 70, 134, 291n42
employment relationship, 14, 126, 190, 245, 247, 268n10, 306n28; in rationalizing industries, 48, 242, 270n19; in "flat" organizations, 240–243. *See also* career employment; personnel management; retirement
Epstein, Abraham, 97
Equitable Life Assurance Company, 68, 146, 148, 164, 167, 180, 276n30, 295n3
equity in pension arrangements, 20, 63, 65, 95, 117, 138, 140, 190, 198, 237, 242, 249, 272n2
equity investments, 154, 166–167, 174–175, 205–206, 220, 223–225, 249, 251, 301nn42,43, 303n54
ERISA. *See* Employee Retirement Income Security Act of 1974
"exclusive benefit" rule, 102–103, 105, 309n51. *See also* discrimination
exculpatory clauses, 16, 57, 187, 272n2
expansion: of the private pension institution, 192ff; of Social Security, 194–195

Farwell, Stanley P., 80
Federal Accounting Department, 270n23
Federal Conciliation Service, 126

Federal Mediation and Conciliation Service, 133
federal pension agency, proposals to create, 196, 198, 211
fiduciary management, 86, 123, 128, 132, 138, 181, 205, 228, 289n29, 320n39; government regulation of, 110, 192–193, 197–199, 203, 205–206, 211, 220, 224, 305n25, 306n27, 309n50; ERISA's "institutional man" standard, 206, 224–225. *See also* "prudent man" standard
flexibility in pension arrangements, 152–153, 160, 165, 245
Ford, Gerald R., 214, 221
Ford, Henry, II, 200, 213, 308n41
Ford Foundation, 306n27
Ford Motor Company, 130, 131, 132, 186, 292n45, 308n41; and UAW, 135, 136, 184, 293n47; use of pension trusts, 155
foreign influences, 32, 259n26; Australia, 63; Britain, 19–23, 25–27, 28, 35, 44, 63, 65, 68, 195, 196, 199, 212, 265n26, 274n12, 275n24; Canada, 48, 195, 196, 199, 211, 212, 262n14; New Zealand, 63
Forster, H. Walter, 107, 157, 158
401(k), 245–246
Franklin, John M., 308n41
funding, 41, 57, 62, 76, 78, 80, 83–85, 95, 96, 123, 128, 132, 136, 139, 140, 153, 160–161, 172–173, 175, 184–186, 200, 201, 215–216, 220–221, 228, 230, 232, 233–235, 255n1, 277n41, 275nn44,46, 279n52, 282n18, 286nn8,10, 310nn54,56, 313n82, 314n5; government regulation of, 108, 197, 201, 206–208, 211, 212, 220–224, 311n68, 314n5, 315n12; tax treatment, 102, 106, 222; in Social Security, 97, 316n17. *See also* contributions; pay-as-you-go
Future of Private Pensions, The (Bernstein), 190, 203

Galambos, Louis, 53
General Electric, 269n17, 276n26
General Foods, 157
General Motors, 130, 184, 186, 269n17, 276n26; and UAW pact, 136, 137
Gifford, Walter S., 269n14, 277n39
Goodman, Isadore, 110

Goodyear, 269n17
Gordon, Michael, 211–212, 216, 218, 219, 303n1, 312n75
government labor policy, 92–94, 126, 127, 131–132, 138, 152, 159
government pension regulation, 81–84, 101–112, 187–226, 234, 278n45. *See also* actuarial assumptions; actuarial costing methods; actuarial valuation; discrimination; fiduciary management; funding; pension benefits; plan participation; taxation; vesting; Internal Revenue Service; Interstate Commerce Commission; National Labor Relations Board; Pension Benefit Guaranty Corporation; Pension and Welfare Administration; Securities and Exchange Commission; U.S. Department of Labor; New York State Insurance Department; New York State Superintendent of Insurance
government pensions, 6, 91, 281n13, 308n35. *See also* Social Security
Graebner, William, 33, 50, 52
Grand Trunk Railway, 23, 31, 35–36, 39, 47, 261n10, 270n21
Grand Trunk Railway of Canada Superannuation and Provident Association, 19, 21–23, 47, 48, 49, 117
Gratton, Brian, 12
gratuity theory of pensions, 187, 272n2
Great Depression, 88–92, 94, 112, 120, 123, 124, 145, 206
Great Western Railway, 26
Greenspan, Alan, 236
Griffin, Frank, 215–216
Griffiths, Martha, 186, 204–206, 211
Gross Domestic Product, 238
"Group Association," 89, 146, 147, 148–149, 159, 295n3
Guaranty Fund for Private Pension Obligations (McGill), 216
Gulf Oil, 156

Haber, Carole, 12
Hagedorn, Homer, 42
Hannah, Leslie, 47, 295n1
Hansen, Arthur S., 107, 299n24
Harrah, Charles J., 15
Harris, Albert W., case, 105
Harrison, George M., 309n41
Hartke, Vance, 207, 211, 218

Harvard Business Review, 155
Harvard University, 52
Heinze v. National Bank of St. Louis, 272n1
Heller, Walter, 203
Hertzberg, Frederick, 191
Hicks, Clarence, 72
Hodges, Luther H., 309n41
Hoffa, Jimmy, 180–184, 191, 192–193
Hoffa and the Teamsters (James/James), 180
Hohaus, Reinhard, 54, 72, 74–75, 76
household wealth, 5, 251, 256n3, 315n8, 320n43
House Labor Committee, 219
human capital, 20, 22–23, 47–48, 50, 241, 243–244, 248
"human depreciation" theory of pensions, 134, 291n42
Humphrey, Hubert, 214
Hunt, E. B., 58, 60, 83

Individual Retirement Accounts (IRAs), 245–246
Industrial Relations Counselors, 162, 270n17
industries, pensions in: banks, 40, 47, 49–50; food processors, 49–50; government, 6, 12, 62–64; insurance 40, 47, 49; manufacturing, 44; metals and machinery firms, 49; mining, 49–51; petroleum firms, 49; public utilities, 40, 47, 49; railroads, 18–40, 49–51, 91–94; street railways, 42–43, 49; universities (*see also* Teachers Insurance and Annuity Association), 47, 52, 64
inflation, 55, 59, 61, 79, 118, 120, 126, 132, 133, 153–154, 185, 196, 220, 230, 247, 248, 287n10, 296n17, 312n80, 316n15
Inland Steel, 308n41; NLRB decision on, 132, 133, 188, 290n38
insurance brokers, 156–159
insurance companies, 9, 65, 86, 145–154, 222; insurance company products, 66–76, 115–117, 285n3, 286n8; group annuity policies, 74; deposit administration policies, 164–165, 300n38; group permanent policies, 149; retirement income policies, 117; individual trust plans, 115; money purchase plans, 65, 90, 146; "immediate participation guarantee," 165; investment-year method, 166; insurance company costs, 116, 117, 298n14; func-

tions performed, 147; competitive position, 76ff, 89, 148ff, 161ff
integration with Social Security, 100, 115, 119, 136, 282n21, 285n3, 292nn43,45
interest rates, 9, 26, 146–147, 220
intergenerational transfers, 64, 97, 100, 140, 250
Internal Revenue Service, 102, 103, 104–105, 106–110, 273n2; plan approval rate of, 118–119; set of values of, 161; Code of, 203; Pension Trust Division, 211, 212; and impact of unions, 294n59; on vesting, 308n33; and underfunding, 314n5
International Association of Machinists, 121
International Brotherhood of Electrical Workers, 200, 309n41
International Brotherhood of Teamsters, 180
International Business Machines Corporation, 308n41
International Foundation of Employee Benefit Plans, 163
International Harvester, 43, 45, 54, 157, 233, 269n17
International Ladies Garment Workers Union, 200, 289n28, 309n41
International Railway Congress, 32
International Union of Automobile, Aerospace, and Agricultural Implement Workers of America, 309n41
Interstate Commerce Commission, 81, 83, 84
investment performance, 152, 154, 182
IPG (immediate participation guarantee), 164–165
Ippolito, Richard, 186, 220–221
Irving Trust, 269–270n17
Ives, Irving, 192

James, Estelle, 180, 181
James, Gorton, 276n30
James, Ralph, 182
Javits, Jacob, 210–213, 218, 311n61
Javits-Williams pension bill, 219
John Hancock, 146, 167, 168
Johnson, Emory, 265n26
Johnson, Lyndon Baines, 202, 213, 214, 218
John Wanamaker (department store), 16
joint-and-survivor annuity, 183–184, 220, 304n8

Joint Committee on Tax Evasion and
Avoidance, 103–104
Joint Economic Committee, Subcommittee
on Fiscal Policy of, 204–206
Joseph, Myron, 203

Keenan, Joseph, 200, 309n41
Kennedy, John F., 193–196, 199, 202,
306n27
Kennedy, Robert, 193
Keogh plans, 311n67
Kerr, Clark, 133, 309nn41,46
Keynesianism, 97
Keynesians, 97–98
Kidder, Tracy, 242
Kimball, Ingalls, 68–73
King, George, 63
King, William Lyon Mackenzie, 45, 46
Knights of Labor, 10
Krug, J. A., 128, 289n29
Kryvicky, Robert C., 232

labor, views on pensions, 61, 121, 228. *See
also* employee demand for pensions
Labor-Management Advisory Committee,
199, 202
labor movement, 124, 129, 201, 229,
292n43
Latimer, Murray Webb, 48, 61, 76, 79, 80,
81, 84, 85, 114, 122, 267n3, 273n3; on
vesting, 191
Lawrence, Helen, 239
Lazear, Edward, 30
legal liabilities, 15–16, 57, 60, 80, 187–
190, 197, 217, 234, 272n2, 277n40,
279n47
level premium deferred annuity (LPDA).
See actuarial costing methods
Lewis, John L., 127–130, 136, 152,
289nn29,30
Licht, Walter, 24
Linton, M. Albert, 97
Lockheed, 157
London and North Western Railway, 19
LPDA (level-premium deferred annuity)
contracts, 64, 73, 82–83, 230
Ludlow Massacre (1914), 45

MacMillan, Clifford, 186
Magill, Roswell, 103–104, 105
managers, 28; managerial self-interest, 79,
114–119, 246

Manley, H. W., 35, 63
Margo, Robert, 5
marketing of pension plans, 74, 149
Marshall Field Company, 149
Martin E. Segal Company, 159–160
Massachusetts Institute of Technology,
270n19
Massachusetts Railroad Commissioners, 26
McCarthy, Eugene, 214
McClellan, John, 192, 193, 205, 211
McClung, Nelson, 310n55
McDonald, David J., 309n41
McGill, Dan, 166, 207, 216, 295n1,
301n41, 303n1; on employer liability,
188–189, 197–198; as consultant to
cabinet commission, 203; on portability,
212
McGill, Ralph, 309n41
McGraw-Hill Publishing Company,
308n41
McNevin v. Solvay Process Company, 272n2.
See also Solvay Process Company
McNulty, James E., Jr., 172–173, 295n1
Meany, George, 200, 309n41
Medicaid, 248
Medicare, 194, 248
Mellon Bank, 155
Melnikoff, Meyer, 296n6, 299n18
Memorandum of Agreement on Retirement
and Health and Security Programs, 135
Merchants Association of New York,
276n30
Merrill, John, 273n3
Metropolitan Life Insurance Company, 68–
73, 79, 86, 89, 108, 146, 157, 275n22,
276n30; Pension Division, 68; as indus-
try standard, 163; and withdrawal rights,
190–191; Pension Conference of,
275n26
Midvale Steel Company, 15
Miller, Ben, 181
Mills, A. G., 71–72
Mills, Wilbur, 212, 213
Minnesota Mutual Life Insurance Com-
pany, 295n3
Minster, Pembroke, 301n41
Moen, Jon, 11
monopoly, 42, 43, 127, 146, 269n12
moral hazard, 209, 217, 232, 234
Morgan, J. P., 41, 43
Morris Packing Company, 56–58, 60, 180,
273nn2,3, 294n59
mortality, 146, 236, 248

multiemployer plans, 128, 138, 159, 192
Munnell, Alicia, 285n1
MUPS (minimum universal pension system), 251–252
Murray, Philip, 127, 292n45
Mutual Benefit Life, 157
Myers, Robert J., 236

National Bureau of Economic Research, 309n41
National City Bank, 48
National Civic Federation, 71; conference of, 276n30
National Commission on Social Security Reform, 236
National Industrial Conference Board, 71, 119
National Industrial Recovery Act, 89
National Labor Relations Act, 131. *See also* Taft-Hartley Act
National Labor Relations Board, 126; and Inland Steel decision, 132, 133, 188, 290n38
National Labor Union, 10
national old age income system, 218, 251. *See also* employee demand for pensions
NBC network, 218
New Deal, 88, 101, 102, 103, 112, 118, 120; labor system of, 127, 142; reforms of, 150
New York Central Railroad, 54, 276n26
New York Chartered Life Underwriters, 102
New York State Insurance Department, 69, 146, 274n21, 295n3
New York State Superintendent of Insurance, 77
New York Stock Exchange, 4
New York Telephone, 276n26
Nixon, Richard M., 214, 217, 218, 221
"normal cost," 108, 133, 136, 152, 160, 185, 197, 206, 232, 298n15

OASDI, 197, 235
Occidental Life Insurance, 295n3
Office of Labor-Management and Welfare Pension Reports, 211
Old Age and Survivors Insurance, 316n16
Old Age Assistance program, 120
Old Age Pension Plan, 70
old age poverty, 11–13, 70
organizational boundary problems, 53, 125, 130

Otis Elevator, 71, 276n26
Ozanne, Robert, 42

Pacific Mutual, 157
Packard Motor Company, 209, 304n9
"past service," 35, 64, 66, 73, 109, 129, 135, 136, 138, 184–185, 197, 199, 206, 215, 230, 278n45, 298nn14,15, 300n33, 310n59, 313n83
Paul, Randolph, 106, 108
pay-as-you-go, 35, 93, 222; Social Security, 97
PBGC. *See* Pension Benefit Guarantee Corporation
Pencavel, John, 42
Pennsylvania Railroad, 28–37, 39, 40, 54, 58–60, 66–67, 78, 80–81, 86, 244, 264n23, 308n41
Pension and Welfare Administration (U.S. Department of Labor), 239
pension assets, 77–78, 84–86, 89, 123, 140–142, 179, 182, 184–185, 222, 232, 234, 283n24. *See also* funding; insurance companies; Teachers Insurance and Annuity Association
Pension Benefit Guaranty Corporation (PBGC), 220, 224, 225, 228, 234, 238, 315n12; claims against, 233; insurance of, 235
pension benefit insurance, 197, 199, 203, 207–213, 216–217, 220, 233–235
pension benefits, 19, 21, 23, 27, 33, 39, 41, 53, 57, 64, 65, 122, 123, 128, 131, 138, 146, 261n10, 263n16, 263n18, 266n29, 268n6, 270n21, 270n23, 276nn29,30, 280n9, 315n8; final salary basis, 66, 79, 116, 282n21, 284n30, 286n6, 287n17, 292n45, 298nn15,16,17; average salary basis, 70, 115; tax treatment, 106, 107; government regulation, 110, 185, 196, 204, 220, 234, 238, 247; liberalization, 185, 294n58; replacement, 194, 285n1, 307n29, 315n8
pension expense, 23, 58, 59, 61, 66, 96, 146, 230, 246, 261n10, 263n18, 266n31, 275n22, 278n42, 287n10, 295n4, 298n14; accrual, 62, 66, 83. *See also* actuarial costing methods; "normal cost"; "past service"
pension fund socialism, 225
pension liabilities, 66, 70, 179, 222, 255n1. *See also* legal liabilities

Pension Protection Act (PPA) of 1987, 234, 315n12

pension put, 189

pension rationales, 66, 98, 100, 111, 113, 122, 128, 140, 141, 221, 232, 235, 237, 240, 245, 265n26, 291n41, 307n32. *See also* welfare capitalism; efficiency movement; retirement; pensions: as fidelity bonds; pensions: as a "gift exchange"; pension tax shelter

Pension Research Council, 162, 203, 295n1, 297n13; study of, 215–216

pensions: as "dissatisfiers," 191; as a "gift exchange," 24, 126, 137, 246; as a "fidelity bond," 47, 69ff, 137, 141, 143, 210, 294n58

pension service industry, 62–76, 111, 145–178; vertical and horizontal integration and disintegration, 86, 112

pension tax expenditure, 195, 307n32

pension tax shelter, 101–110, 115, 116, 118, 203, 237, 250, 283n28, 307n32

pension trust, 223–225, 283nn25,29, 285n4, 299n21, 284n30, 309n51; revocable, 104; tax treatment, 104, 107, 299n21. *See also* fiduciary management; Section 165 of the Internal Revenue Code

Perkins, George W., 43–44

personnel management, 10, 13, 20, 31, 34, 40, 42, 54, 76, 78, 118, 119, 126, 130–131, 187, 221, 227, 237, 239, 242, 244, 246, 265n24, 290n38, 317n24, 318n27; employee relations, 72, 115; turnover, 72. *See also* career employment; collective bargaining and collectively bargained plans; employee relief associations; employee representation plans; employment relationship; industries, pensions in; pension rationales; seniority

Peterson, Ray, 180, 296n6, 299n18

Philadelphia and Reading Railroad, 265n23

plan administration, 65, 123, 288n18

plan document, 57, 187, 272n2

plan maturity, 59

plan participation, 122, 187, 228, 229, 247; compulsory, 26; government regulation of, 107, 204; voluntary, 72, 131, 135. *See also* discrimination; "exculsive benefit" rule

plan soundness, 62ff, 78ff, 197–199, 218

plan termination, 56–57, 184, 209, 260,

304n9. *See also* pension benefit insurance; reversion of pension fund assets

politics, 12, 92, 213–221; presidential, 88, 95, 103, 114, 126, 128, 132–135, 202, 214, 218, 221, 233, 251, 290n39, 311n66, 312n81; congressional, 95–96, 127, 218, 219–220

portability, 65, 196. *See also* vesting

Priest, William W., 189

Principal Financial Group, 148

Principles of Scientific Management (Taylor), 50–51

Pritchett, Henry C., 52, 64–67, 68, 88, 270n19

private pension coverage, 15, 35, 38, 54, 75, 90, 99, 115, 118–119, 122, 129, 139, 146, 149, 154, 179, 217, 245–246, 314n4, 319n35

Proctor & Gamble, 16, 17

professionals, 52, 157, 162, 155–178, 240–243

profit-sharing, 16

prohibited transactions, 206. *See also* fiduciary management; "prudent man" standard

promisory estoppel, 187

Prouty, William C., 301n41

Prudential, 146, 148, 157, 167, 295n3

"prudent man" standard, 180–181, 205. *See also* fiduciary management

public opinion, 191, 202, 218. *See also* scandals

Public Service Corporation of New Jersey, 276n26

Pure Oil, 157

R. D. Wood (company), 276n26

R. H. Macy (department store), 276n26

Rahde, Mr., 63

Railroad Brotherhoods, 121–123, 288n19

Railroad Employees' National Pension Association (RENPA), 92–94, 280n9

railroad pension plans, 18–40, 49–51, 91–94

Railroad Retirement Act, 98, 281n15; program of, 208

Railroad Retirement Board, 159

Railway Accounting Officers Association, 81

rationalization of the economy, 6–13, 28–29, 34, 44, 51–53, 225, 227, 242, 271nn26,28; dynamic rationalization, 52, 80, 241

Reagan, Ronald, 233, 236, 251
recessions, 8; the Great Depression, 89ff, 220, 229, 233
Regan, Patrick J., 189
RENPA. *See* Railroad Employees' National Pension Association
replacement ratio. *See* pension benefits
retirement, 11, 19, 21, 28–37, 44, 128, 138, 140, 244; conditions, 41, 57–58, 267n3, 268n6; compulsory, 33, 39, 49–53; discretionary, 90; early, 231, 242
retirement savings plans, 245, 248–250. *See also* thrift plans; profit-sharing
Reuther, Walter, 130–131, 136, 183, 290n32, 292n43, 309n41; on mandatory vesting, 201–202
Revenue Act: of 1921, 102; of 1928, 102; of 1938, 104–105; of 1942 (*see also* Section 23p and Section 165), 106–110, 188; of 1986, 247
reversion of pension fund assets, 105, 245, 283n29
Reynolds, Richard S., 308n41
Reynolds Metals Company, 308n41
Riebenack, Max, 31, 32, 33, 34–35, 39, 40, 42, 58–60
risk and risk management, 12, 21, 60, 61, 70, 77–78, 89–90, 136, 145, 147, 151–153, 156, 162, 164, 180, 249, 250, 296nn5,6, 301n42, 310n52, 320n39
Robbins, Rainard B., 64–67, 141
Rockefeller, John D., Jr., 45–46, 53, 271n32
Roosevelt, Franklin D., 88, 95, 103, 114
Roth, E. C., 276n30
Royce, Robert E., 208–209
Rubinow, Isaac, 97
Rule of X, 204
Russell, Charles T., 104

Sacher, Steven J., 221, 313n81
St. Joseph Lead, 276n26
Saunders, Stuart T., 308n41
saving(s), 5, 19, 26, 49, 65, 90, 120, 250, 257nn10,11, 306n28, 320n40
scandals, 56–58, 180–191, 192, 218
Schulz, James, 194, 285n1
scientific management, 50–51. *See also* efficiency movement
Seargeant, L. J., 22
Sears Roebuck, 276n26
Section 23(p) of the Internal Revenue Code, 108–109

Section 165 of the Internal Revenue Code, 107
Securities and Exchange Commission (SEC), 167, 203, 205, 305–306n25
Select Committee on Improper Activities in the Labor or Management Field, 192
Selekman, Benjamin, 125, 131
Senate Finance Committee, 219
Senate Labor and Public Welfare Committee, 192, 193, 210
Senate Labor Committee, 216, 219
Senate Subcommittee on Welfare and Pension Funds, 305n25
seniority, 29, 33, 35, 92, 242, 244, 264n22
Single Employer Pension Plan Amendments of 1986, 234
single premium deferred annuity (SPDA). *See* actuarial costing methods
Smith, Adam, 28
Smith, R. F., 25, 26
social insurance, 94, 134, 193, 217, 221. *See also* Social Security; national old age income system
Social Security, 94–101, 120, 194–195, 233, 236–237, 280n13, 314n7; private plans as "supplemental," 93
Social Security Act, 96–101; amendments to, 98
Social Security Administration, 94, 95, 111–112, 119, 143, 180, 218, 280n13, 281n15, 282n22; and corporate pensions, 114, 115; decline in benefits of, 120; funding of, 124; and Ford-UAW plan, 131; benefits raised, 136, 137; and blue-collar pensioning, 140; impact of, 150–151; and employer pensions, 191; benefits, 194; and portability, 196–197; and reduction in allowance, 231; 1972 increases, 232; reduction in, 233; use of surpluses of, 236–238; out of balance, 237–238; and benefits index, 248; and inflation, 308n34; on funded plan, 313n82
Society of Actuaries, 162
Solenberger, Willard, 304n8
Solvay Process Company, 16, 259n26
Soul of a New Machine, The (Kidder), 242
Southern Pacific Railroad, 83
SPDA (single-premium deferred annuity) contract, 69–70, 74, 82–83; as costing method, 300n33
Special Conference Committee, 46, 269n17
SPIA (single-premium immediate annuity)

contract, 81; as funding program, 278n46

Standard Oil Company, 45, 53, 67, 85, 88, 269n17, 271n32; and money purchase pension plan, 296n4

Stanley Rule and Level, 276n26

Steel Industry Board, 133–135, 290n39, 291nn41,42, 292n45

Studebaker: collapse of, 183, 184–186, 191, 206, 210, 304n9; and pension liability, 189, 203; and terminal funding, 232

Subcommittee on Fiscal Policy (Joint Economic Committee), 204–206

Sunley, Emile, 237

Sun Life, 146

Superannuation Act of 1834 (Great Britain), 19–20, 21

Supreme Court, 93; on collective bargaining, 132

Surrey, Stanley, 195, 202, 204, 212, 217

Taft, Philip, 43

Taft, Robert, 106

Taft-Hartley Act of 1947, 127, 138, 159, 289n29

taxation, 101–110, 118, 119, 152–153, 163, 204, 245, 298n14. *See also* pension tax expenditure; pension tax shelter

Tax Equity and Fiscal Responsibility Act of 1982, 238

Taylor, Frederick, 50–51

Taylor, George W., 309nn41,46

Teachers Insurance and Annuity Association (TIAA), 65–66, 67, 68, 70, 79, 138, 274n15, 301n43. *See also* TIAA-CREF model

Teagle, Walter, 53

terminal funding, 81, 232

Thayer, H. B., 269n14

"thirty-and-out," 231

Thompson, James, 241

"three-legged stool," 101

thrift plans, 45, 49

TIAA-CREF model, 251

Tilove, Robert, 159, 215

TNEC (Temporary National Economic Committee), 149, 295n3

"topheavy" plans, 238

top-tier plans, 101–111, 114–119, 238, 284n30

Towers, Perrin, Forster & Crosby (TPFC), 156–159, 299n25

Townsend, Francis, 94

TPF&C *Letter*, 157

TPF&C *Tax Manual*, 157

Trapp, Robert K., 168

Travelers, 146

Treasury (U.S. Department of), 104, 105, 106–110, 203; 1942 restrictions of, 117; Eisenhower's, 143; on pension taxation, 204. *See also* Internal Revenue Service

Treynor, Jack L., 189

Trowbridge, Charles, 215, 299n18

Truman, Harry S, 126, 128, 132; establishes Steel Industry Board, 133–135, 290n39

unfunded liabilities. *See* funding; "past service"

"unilateral contract" theory, 188, 190

Union Carbide and Carbon, 157, 276n26, 299n25

unions, 10, 24, 26–29, 46, 60, 121, 133, 135, 139, 159–160, 180–186, 188, 192, 200–202, 213–214, 215, 216, 229–234; union plans, 121–124, 287n17, 288n19; single-employer plan, 130. *See also* collective bargaining and collectively bargained plans; multiemployer plans

United Auto Workers (UAW), 129–131, 136, 137, 183, 233, 304n9; and Studebaker collapse, 184–186; pension insurance scheme of, 199, 207; Social Security department of, 290n32

United Mine Workers (UMW), 127–129, 136, 183, 200, 231, 233, 309n41; Welfare and Retirement Fund of, 128, 201, 289n28; pension program of, 293n47

United Rubber Workers, 183

United Steelworkers of America, 133, 231, 233, 290n38, 309n41; and Steel Industry Board recommendations, 135

U.S. Bureau of Labor Statistics, 209, 215

U.S. Chamber of Commerce, 162, 209–210

U.S. Department of Commerce, 238–239

U.S. Department of Labor, 192–193, 203, 205, 212, 218, 220; explores vesting requirements, 204

U.S. government, military pensions from, 3, 63

U.S. Industrial Commission, 15

United States Lines Company, 308n41

U.S. Rubber, 78, 169n17, 276n26

U.S. Steel, 43, 45, 53–54, 58, 133, 269n17, 276n26; and Steel Industry Board proposals, 135; salaried plan of, 155

Vail, Theodore N., 269n14, 272n33
Vanderlip, Frank, 48, 50
Vaughn, Roger, 116
vesting, 62, 83, 90, 142, 183, 185, 187, 188, 189–190, 200, 215–216, 217, 228, 311n69; tax treatment, 105, 106, 196; government regulation, 110, 199, 203, 211, 212, 214–215, 220, 247, 312n79
Virginia Railway and Power, 276n26
Voorhees, Enders, 291n42

wage and price controls, 118, 119
Wagner Act of 1935, 94, 127, 152; and collective bargaining, 113–114; and revised labor leadership, 124, 125; and bilateral monopolies, 126; impact of, 150–151
Walker Commission, 270n23
War Labor Board, 118
War Labor Disputes Act, 128
War Powers Act, 218
Watson, Thomas J., 208n41
Ways and Means Committee, 212, 219
Welfare and Pension Plan Disclosure Act of 1958, 192, 193, 205–206, 305n25
welfare capitalism, 14–15, 18, 22, 23–27, 30, 40, 49. *See also* pensions: as a "gift exchange"; pension rationales

Western Clock Company, 73–74, 276n30
Western Conference of Teamsters, 183
Western Electric, 40, 44, 276n26
Western Union, 276n26
Westinghouse, 269n17
Wharton School, Insurance Department of, 162
"Why Is There Mandatory Retirement?" (Lazear), 30
widows, 248
Wiebe, Robert, 13
Winklevoss, Howard, 216
Wirtz, W. Willard, 202, 213–214, 309n41
withdrawal rights, 19, 48–49, 65, 73, 116–117. *See also* portability; vesting
Witte, Edwin, 95
Wooten, James, 309n51, 310n54
Workingmen's Party, 10
World War II, 113, 143, 145; and pension arrangements, 117–119; and wage and price controls, 125
Wyatt, Birchard E. (Byrd), 158
Wyatt Company, 158–159, 173, 215–216

Yale University, 52, 190
Yarborough, Ralph, 214, 218
YMCA, 31
Young, Howard, 207–208, 210, 310–311nn54,55,56,60

Zebrowitz, Harry, 299n24

To order other Pension Research Council Books:

Pension Research Council
The Wharton School
3641 Locust Walk, room 304
Philadelphia, PA 19104-6218
fax: 215-898-0310

web site:
http://prc.wharton.upenn.edu/prc/prc.html